P9-COO-104

The 21st Century Webster's
Family Encyclopedia

The 21st Century Webster's Family Encyclopedia

Volume 9
Seal - Toxi

1999 Edition

IMPORTED BY/IMPORTE PAR
DS-MAX CANADA
RICHMOND HILL, ONTARIO
L4B 1H7

ENGLAND
WENTWALK LTD.
278A ABBEYDALE ROAD, WEMBLEY
MIDDLESEX, HA0 1NT

MALAYSIA
PRO ENTERPRISE SDN BHD
LOT 605, SS13/1K, OFF JLN.
KEWAJIPAN, 47500 SUBANG JAYA
SELANGOR D.E., MALAYSIA

DS-MAX
IRVINE, CA 92618
IMPORTER: #16-1241510
949-587-9207

TRIDENT PRESS INTERNATIONAL
Copyright © 1999, Uitgeverij Het Spectrum BV, Utrecht

ISBN 1-55280-464-X

All rights reserved

Copyright under the Universal Copyright Convention; the International Copyright Union; Pan-American Conventions of Montevideo, Mexico, Rio de Janeiro, Buenos Aires and Havanna

Printed in Peru

The 21st Century Webster's Family Encyclopedia
is based on the Spectrum Database

editors:
Bart Drubbel
Tjeerd van der Velde
Saskia van Iperen

Seal, stamping device with an inscription or emblem in relief or cut into its surface, used to make impressions in wax, paper, or other materials, for certification or authentication of documents. "Seal" also refers to the impression made, as well as to the proprietary design itself.

Seal, fin-footed mammal of the order Pinnipedia, which includes both the sea lions (family *Otariidae*) and the true seals (*Phocidae*). True seals have no external ears and have a thick coat of strong guard hairs. Seals are animals of the colder seas of both hemispheres. Northern species (subfamily *Phocidae*) include the bearded seal, the gray seal, and the common, or harbor, seal. Southern species (subfamily *Monachinae*) include the monk seals, elephant seals, crabeater, and Weddell seals. Most seals are gregarious; all live on the open seas and many go ashore only to breed. A single, light-colored pup is born, and further mating takes place immediately afterward. Males form harems of females on the breeding grounds. Many species are now endangered, having been extensively hunted for their skins and meat.

Sea lily, delicate, deep-sea echinoderm (class *Crinoidea*) shaped like a plant. It is related to the starfishes. Its body has a skeleton of chalk and consists of a stalk with five arms at one end. The arms branch repeatedly so that the animal has a feathery appearance and is often called the feather star. The largest star lily is 2 ft (61 cm) long, but 70-ft (21-m) fossils have been found. They used to be thought rare, but now they are sometimes dredged up by the ton.

Sealing wax, wax once used for sealing letters and still used for taking impressions from seals and for sealing bottles. Sticks of sealing wax, originally made of beeswax, turpentine, and coloring, are held over the material to be sealed and heated by a flame. The wax drips onto the paper or other surface; an impression can be made in the drops before they cool and harden. *See also:* Wax.

Sea lion, fin-footed seal (family *Otariidae*) differing from the true seals in having external ears and an almost hairless body. Sea lions are found in the northern Pacific Ocean and oceans of the Southern Hemisphere. Males may measure between 6 and 10 ft (1.8 and 3.0 m). They are active marine carnivores, feeding on fishes, squids, and other mollusks.

Sealyham terrier, short-legged dog originally bred in 19th-century Wales for hunting small burrowing animals. The terrier is of sturdy build, about 11 in (28 cm) tall and 23-25 lb (10-11 kg), with a large head and strong jaws. Its wiry coat is white, sometimes with darker markings around its head.

Seaman, Elizabeth Cochrane *See:* Bly, Nellie.

Sea onion *See:* Squill.

Sea otter (*Enhydra lutris*), marine mammal of the weasel family that lives near shores in the North Pacific Ocean. The animal averages 4-5 ft (1.2-1.5 m) and 60-85 lb (27-39 kg), and is covered with a thick, soft brown fur that insulates it against cold. It swims on its back, paddling with its hind feet, the pup carried on the chest of the female, sleeping in masses of kelp. Sea otters dive to a depth of 180 ft (55 m) for food, consisting of shellfish and other sea animals. They eat on their backs, breaking open shells by pounding them together. Sea otters have been hunted for their fur since the 1700s; a 1911 treaty saved them from extinction.

Search warrant, in law, court order issued to give law officers the authority to enter and search private premises for evidence, persons, contraband goods, or illegal equipment, such as counterfeiting machinery. "Unreasonable searches and seizures" are forbidden in the Fourth Amendment to the U.S. Constitution, and the scope of such a warrant is severely limited.

Sears, Roebuck and Company, large U.S. retail firm. Originally a mail-order company, it was founded in Chicago in 1893 by Richard W. Sears and Alvah C. Roebuck. Its mail-order business flourishing, the company began opening retail stores in 1925. It now also includes the Sears Financial Network, comprising the Allstate Insurance Company, the Coldwell, Banker & Company real estate brokerage, and the Dean Witter Reynolds stock brokerage firm, all operating out of Sears retail stores.

Sears Tower, in Chicago, Ill., tallest building (1,454 ft/443 m) in the world. It is over 100 ft (30 m) taller than the World Trade Center in New York City. Designed by Skidmore, Owings and Merrill, the office building was erected in the mid-1970s as the headquarters of Sears, Roebuck and Company. Prefabricated welded steel frames form a vertical core for the 110 stories. *See also:* Skyscraper.

Sea serpent, in myths and legends from many parts of the world, large, snakelike sea animal. Sea monsters of various description appear in ancient myths of the Middle East. Sightings of sea serpents, especially in the North Atlantic, have been common but have never been confirmed by material evidence. It is thought that what have appeared to be sea serpents have actually been giant squid, masses of seaweed, schools of porpoises, and other natural phenomena. The Loch Ness Monster is a similar freshwater creature thought to inhabit a lake in northern Scotland.

Seashore, land at the edge of a sea, alternately submerged and exposed by the tides. This land-water environment produces a rich variety of life forms. Tiny plankton (animals and plants floating in the tides) are the basis of shore life, both as larvae for shore animals and as food near the bottom of the food chain. The mollusks, sponges, and other animals that feed on plankton serve as food for shorebirds and other larger animals. Rocky seashores provide surface for seaweeds, mussels, sea urchins, and other organisms to attach themselves. Tide pools left by retreating tides shelter fish and other aquatic animals. Sandy shores are less hospitable, but some clams and crabs can make their home in the loose sand. Where protected bays create muddy shores and sea water mixes with fresh river water, plants thrive and crabs and turtles are common.

Season, one of several divisions of the year, characterized by cyclical changes in the predominant weather pattern. In the temperate zones there are four seasons; spring, summer, autumn (fall), and winter. These result from the constant inclination of the earth's polar axis as the earth orbits the sun:

during summer in the Northern Hemisphere the North Pole is tilted toward the sun; in winter, when the solar radiation strikes the hemisphere more obliquely, it is tilted away from the sun. The summer and winter solstices (about June 21 and Dec. 22), popularly known as midsummer and midwinter, mark the beginnings of summer and winter, respectively. Spring begins on the day of the vernal equinox (about Mar. 21) and autumn at the autumnal equinox (about Sept. 23).

Sea squirt, any of a group of marine animals (class Ascidiacea), also known as ascidians, that squirt water when squeezed. The sea squirt's body is enclosed in a jellylike coat; there are two openings, at the top and side, from which the water squirts. When the sea covers it, the sea squirt takes water in through one opening sieving off minute food particles. The waste water is passed out of the other opening. Sea squirts are found alone or in clusters, sometimes with individual animals joined together. Each sea squirt is both male and female; in the larval stage it looks like a tadpole.

SEATO *See:* Southeast Asia Treaty Organization (SEATO).

Seattle (pop. 519,600), largest city in Washington, situated on hills between Elliott Bay (Puget Sound) and Lake Washington; seat of King County. Seattle is the financial, cultural, commercial, industrial, and transportation center of the Pacific Northwest. Its chief industries are aerospace production, steel, shipbuilding, food processing, and chemicals. Settled in 1852, Seattle rapidly expanded with the coming of the railroad, the 1897 Alaska gold rush, and following the boom created by World War II. Its port is important in trade with Asia and serves as the main connection with Alaskan oil. This scenic city has a thriving recreational industry and is a cultural hub for theater, music and art. Seattle, host of the 1962 World's Fair, still boasts the landmark Space Needle, a 600-ft (183-m) structure built for the fair.

Sea urchin, any of a class (Echinoidea) of spiny marine animals related to the starfish and the sand dollar, occurring worldwide. The basic structure of the sea urchin is a sphere of 20 columns of calcareous plates, the "test," within which the gut, gonads, and water-vascular system are looped around the inside wall. The center of the sphere is empty. The test bears tubercles and short spines, and pedicellaria—pincer-like organs that clear the surface of detritus. Tube feet protrude through pores in the test, arranged in double rows down the sides.

Seaweed, algae found around coasts from the shore to fairly deep water. Most common are the brown algae, or wracks. Some, such as bladderwrack, clothe the rocks between tides; others live up to 40 ft (12m) deep. The large brown algae (kelps) sometimes form thick beds of long, tangled fronds, with tough, well-anchored stems. Gulfweed is another widespread species. Delicate green and red seaweeds live mainly in rock pools. Seaweeds provide oxygen through photosynthesis. Some seaweeds also provide food and shelter for sea animals, and many are used for food, fertilizer, iodine, and gelatin.

Sebastian, Saint (d. A.D. 288), early Christian martyr. Stories about him are mostly legends. According to these legends, Sebastian joined the Roman army with the intention of helping Christians. He became popular with Emperor Diocletian, who made him a military commander. When his religious faith was discovered, Sebastian was tied to a tree and shot with arrows. Left for dead, he recovered only to be captured later and put to death in the Roman amphitheater. Scenes of his martyrdom were popular subjects of early Italian painters. His feast day is January 20.

Sebastopol *See:* Sevastopol.

Secession, in U.S. history, withdrawal of the Southern states from the Federal Union, 1860-1. A right of secession, arising from a states' rights interpretation of the Constitution, was claimed in the early 19th century by the defeated Federalist Party in New England. The concept died in the United States when the Civil War ended in the Southern states' defeat.
See also: Civil War, U.S.

Second, measurement of time and angles in the metric system. In time, 60 seconds make up 1 minute; 60 minutes make up 1 hour. In measuring angles, 60 seconds make up 1 minute and 60 minutes make 1 degree. According to the standard established by use of an atomic clock, a second is defined as 9,192,631,770 times the vibration of radiation from a cesium atom.
See also: Metric system.

Secretariat, U.S. thoroughbred racehorse. Born in 1970, he raced only in 1972 and in 1973, when he became the first horse since Citation (1948) to win the racing Triple Crown (Kentucky Derby, Preakness, and Belmont Stakes; Affirmed became the next Triple Crown winner, in 1978). Secretariat retired from racing with lifetime winnings of $1,316,808.

Secretary bird (*Sagittarius serpentarius*), tall bird of prey of the dry African plains. It nests in trees but is the only predatory bird to hunt on the ground, using its long legs to stalk and stamp on snakes and other prey. Standing over 40 in (1 m) tall, it is mostly gray above and black below, with a red or orange face. The black feathers that stand out from the back of its head resemble quill pens, thus its name.

Secretion, complex substance produced in certain cells or glands in the body and discharged into or expelled from the body; also, the process of forming and discharging the substance. External secretions, those released through ducts from the exocrine glands onto an internal or external surface of the body, include tears, mucous, sweat, bile, saliva, and pancreatic juice. Internal secretions, or hormones, are released from the endocrine glands directly into the blood or lymph and effect processes distant from the point of origin. These include thyroxine, insulin, epinephrine, androgens, and estrogens.

Secret Service, United States, branch of the U.S. Treasury Department. Established 1865 to suppress the counterfeiting of currency, it became responsible for protecting the president after the assassination of President William McKinley (1901). It now also guards the vice president, the president-elect, presidential candidates, and former presidents.

Securities and Exchange Commission (SEC), independent agency of the U.S. government set up in 1934 to protect investors in securities (stocks and bonds). It requires disclosures of the structure of all public companies and registration of all securities exchanged. Its 5-member panel, appointed by the U.S. president, hears complaints, initiates investigations, issues brokerage licenses, and has broad powers to penalize fraud.
See also: Stock exchange.

Securities Exchange Act, U.S. law passed in 1934. The Securities Exchange Act established the Securities Exchange Commission, a federal agency charged with regulating the issuance and trade of corporate stocks and bonds. The Securities Exchange Act also allows the Federal Reserve to set margin requirements, the amount a buyer of securities must pay before receiving credit. The Securities Exchange Act replaced the Securities Act of 1933. Its purpose is to prevent the fraud and other financial practices that led to the Great Depression.
See also: Securities and Exchange Commission.

Security Council *See:* United Nations.

Sedative, any of several drugs that reduce anxiety and induce relaxation without causing sleep. Many are also hypnotics, drugs that in adequate doses may induce sleep. Barbiturates, among the earlier drugs used in sedation, have fallen into disfavor because of addiction, side-effects, dangers of over-dosage, and the availability of safer alternatives. Benzodiapezines (e.g., Valium, Librium), classified as minor tranquilizers, are now used more often.
See also: Barbiturate.

Seddon, James Alexander (1815-80), U.S. politician, Confederate secretary of war (1862-65). He was a close friend of Jefferson Davis, the Confederate president, but unpopular with the Confederate Congress. He supported an offensive military effort in the West and the conscription act. Seddon was born in Fredericksburg, Va., studied law at the Univ. of Virginia, and served in the U.S. House of Representatives before the Civil War.
See also: Civil War, U.S.

Sedge, any of a family (Cyperaceae) of grasslike plants found in damp places worldwide in temperate regions. They have triangular, flattened or cylindrical stems, and the leaves arise from sheaths that enclose the stem. The flowers are in clusters grouped in a spikelet. True sedges have triangular stems. Some are used for making matting. Other sedges include the bulrushes (genus *Scirpus*), cotton grass (genus *Eriophorum*), and papyrus (*Cyperus papyrus*).

Sedimentary rock, one of three main rock classes of the earth's crust; the others are igneous rock and metamorphic rock. Sedimentary rocks consist of weathered fragments of rock transported usually by water and deposited in distinct strata. They may also be of organic origin, as in coal and some organic limestone, or they may be formed by chemical processes, as in the evaporites. About three-quarters of the earth's land area and most of the ocean floor are covered by sedimentary rock. Most common are shale, sandstone, and limestone. Sedimentary rocks frequently contain fossils as well as most of the earth's mineral resources.

Sedition, incitement of the violent overthrow of the government. During World War I Congress passed sedition and espionage acts that banned communications attacking the U.S. government. In appealing convictions under these acts to the U.S. Supreme Court, defendants claimed a violation of their freedom of speech and press. The Court paid some attention to Justice Oliver Wendell Holmes's "clear and present danger" test but gave more weight to the "evil intent" of the defendants and, without exception, upheld their convictions.

Sedum, genus of succulent plants of the Crassulaceae family. Sedums are native to the temperate zone and tropical mountains of the Northern Hemisphere. Low-grading sedums are planted as ground and rock cover. Sedums are also called stonecrops and live-forevers.

See, Holy *See:* Pope.

Seed, mature reproductive body of angiosperms and gymnosperms (seed-bearing plants). It also represents a resting stage that enables plants to survive through unfavorable conditions. Seeds develop from the fertilized ovule. Each seed is covered with a tough coat called a testa, and contains a young plant or embryo. In most seeds three main regions of embryo can be recognized: a radicle, which gives rise to the root; a plumule, which forms the shoot; and one or two seed leaves, or cotyledons, which may or may not be taken above ground during germination. Plants that produce one seed leaf are called monocotyledons and those that produce two, dicotyledons. The seed also contains enough stored food to support embryo growth during and after germination. It is this stored food that is of value to animals. Flowering plants produce their seeds inside a fruit, but the seeds of conifers lie naked on the scales of the cone. Distribution of seeds is usually by wind, animals, or water, and the form of seeds is often adapted to a specific means of dispersal.
See also: Reproduction.

Seeger, Alan (1888-1916), U.S. poet. He joined the French Foreign Legion at the outbreak of World War I and was killed in France. Among his *Collected Poems* (1916) is the well-known "I Have a Rendezvous with Death."

Seeger, Pete (1919-), U.S. folksinger and conservation activist. A master of the 5-string banjo and 12-string guitar, he led the 1950s revival of interest in folk music with his group the Weavers. Many of his own songs, including "Where Have all the Flowers Gone?" (1961), have become classics of folk music.

Seeing Eye dog, animal trained to guide the blind. Most U.S. guide dogs are German shepherds and are schooled by The Seeing Eye Inc., founded (1929) by Dorothy Harrison Eustis.

Segal, George (1924-), U.S. sculptor. He is best known for his life-size white figures, resembling plaster casts of his subjects, placed in natural settings, such as a doorway or behind a steering wheel.

Sego lily, one of the mariposa lilies (*Calochortus nuttallii*) native to the dry areas of western North America. Its long stems (18 in/46 cm) grow from corms and bear narrow leaves and large 3-petaled flowers. The white petals are marked with yellow-green, purple, or lilac, with a purple spot at the center. The Mormon settlers in Utah used the edible corms as food. The sego lily is Utah's state flower.

Segovia, Andrés (1893-1987), Spanish classical guitarist, most celebrated of modern players. He did much to revive serious interest in the guitar, transcribing many pieces for it. Manuel de Falla, Heitor de Villa-Lobos, and others have composed works for him.

Segregation, separation of people according to race, religion, or ethnic origin. Custom or law may restrict the group's place of residence, use of public facilities and institutions, employment, movement, ownership of property, marriage, and the exercise of citizenship. Segregation has occurred throughout history and in most multiracial societies, especially those in which one group has seized or attained social, economic, and political dominance. In the United States from the early 1800s to the mid-1900s, laws required blacks and whites to use separate public facilities. This is known as *de jure* (by law) segregation. From the mid-1950s on, several Supreme Court decisions were made and federal laws passed that forbade segregation in voting, education, and the use of public facilities, and prohibited job discrimination in federally funded programs. While legal reforms and social patterns have made racial segregation less common in the world, it has not been eradicated. *De facto* segregation—segregation passed along through customs, not laws—actually increased in the mid-1900s and was one of the main causes of the race riots of the 1960s and early 1980s.

Seiche, standing wave that occurs in a lake, bay, or similar basin. A seiche is most often started by wind or a change in air pressure, and sometimes by an earthquake or ocean swell, that suddenly alters the basin's surface. While the surface regains stability, a simple harmonic wave is set in motion along the length of the basin. This wave is reflected by the basin's walls, creating interference. The repeated reflections produce a standing wave, a wave having fixed points with no vertical motion, with a wavelength equal to twice the length of the basin. Lasting a few minutes to an hour, seiches can interfere with shipping, damage property, and imperil lives.

Seifert, Jaroslav (1901-85), Czechoslovakian poet who was awarded the 1984 Nobel Prize for literature. His early work concentrated on revolutionary themes. *City in Tears*, his first book of poems, was published when he was 20.

Seigneurial system, feudal system of landholding practiced in France and in the French colonies in eastern Canada. Beginning in the early 1600s, the French king granted land in Canada to nobles, religious groups, merchants, and military officers. The *seigneury*, often narrow strips of land touching the St. Lawrence River, generally covered 12-100 sq mi (31-259 sq km). The owners, or *seigneurs*, rented the land to farmers in return for an annual payment, a share of the harvest, and several days' free labor. The seigneurs and tenants provided the king with military service and contributed material and labor to such works as the building and maintenance of public roads. The seigneurial system at first spurred French settlement of Canada, but it

later proved an impediment to industrialization and urban expansion. The system was abolished by the Canadian government in 1854.
See also: Feudalism.

Seine River, France's principal waterway. Rising on the Langres Plateau 18 mi (29 km) northwest of Dijon, it winds 475 mi (764 km) northwest to Paris, where over 30 bridges span it, through Rouen and Normandy, to the English Channel. It is the main artery of a far-reaching river system converging on Paris. Canals link it to the Loire, Rhône, Rhine, and Schelde rivers.

Seismograph, instrument used to detect and record seismic waves caused by earthquakes, nuclear explosions, etc.; the record it produces is a seismogram. The simplest seismograph has a horizontal bar, pivoted at one end with a recording pen at the other. The bar, supported by a spring, bears a heavy weight. As the ground moves, the bar remains roughly stationary owing to the inertia of the weight, while the rest of the equipment moves. The pen traces the vibrations on a moving belt of paper. Seismographs are used in seismic prospecting.
See also: Richter scale.

Seismology, branch of geophysics concerned with the study of earthquakes, seismic waves and their propagation through the earth's interior. Seismologists use seismographs to detect the location and severity of earthquakes and to locate oil and minerals.
See also: Geophysics.

Selassie, Haile *See:* Haile Selassie.

Selective Service System *See:* Draft, military.

Selene, in Greek mythology, goddess of the moon, called Luna in Roman mythology. At night, her crescent-shaped crown shining gold, she drove a 2-horse chariot across the sky. She figures in magic rituals held at the full and new moons. There are few myths about her and her relationship to the other Greek gods and goddesses is unclear. Helios, the sun god, was her brother, or possibly her father. She was the daughter of Hyperion and Theia or Zeus and Leto. Some Greek writers added to the confusion by identifying Selene with Artemis, a goddess also associated with the moon.
See also: Mythology.

Selenium, chemical element, symbol Se; for physical constants see Periodic Table. Selenium was discovered by Jöns J. Berzelius in 1817. It occurs in nature in the minerals crooksite and clausthalite. It is obtained commercially from the anode muds left from electrolytic copper refining, from which selenium is prepared by roasting with soda or sulfuric acid. Selenium is a lustrous gray metalloid which exists in several allotropic forms. It can be amorphous or crystalline. The most stable form is the crystalline hexagonal form. Selenium is an essential trace element for humans, however selenides resemble arsenic in their extreme toxicity. Selenium and its compounds are used in photocells, light meters, solar cells, rectifiers, special glasses, and xerography.

Seleucid dynasty (312-64 B.C.), dynasty in southwestern Asia, founded by Seleucus I (c.358-354 B.C.-218 B.C.). A general under Alexander the Great, Seleucus gained control of the eastern part of the Macedonian empire following Alexander's death (323 B.C.). The Seleucids came to rule the area between what is now Turkey and India. In the 200s B.C., the Parthians overran their eastern lands. In the 100s B.C., the Romans began to take over their western regions and brought the dynasty to a close with the occupation of Syria (64 B.C.). The Seleucids helped to spread Greek culture to western Asia.

Seljuks, members of the ruling family of Ouz Turkmen tribes. The warlike and nomadic Seljuks originated in Turkestan, in central Asia, and were named for Seljuk, their first leader. The Seljuks invaded western Asia in the mid-11th century. By 1092 they controlled most of Iran and all of Mesopotamia, Syria, and Palestine. But the Seljuks' territory soon was splintered into small states, one of which, in Anatolia, gave rise to the Ottoman Turks and the modern Turkish state. During the Crusades of the 11th, 12th, and 13th centuries, the Islamic Seljuks defended the Holy Land against the European Christians.

Selkirk Mountains, subdivision of the Columbia Mountains and considered part of the Rocky Mountain system. Mostly in British Columbia, Canada, and touching Idaho and Montana in the United States, the Selkirk Mountains extend for 200 mi (322 km) between the Columbia River, on the west and north, and the Purcell Mountains, on the east. The Selkirk's higher northern peaks include Mt. Sir Sanford (11,590 ft/3,533 m), the range's highest. Glacier and Mt. Revelstoke national parks are also in the northern end. Illecillewaet is the Selkirk's largest glacier.

Selye, Hans (1907-82), Austrian-born Canadian physician best known for his work on the physiological effects of environmental stress, which he suggested might cause certain diseases.
See also: Physiology.

Semantics, study of meaning, concerned both with understanding the relationship of words and symbols to the ideas or objects that they represent and with tracing the histories of meanings and changes that have taken place in them. Semantics is thus a branch both of logic and linguistics. General semantics, propounded primarily by Alfred Korzybski, holds that habits of thought have lagged behind the language and logic of science.
See also: Linguistics.

Semaphore, system of visual signaling using flags or lights to represent letters and numbers. The first such system was introduced by Claude Chappe (1763-1805) used 5-10 mi (8-16 km) apart. Semaphore is still used for signaling between ships and on some railroads.

Semiconductor, solid with an electrical conductivity that lies between the high conductivity of metals and the low conductivity of insulators. A semiconductor device is an electronic element fabricated from crystalline materials, such as silicon or germanium, that in the pure state, are neither good conductors nor good insulators and are unusable for electronic purposes. When certain impurity atoms, such as phosphorus or arsenic, are diffused into the crystal structure of the pure metal, the electrical neutrality is upset, introducing positive or negative charge carriers.

Seminole, last Native American tribe to make peace with the U.S. government. Seminole formed in Florida out of an alliance including refugee Creek from Georgia, native Apalachee and runaway slaves. They fought Andrew Jackson's troops in 1817-18 while Florida was still a Spanish territory. The major Seminole War began in 1835 when the U.S. government ordered their removal to west of the Mississippi. A fierce guerrilla war against overwhelming odds ended in 1842, after which most Seminoles were moved to Oklahoma. However, a small band held out in the Everglades until 1934, when they agreed to a settlement.

Semiramis, mythical Assyrian queen who supposedly founded the city of Babylon. Born of the union of a Syrian youth and a fish goddess, she was raised by doves. She married King Ninus of Assyria, and became queen when he died. During her long reign, she conquered Persia and Egypt. She was overthrown by her son and became a dove. Her story may be based on the life of Sammuramat, regent of Assyria (810-805 B.C.).
See also: Babylon.

Semites, in the Old Testament, the "sons of Shem" (who was the son of Noah). The term now generally applies to speakers of Semitic languages, including ancient Akkadians, Babylonians, Assyrians, and Phoenicians and modern Arabs and Israelis.
See also: Old Testament.

Semitic languages, group of the Hamito-Semitic language family found in the Near East and North Africa. Most of the group is now extinct; extant members include Hebrew, Arabic and Maltese. A few were written in cuneiform, but most used alphabets. Most of the letters of the Latin alphabet have descended from the North Semitic alphabet, the first fully formed alphabetical writing system.

Semmelweis, Ignaz Philipp (1818-65), Hungarian obstetrician. He was the first doctor to use antiseptic methods in childbirth, after his discovery that puerperal fever was transmitted by obstetricians who had failed to thoroughly clean their hands after performing autopsies on mothers who had died of the disease and then had made examinations of living mothers.
See also: Obstetrics.

Senate, one of the two lawmaking bodies in the United States. It consists of two senators from each state who serve six-year terms. Every two years, one-third of the Senate is elected. The presiding officer of the Senate is the vice president. Both the House of Representatives and the Senate have an equal voice in legislation. The Constitution requires that a U.S. senator be at least 30 years old, be a citizen for at least nine years, and maintain legal residence in the state represented.
See also: Congress of the United States.

Sendak, Maurice (1928-), U.S. illustrator and author of children's books whose inventive renderings both delight and startle. His works include the

Caldecott Medal winners *Where the Wild Things Are* (1963) and *In the Night Kitchen* (1970). His lively art became known to a wider public in the 1980s through his stage sets for operas, including *Così fan tutte*.

Seneca, Native American tribe (*O-non-dowanagh*, "people of the great hill") of western New York and eastern Ohio, once the largest nation of the Iroquois League (5 tribes that banded together in the 1400s). The Seneca built their villages on hills above a river and surrounded them with tall wooden stake fences for protection. They lived in large rectangular dwellings (longhouses), 30-50 per village, which gave shelter to several related families. Today most Seneca live on 3 reservations in western New York; they make up the Seneca Nation (a republic) and the Tonawanda Band of Seneca (ruled traditionally by chiefs).

Seneca, Lucius Annaeus (4 B.C.?-A.D.65), Roman statesman, philosopher, and writer. As Nero's tutor, he restrained the worst excesses of the young emperor. Writing in highly rhetorical, epigrammatic style, Seneca advocated stoicism in his *Moral Letters*, essays, one masterly satire, and nine bloody, intense tragedies. After implication in a conspiracy, he was commanded to commit suicide.
See also: Nero; Rome, Ancient.

Senefelder, Alois (1771-1834), German lithographer. He invented the process of lithography in Munich when he inked and printed some wax crayon marks he had made on a stone slab (c.1796). He published a history of the method in 1818. Senefelder was also a playwright.
See also: Lithography.

Senegal, westernmost country in Africa, formerly part of French West Africa.
Land and climate. Bordering on the Atlantic Ocean, Senegal is flanked on the north by Mauritania, on the east by Mali, and on the south by Guinea. The small independent country of Gambia cuts deeply into southern Senegal from the Atlantic coast, forming a long, narrow enclave along the Gambia River. Senegal has an area of 75,955 sq mi (196,722 sq km). The country is mostly plain, with the semi-desert Ferlo area in the northeast and savanna grassland elsewhere. In the north, the Senegal River has a broad flood plain which is cultivated. The south is drained by the Gambia, Casamance, Sine, and Saloum rivers. The coastline is sandy in the north and muddy in the south. Climate varies, but is relatively cool along the coast most of the year. Inland temperatures are much higher, especially in the northeast.
People. The people are black African, the most numerous ethnic groups being the Wolof, Fulani, Serer, Toucouleur, and Diola peoples. More than 80% of the people are Muslim. Dakar, the capital, is a modern port city. The official language is French.
Economy. The majority of the people are employed in agriculture, the mainstay of Senegal's economy. Peanuts are the major crop, and peanut processing is the leading industry. Senegal's industrial sector is growing. Limestone and phosphates are important mineral exports, and oil and natural gas deposits have yet to be exploited.
History. Parts of Senegal were within the medieval empires of Ghana, Mali, and Songhai. Under French control and part of French West Africa from

Senegal

Capital:	Dakar
Area:	75,955 sq mi (196,722 sq km)
Population:	9,723,000
Language:	French, Wolof
Government:	Presidential republic
Independent:	1960
Head of gov.:	Prime minister
Per capita:	U.S. $600
Mon. unit:	1 CFA franc = 100 centimes

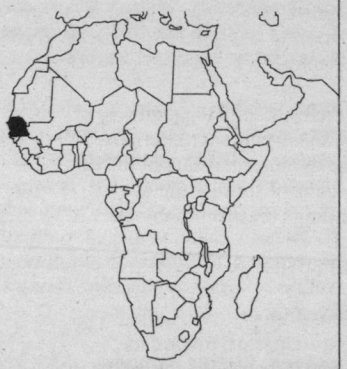

1895, Senegal became part of the Federation of Mali from 1959 to 1960, but declared independence in 1960. Under the presidency of Leopold-Sédar Senghor for two decades following independence, Senegal elected Abdou Diouf to succeed Senghor in 1981. Diouf was reelected in 1988. In the 1990s Diouf had to deal with a secession movement in Casamance.

Senghor, Léopold Sédar (1906-), Senegalese statesman and poet, Senegal's first president (1960-80), and first black member of the French academy (1984). He became known for his philosophy of *négritude*, a concept of socialism incorporating black African values and rejected the French policy of assimilation.
See also: Senegal.

Senility, general mental and physical deterioration often (but not always) seen in the elderly. Because the term refers to several conditions and causes, experts on the elderly avoid using it. Failure of recent memory, dwelling on the past, episodic confusion, and difficulty in absorbing new information are common conditions associated with so-called senility. Permanent damage can be caused by the brain diseases multi-infarct dementia and Alzheimer's disease.
See also: Alzheimer's disease; Geriatrics.

Senna (*Cassia marilandica*), perennial plant of which the leaves are used for medicinal purposes. Senna is an effective laxative when combined with other herbs.

Sennacherib (d.681 B.C.; r.704-681 B.C.), Assyrian king who succeeded his father, Sargon II. Sennacherib's reign was characterized by war. He put down a revolt by the Elams and the Babylonians led by Merodach-Baladan, the former Babylonian king (703 B.C.). He defeated Egypt and, except for Jerusalem, crushed revolts in Syria and Palestine (701 B.C.). He again fought Babylon and razed the city in 689 B.C. He made Nineveh the Assyrian capital and a magnificent city. Sennacherib was murdered by his sons.
See also: Assyria.

Sennett, Mack (1884-1960), Canadian-born U.S. silent movie director-producer, a pioneer of slapstick humor on the screen. After working with D.W.

Griffith, he formed his own Keystone Co. and made over 1,000 short subjects ("shorts") with his Keystone Kops, Bathing Beauties, and stars like Charlie Chaplin, W.C. Fields, and Gloria Swanson.

Senses, media through which stimuli in the environment of an organism act on the organism (external senses); also, the internal senses, which report on the the internal state of the organism (through thirst, hunger, pain, etc.). The organs of sense—the eye ear, skin, etc.—contain specialized cells and nerve endings that communicate with centers in the nervous system. Sense organs may be stimulated by pressure (in touch, hearing, and balance), chemical stimulation (smell, taste), or electromagnetic radiation (vision, heat sensors).

Sensitive plant, small shrub (*Mimosa pudica*) of the pea family. Its leaves and stems curl toward the main stem when touched or exposed to fumes. The plant is native to the tropics of the Western Hemisphere and is grown in greenhouses.

Sensitivity training, technique using group discussion and interaction intended to increase one's awareness of self and others and how one behaves with others. Sensitivity training takes many forms and goes by many names: encounter group, T-group, human relations, and group dynamics training. The group has 8-20 participants. The leader, who is trained in psychotherapy, establishes a psychologically safe environment and encourages participants to speak frankly about their feelings and each other, but remains neutral and outside the discussion. The participants choose the topics and direct the discussion. They examine their reactions to each other and test new ways to communicate. The goal of sensitivity training is to develop trust and improve communication and intrapersonal behavior. The techniques of sensitivity training have been applied to education and to training businesspeople. Sensitivity training was developed at the Esalen Institute, Big Sur, Calif., and was popular in the 1960s.

Seoul (pop. 10,612,600), or Kyongsong, capital, largest city, and industrial and cultural center of South Korea, on the Han River, 25 mi (40 km) east of Inchon, its seaport. It was founded in 1392 as capital of the Yi dynasty, and remained so until 1910. Seoul changed hands several times in the Korean War and suffered great damage. Largely built, it has grown rapidly. The 1988 Summer Olympic Games were held in Seoul.
See also: Korea.

Separation of powers, political theory developed by Montesquieu from his studies of the British constitution, arguing that the arbitrary exercise of government power should be avoided by dividing it between distinct departments: the executive, legislature, and judiciary. This was a basic principle of the Founding Fathers in producing the U.S. Constitution; legislative powers were vested in Congress, judicial powers in the Supreme Court and subsidiary courts, and executive powers in the president and his governmental machinery. Each branch was to have its functions, duties, and authority, and in theory no branch could encroach upon another. In practice there has always been a degree of necessary overlap. The legislature can oppose and impeach members of the executive, the president can veto legislation, and the Supreme Court can adjudicate the actions of the other branches; its members, in turn,

are presidential appointees subject to congressional approval. In U.S. history one branch has always tended to dominate others for long periods, but this "checks and balances" ensures that power can and does shift between them.
See also: Montesquieu.

Separatists, in religion, English Christian congregations that sought independence from the state and Established Church, beginning in 1580 with the Norwich Brownists. John Robinson led refugee Separatists in Leyden, the Netherlands, who were later prominent among the Pilgrims.

Sepoy Rebellion, or Indian Mutiny, mutiny of Sepoys (Hindi, "troops") in the Bengal Army of the East India Company. It began at Meerut, near Delhi, in May 1857 and spread over northern India. The immediate cause was the issuing of cartridges greased with the fat of cows (sacred to Hindus) and pigs (unclean to Muslims), but the underlying cause, years of increasing British domination, led to a general revolt that was not suppressed until Mar. 1858. As a result, the British government took over the rule of India.
See also: India.

Septicemia *See:* Blood poisoning.

Septuagint, oldest Greek translation of the Hebrew Old Testament, probably from an older source than any now extant. The Pentateuch was translated in Alexandria at the behest of Ptolemy II (250 B.C.), according to legend by 70 scholars (hence the name *septuagiht*, Latin for "seventy"). It was completed, including the Apocrypha in 130 B.C.
See also: Old Testament.

Sequoia, genus including the two largest trees, the redwood (*Sequoia sempervirens*) and the giant sequoia (*Sequoiadendron giganteum*), both found only in the Pacific Northwest of the United States. Only the bristlecone pine lives longer. The largest living organism in the world is the General Sherman giant sequoia in Sequoia National Park, which is over 270 ft (82 m) high with a circumference at the base of over 100 ft (30.5 m).

Sequoia National Park, park in south-central California (administered with the adjacent Kings Canyon National Park), established in 1890 to preserve the groves of giant sequoia. It covers 402,482 acres (162,879 hectares). Lying in the southern Sierra Nevada, it includes Mount Whitney, the highest U.S. peak outside Alaska.

Sequoyah (c.1770-1843), Cherokee silversmith who devised an alphabet whose 85 characters represented every sound in the Cherokee language, enabling thousands of Cherokee to read and write. The sequoia tree is named for him.

Serapis, Egyptian god, worshipped also in Greece and Rome. He ruled the underworld and the universe and was lord of the Nile. He was a source of fertility and healing and gave the oracles speech. The god may have derived his traits and name from the more ancient gods Osiris and Apis. Osiris was

also a fertility god, ruled the underworld, and associated with Isis. Apis was the earthly form of Osiris. The Ptolmaic rulers of Egypt (323-330 B.C.) built temples to Serapis and encouraged his worship.
See also: Mythology.

Serbia, Balkan state. The Serbs were Slavs who settled the Balkans from the 600s onward. Stephen Nemanja (r.1168- 96) created the first united kingdom, which became a great empire under Stephen Dushan (r.1331-55), but after the battle of Kosovo (1389) Serbia remained under Turkish rule until independence was restored in 1878. After World War I occupation by Austria, it became the core of the kingdom of Yugoslavia. After 1992 it formed the Federal Republic of Yugoslavia together with Montenegro. Serbia (34,00 sq mi/88,060 sq km) is mountainous and mainly agricultural. Its capital is Belgrade.
See also: Yugoslavia, Federal Republic of.

Serf, medieval peasant generally bound to the land. A serf held the lowest status in the feudal hierarchy and owed allegiance, service, and often certain payments to the lord. The serf retained a number of hereditary rights that were usually determined by local custom. With the development of a money economy and the growth of towns, many serfs escaped or purchased their freedom, and by the 18th century serfdom had largely died out. In Russia and parts of eastern Europe, however, forms of serfdom survived into the 19th century.
See also: Manorialism.

Sergeant at arms, officer who preserves order in a legislative, judicial, or social organization. The sergeant at arms has the power to execute commands, such as serving legal papers, and to require the body's members to attend meetings. Anyone who disregards the sergeant at arms is guilty of contempt. Each house of the U.S. Congress has a sergeant at arms. The office of sergeant at arms is believed to have been instituted by Richard I of England.

Series, in mathematics, sum of a sequence of terms (numbers or algebraic expressions). The terms in a sequence have a specific relationship and order based on how the terms are formed. The series may be finite (with a definite sum), or infinite. As more terms from an infinite series are added, the sum may approach a value called the limit. Series with a limit are said to converge; those without a limit diverge. Mathematicians have devised formulas and notations to express the values of a series and individual terms in a series.
See also: Mathematics.

Serkin, Rudolf (1903-91), Bohemian-born U.S. pianist. He studied with Arnold Schoenberg in Vienna, made his U.S. debut in 1933, and joined the Curtis Institute of Music, Philadelphia, in 1939. A noted Beethoven interpreter, he played in concerts all over the world. His son Peter (1947-) is also a prominent pianist.

Sermon on the Mount *See:* Beatitudes; Golden rule.

Serpentine, hydrous magnesium silicate mineral, $Mg_3(Si_2O_5)(OH)_4$, that occurs in 2 forms: chrisotile, the fibrous variety which is the primary source of asbestos, and antigorite, the flaky variety. Serpentine, usually green, may also be black, red, yellow, gray, or white. It is used as an indoor building or decorative stone or as a gemstone. Serpentine is widely distributed and is quarried in Quebec, the USSR, South Africa, and the United States.

Serra, Junípero (1713-84), Spanish Franciscan missionary who founded 9 of California's 21 missions. Serra was ordained (1738) and taught philosophy on the island of Majorca, Spain. He traveled to Mexico City (1749) and then to Sierra Gorda, Mexico to help staff the mission there (1750-59). He joined Gaspar de Portolá's expedition to upper California (1769) and established the mission of San Diego de Alcalá, now the city of San Diego. Between 1770 and 1782 Serra ordered the founding of 8 more missions, including San Luis Obispo and San Juan Capistrano.
See also: Franciscans.

Serum, clear yellowish fluid that separates from blood, lymph, and other body fluids when they clot. It contains water, proteins, fat, minerals, hormones, and urea. Serum therapy involves injecting serum (obtained from humans or horses) containing antibodies (globulins) that can destroy particular pathogens. Occasionally injected serum gives rise to an allergic reaction known as serum sickness; a second injection of the same serum may induce anaphylaxis (hypersensitivity).
See also: Gamma globulin; Plasma.

Serval (*Felis capensis*), large, black spotted, nocturnal wildcat of Africa. It has long legs, a small head, and pointed ears. Its prey is mainly rodents and sometimes birds, reptiles, or insects.

Servetus, Michael (Miguel Serveto; 1511-53), Spanish theologian and physician whose religious work *Christianismi restitutio* (1553) contains the earliest known description of the pulmonary circulation of blood. As a theologian, Servetus antagonized Roman Catholics and Protestants alike by denying the doctrines of the trinity (*De trinitatus erroribus*, 1531), transubstantiation, and original sin. He eventually embraced pantheism, believing that a supreme intelligence orders the universe. He was tried for heresy by the Inquisition (1553) and condemned to death, but escaped from prison. Passing through Geneva, Switzerland several months later, Servetus was arrested on the orders of John Calvin, retried, and burned at the stake.
See also: Inquisition.

Serviceberry, also called shadbush, shadblow, or Juneberry, wild rose tree or shrub found in many parts of North America and in the Mediterranean region and eastern Asia. It bears clusters of small white flowers and blue fruits.

Service industries, commercial, government, or nonprofit occupations performed without involving the sale of commodities. Service industries may be classified as several types: business services, including advertising, bookkeeping, or banking; personal services which might include recreation, travel, housekeeping, and beauty or barbershops; art, including theaters and museums; the professions, including legal, medical, or educational services; and government. Economists consider service occupations an indicator of a country's economic development: the greater the growth, the more advanced the nation. In the late 1950s services accounted for 25% of the U.S. gross national product, and in the 1980s for 66%.

Servomechanism, or feedback control system, automatic device that detects and corrects errors and maintains constant performance of a mechanism, for example an automatic pilot.
See also: Automation.

Sesame (*Sesamum indicum*), tropical plant cultivated mainly in China and India for its flat seeds; also, the seeds themselves. Sesame seeds yield an oil used as a salad or cooking oil and in margarine, cosmetics, and ointments. The residue left after oil extraction is used as a cattle feed and fertilizer.

Sesshu (1419-1506), Japanese Buddhist monk and landscape artist. Combining Chinese ink-painting technique with Japanese aesthetics, Sesshu's style is characterized by strong composition, straightforward forms, and vigorous brushstrokes. He produced his greatest works, including screens, scrolls, and religious paintings, after 1469, following a period of study in China.

Sessions, Roger (1896-1985), U.S. composer, winner of the Pulitzer Prize for music (1982). He was professor of music at the University of California, Berkeley (1945) and Princeton University (1935-45, 1953-65). Sessions's compositions include operas, symphonies, piano sonatas, and chorus music. He is best known for *The Black Maskers* (1923) and *Concerto for Orchestra* (1981). His written works include *The Musical Experience of Composer, Performer and Listener* (1950) and his collected essays, *Roger Sessions on Music* (1979).

Sessions, William Steele (1930-), U.S. Federal Bureau of Investigation (FBI) director since 1987. After practicing law, he worked as a criminal prosecutor for the U.S. Justice Department (1969-71), actively prosecuting Vietnam draft evaders. He was named by President Richard Nixon as a district attorney for western Texas (1971-74) and by President Gerald Ford as a U.S. district judge (1974-87).
See also: Federal Bureau of Investigation.

Seth, or **Set**, in Egyptian mythology, god of evil, represented with an ass's head and a pig's snout. Originally a royal deity, he came to personify evil as killer of Osiris, god of goodness. Osiris's son Horus fought and killed Seth.
See also: Mythology.

Seti I, Egyptian ruler of the 19th dynasty who reigned about 1303-1290 B.C. Seti I established his seat of government at Memphis and directed several military campaigns into Syria against the Hittites. He built his mortuary temple at Abydos in the Valley of the Kings and continued work on the temple of Amon at Karnak. Seti I was the father of Ramses II.
See also: Egypt, Ancient.

Seton, Saint Elizabeth Ann, or Mother Seton (1774-1821), first native-born U.S. saint. A devout Episcopalian, she was widowed at 28 with five children. In 1805, she converted to Catholicism. She opened an elementary school (1808), regarded as the basis of the U.S. parochial school system, and in 1813 founded the first U.S. religious society, the Sisters of Charity. She was canonized in 1975. Her feast day is Jan. 4.

Setter, 3 breeds of long-haired dog used in bird hunting: the English, the Gordon, and the Irish setter. Classified in the United States as sporting dogs, setters are derived from the medieval setting spaniel. They have long heads and tails, silky coats, and hanging ears. A setter is trained to locate game by smell, come to a point with its nose directed toward the bird, and retrieve the game after the shot.

Set theory, branch of mathematics or symbolic (mathematical) logic in which systems are analyzed by membership in and exclusion from *sets*. A set is any specified collection of *elements* or *members*. In the notation of set theory, members of a set are enclosed in braces as, {a,b,d,x}. Alternatively, a rule defining inclusion in the set may appear in braces. The expression {xx is a U.S. state bordered by 3 or more other states} defines the set of all U.S. states bordered by 3 or more other states; this is a *finite set*, having a definite number of members. The set of all positive even numbers is an example of an *infinite set*, one with an infinite number of members. It might be represented as {2,4,6,8,...} or as {xx/2 is an integer greater than 0}. *Null sets*, those with no members (e.g., all U.S. presidents who are female, nonwhite, or non-Christian) are represented as { }. Sets that have exactly the same members (the set of all U.S. presidents who have served more than 2 terms, the set of all presidents crippled by polio) are said to be *equal sets*, while those with the same number of members but not necessarily the identical membership are *equivalent*. Set A is a *subset* of set B if all of the members of set A are contained in set B. (The set of all equal sets is thus a subset of the set of all equivalent sets, but not vice versa). The *union* of 2 sets A and B (A B) is the combined membership of those 2 sets. The *intersection* of sets A and B ($A \cap B$) is the set of those elements belonging to both set A and set B. *Disjoint* sets have no common members and thus their intersection is a null or empty set (the set of all women, the set of all U.S. presidents). If A is a subset of B, the *complement* of A consists of all members of B not in A. Set theory, which owes much to the techniques of symbolic logic established by 19th-century English mathematician George Boole, was developed by 19th-century German mathematician Georg Cantor. It is of particular importance in representing logical relationships and approaches to algebraic solutions.
See also: Mathematics.

Settlement house, neighborhood center established to provide social services to inner-city communities and usually staffed by social workers. Samuel A. Barnett, an English clergyman, founded the first settlement house, Toynbee Hall (1884) in London, to restore the neighborhood order disrupted by the Industrial Revolution. The original U.S. settlement house was University Settlement, founded (1886) by Stanton Coit, in New York City. Jane Addams's Hull House in Chicago began (1889) as a settlement. Settlement house programs include counseling, rehabilitation for the disabled, child welfare, athletics and recreation, hobby and interest groups, classes in citizenship and English, and manual training. Originally privately funded, settlement house services were forerunners of tax-supported public welfare

programs. There are now some 300 settlement houses in the United States overseen by the United Neighborhood Centers of America.
See also: Hull House.

Seurat, Georges (1859-91), French painter, one of a small group representing neoimpressionism or postimpressionism. Interested in color both scientifically and artistically, he invented pointillism, in which discrete points of color are placed to create patterns that are perceived at a distance as complex tones. His works include *A Sunday Afternoon on the Island of La Grande Jatte* (1884-46).
See also: Impressionism.

Seuss, Dr. (Theodor Seuss Geisel; 1904-), U.S. author-illustrator of children's books. His many imaginative verse tales—*Horton Hears a Who* (1954), *How the Grinch Stole Christmas* (1957)—and humorous pictorial fantasies are tremendously popular. In 1984 he was acknowledged by the Pulitzer committee for having contributed for nearly half a century to the education and reading enjoyment of U.S. children.

Sevastopol (pop. 335,000), Black Sea port of the Crimea peninsula in Ukraine, southeast Europe. Now an industrial city, and railroad terminal with lumber milling and shipbuilding industries, the city suffered long sieges in the Crimean War (349 days; 1854-55) and World War II (8 months; 1941-42). During the Soviet period there was a major naval base. Sevastopol is situated near the site of the ancient Greek colony Chersonesus, founded in 421 B.C. It eventually became part of the Roman Empire (first century B.C.) and Byzantine Empire (4th century A.D.).

Seven Cities of Cibola *See:* Cibola, Seven Cities of.

Seven seas, archaic collective term for the world's large bodies of water. The term is usually thought to refer to the Arctic, Antarctic, North and South Atlantic, Indian, and North and South Pacific oceans.

Seventh-day Adventists, Christian religious group, organized in 1863 in both Europe and the United States, who believe that Christ will return in person. They observe the Sabbath on Saturday, the seventh day of the week. There are about 2 million members in 150 countries.
See also: Christianity.

Seven Weeks' War (Austro-Prussian War, June 16-August 23, 1866), conflict between Austria (and its German allies), led by Field Marshal Lieutenant von Benedek, and Prussia (and its Italian ally) under Helmuth Karl von Moltke, over control of the Danish duchies of Schleswig and Holstein. Austria declared war on Prussia on June 14, 1866, and the decisive battle was fought July 3 at Königgrätz in Bohemia, resulting in a Prussian victory. The war ended formally on Aug. 23 with the Treaty of Prague. It gave Prussia undisputed leadership of the new North German Confederacy, effectively ending Austrian influence in German affairs.

Seven Wonders of the Ancient World, seven magnificent structures of the ancient world, as listed by Greek scholars. The oldest and only to survive are the pyramids of Egypt. The others were the Hanging Gardens of Babylon, the 30-ft (9-m) statue of Zeus at Olympia, the great temple of Artemis at Ephesus, the mausoleum at Halicarnassus, the Colossus of Rhodes, and the Pharos lighthouse of Alexandria.

Seven Years' War (1756-63), war between Austria, France, Russia, Saxony, Sweden (from 1757), and Spain (after 1762) on the one side and Britain, Prussia, and Hanover on the other. In the United States the struggle centered on colonial rivalry between Britain and France, and formed part of the French and Indian Wars. In Europe the main dispute was between Austria and Prussia for supremacy in Germany. Austria's Maria Theresa aimed to recover Silesia (lost in the War of the Austrian Succession). This provoked Prussia to attack Saxony and Bohemia. Although severely pressed, the Prussians avoided complete defeat. By the treaties of Hubertusberg and Paris (1763), Britain emerged as the leading colonial power and Prussia as a major European force.

Severn, River, Britain's longest river, 220 mi (354 km) long. It rises in eastern Wales and flows east and south into the Bristol Channel. The Severn Bridge is one of the world's longest suspension bridges.

Sevier, John (1745-1815), U.S. pioneer and first governor of Tennessee (1796-80, 1803-09). He was prominent in the Carolina Campaign of the Revolutionary War and became head of the temporary state of Franklin (1785-88). He represented Tennessee in the U.S. Congress (1789-91, 1811-15).
See also: Franklin, State of.

Seville (pop. 663,000), city of southwest Spain, capital of Seville province, and an important industrial center and port on the Guadalquivir River. Seville produces tobacco, machinery, and perfume, among other products, and exports wine and olives. The city is famous for its historic buildings, including the Gothic cathedral (1401-1519), and Holy Week processions. It was the birthplace of the painters Diego Velázquez and Bartolomé Murillo.
See also: Spain.

Sèvres, Treaty of (1920), peace pact between the Allies and Turkey after World War I, signed at Sèvres, France. It redistributed almost all of the Turkish Ottoman Empire, leaving only Istanbul and Anatolia under Turkish control. Though signed by the representatives of Sultan Mohammed VI, the treaty was never ratified by the Turkish National Assembly. After the overthrow of the government by Kemal Atatürk and the nationalists (1922), the Treaty of Sèvres was superseded by the Treaty of Lausanne (1923), which offered Turkey more acceptable terms.
See also: World War I.

Sewage, liquid and semisolid wastes from dwellings and offices, industrial wastes, and surface and storm waters. Sewage systems collect the sewage, transport and treat it, then discharge it into rivers, lakes, or the sea. Vaulted sewers had been developed by the Romans, but from the Middle Ages until the mid-19th century sewage flowed through the open gutters of cities, constituting a major health hazard. Later sewage was discharged into storm-water drains that were developed into sewers. Because the dumping of large amounts of untreated sewage into rivers led to a serious water pollution, modern treatment methods arose, at least for major cities. An early solution (still sometimes practiced) was sewage farming, in which raw sewage was used as fertilizer. Noting that natural watercourses can purify a moderate amount of sewage, sanitary engineers imitated natural conditions by allowing atmospheric oxidation of the organic matter by the activated-sludge process, in which compressed air is passed through a sewage tank, where the sludge is decomposed by the many microorganisms that it contains. A by-product is sludge gas, chiefly methane, burned as fuel to help power the treatment plant. Sedimentation is carried out before and after decomposition; the filtered solids are buried, incinerated, or dried for fertilizer. Dwellings not connected to the sewers have their own septic tanks.

Sewall, Samuel (1652-1730), colonial American politician and jurist best known as one of the judges in the Salem, Mass., witchcraft trials (1692). He was also justice of the colony superior court (1692-1718) and chief justice of the province (1718-25). A liberal, Sewall later publicly repented his part in the witchcraft trials, in which 19 people were condemned to death. His writings include an early antislavery tract *The Selling of Joseph* (1700), *A Memorial Relating to the Kennebeck Indians* (1721), and his 3-volume *Diary* (1878-82).
See also: Salem witchcraft trials.

Seward, William Henry (1801-72), U.S. politician famous for his purchase of Alaska from Russia in 1867. A prominent antislavery senator, he was appointed secretary of state by President Abraham Lincoln in 1861. He did much to keep Britain out of the Civil War. Seward survived an assassination attempt by an accomplice of John Wilkes Booth, and served as President Andrew Johnson's secretary of state.

Sewing, use of a needle and thread to attach, repair, fasten, or decorate fabric or other materials. Sewing dates from the second Stone Age period, when stone or bone needles and hair or animal ligament thread were used to stitch pieces of skin together. Sewing now may be accomplished by hand or machine. The most basic hand-sewing stitches are basting, running, slip-stitch, blindstitch, overcast, and catch stitch. Isaac Merritt Singer, improving on earlier inventions, produced the first sewing machine practical for home use (1851). Singer's machine used a top thread with a bobbin thread, allowing continuous stitching. Modern machines commonly provide 3 types of stitches: straight, zigzag, and embroidery. Mechanical sergers can sew, trim, and finish straight seams in a single operation.

Sewing machine, machine for sewing cloth, leather, or books. There are two main types: chainstitch machines, using a needle and only one thread, with a hook that pulls each looped stitch through the next, and lockstitch machines, using two threads, one through the needle eye and the other interlocking with the first in the material, from a bobbin/shuttle system. Chain-stitch machines—the first to be invented, by Barthélemy Thimmonier (1793-1859)—are now used chiefly to make sacks or bags. The lockstitch machines now in general use are based on the one invented by Elias Howe (1846). Isaac M. Singer invented the foot treadle and the presser foot (1850), which holds the fabric down. Zigzag machines differ from ordinary straight-stitch machines in having variously shaped cams that move the needle from side to side. Almost all U.S. machines are electrically powered, but foot-treadle machines are common elsewhere.

Sex (sexual behavior), term covering a wide range of behavior derived from or analogous to sexuality and sexual drive. To the psychologist "sex" and "sexual behavior" are used in connection with human drives linked to reproduction, including fantasies, sensations, etc. To the psychoanalyst, sexual behavior has its roots in infantile sexuality as well as instinct.

Sex education, study of human sexuality and how it is acquired and expressed. Sex education begins in early childhood when children first show curiosity about their sexuality and body processes. Until the mid-20th century, satisfaction of that curiosity was solely a function of a child's parents, and information from outside the family was discouraged. Today children may receive sexual information from their peers, the media, churches, or schools and rely less on traditional sources. Sex education has generated controversy between those who believe that home sex education may be inadequate and those who believe it may encourage premarital sex or fail to teach moral responsibility. Many sex education curricula are available to schools and other agencies, beginning with programs for kindergarten and continuing through high school. They cover aspects of human sexuality including social, physical, and psychological aspects, rudimentary anatomy, marriage, and parenthood.
See also: Calderone, Mary Steichen.

Sextant, instrument for navigation, invented in 1730, superseding the astrolabe. The sextant is named for its shape ($^1/_6$ of a circle). A fixed telescope is pointed at the horizon, and a radial arm bearing a mirror is moved against an arc graduated in degrees. The mirror reflects an image of a known star or the sun down the telescope to coincide with the image of the horizon. The angular elevation of the star, with the exact time, gives the latitude. The air sextant is a similar instrument, usually periscopic, designed for use in aircraft; it has an artificial horizon, generally a bubble level.
See also: Navigation.

Sexton, Anne (1928-74), U.S. poet. Her work was largely confessional and explicitly personal (*To Bedlam and Part Way Back*, 1960; *Live or Die*, 1966, Pulitzer Prize). *Transformations* (1971) is her ironic retelling of Grimms' fairytales. Sexton struggled with mental illness, ultimately committing suicide.

Seychelles, African republic consisting of about 85 islands in the Indian Ocean 1000 mi (1600 km) east of Kenya. Part of the British Commonwealth. Seychelles's total area is 175 sq mi (454 sq km) scattered over 400,000 sq mi (1 million sq km) of ocean. The climate is tropical. Victoria, on Mahé Island, is the capital and only city. Most of the population is Roman Catholic, of African and French descent, and speaks Creole, a French patois. Tourism, construction, agriculture, and fishing are the primary occupations. Cinnamon, coconuts and copra, vanilla, livestock, and poultry are the chief products. Portuguese explorer Vasco da Gama discovered Seychelles (1502),

Seychelles

Capital:	Victoria
Area:	175 sq mi (454 sq km)
Population:	79,000
Language:	Creole
Government:	Presidential republic
Independent:	1976
Head of gov.:	President
Per capita:	U.S. $6,620
Mon. unit:	1Rupiah = 100 cents

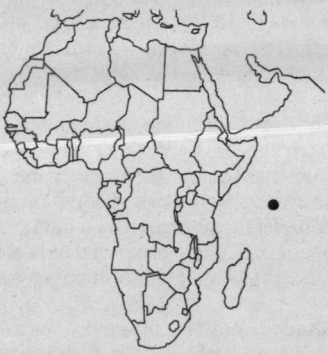

and French planters began colonizing the area in 1768. Britain controlled the islands from 1794 to 1976, when they achieved independence. The one party government established in 1979, was replaced by a multi party government in 1993, which was overthrown by a military coup in 1995.

Seymour, Horatio (1810-86), U.S. politician. As Democratic governor of New York (1862-64), he declared the Emancipation Proclamation unconstitutional and opposed national conscription, although he encouraged voluntary enlistment. He was defeated by Ulysses S. Grant in the 1868 presidential election.
See also: Copperheads.

Seymour, Jane (1509?-37), third wife of England's Henry VIII (from 1536). She died soon after the birth of her son, Edward VI.

Seyss-Inquart, Arthur von (1892-1946), Austrian Nazi leader, governor of Austria (1938-39), and deputy governor of Poland (1939-40). As a high commissioner for the Netherlands (1940-45), his cruelty was notorious. He was executed for war crimes.
See also: Nazism.

Shabuot *See:* Shavuot.

Shackleton, Sir Ernest Henry (1874-1922), Irish explorer who commanded 3 Antarctic expeditions (1907, 1914, 1921), the first of which came within 97 mi (156 km) of the South Pole and located the south magnetic pole. His 1914 expedition was marked by an open-boat crossing from Elephant Island to South Georgia Island and a winter traverse of that island's crest after his ship was crushed by ice. Written works include *Heart of the Antarctic* (1909), *South: The Story of Shackleton's 1914-1917 Expedition* (1919), and *Adventure* (1928).
See also: Antarctica.

Shad, deep-bodied food fish of the herring family (genus *Alosa*), which grows to about 3 lb (1.4 kg) and 2 ft (61 cm). Native to Atlantic waters from

Newfoundland to Florida, the shad was successfully introduced to Pacific waters (c.1871). Characterized by bluish coloring with silver sides and a spineless upper fin, it swims up freshwater rivers to spawn. Some shad is smoked and sold as kippers.

Shadow, reduction of light on an area caused when an opaque object interrupts the light source. The shadow appears on the side of the body away from the source; the brighter the light, the darker and crisper the shadow seems. A very dark shadow, called an umbra, occurs when the light is completely obstructed. A lighter area surrounding the umbra, called the penumbra, occurs when the light source is larger than the interrupting object, allowing some light to shine beyond it.

Shadow matter, in science, term to describe a theoretical form of matter that neither reflects nor absorbs light and interacts with ordinary matter only through the force of gravity. The existence of shadow matter (a type of dark matter) has not been proved, but physicists theorize that as much as 90% of the mass of the universe may be comprised of this kind of invisible particle.
See also: Dark matter.

Shafter, William Rufus (1835-1906), U.S. soldier. In the Spanish-American War, he led the U.S. expeditionary force that eventually gained the surrender of Santiago, Cuba (1898).
See also: Spanish-American War.

Shaftesbury, 3 important English earls, each bearing the name **Anthony Ashley Cooper**. The **1st earl** (1621-83) was a founder of the Whig Party and a staunch Protestant. After supporting both Cromwell and the Restoration, he became Lord Chancellor (1672) but was dismissed (1673) for supporting the Test Act. He then built up the Whig opposition to Charles II, supporting the duke of Monmouth, the pretender, and opposing James II's successor. He was acquitted of treason (1681) but fled to the Netherlands (1682). The **3rd earl** (1671-1713), grandson of the 1st, was a moral philosopher and pupil of John Locke. He aimed to found an ethical system based on an innate moral sense. The **7th earl** (1801-85) was a politician and leading evangelical Christian who promoted legislation to improve conditions in mines and factories and supported movements for better housing and schools.

Shah (Persian, "king"), title borne by the rulers of Middle Eastern and some Asian countries. It is used especially to refer to rulers of Iran (Persia) until 1979.

Shah Jahan (1592-1666), fifth mogul emperor of India (1628-58), under whose rule the Moguls achieved their cultural peak. He built New Delhi and is best known for construction of lavish buildings, particularly the Taj Mahal (1632-45) at Agra, a tomb for his wife, Mumtaz Mahall. He was deposed (1658) by his son Aurangzeb and imprisoned at Agra until his death.
See also: India.

Shahn, Ben (1898-1969), Lithuanian-born U.S. artist whose realistic works treated social and political themes. Influenced by Diego Rivera and painters of the Parisian school, Shahn's style is characterized by harsh colors and simplified linear forms. Shahn created his own murals, posters, advertising art, and photography. He is particularly known for his series of political paintings on the Dreyfuss Affair, the Sacco-Vanzetti trial, and the Tom Mooney labor disputes.

Shah Namah *See:* Firdausi.

Shakers, originally an abusive term for the United Society of Believers in Christ's Second Appearing, a religious sect whose members shook with ecstatic emotion in their worship. Originating among the Quakers of England, they were brought by "Mother" Ann Lee to the United States in 1774, where they formed celibate communes that flourished until the mid-19th century. There are still a few remaining Shakers living in Maine and New Hampshire.

Shakespeare, William (1564-1616), English playwright and poet, considered the greatest dramatist ever as well as the finest English language poet. Shakespeare was born of middle class parents in Stratford-upon-Avon where he spent his school years. At 18 years of age he married Anne Hathaway, with whom he had 3 children. In the years 1594 to 1608, Shakespeare was heavily involved in the world of London theater as a stockholder and an actor in the Lord Chamberlain's Company—renamed the King's Men in 1603—which performed at the Globe Theater. He also wrote an average of 2 plays a year in this period, including several comedies and virtually all of his famous tragedies.

All of Shakespeare's plays have been grouped into 4 periods reflecting general phases of his artistic development. In the first period (1590-94) he wrote comedies, histories, and tragedies. *The Comedy of Errors*, *Henry VI* (parts I, II, and III) *Richard III*, *The Taming of the Shrew*, *Titus Andronicus*, *The Two Gentlemen of Verona*, and *King John* were all written in the first period.

The second period (1595-1600) consists primarily of historical drama and romantic comedies. Included in this period are *A Midsummer Night's Dream*, *Richard II*, *Love's Labour's Lost*, *Romeo and Juliet*, *The Merchant of Venice*, *Henry IV* (parts I and II), *As You Like It*, *Julius Caesar*, *Much Ado About Nothing*, *Twelfth Night*, and *The Merry Wives of Windsor*.

Shakespeare's great tragedies were written in the third period (1601-08). At the height of his artistry his writing now moved back and forth easily between verse and prose in portraying his characters. *Hamlet*, *All's Well That End's Well*, *Measure for Measure*, *Othello*, *King Lear*, *Troilus and Cressida*, *Macbeth*, *Timon of Athens*, *Pericles*, *Antony and Cleopatra*, and *Coriolanus* all were written in this period.

In the fourth and final period (1609-13) Shakespeare wrote 3 comedies and a history. They are *Cymbeline*, *The Winter's Tale*, *The Tempest*, and *Henry VIII*.

Shakespeare began to write poems between 1592 and 1594 partly because poetry was considered to be of greater importance than drama by the Elizabethans. His 2 long narrative poems were *Venus and Adonis* (1593) and *The Rape of Lucrece* (1594).

The sonnets were probably written over a period of several years. The first 126 are addressed to a young nobleman and the next 26 to a young woman with whom Shakespeare may have been having a love affair. The common theme of the sonnets concerns the destructive effects of time, the quickness of physical decay, and the loss of beauty, vigor, and love. Although the poems celebrate life, they do so with a keen sense of death.

Shakespeare shaped and used language with great power. He invented, changed, and borrowed words from other languages and employed rhetorical devices such as alliteration and repetition to produce dramatic effect.

Shakespeare's plays and poems have been the subject of critics and scholars who have examined every aspect of the man himself, his works, and his influence. His works have long been a required component of liberal education. His brilliant portrayal of historical figures and events has caused many people to visualize the likes of Julius Caesar, Mark Antony, and Cleopatra not as they have been described in history books but as Shakespeare envisioned them.

Shakespeare was knowledgeable in a wide variety of subjects, including music, the law, the Bible, military science, the stage, art, politics, history, hunting, woodcraft, and sports. He displayed a keen sense of human nature with vivid characters, including kings, pickpockets, drunkards, generals, hired killers, and philosophers. His genius seems all the more amazing considering that as far as scholars have been able to determine, Shakespeare had no experience in any field other than theater.

Shale, fine-grained sedimentary rock formed by compaction and drying-out of mud (clay and silt). Shales are sometimes rich in fossils and are laminated (they split readily into layers, or laminae). Their metamorphism produces slate.

Shallot, edible hardy perennial (*Allium ascalonicum*) of the Liliaceae family, used in cooking. The plant has edible stems, bulbs, and leaves, and grows like garlic or onions. The bulb, composed of cloves attached to a common disk, is green, shading to lavender with a thick grayish skin. Shallots probably developed by cultivation as early as the 9th century.

Shamanism, primitive religious system centered around a shaman, or medicine man. (The word *shaman* is from the language of the Tungus of Siberia). In a trance state, he is believed to be possessed by spirits who speak and act through him; he is expected to cure the sick, protect the tribe, and foretell the future, among other mystical activities.

See also: Religion.

Shamir, Yitzhak (1915-), prime minister of Israel (1983-92), successor to Menachem Begin. Born in Poland, he went to Palestine in 1935, where he joined the underground military organization Irgun Zvai Leumi and later the more radical Stern Gang in combating British rule. From 1955 to 1965 he worked for the Israel intelligence agency. As foreign minister (1980-83), he was identified as a strong supporter of Begin's policies. In 1984 and 1988 his Likud Party formed coalition governments with the Labour Party.

See also: Israel.

Shamrock, popular name in Ireland for several leguminous plants, the trifoliate leaves of which were cited by St. Patrick as a symbol of the Christian Trinity. Among the plants called shamrock are the wood sorrel (*Oxalis* *acetosella*), white clover (*Trifolium repens*), and black medic (*Medicago lupulina*).

Shang dynasty, first historic Chinese dynasty, traditionally said to have lasted from 1766 to 1122 B.C. The legendary founder was T'ang. The Shang civilization was agriculturally and technically advanced and is famed for the artistic quality of its bronzes.
See also: China.

Shanghai (pop. 13,450,000), China's largest city, in the southeastern region of Jiangsu province. It is a major seaport and a leading commercial and industrial center, producing textiles, iron and steel, ships, petroleum products, and a wide range of manufactured goods. In 1842 it was one of the first Chinese ports opened by treaty to foreign trade. Great Britain (1843), France (1849), and the United States (1862) gained concessions to develop the city, and most of it remained under foreign control until after World War II. The British and U.S. concessions were renounced in 1945. Shanghai is now China's film capital and the home of 190 research institutes, colleges, and universities.
See also: China.

Shanker, Albert (1928-), U.S. labor leader. A New York City public school teacher (1952-59), he was active in the teachers' drive for unionization and, as president of the United Federation of Teachers (1964-74), led strikes over pay and pedagogical issues. He has headed the American Federation of Teachers since 1974.
See also: Labor movement.

Shannon River, chief river in Ireland and longest (240 mi/386 km) in the British Isles. It rises in northern Cavan county, Ulster, and flows south and west through several loughs (lakes) into the Atlantic Ocean. From Limerick westward, it is navigable by all but the largest vessels.

Shapiro, Karl Jay (1913-), U.S. poet and literary critic. His early poetry, such as *V-Letter and Other Poems* (1944; Pulitzer Prize), shows the influence of W. H. Auden and was admired for its verbal conceits. Later work, such as *The Bourgeois Poet* (1964), became more Whitmanesque. His *Collected Poems: 1948-1978* appeared in 1978.

Shapley, Harlow (1885-1972), U.S. astronomer whose work on pulsating stars (Cepheid variables) and globular clusters established the position of the sun in the galaxy and the size of the Milky Way. Shapley discovered 2 star systems in distant galaxies and was director of the Harvard Observatory (1921-52). Shapley's written works include *Star Clusters* (1930), *Galaxies* (1943), and *Cosmic Facts and the Human Response* (1957).
See also: Astronomy.

Sharaku (fl. late 1700s), professional name of a Japanese woodcut artist known for color portraits of Kabuki actors, produced in 1794 and 1795. The actors, shown dressed for their roles, have enlarged heads and exaggerated expressions. The backgrounds are plain. Little is known about the artist.

Sharecropping, arrangement whereby a share of a tenant farmer's yearly land yield (usually 50%) went to the landowner in lieu of rent. The tenant provided the labor, while the landowner provided land, equipment, and often loans to buy seed. The system was notorious for its abuses.

Sharif, Nawaz (1949-), prime minister of Pakistan (1990-93 and 1997-), president of the Islamic Democratic Alliance (IDA), a right-wing Pakistani coalition. He has shown special interest in accelerating Pakistan's economy while at the same time reducing the country's dependence on foreign aid. He served as Punjab's finance minister under former President Zia ul-Haq (1981). In February 1997 he was elected president for the second time.

Shark, any of about 250 species of cartilaginous fishes of marine and fresh waters, order Selachii. Sharks, with the related rays and chimeras, have a skeleton formed entirely of cartilage rather than bone. Other distinguishing features are that the gills open externally through a series of gill slits, rather than through a single operculum, and reproduction is by internal fertilization, unlike that of bony fishes. The body is fusiform, and the upper lobe of the tail is usually better developed than the lower lobe. Sharks swim by sinuous movements of the whole body; there is no swim bladder, so they must swim constantly to avoid sinking. All are extremely fast swimmers and active predators. Despite a universal reputation for unprovoked attack, only 27 out of the 250 known species have been definitely implicated in attacks on humans.

Shar-pei, dog of Chinese origin first bred from c.200 B.C. as a guard or fighting dog. The Shar-pei is characterized by a compact body, small flat ears, and a loose, wrinkled skin. It grows 16-20 in (41-51 cm) high and weighs 35-55 lb (16-25 kg). The coat is short, of a solid color, and may be tan, black, cream, or red.

Shavuot, Jewish holiday known as the Festival of Weeks, held on the sixth and seventh days of the month of Sivan (May-June). Originally an agricultural celebration of the harvest, it was observed by presenting the season's first fruits and bread baked from the first wheat at the Temple in Jerusalem. Later it came to commemorate the receipt of the Ten Commandments.
See also: Passover.

Shaw, Anna Howard (1847-1919), English-born U.S. leader of women's suffrage and temperance movements. Shaw became a Methodist minister (1880) and a medical doctor (1886). An associate of Susan B. Anthony, she worked for the passage of an amendment to the United States Constitution that would secure voting rights for women. Shaw served as president of the National American Woman Suffrage Association (1904-15).
See also: Woman suffrage.

Shaw, George Bernard (1856-1950), Irish dramatist, critic, and political propagandist whose witty plays contained serious philosophical and social ideas. Born in Dublin, he moved to London (after 1876), where he became a music and theater critic and a leader of the Fabian Society. He began writing his brilliantly witty, ironical, and polemical comedies in the 1890s. Success came with such plays as *Major Barbara* (1905), *Caesar and Cleopatra*

(1906; written 1899), *Androcles and the Lion* (1912), and *Pygmalion* (1913; adapted as the musical *My Fair Lady*, 1956). He lost popularity for his opposition to World War I, but regained it with *Back to Methuselah* (1921). *Saint Joan* (1921), his greatest success, was followed by the 1925 Nobel Prize in literature.

Shaw, Robert Gould (1837-63), Union hero of the U.S. Civil War. Colonel Shaw led the first regiment of black troops (54th Massachusetts volunteers) to be mustered in a free state. He was killed attacking Fort Wagner, S.C. (July 18, 1863). The heroic deeds of Shaw and his men were retold in the motion picture *Glory* (1990). A statue of Shaw by Augustus Saint-Gaudens stands in his honor in the Boston Commons.
See also: Civil War, U.S.

Shawn, Ted (Edwin Meyers Shawn; 1891-1972), U.S. dancer, choreographer, and teacher. With his wife, Ruth St. Denis (1877-1968), he founded the Denishawn school and company. He led an all-male company of dancers (1933-40), and in 1941 established an international dance center at Jacob's Pillow, in Massachusetts.

Shawnee, Native North Americans of the Algonquian language group. They settled in the Ohio Valley during the 18th century, hunting and cultivating maize. In 1811 the Shawnee chief Tecumseh attempted to unite the Native Americans of the region, but his plan failed when the Shawnee were defeated at Tippecanoe by Gen. William Henry Harrison's army. The Shawnee were eventually resettled in Oklahoma, where about 2,250 still live.

Shawnee Prophet (1775?-1837), Shawnee religious leader who (c.1805) had visions that led him to take the name Tenskwatawa, meaning "the open door." He began to preach to Native Americans, urging them to quit alcohol and to rededicate themselves to their own traditions. Members of many tribes rallied behind him and his brother, the chief Tecumseh. Tenskwatawa and his followers were defeated in the Battle of Tippecanoe (1811).
See also: Indian wars.

Shays, Daniel *See:* Shays' Rebellion.

Shays' Rebellion, uprising in Massachusetts that lasted intermittently from Aug. 1786 to Feb. 1787. At that time the country was suffering a postwar depression, and taxes in Massachusetts were very high and unequally levied. After the legislature ignored local petitions for tax reductions, an easing of legal action against debtors, a halt to mortgage foreclosures, and a proposal to inflate currency by printing paper money, many rebelled. Led by Daniel Shays, they threatened several local courthouses and forced them to close, attempted to capture a state armory, and resisted the state militia until a final defeat by Maj. Gen. Benjamin Lincoln on Feb. 2. Shays escaped and was later pardoned. The uprising led to some of the reforms that farmers had demanded. It also helped bring about the Constitutional Convention of 1787 by pointing up the need for a strong national government and army, because many of the local militia had either deserted to the rebels or refused to fight them.
See also: Annapolis Convention.

Shcharansky, Anatoly Borisovich, (1948-), Soviet mathematician and political dissident. Jailed in 1974, he was sentenced in 1978 in Moscow to 13 years in a labor camp for anti-Soviet agitation, espionage, and treason. In 1986 he was released as part of a "spy trade" and was welcomed in Israel as a hero.

Shearwater, any of about 12 species of oceanic birds related to the petrel and the albatross. They are brown or dark gray, sometimes with a white belly, 10-26 in (25-66 cm) in length with long, slender wings. Shearwaters land only to reproduce, congregating in huge colonies on offshore islands and the rugged coasts of the Atlantic and Pacific oceans and the Mediterranean. They nest in burrows. The female lays one egg, and the chick is tended by both parents.

Sheeler, Charles (1883-1965), U.S. painter and photographer whose linear treatment of architectural forms, interiors, and industrial settings shows the influence of cubism. In 1913, six of Sheeler's paintings were shown at the New York Armory Show, the exhibition that first introduced European modernism to Americans. Among his paintings are *Upper Deck* (1929) and *American Interior* (1934).

Sheen, Fulton John (1895-1979), U.S. Roman Catholic archbishop widely known for his popular inspirational radio and TV talks and for his conservative stances on many issues.

Sheep, diverse genus of mammals best known in the various races of domestic sheep (*Ovis aries*), bred for both meat and wool. Wild sheep are a diverse group of mountain-dwelling forms with about 37 races alive today, divided into 2 large groups: the Asiatic sheep, which include the mouflons, urials, and argalis; and the American sheep, the thinhorns and bighorns. Asiatic sheep are long-legged, lightly built animals that prefer a gently rolling terrain. American-type sheep by comparison are heavyset and barrel-chested and characteristic of steep slopes and rocky areas, in part filling the role played in Europe and Asia by the ibex. Sheep are social animals; males usually form bands following a dominant ram, and females form separate parties following a mature ewe. The rams use their horns and the specially thickened bone of their foreheads for combat, not only when sexually excited but also in dominance struggles.

Sheepdog, type of dog bred to herd and protect sheep. The American Kennel Club lists these 9 breeds of sheepdogs: Belgian sheepdog, Briard, collie, German shepherd, Great Pyrenees, Komondor, old English sheepdog, puli, and Shetland sheepdog.

Sheffield (pop. 531,000), city in South Yorkshire, northern England. Known worldwide for its high-grade steel, metal products, cutting tools, cutlery, and silverware, Sheffield probably began as an Anglo-Saxon farming settlement in the 1000s. It grew into a center of steel production during the Industrial Revolution.
See also: England.

Sheik (more properly spelled "sheikh"), Arabic term for the leader or elder of a family, tribe, or village, also applied to some Muslim religious leaders.

Shell, any hard external covering secreted by an invertebrate, enclosing and protecting the body. The term is used particularly for the coverings of mollusks, but it also refers to those of foraminifers and may be used loosely to describe the exoskeleton of crustaceans and insects.

Shellac, resin produced by the lac insect (*Laccifer lacca*). It softens when it is heated to about 158° F (70° C), a property that makes it useful for making sealing wax. Shellac is also used as a binder in the manufacture of mica board and stiffening materials, and to make polishes, varnishes, and insulating materials. Shellac once had many uses, including the manufacture of phonograph records, but it has mostly been superseded by plastics.

Shelley, Mary Wollstonecraft (1797-1851), English writer, daughter of philosophical radical William Godwin and Mary Wollstonecraft and wife of poet Percy Bysshe Shelley. Her best-known work is the Gothic horror story *Frankenstein* (1818). She wrote several other novels and edited her husband's works (1839-40).

Shelley, Percy Bysshe (1792-1822), English romantic poet whose work reflects his revolutionary political idealism and his strong faith in the spiritual power of the imagination. It includes long narrative poems, such as *Queen Mab* (1813), *The Revolt of Islam* (1818), and *Epipsychidion* (1821); the verse drama *Prometheus Unbound* (1820); and such famous lyrics as "Ode to the West Wind" (1819) and "To a Skylark" (1820). He was drowned in a boating accident in Italy, were he had settled with his second wife, Mary Wollstonecraft.

Shelter, structure to protect people from the weather, animals, insects, and other threats. A shelter can be a house, tent, cave, houseboat, or a lean-to. Shelters have been made from animal skins, cloth, grass, vines, timber, stones, mud, clay, brick, glass, steel, concrete, and plastic. The materials, forms, and method of construction vary worldwide.

Shelter belt, planted or natural line of trees that protects soil and crops from wind erosion. In 1934 the U.S. government started a program under the Forest Service called the Shelter Belt Project and later the Prairie States Forestry Project. Under this program, trees were planted as wind barriers in the farmlands of the Dakotas, Nebraska, Kansas, Oklahoma, and Texas, areas that had been badly damaged by erosion and dust storms. In 1942 the program was transferred to the Soil Conservation Service.

Shenandoah National Park, area in the Appalachian Mountains, northern Virginia. Covering approximately 300 sq mi (777 sq km) along the crest of the Blue Ridge Mountains, it is heavily crested and affords magnificent views along the Skyline Drive, which runs its whole length.

Shenandoah River, river in Virginia and West Virginia, a major tributary of the Potomac. Its North Fork, 117 mi (188 km) long, and South Fork, 155 mi (249 km) long, meet at Riverton, Va., to form the Shenandoah proper, which flows 55 mi (88 km) to the Potomac at Harper's Ferry, W. Va.

Shenandoah Valley, area between the Allegheny and Blue Ridge mountains in northeastern Virginia. About 150 mi (241 km) long and up to 25 mi (40 km) wide, it is a rich farming area famed for its natural beauty. During the Civil War it was the site of the Shenandoah Valley campaign (1862-64).

Shenyang (pop. 4,540,000), formerly Mukden, capital of Liaoning province in northeastern China, on the Hun River. A major industrial city, its products include steel and steel products, tools, chemicals, and processed food. It is also a transportation hub. The city dates from the Middle Ages. It was the capital of Manchu China and the site of the Japanese invasion of Manchuria (1931).
See also: China.

Shepard, Alan Bartlett, Jr. (1923-) first U.S. astronaut in space (May 5, 1961). He was later grounded for medical reasons but overcame them to command the *Apollo 14* moon landing (1971).

Shepard, Sam (1943-), U.S. actor and playwright noted for almost cinematic inventiveness in such plays as *Buried Child* (1978; Pulitzer Prize), *True West* (1980), and *Lie of the Mind* (1987). Other works are collected in *Mad Dog Blues and Other Plays* (1972). Shepard appeared in the films *Frances* (1982), *The Right Stuff* (1983), *Country* (1984), and *The Pelican Brief* (1993).

Sheraton, Thomas (1751-1806), English furniture designer. Sheraton's furniture is noted for its delicacy and simplicity of shape. It may be decorated with inlays, oval or diamond shapes, or classical motifs such as lyres and urns. Sheraton published his designs in *The Cabinet-Maker and Upholsterer's Drawing Book* (1791-94). His style of furniture was popular in England (1790-1805) and in the United States (1795-1810).

Sheridan, Philip Henry (1831-88), U.S. general and Union Civil War hero. After successes in the Chattanooga and Wilderness campaigns, he commanded the army that defeated Gen. Jubal Early and devastated the Shenandoah Valley (1864). In 1865 he won the Battle of Five Forks in Virginia and helped end the war by cutting off Robert E. Lee's line of retreat from Appomattox. He became commander of the U.S. Army in 1884.
See also: Civil War, U.S.

Sheridan, Richard Brinsley (1751-1816), Irish-born English dramatist and politician famous for his witty comedies of manners, including *The Rivals* (1775), *School for Scandal* (1777), and *The Critic* (1779). A Whig member of Parliament (1780-1812), he played a leading part in the impeachment trial (1787) of Warren Hastings.

Sheriff, executive officer of a county, a post that has existed in England since before 1066. Today the duties of a sheriff entail the execution of writs, the preparation of jurors, and the custody of prisoners. In the United States a sheriff functions as a peace officer in areas of a county not protected by city police. The office of sheriff is also found in Canada, Scotland, and Northern Ireland.

Sherman, brothers important in the U.S. Civil War era. **William Tecumseh Sherman** (1820-91) was a Union commander, second in importance only to

Gen. Ulysses S. Grant. He fought in the battles of Bull Run (1861) and Shiloh (1862) and in the Vicksburg campaign (1862-63). He was given command of the Army of Tennessee and, with Grant, took part in the Chattanooga campaign (1863). As supreme commander in the West (1864) he invaded Georgia, capturing Atlanta and marching on to Savannah. Turning north, he pushed Gen. Joseph Johnston's army before him and accepted its surrender at Durham, N.C. (1865). The destruction Sherman wrought in obliterating Confederate supplies and communications and breaking civilian morale made him a hero in the North and a villain in the South. He was U.S. Army commander 1869-84. **John Sherman** (1823-1900) was a founding member of the Republican Party. A senator (1861-77, 1881-97) and secretary of the treasury (1877-81), he introduced the Sherman Antitrust Act and the Sherman Silver Purchase Act.
See also: Civil War, U.S.

Sherman, James Schoolcraft (1855-1912), U.S. Republican politician, member of the House of Representatives (1887-91, 1893-1909) and vice president under William H. Taft (1909-12).
See also: Antitrust laws.

Sherman, Roger (1721-93), American patriot who helped draft and signed the Declaration of Independence. He was a member of the 1787 Constitutional Convention and, with Oliver Ellsworth, introduced the Connecticut Compromise. He was a member of the House of Representatives (1789-91) and Senate (1791-93) from Connecticut.

Sherman Silver Purchase Act (1890), compromise measure aiming to placate mine-owners and the advocates of free silver, which required the U.S. government to double its monthly silver purchases. It threatened to undermine gold reserves and was repealed when the panic of 1893 began.

Sherpas, Buddhist people of northeast Nepal, famous as Himalayan guides. Of Tibetan origin and speaking a Tibetan language, they number some 85,000 and raise cattle, grow crops, and spin wool in the high valleys of the Himalayas.

Sherrington, Sir Charles Scott (1857-1952), British neurophysiologist who shared with Edgar D. Adrian the 1932 Nobel Prize in physiology or medicine for studies of the nervous system that form the basis of our modern understanding of its action. He established the use of the word "synapse," explained the functions of the spinal cord, and made vital contributions to the understanding of muscles. He is the author of *The Integrative Action of the Nervous System* (1906).
See also: Nervous system.

Sherry, alcoholic beverage named for Jérez de la Frontera, Spain, where it originated. It is an aperitif wine, matured in wooden casks and fortified with brandy to bring the alcohol level to 15%-23% by volume.

Sherwood, Robert Emmet (1896-1955), U.S. playwright. His plays *Idiot's Delight* (1936), *Abe Lincoln in Illinois* (1938), and *There Shall Be No Night*

(1940), and his biography *Roosevelt and Hopkins: An Intimate History* (1948) won Pulitzer Prizes for drama or biography.

Shetland Islands, archipelago of about 200 islands, covering 550 sq mi (1,425 sq km) northeast of Scotland's mainland, constituting its northernmost county. Lerwick, on Mainland Island, is the chief port and administrative center. Along with the Orkneys, the Shetlands are the center of the North Sea oil industry. Fishing and cattle and sheep raising are the main occupations of the some 18,500 Scots on the 24 inhabited islands. The Shetlands are noted for their knitted woolen goods and the Shetland pony.

Shetland pony, smallest of the ponies, probably a relic of prehistoric British and Scandinavian horses. Tiny, shaggy, and once restricted to the Shetland Islands, it has now been widely bred as a riding pony for children.

Shetland sheepdog, small dog, developed (19th century) in the Shetland Islands to herd sheep. Measuring 13-16 in (33-41.6 cm) at the shoulder and weighing about 15 lb (7 kg), the Shetland sheepdog resembles a miniature collie. Agile and hardworking, it can cover great distances without tiring and is also kept as a pet or watchdog.

Shevardnadze, Eduard Amvrolyevich (1928-), president of the Republic of Georgia (1992-). USSR foreign minister 1985-90. He was head of the ministry of internal affairs of the Republic of Georgia, 1965-72. He became foreign minister after being promoted to a full voting member of the Politburo in 1985. Shevardnadze was known as a liberal on friendly terms with the West. He resigned Dec. 20, 1990 over disagreements with other members of the Soviet government. Since 1995 he is also prime minister of Georgia.
See also: Georgia; Union of Soviet Socialist Republics.

Shevchenko, Taras (1814-61), Ukrainian patriot and poet. He was also a realist painter and a publisher of Ukrainian ballads in Russian. He opposed serfdom and was active in the Ukrainian independence movement. As punishment, the Russian government sentenced him to military service in the Ural Mountains (1847-57). His nationalistic poems include *Katerina* (1840), *Haydamaki* (1841), and *The Dream* (1844). He was born in Kiev.

Shield, defensive armor, usually carried on the left arm to leave the right arm free for fighting. The ancient Greeks and early Romans used large, circular wooden shields covered with bronze. The later Romans, for the sake of greater mobility, switched to smaller, rectangular shields that were curved to half encircle and thus protect the body more effectively. Kite-shaped shields were employed during the Middle Ages. The introduction of body armor and then firearms (requiring the use of both hands) gradually made the shield obsolete. In modern times shields have been reintroduced by riot police as protection against urban rioters.

Shih Huang-ti *See:* Shi Huangdi.

Shih Tzu, breed of toy dog. It stands 8-11 in (20-28 cm) at the shoulder and weighs 9-18 lb (4-8 kg). The dog has a broad head, a short, square muzzle, and drooping ears. The thick coat varies in color. The breed originated in Tibet and is related to the Pekingese and Lhasa apso.

Shi Huangdi (259?-210 B.C.), emperor of the first Chinese empire and founder of the Qin dynasty. He became ruler of the kingdom of Qin (246 B.C.), conquered Qin's rival states, and declared himself emperor of China (221 B.C.). He established a strong central government. He had his opponents executed and potentially inciteful books burned. He ordered the construction of roads and canals and the completion of the Great Wall of China, a defense along China's northern frontier.
See also: Qin dynasty.

Shiloh, Battle of, major conflict of the U.S. Civil War, fought at Pittsburgh Landing, Tenn. (Apr. 6-7, 1862). The Union army under Gen. Ulysses S. Grant was forced back by a surprise onslaught of the 40,000-strong Confederate army under Gen. Albert S. Johnston. The reinforced Union army routed the Confederates in a counterattack the next day. On each side casualties were over 10,000.
See also: Civil War, U.S.

Shingles, or herpes zoster, viral disorder of a nerve center, characterized by pain, a vesicular rash, and later scarring of the skin of the abdomen or trunk. The disorder is caused by the same virus that causes chickenpox. Predominantly striking people past age 50, it leads to an acute skin eruption that follows the path of the nerve involved.
See also: Herpes.

Shinn, Everett (1876-1953), U.S. painter, member of the Ashcan School. He is best known for his pictures of the theater and music hall world, such as *Revue* (1908).
See also: Ashcan School.

Shinto (Japanese, "way of the gods"), indigenous religion of Japan originally based on worship of nature's forms and forces. As this worship evolved, entering a stage of polytheism, its most revered deity became the sun goddess, Ama terasu-o-mi-kami, from whom it was believed the emperors descended. They were regarded as chief priests by divine right, until the disavowal of divinity by Emperor Hirohito in 1946. The blending of church and state occurred in 1882, when the religion was organized into state shrines (supervised by the government) and sectarian shrines. (The imperial shrine is at Ise.) State Shinto was used by the militarists of Japan until its dismantling after World War II. Shinto beliefs, rituals, and prayers, transmitted orally before the introduction of writing by the Chinese in the 5th century, are recorded in 3 texts: the *Kojiki*, the *Nihongi*, and the *Yengishiki*. Today Shinto, influenced by Buddhism and Confucianism, is practiced through rituals and customs involving celebration of festivals, pilgrimages to shrines, and the honoring of ancestors. The practice of pure Shinto involves prayer, food offerings, and dances.
See also: Religion.

Ship, large seagoing vessel for transport of people and goods. The wooden ships of ancient times were propelled by oars, sails, or a combination of the two. In the history of ships, highlights include the triremes (warships) of the Greeks and Romans, the Viking ships of the Middle Ages, and the ships of such powers as Spain, Portugal, and England during the 1400s and 1500s. Transoceanic voyages (of Columbus and others), made possible by improved navigational instruments, and the continued use of the seas to conquer new lands and expand empires prompted a booming shipbuilding industry of a wide variety of ships. With the introduction of steel, as well as the steam engine, the steam turbine, and then the diesel engine of the 20th century, the endurance and speed of ocean craft improved markedly. Nuclear engines for ships came into use in the 1950s. Despite competition from the airplane, railroad, and truck, ships still transport the bulk of the world's freight. Half the cargo at sea is oil, carried by supertankers that can hold millions of gallons of crude oil. Luxury cruise ships continue to hold their own in the travel/vacation industry. Ships, including destroyers, cruisers, and frigates, have also maintained an important position in the defense forces of many nations.

Ship, model, small copy of a ship. Some models are built and sailed by hobbyists for pleasure. Historically, shipbuilders have made models as plans for a larger ship's construction. Ship models also are made so the hull's design can be tested in different wave conditions.

Shipworm, bivalve mollusk (*Teredo navalis*) notorious for burrowing into the timbers of piers and wooden ships. The body is long and wormlike, with the shell reduced to a tiny pair of abrasive plates at the head end. These are used for rasping into wood—at a rate sometimes exceeding 1 ft (30.5 cm) per month.

Shire, administrative division in Great Britain. The Anglo-Saxon shires, first organized in the A.D. 800s, were made up of smaller divisions called *hundreds*. A shire was headed by an ealdorman and a sheriff. The term *shire* was eclipsed in the 1400s by the word *county*.

Shi'te (Arabic, "sectarian"), member of one of Islam's two great sects, the other being the orthodox Sunni. The schism arose over disagreement about Muhammad's successor. The Shi'te reject the first 3 caliphs and recognize Ali (Muhammad's son-in-law) and his descendants as rightful successors. They are concentrated principally in Iran, but also with communities in Iraq, Yemen, Pakistan, Oman, and Lebanon.
See also: Islam; Sunni.

Shiva, Hindu deity representing that aspect of the Godhead connected with the destruction necessary for renewal of life. He is sometimes depicted as an ascetic youth. In the role of re-creator he is called "the happy one." His phallic emblem is worshipped.
See also: Brahmanism; Hinduism.

Shock, specifically refers to the development of low blood pressure, inadequate to sustain blood circulation, usually causing cold, clammy, gray skin and extremities, faintness, mental confusion, and decreased urine production. It is caused by acute blood loss, burns with plasma loss, acute heart failure, massive pulmonary embolism, and septicemia. If untreated, death ensues. Early replacement of plasma or blood and administration of drugs to improve blood circulation are necessary to prevent permanent brain damage and acute kidney failure.

Shock absorber, any mechanism used to lessen impact in vehicles, aircraft, or stable structures. Most shock absorbers are hydraulic: They operate by forcing liquid through a small opening, an action that sets up resistance to both contraction and expansion of the spring mountings. In automobiles, shock absorbers control up-and-down vibrations and absorb impact on the car body. They are made of a piston inside an oil-filled cylinder. When the piston slides, it allows the fluid to flow through a spring-loaded valve.

Shockley, William (1910-89), U.S. physicist who shared with John Bardeen and Walter H. Brattain the 1956 Nobel Prize in physics for their joint development of the transistor. He is also known for promoting the erroneous belief that black people are intellectually inferior to Caucasians.
See also: Transistor.

Shock treatment, any of several types of therapy for mental illness that involve subjecting the patient to convulsions or seizures produced by electricity. It is now generally used only for hospitalized patients who are suicidal or severely depressed. Controversial because of its negative side effects, particularly amnesia and cardiac damage, shock therapy has been widely replaced by the use of tranquilizers.

Shoe, protective covering for the foot. The various types include the boot, whose upper extends above the ankle; the clog, a simple wooden-soled shoe; the moccasin, a hunting shoe whose sole extends around and over the foot; the sandal, an open shoe whose sole is secured to the foot by straps; and the slipper, a soft indoor shoe. Shoes have been made from earliest times, the type depending mainly on the climate; clogs, sandals, and moccasins predominated until the early Middle Ages. Since then boots and typical shoes in widely varying styles have been most popular. Leather has always been the main material used, shaped on a wood or metal form (*last*) and hand sewn, the sole being nailed to the upper. In the mid-19th century the sewing machine was adapted for sewing shoes, and nailing and gluing were also mechanized, allowing mass production. Other materials have to some extent displaced leather: natural and synthetic rubber for the sole and heel and various plastics and synthetic fibers for the upper.

Shoebill, African wading bird (*Balaenicips rex*), native to the White Nile area of the Sudan. The shoebill is gray, long legged, and has a large, wide bill ending in a hook. It stands 3-4 ft (90-120 cm) high and eats small frogs and shallow-water fish. Shoebills live in pairs and nest on the ground in grass-lined reed platforms.

Shoemaker, Willie (William Lee Shoemaker, 1931-), U.S. jockey. The most successful jockey in U.S. history, he rode 4 Kentucky Derby winners (1955, 59, 65, 86) and was the first jockey to win more than $2 million in a single year (1956). Shoemaker began his career at age 18 and had ridden nearly 9,000 winning mounts when he retired in 1990. He was elected to the National Racing Hall of Fame in 1958.

Shogun, title of the hereditary military commanders of Japan who usurped the power of the emperor in the 12th century and ruled the country for about 700 years. In 1867 the last Tokugawa family shogun was forced to resign and restore sovereignty to the emperor.
See also: Japan.

Sholem Aleichem (Solomon Rabinovitz; 1859-1916), Russian-born Yiddish humorous writer. His pseudonymous first name is Hebrew for "Peace be unto you." He was an immensely prolific and popular author, and his novels, short stories, and plays tell of the serious and absurd aspects of Jewish life in Eastern Europe. His works include *The Old Country* and *Tevye's Daughters* (1894; the basis for the musical *Fiddler on the Roof*, 1964).

Sholes, Christopher Latham (1819-90), U.S. inventor (with Carlos Glidden and Samuel Soulé) of the typewriter (patented 1868). He sold his patent rights to the Remington Arms Co. in 1873.
See also: Typewriter.

Sholokhov, Mikhail (1905-84), Russian novelist awarded the 1965 Nobel Prize in literature. He is best known for his stories about the Don Cossacks of southern Russia. His greatest work is *And Quiet Flows the Don* (1928-40).

Shooting star *See:* Meteor.

Shoplifting, crime of stealing displayed items from a store. It is estimated that $8 billion worth of merchandise is shoplifted in the United States annually, and that fewer than one shoplifter in 1,000 receives a jail sentence. The merchandise most frequently stolen is beauty and health aids, cigarettes, and fresh meat.
See also: Crime.

Shoran, acronym for short-range navigation, an electronic system for establishing the position of a ship or aircraft. The craft being monitored sends a radio signal to 2 separate land stations, and the stations return the signals. Shoran calculates the distance to the craft by the time between transmission and reception of the signal. It can pinpoint the craft's position to within 1 part in 10,000. Its range is limited to 500 mi (800 km). First used during World War II, shoran has largely been replaced by more accurate systems.
See also: Navigation.

Shore Patrol, military police of the U.S. Navy, Marines, and Coast Guard. The Shore Patrol enforces laws involving military personnel while they are ashore. It is made up of trained officers and enlisted personnel empowered to arrest suspected offenders, who are then placed in the custody of their commanding officers. The Shore Patrol has no authority to try or punish those it arrests.

Shorthand, or stenography, any writing system permitting the rapid transcription of speech. Most used today are Speedwriting, which uses abbreviations; (Isaac) Pitman shorthand, the first to be commercially developed (1837); and Gregg shorthand, by John Robert Gregg (published 1888). Pitman and Gregg shorthands are both phonetic, using symbols to represent

recurring sounds. Shorthand is much used by secretaries, journalists, and court reporters.
See also: Speedwriting.

Shorthand machine, any of several mechanical devices that use keyboards to record dictation. Invented (1912) by a court stenographer, Ward Stone Ireland, the shorthand machine is used chiefly to record court testimony, legislation, and speeches. The operator works by touch, typing words phonetically while watching the speaker. The keyboard is arranged to allow any number of the 21 lettered keys to be struck simultaneously, so that an entire word or phrase can be typed with 1 stroke. The shorthand machine is portable and operates silently.
See also: Court reporter.

Short story, form of prose fiction, usually limited in character and situation and between 500 and 20,000 words long. Chaucer's *Canterbury Tales* and Boccaccio's *Decameron* of the 14th century are prototypes of short stories. The art form was revived in the 19th century, and prominent short-story writers include Anton Chekhov, O. Henry, Ernest Hemingway, Henry James, Katherine Mansfield, Guy de Maupassant, John O'Hara, Edgar Allen Poe, Jean Stafford, and Eudora Welty.

Short waves, electromagnetic (radio) waves having a wavelength from about 32 to 328 ft (10 to 100 m) and a frequency between about 3,000 and 30,000 kilohertz—shorter and of higher frequency than the wavelengths of amplitude modulation (AM) transmissions. Short waves are used to carry international broadcasting, FM (frequency modulation) radio stations, and transoceanic telephone calls. Shortwave radios that can receive and transmit signals are used by pilots, the police, and amateur and citizens band operators.
See also: Radio, amateur.

Shoshone, group of Native North Americans originally inhabiting the territory between southeastern California and Wyoming. The Shoshone of eastern Utah and Wyoming were typical buffalo hunters of the plains. In the 18th century the Comanche split off and moved south to Texas. There are about 8,000 Shoshone on reservations.

Shostakovich, Dmitri (1906-75), Soviet composer. His works include the opera *Lady Macbeth of Mtsensk* (1930-32) and 15 symphonies, the most famous of which are the Fifth (1937), the Seventh—"Leningrad," written during the siege of the city (1941)—and the Tenth (1953). Some of his music is notably patriotic. The Piano Quintet (1940) is one of his leading chamber music pieces.

Shotgun, smoothbore shoulder firearm that discharges pellets (shot) designed to disperse as they leave the gun muzzle. Used primarily in hunting small game and birds and in skeet, or trapshooting, the shotgun evolved from the early fowling guns of 16th century Europe, becoming lighter and shorter and benefitting from the addition of a choke to control the spread of the shot and from the patent of the shotgun cartridge (1831). The repeating shotgun appeared c.1880. A shotgun's caliber is measured by its gauge, the most popular U.S. gauges being 12, 16, 20, and the 410 bore. Models may be single or double barreled.

Shot-put, track-and-field competition in which a weight, generally a solid metal ball, is thrown one-handed from the shoulder, using the whole weight of the body in the heave. Dating from ancient times, when stones were used as shots, the shot-put was made an official event of the first modern Olympic Games (1896). The shot is tossed (or put) from a 7-ft (2.1-m)-diameter circle and weighs 16 lb (7.3 kg) in men's competitions and 8 lb 13 oz (4 kg) in women's. The distance of the put is measured from the inside edge of the throwing circle to the nearest edge of the shot's first ground contact. The put is disqualified if the athlete steps on or outside the circle or allows the shot to fall below shoulder level.

Shoulder, term for the area of the body between the trunk and the arm, including bones, joints, and the adjacent tissue. There are 2 bones in the shoulder: the clavicle (collarbone), which is the horizontal bone that connects to the breastbone, and the scapula (shoulderblade), the flat triangular bone of the back. The upper arm bone (humerus) fits into the socket formed by the scapula. There are several muscles in the shoulder, primarily the trapezius, which helps turn the scapula, and the deltoid, which moves the upper arm. In primates the shoulder protrudes; in other mammals, it slopes.

Shoveler (*Anas clypeata*), common duck of the family Anatidae native to marshes and lakes of North America, particularly west of the Mississippi River. The shoveler also lives in Asia and Europe and migrates to the Southern Hemisphere. The shoveler has a broad bill longer than its head. The drake has a green head and neck, a white breast, and a black tail. The female is mottled brown. The shoveler feeds in shallow water and nests on the ground. It migrates in small flocks of 5 to 10 birds.

Shrapnel, type of antipersonnel artillery shell made of a hollow metal sphere filled with musket balls or other large shot and an explosive charge detonated by an adjustable fuse. Shrapnel was invented by Lt. Henry Shrapnel (1761-1842) and first used (1804) by British forces in the Napoleonic Wars. Since World War II, the term *shrapnel* has usually been understood to mean exploded fragments of the shell casing.
See also: Artillery.

Shreveport (pop. 334,341), city in northwest Louisiana on the Red River, seat of Caddo Parish. A major industrial and agricultural center with more than 250 factories, Shreveport produces primary and fabricated metals, telephones, glassware, timber and wood products, cotton, beef, petroleum products, and natural gas. It is the site of Centenary College (1825), Saint Vincent's Academy, and a branch of Louisiana State University.
See also: Louisiana.

Shrew, small, mouselike, insect-eating mammal with short legs, and long, pointed nose. Shrews have narrow skulls and sharp, rather unspecialized teeth for feeding on insects, earthworms, and small-mammal carrion. They are highly active creatures. The somewhat indigestible nature of their food combined with the high energy consumption of their constant activity means that they may eat 2-3 times their own weight of food in a day. Having a pulse rate that sometimes approaches 1,000 beats a minute, few shrews live longer than a year.

Shrike, aggressive and predatory passerine bird of the family Laniidae that kills insects, birds, or small mammals with its hooked bill. Because shrikes store their victims impaled on thorns like the carcasses hung in a butcher's shop, they are often called butcherbirds. They live on the edges of woods and forests worldwide.

Shrimp, decapod crustacean (suborder Natantia) that uses its abdominal limbs to swim instead of crawling like a lobster or crab. The body, more or less cylindrical and translucent, bears 5 pairs of walking legs and 2 pairs of very long antennae. The eyes are stalked. Shrimp are mostly scavengers or predators and may be found in the open ocean, near shore, in estuaries, and even in fresh water. They are fished for food worldwide.

Shrine, The, fraternal order and service branch of the Masons (officially called the Ancient Arabic Order of Nobles of the Mystic Shrine for North America) open to men who have achieved the rank of Knights Templar or the 32nd Masonic degree. Founded in 1872, the Shrine supports a number of philanthropies, including 22 hospitals offering free services to burned and crippled children. There are over 800,000 North American Shriners.
See also: Masonry.

Shriver, Sargent (1915-), U.S. politician, first Peace Corps director (1961-66), head of the Office of Economic Opportunity (1964), ambassador to France (1968-70), and unsuccessful Democratic candidate for vice president (1972).
See also: Peace Corps.

Shroud of Turin, linen cloth bearing the image of a crucified man, believed to be Jesus' burial cloth. Stored at the Cathedral of Turin since 1578, the shroud measures 14 ft 3 in by 3 ft 7 in (434 cm by 109 cm). It received publicity in the 1970s and 1980s when it became available for scientific research. Tests proved that the negative image was not painted but did not determine how it was produced. They also showed, from pollen and dust samples, that the linen could have been in the Palestine area where Jesus died and that bloodstains on the fabric were genuine. However, radiocarbon dating (1988) seemed to prove that the cloth is no older than about 500 years. Theologians, historians, and scientists have sustained the controversy surrounding the shroud, particularly since no early accounts of an imaged burial cloth exist. Historians usually agree that the shroud's whereabouts can be traced from the 500s with a gap from 1204 to 1355. However, recent research has shown that it is in fact possible that the shroud dates from the beginning of our era. In April 1996 the shroud was saved from a fire which destroyed the chapel.

Shrove Tuesday, last day before Lent begins. It is a traditional day for Mardi Gras (Fat Tuesday) carnivals, such as those in New Orleans, Rio de Janeiro, and Nice.
See also: Lent.

Shrub, term for a woody plant that is shorter than a tree and usually has branching stems that give it a bushy appearance.

Shuffleboard, game played by 2 or 4 persons who use cues (long sticks) to slide disks down a long, narrow court, 52 x 6 ft (15.8 x 1.8 m), that has a triangular scoring area at either end. The game is generally played outdoors on pavement, a ship deck, or other smooth surface. Players try to knock their opponents' disks into the penalty section, while leaving their own disks in one of the scoring positions on the triangle.

Shultz, George Pratt (1920-), U.S. secretary of state (1982-89). A former dean of the Graduate School of Business at the University of Chicago, in Pres. Richard Nixon's administration he was secretary of labor (1969-70), director of the Office of Management and Budget (1970-72), and secretary of the treasury (1972-74). He was president of the Bechtel Corp. when Pres. Ronald Reagan appointed him to succeed Alexander Haig as secretary of state. He was awarded the 1992 Seoul Peace Prize.

Shumway, Norman Edward (1923-), U.S. surgeon who performed the first adult cardiac transplant in the United States, Jan. 6, 1968, at Stanford Medical Center. Shumway is also known for pioneering research in measuring and combating rejection of transplanted hearts and in other open-heart surgery, such as valve transplantation.

Shush *See:* Susa.

Siam *See:* Thailand.

Siamese fighting fish *See:* Fightingfish.

Siamese twins, identical twins joined most commonly at the hip, chest, abdomen, buttocks, or head. Some share one internal organ, such as the heart or the liver. Originating from a single fertilized egg that has developed imperfectly, Siamese twins occur about once in every 50,000 births. Surgery in some cases can successfully separate these twins.

Sibelius, Jean (Julius Christian Sibelius, sometimes Jan; 1865-1957), Finnish composer. His best-known work is *Finlandia* (1900), which expressed his country's growing nationalist feeling. He composed several tone poems, such as *En Sagà* (1892), that evoke the physical beauty and ancient legends of Finland. He wrote 7 symphonies and many violin and piano pieces.

Siberia, vast, indefinite area of land (about 2.9 million sq km/7.5 million sq km) in northern Russia between the Ural Mountains in the west and the Pacific Ocean in the east, forming most of the Russian Republic. The landscape varies from the Arctic tundra to the great forest zone in the south and the steppes in the west. Summers are mild in most parts, winters extremely severe (as low as –90° F/–67.8° C in some parts). Most of the people are Russian or Ukrainians; Yakuts, Buryats, and Tuvans form autonomous republics. The largest cities are Novosibirsk, Omsk, Krasnoyarsk, and Novokuznetsk. Siberia has rich natural resources—farmland, forests, fisheries, natural gas, and such minerals as coal, iron ore, tungsten, and gold. Industrial centers have developed in the regions of Krasnoyarsk and Lake Baikal (the world's deepest lake), and one of the world's largest hydroelectric plants is near Bratsk. Siberia was inhabited in prehistoric times. Russians

conquered much of Siberia by 1598. Political prisoners were first sent to Siberia in 1710 and forced-labor camps still exist. The Trans-Siberian Railroad (completed 1905) led to large-scale colonization and economic development. There are now a number of large industrial centers. A pipeline has been placed in order to transport natural gas to Western Europe.
See also: Union of Soviet Socialist Republics.

Siberian husky, arctic working dog bred to pull sleds. The husky stands 20-23 in (51-58 cm) high at the shoulder and weighs 35-60 lb (16-27 kg). It has a dense undercoat and a smooth outercoat, of colors ranging from white through tan and gray to black. Originally raised by the Chukchi tribe of northeastern Siberia, the husky was introduced to Alaska (1909) as a sled-racing dog. It is related to the Samoyed and the malamute.

Sibyl, in Greek and Roman mythology, female prophet, usually divinely inspired and associated with a shrine or temple. There were sibyls throughout the ancient world, the most famous being the Cumaean sibyl, who accompanied Aeneas to Hades and sold the books of the Sibylline Prophecies to King Tarquin of Rome. Her caverns still exist in Mount Cuma in southern Italy. Medieval monks adapted the sibyls to Christianity, making them 12 in number and giving each a separate prophecy regarding Jesus.
See also: Mythology.

Sicilies, Kingdom of the Two, name taken by the kingdoms of Sicily and Naples when they merged in 1816 under Ferdinand I. The Two Sicilies were conquered by the Italian revolutionary leader Guiseppe Garibaldi in 1860, and subsequently absorbed, by popular vote, into the kingdom of Italy.
See also: Italy.

Sicily, largest Mediterranean island (9,925 sq mi/25,706 sq km), part of Italy, but with its own parliament at the capital, Palermo. Its most notable feature is the active volcano, Mt. Etna (height varies around 10,750 ft/3,277 m). Much of the island is mountainous, but there are lowlands along the coasts. About half the population live in the coastal towns Palermo, Catania, Messina, and Siracusa. Agriculture is the mainstay of the economy, though hampered by the low rainfall and feudal land tenure system. Wheat is the staple crop; grapes, citrus fruits, and olives are also grown. Main exports, from Ragusa, are petroleum products. Sicily was the site of Greek, Phoenician, and Roman colonies before conquests by the Arabs, who in turn were ousted by Robert Guiscard, the Norman conqueror. The Sicilian Vespers rebellion (1282) led to Spanish rule, ended by Garibaldi (1860), when Sicily became part of the kingdom of Sardinia, then of unified Italy. In World War II, Sicily was conquered by the Allies (1943) and used as a base for attack on Italy.

Sickle-cell anemia, one of many hereditary blood diseases caused by chemically abnormal hemoglobin in the red blood cells, occurring almost exclusively among blacks. Rather than the normal disk shape, the red cells have distorted (crescent) shapes when their oxygen supply is low. It is from this unusual appearance of the red blood corpuscles that the disease and its abnormal hemoglobin derive their names, the hemoglobin being known as the sickle hemoglobin, or hemoglobin S. The disease was first described by

J. B. Herrick in 1910, but it was not until 1949 that Linus Pauling and his associates demonstrated the basic defect to be in the hemoglobin molecule of the red blood cells. Since the discovery of the sickle hemoglobin, more than 100 other abnormal hemoglobins have been described. Characteristics of the disease, for which there is no cure, include fever, anemia, and pain in the joints and abdomen.

Siddhartha Gautama *See:* Buddha, Gautama.

Sidereal time, time as measured by the rotation of the earth relative to the fixed stars rather than relative to the sun. The sidereal day is the time it takes the earth to complete one rotation on its axis, such that a given star reappears on the observer's celestial meridian. The sidereal day (23 hr, 56 min, 4 sec) is slightly shorter than the solar day. The difference is caused by the earth's movement around the sun.

Sidewinder, any of several species of snake, especially rattlesnakes, that exhibit a peculiar sideways looping motion when moving rapidly. The name is particularly applied to the horned rattlesnake (*Crotalus cerastes*) of the southwestern United States.

Sidney, Sir Philip (1554-86), Elizabethan poet and courtier, a favorite with Queen Elizabeth I and a classic example of Renaissance chivalry. He had great influence on English poetry, both through his poems, of which the best known are *Arcadia* (1590) and the love sonnets *Astrophel and Stella* (1591), and through his critical work *The Defence of Poesie* (1595), all published posthumously.

Sidon, or Saida (pop. 80,000), city in southern Lebanon, on the Mediterranean Sea. Founded by the ancient Phoenicians, Sidon was prominent in shipbuilding and trade, and was famous for its bronzeware and purple dyes. The art of glassblowing probably originated in the city. Today, as a result of conflict within Israel, it has a large population of Palestinian refugees.

SIDS *See:* Sudden infant death syndrome.

Siegbahn, Karl Manne Georg (1886-1978), Swedish physicist who was awarded the 1924 Nobel Prize in physics for his pioneer work in X-ray spectroscopy. He devised a way of measuring X-ray wavelengths with great accuracy and developed an account of X-rays consistent with the Bohr theory of the atom. His son, **Kai M. Siegbahn** (1918-), also a Swedish physicist, and a professor at Uppsala University (from 1954), shared the 1981 Nobel Prize in physics with U.S. physicists Nicolass Bloembergen and Arthur Schaalow for work in developing high-resolution electron spectroscopy.

Siegfried, or Sigurd, legendary figure of Germanic mythology possessing outstanding strength and courage. He appears in both the Icelandic *Edda* and the 13th-century German *Nibelungenlied*, and is the hero of Richard Wagner's "Ring" operas *Siegfried* and *Die Götterdämerung*.
See also: Nibelungenlied.

Siegfried Line, defensive line of fortifications built on Germany's western frontier. The first Siegfried Line was constructed in the winter of 1916-17 and ran through northern France and Belgium. The Allies called it the Hindenburg Line and finally breached it at the end of World War I. The second line, built in the 1930s along the German-French border, was smashed by the Allies in World War II.
See also: World War II.

Siemens, German family of technologists and industrialists. **Ernst Werner von Siemens** (1816-92) invented, among other things, an electroplating process (patented 1842), a differential governor (c.1844), and a regenerative steam engine. The principle for it was developed by his brothers **Friedrich** (1826-1904) and then **Karl Wilhelm** (1823-83) to form the basis of the open-hearth process. Karl later became Sir Charles William Siemens after obtaining British citizenship (1859). He and Ernst both made many innovative contributions to telegraph science, culminating in the laying of the Atlantic Cable (1874) by the company Sir William owned—done from the *Faraday*, a ship he designed.

Siena (pop. 61,900), city in Tuscany, central Italy. Siena is an agricultural and tourist center and produces wine, cotton goods, marble, and chemicals. An ancient Etruscan settlement, Siena was occupied by the Gauls (c.400 B.C.) and became a free commune in the 12th century. It was attached to Tuscany after 1555. Home to the medieval Sienese school of painting (13th-14th centuries), its attractions include the public square (Piazza del Campo), the 14th-century cathedral, and the Piccolomini Library. It is the scene of 2 medieval, pageant-like horseraces, known as the Palio, held every summer.

Sienkiewicz, Henryk (1846-1916), Polish novelist awarded the 1905 Nobel Prize in literature. His greatest works are a trilogy about 17th-century Poland—*With Fire and Sword* (1883), *The Deluge* (1886), and *Pan Michael* (1887-88)—and the internationally famous *Quo Vadis?* (1896).

Sierra Club, environmental organization of North America. Various committees and publications of the Sierra Club work to educate the public and protect the environment. Its founder, the naturalist John Muir, held that its purpose was to protect the Sierra Nevada mountain range of California, but today the club, with a main office in San Francisco, has branches across the United States and Canada. Total membership is about 350,000. The Sierra Club organizes outdoor recreational activities such as mountain climbing and wilderness trips. The club also sponsors lectures, films, and special exhibits and publishes beautifully illustrated books and calendars to promote an appreciation of wildlife and conservation.

Sierra Leone, small, independent country in West Africa; a former British colony, borders Guinea to the north, Liberia to the southeast and the Atlantic Ocean to the southwest.
Land and climate. Bordering on the Atlantic Ocean and situated between the republics of Guinea, to the north and east, and Liberia, to the south, Sierra Leone has an area of 27,699 sq mi (712,740 sq km). The coastal area consists of mangrove and freshwater swamps that are gradually being transformed into rice fields. The inland plains, in places as much as 100 mi (161 km) wide,

Sierra Leone

Capital:	Freetown
Area:	27,699 sq mi (71,740 sq km)
Population:	5,080,000
Language:	English
Government:	Presidential republic
Independent:	1961
Head of gov.:	President
Per capita:	U.S. $180
Mon. unit:	1 Leone = 100 cents

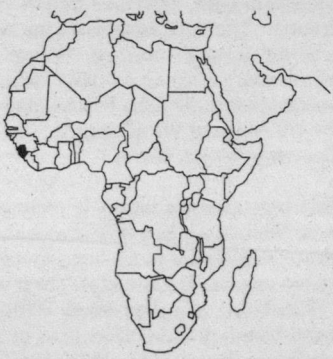

are crossed by many rivers draining westward to the Atlantic. The land to the north and northeast rises in a series of irregular steps reaching 6,390 ft (1,948 m) in Loma Mansa. The climate is tropical.

People. The population is mostly black African with the Mende people of the south and the Temne people of the north predominating. Creoles, descendants of freed slaves, mainly from the Americas, live around Freetown, the country's capital and chief port. Most of the people adhere to traditional beliefs, but there are also sizable minorities of Christians and Muslims. The official language is English. Education is not compulsory in Sierra Leone and the literacy rate is 20%.

Economy. Sierra Leone's economy is heavily dependent for export revenue upon diamond mining and the production of cocoa and coffee. Rice is the chief food crop. Cattle are raised in the north, pigs and poultry in the west. Fishing and tourism also contribute to the economy.

History. Named by the Portuguese who first arrived in 1460, the coastal area of present-day Sierra Leone was long the haunt of slavers. In 1787 the English abolitionist Granville Stamp settled freed slaves there. In 1808 Sierra Leone became a British colony, and in the years following thousands more freed slaves settled there. Independent since 1961, Sierra Leone has seen much internal political unrest. It was declared a republic in 1971 under the presidency of Dr. Siaka Stevens, who sought to establish a one-party regime in the face of more than a decade of protest and resistance. In 1985 Maj. Gen. Joseph Saidu Momoh was elected president. Despite several initiatives the democratization process that started in 1991 progressed slowly and without real accomplishments. In 1992 Momoh was ousted by the army and the new head of state was Valentine Strasser. The latter was ousted in 1996. Since 1992 the country is plagued by a devastating civil war. In 1997, a military coup resulted in the ousting of president Ahmad Tejan Kabbah. Major Johnny Paul Koroma took over but was ousted in 1998, after which Kabbah returned as president.

Sierra Madre, vast mountain system of Mexico. The Sierra Madre Oriental, the eastern range, stretches 1,000 mi (1,609 km) south from the Rio Grande, forming the eastern edge of the central plateau and reaching 18,700 ft (5,700 m) in Orizaba. The Sierra Madre Occidental, running southward from

Arizona and New Mexico, borders the plateau on the west, rising to over 10,000 ft (3,048 m). The Sierra Madre de Sur parallels the southwest coast. *See also:* Mexico.

Sierra Nevada, mountain range, 420 mi (676 km) long, in eastern California, including Mt. Whitney (14,494 ft/4,418 m), the highest mountain in the United States outside Alaska.

Sieve of Eratosthenes, mathematical process for discovering prime numbers. The ancient Greek mathematician Eratosthenes worked out this method by which whole numbers are eliminated—as if filtered through a sieve—until only prime numbers (those that can be divided evenly by themselves and 1) remain. The sieve starts as a string of consecutive whole numbers, beginning with 2. Every even number (except 2 itself) is eliminated, since each of them can be divided by 2. Next, beginning after the first untouched number after 2 (namely 3), every third number is eliminated, because they can all be divided evenly by 3. The next prime is the next untouched number. Since there is no largest prime number, the process can go on indefinitely.
See also: Eratosthenes.

Sieyès, Emmanuel Joseph (1748-1836), French revolutionary, legislator, and author. He participated in drafting such basic documents of the French revolution as the Declaration of the Rights of Man and Citizen and the Constitution (1791). His pamphlet *What is the Third Estate?* (1789) helped inspire the revolution. He served in various legislative bodies throughout the changing post-revolutionary governments, and he ended his life as an exile in Brussels, Belgium, following the Bourbon restoration in France.
See also: French Revolution.

Sight *See:* Eye.

Sigismund (1368-1437), Holy Roman emperor (1433-37), king of Germany (1410-37), Hungary (1387-1437), and Bohemia (1419-37). His coronation as German king was challenged by his half-brother, the former King Wenceslaus of Germany. Sigismund was an important organizer of the Council of Constance (1417), which ended the Great Schism in the Catholic church over papal elections. His coronation as king of Bohemia was contested by the Czech religious reformer John Hus. When Sigismund offered Hus safe-conduct and then went back on the pledge and had Hus executed, the Hussite Wars broke out.
See also: Holy Roman Empire; Hus, Jan.

Sigma Xi, honorary scientific society founded at Cornell University in 1886. It encourages the study of both pure and applied science.

Signac, Paul (1863-1935), French painter, leading theorist of neoimpressionism. A friend of Georges Seurat, he developed pointillism and painted many views of ports, like *Port of St. Tropez* (1916).

Signaling, any of various methods of nonverbal communication. Early visual and sound signals included smoke signals, drum calls, whistles, torch fires, and buoys. Sailors position flags in specific arrangements to communicate through the international flag code. Electrical signals are transmitted through various electronic devices, including radios, radar, computers, and telephone-operated facsimile (FAX) machines.

Sign language, any system of communication using gesture (usually of the hand and arm) rather than speech. The most comprehensive sign language in modern use is that employed by the hearing- or sight-impaired, but sophisticated sign languages are also used by many primitive peoples to communicate with one another.

Sikhism, religion combining elements of Hindu and Muslim beliefs. Founded by the guru Nanak at the turn of the 16th century, Sikhism is a monotheism whose teachings are embodied in its holy book, *The Adi Granth.* The word *sikh* means "disciple." Among the beliefs of the Sikhs is the Hindu concept of reincarnation. Their tenth and final guru, Gobind Singh (1666-1708), led a fight against Muslim persecution, creating the warrior image with which Sikhs are still identified today. Additional characteristics are their turbans and their uncut hair. After the partition of India (1947), a war between Sikhs and Muslims resulted in the transfer of several million Sikhs from the western Punjab, which became part of Pakistan, to the eastern Punjab, in India. There the Sikhs, numbering some 14 million, have played a major role in the economy and in politics, often clashing with the central government in New Delhi. The Indian government's 1984 military occupation of the Golden Temple, the major shrine of Sikhism, has led to continuing conflict.
See also: Punjab; Ranjit Singh.

Sikkim, state in northeast India, located in the Himalaya Mountains, bordered by Tibet on the north, Nepal on the west, and Bhutan on the east. The altitude of the state ranges from sea level rain forests to Mount Kanchenjunga, at over 28,000 ft (8,530 m), the world's third tallest mountain. The capital city, Gangtok, is also the only significant town. The official religion is Buddhism, although many practice Hinduism. Major products of the country are agricultural, although there is some mining of copper, lead, and zinc. A Sikkim monarchy was established by neighboring Tibet in 1642 and lasted until Indian statehood (1975), functioning under British rule from 1861 to 1947.
See also: India.

Sikorsky, Igor Ivanovich (1889-1972), Russian-born U.S. aircraft designer best known for his invention of the first successful helicopter, flown in 1939. He also designed several airplanes, including the first to have more than one engine (1913).
See also: Helicopter.

Silanpää, Frans Eemil (1888-1964), Finnish novelist awarded the 1939 Nobel Prize in literature. His best-known works are *Meek Heritage* (1919) and *The Maid Silja* (1931).

Silesia, region of central Europe, mostly in Poland but extending to the Czech Republic and eastern Germany. Known for the mineral and coal deposits of heavily industrialized Upper Silesia, the region is heavily forested and traversed by the Oder River. The Sudetes Mountains rise in the south. The largest cities are Polish: Wroclaw and Katowice. Silesia became part of

Poland in the 10th century. It was later conquered by Austria (1526) and Prussia (1742). The present borders were redrawn at the end of World Wars I and II.

Silica, chemical compound (SiO_2), properly called silicon dioxide. Sand, clay, granite, and sandstone contain forms of silica, which is also the major ingredient in glass. Quartz is an important crystalline form of silica used in optical tools and communications instruments. Opals are forms of amorphous silica polished and used in jewelry.

Silica gel, chemical substance (SiO_2) forming a noncrystalline form of silica. Silica gel absorbs moisture and this is its prime use. It was used in World War I in gas masks and now serves to dehumidify foods.

Silicate, any of various metallic compounds containing silicon and oxygen, generally with tetrahedral structures. This material makes up 95% of the earth's crust, including soil and rocks. Its basic structure consists of 4 oxygen atoms forming a pyramid-type shape with a silicon atom at the center. This structure may adhere to metals with positively charged ions.

Silicon, chemical element, symbol Si; for physical constants see Periodic Table. Silicon was isolated by Jöns J. Berzelius in 1823. It occurs in nature as sand, quartz, granite, feldspar, asbestos, and many other minerals. It is the second most abundant element and makes up 25.7% of the earth's crust by weight. Silicon is prepared by heating silicon dioxide in an electric furnace, using carbon electrodes. Silicon is a gray, lustrous, unreactive metalloid. It can be amorphous or crystalline. Silicon transmits more than 95% of all wavelengths of infrared radiation. Single crystals of silicon are used for solid-state or semiconductor devices. Silicones, a class of compounds prepared by hydrolyzing organic chlorides, are numerous with hundreds of useful properties, especially in the form of pottery, glass, and building materials. Silicon and its compounds are used in steel, as abrasives, and in lasers.

Silicone, polymer with alternate atoms of silicon and oxygen and organic groups attached to the silicon. Silicones are resistant to water and oxidation and are stable to heat. Liquid silicones are used for waterproofing, as polishes and antifoam agents. Silicone greases are high- and low-temperature lubricants, and resins are used as electrical insulators. Silicone rubbers remain flexible at low temperatures.

Silicon Valley, area around Sunnyvale, in the Santa Clara Valley, Calif., where many semiconductor manufacturers are located. More generally, it contains the greatest concentration of electronics industries in the United States. The region acquired the name because silicon is a material used in the fabrication of electronic equipment.
See also: Semiconductor.

Silicosis, form of pneumoconiosis, or fibrotic lung disease, in which long-standing inhalation of fine silica dusts in mining causes a progressive reduction in the functional capacity of the lungs. The normally thin-walled alveoli and small bronchioles become thickened with fibrous tissue, and the

lungs lose their elasticity. Characteristic X-ray appearances and changes in lung function occur.
See also: Pneumoconiosis.

Silk, natural fiber produced by certain insects and spiders to make cocoons and webs, a glandular secretion extruded from the spinneret and hardened into a filament on exposure to air. Commercial textile silk comes from various silkworms. The cocooned pupae are killed by steam or hot air, and the cocoons are placed in hot water to soften the gum (sericin) that binds the silk. The filaments from several cocoons are then unwound together to form a single strand of "raw silk," which is reeled. Several strands are twisted together (thrown) to form yarn. At this stage, or after weaving, the sericin is washed away. The thickness of the yarn is measured in denier. About 70% of all raw silk is produced in Japan.

Silk-screen printing, method of printing derived from the stencil process. A stencil is attached to a silk screen, or fine wire mesh, or formed on it by a photographic process or by drawing the design in tusche (a greasy ink). The screen is sealed with glue and then the tusche and its covering glue are washed out with an organic solvent. The framed screen is placed on the surface to be printed, and viscous ink is pressed through by a rubber squeegee. Each color requires a different screen. The process, which may be mechanized, is used for printing labels, posters, and fabrics, and on bottles and other curved surfaces. Since 1938 it has been used by painters, who call it *serigraphy*.

Silkworm, caterpillar of a moth (*Bombyx mori*) that, like many other caterpillars, spins itself a cocoon of silk in which it pupates. The cocoon is, however, especially thick and may be composed of a single thread commonly 3,000 ft (915 m) long. This is unraveled to provide commercial silk. Originally a native of China, *B. mori* has been introduced to many countries. The caterpillar, which takes about a month to develop, feeds on the leaves of the mulberry tree.

Silky terrier (formerly called Sydney Silky), breed of toy dog from Australia. Weighing up to 10 lb (4.5 kg), the silky terrier has long dark hair with tan markings. The tail is normally cut, or "docked," and the ears are erect and pointed. It was bred in the early 20th century from the Yorkshire and Australian terriers. Like most terriers, it is attentive and friendly.

Silliman, Benjamin (1779-1864), U.S. chemist and geologist who founded *The American Journal of Science and Arts* (1818). The mineral sillimanite is named for him.
See also: Geology.

Sillimanite, relatively rare silicate mineral (Al_2SiO_5) found in France, Madagascar, Brazil, and the eastern United States. It is glassy in appearance, white, green, or brown in color, and often located in areas where metamorphic rock has formed under thermal pressure.

Sills, Beverly (Belle Silverman; 1929-), U.S. coloratura soprano. She made her debut at the New York City Opera in 1955, and ultimately became internationally acclaimed both as a singer and an actress in a broad variety

of roles, ranging from bel canto to modern works. After retiring she was general director of the City Opera (1979-89).
See also: Opera.

Silo, structure used on farms to preserve grasses, or silage, for livestock feed. Most silos are cylindrical and up to 50 ft (15 m) high. They are made of an air-tight material, such as glass or porcelain on the inside, and a sturdy material such as metal, brick, tile, concrete, or wood on the outside. The sweetness of certain grasses or the addition of a solution (such as sulfur dioxide) promotes fermentation, a natural process that prevents spoilage. Steady deposit and removal of silage keeps the grasses in the silo fresh for year-round feeding of livestock.

Silone, Ignazio (Secondo Tranquilli; 1900-78), Italian writer and social reformer. Opposed to fascism, he spent 1931-44 in exile in Switzerland. His novels include *Fontamara* (1933), *Bread and Wine* (1937), and *A Handful of Blackberries* (1952).

Silt, fine deposit, or sediment, found on river or lake bottoms. Over long periods of time, natural forces break down rock into silt, which generally has a diameter of 0.00008 to 0.002 in (0.002-0.05 mm), approximately half that of a grain of sand. During floods, silt is deposited on land, helping to make it fertile.

Silurian, third period of the Paleozoic era, which lasted between c.435 and 395 million years ago.

Silver, chemical element, symbol Ag; for physical constants see Periodic Table. Silver has been known and used since ancient times. It occurs in nature as argentite and horn silver, and is sometimes found uncombined. The element is produced as a byproduct from ores. It has the highest electrical and thermal conductivity of all metals. In the past silver was used as a coinage metal, but its value as bullion has driven silver coins from circulation. Silver is the best reflector of visible light known and a poor reflector of ultraviolet. Silver and its compounds are used in photography, jewelry, for mirrors and in dentistry.

Silverfish, any of various wingless insects of the order Thysanura. One common variety, *Lepisma saccharina*, has 2 long antennae, 3 barbed tail parts, and silver-to-gray scales. It is a pest that lives in damp areas of houses, feeding on wallpaper, books, clothes, or food.

Silver nitrate, chemical compound ($AgNO_3$) made from silver and nitric acid, used medically and industrially. As a medicine it helps prevent blindness in newborn babies and works as an antiseptic. In the form of lunar caustic, a crystalline mass, it helps cauterize wounds and ulcerations. The material called emulsion that coats photographic film is made from silver nitrate, which is also used in the manufacture of silver-plated mirrors and indelible ink.

Simenon, Georges (Georges Joseph Christian Sim; 1903-89), Belgian-born French author of over 200 novels and thousands of short stories. He is best known for his detective novels about Inspector Maigret, works of tightly plotted suspense and psychological insight.

Simhat Torah, Jewish holiday celebrated on either the 22nd or 23rd day of the Hebrew month of Tishri. It marks the end of the annual cycle of Sabbath readings from the Torah in the Jewish house of worship, the synagogue. The festival falls in September or October of the Roman calendar. The Saturday morning Torah readings recommence the Saturday after Simhat Torah.
See also: Bible; Sukkot.

Simms, William Gilmore (1806-70), U.S. author whose writings on the South include historical novels, short stories, biographies, and poetry. His most important work was *The Yemassee* (1835).

Simon, Claude (Eugene-Henri) (1913-), French writer. Author of *Le tricheur* (1945), *L'herb* (1958), *Tryptyque* (1973), and *L'Acacia* (1989), he won the 1985 Nobel Prize for literature as a major figure in France's *nouvelle roman* ("new novel") movement of the 1950s and 1960s.

Simon, Neil (1927-), U.S. playwright whose career began with successful comedies such as *Come Blow Your Horn* (1961), *Barefoot in the Park* (1963), and *The Odd Couple* (1965). Many of his plays are autobiographical—including the trilogy made up of *Brighton Beach Memoirs* (1983), *Biloxi Blues* (1985), and *Broadway Bound* (1986)—and several have been made into movies. Simon has also written lyrics for Broadway musicals, such as *Sweet Charity* (1966) and *They're Playing Our Song* (1979). He received the Pulitzer Prize for *Lost in Yonkers* (1991).

Simon, Saint, one of the twelve disciples (apostles) of Jesus. Called Zelotes, he may have been associated with the fanatical Zealots. His feast day is Oct. 28.
See also: Apostles.

Simon Peter *See:* Peter, Saint.

Simplon Pass and Tunnel, Alpine route, 6,590 ft (2,009 m) high and 29 mi (46.7 km) long, between Brig, Switzerland, and Isella, Italy. Napoleon I built a road across it (1800-06).

Simpson, O.J. (Orenthal James Simpson; 1947-), U.S. football player. Known for his speed and elusive running style, he won the Heisman Trophy as the top national college player (1968). Simpson led the National Football League (NFL) in rushing 4 times (1972, '73, '75, '76), and he is 6th on the alltime rushing list (11,236 career yards). He played in the NFL for the Buffalo Bills (1969-77) and San Francisco 49ers (1978-79) and was inducted into the Pro Football Hall of Fame (1985). In 1994 he was charged with the brutal slaying of his ex-wife, Nicole Brown Simpson, and Ronald L. Goldman. After an extensive 9-month-long trial and accompanying media frenzy, he was declared not guilty in October of 1995. However, in a civil case in 1997 he was declared guilty and sentenced to pay damages to the next of kin.

Simpson, Wallis Warfield *See:* Edward.

Sin, or transgression, in Judeo-Christian tradition, unethical act considered as disobedience to the revealed will of God. Sin may be viewed legally as crime—breaking God's commandments—and so deserving punishment, or as an offense that grieves God the loving Father. According to the Bible, sin entered the world in Adam's fall and all humankind became innately sinful. Both for this and for actual sins committed, people become guilty and in need of salvation. Since sin is rooted in character and will, each sinner bears personal responsibility; hence the need for repentance, confession, and absolution. Views as to what constitutes sin vary, being partly determined by church authority, social standards, and one's own conscience. The traditional "7 deadly sins" are pride, covetousness, lust, envy, gluttony, anger, and sloth. The Roman Catholic church defines a mortal sin as a serious sin committed willingly and with clear knowledge of its wrongness; a venial sin is less grave, does not wholly deprive the perpetrator of grace, and need not be individually confessed.

Sinai, in the Bible, mountain on the Sinai Peninsula where Moses received the Ten Commandments.

Sinai Peninsula, triangular desert-mountain area, nearly 150 mi (241 km) at its widest and about 230 mi (370 km) north to south, bounded by the northern arms of the Red Sea, i.e., the Gulf of Suez on the west and the Gulf of Aqaba on the east. It is believed that the Bible's Mt. Horeb, where Moses is said to have received the Ten Commandments, is one of the granitic southern peaks, either Jebel Serbal or Jebel Musa (Arabic, "mount of Moses"; also named Mt. Sinai).

Sinatra, Frank (Francis Albert Sinatra; 1915-98), U.S. singer and film star. A master of timing and communication, he achieved fame as a crooner with Tommy Dorsey's band, and then as a solo performer was a teen-age idol during World War II. He starred in several movie musicals, then became a dramatic actor of note in *From Here to Eternity* (1953), for which he received the Academy Award for best supporting actor, as well as other films. He remained one of the world's most popular vocalist-entertainers.

Sinclair, Upton (1878-1968), novelist and social reformer. He is best known for *The Jungle* (1906), a muckraking expose of the horrors of the Chicago meat-packing industry, and for an 11-novel cycle, beginning with *World's End* (1940), about world events and centered on the fictional Lanny Budd. *Dragon's Teeth* (1942), the cycle's third novel, won a Pulitzer Prize.

Singapore, small island republic in southeast Asia lying at the southern end of the Malay Peninsula.
Land and climate. Consisting of Singapore Island and several adjacent islets, Singapore has a total area of about 240 sq mi (622 sq km). Singapore Island is separated from the Malay Peninsula by the narrow Johore Strait crossed by a road and a railroad causeway that also has a pipeline bringing fresh water to the island. South of the island is the Singapore Strait. Mostly fringed by mangrove swamps, Singapore Island is largely low-lying, but has a central plateau bounded on the west by low hills. The climate is hot and humid and has no distinctive seasons.

Singapore

Capital:	Singapore
Area:	240 sq mi (622 sq km)
Population:	2,987,000
Language:	English, Malayan, Chinese, Tamil
Government:	Republic
Independent:	1965
Head of gov.:	Prime minister
Per capita:	U.S. $26,730
Mon. unit:	1 Singapore dollar = 100 cents

People. The people of Singapore are predominantly Chinese with large Malay and Indian minorities. Principal religions are Buddhism, Islam, Hinduism, and Christianity. Malay, Tamil, Chinese, and English are spoken.
Economy. The capital of the republic, Singapore city, has a fine natural harbor and is southeast Asia's foremost commercial and shipping center, conducting a flourishing international trade as a free port. It trades in textiles, rubber, petroleum, timber, and tin and produces electrical goods, petroleum products, and textiles. Shipbuilding and repair are also important industries.
History. Singapore was founded as a trading port by Sir Thomas Raffles in 1819 and became part of the Straits Settlements in 1826. Occupied by the Japanese during World War II and self-governing since 1959, Singapore joined the Federation of Malaysia in 1963 but withdrew and has been independent since 1965, under the leadership of the strong prime minister (1959-90) Lee Kuan Yew. In 1997 the economy started to deteriorate due to a decline in export.

Singer, Isaac Bashevis (1904-86), Polish-born U.S. Yiddish novelist and short-story writer, known for his portrayal of European Jewish life. His work includes *The Family Moskat* (1950), *The Magician of Lublin* (1960), *The Estate* (1969), and *The Collected Short Stories of Issac Bashevis Singer* (1981). He was awarded the 1978 Nobel Prize for literature.

Singer, Isaac Merrit (1811-75), U.S. inventor of the first viable domestic sewing machine (patented 1851). Although he lost a legal battle with the earlier inventor, Elias Howe, the Singer sewing machine soon became the most popular in the world.
See also: Sewing machine.

Singer, Israel Joshua (1893-1944), Polish-born U.S. Yiddish novelist, playwright, and journalist, best known for his epic novel *The Brothers Ashkenazi* (1936). He was the brother of novelist Isaac Bashevis Singer.

Singing, music created with the voice. In humans, vibrations of the vocal cords in the throat result in sounds whose mechanics are similar to those of wind instruments. The length and thickness of vocal cords as well as their tension in the throat affect the kind of sound that is made. Classifications of women's voices—from highest to lowest in pitch—are soprano, mezzo-soprano, and contralto. For men the classifications are tenor, baritone, and bass.

Singing Tower, tower in central Florida with the biggest bell chimes in the world. Located in Mountain Lake park, which also serves as a bird sanctuary, the tower, designed by Milton B. Medary with doors and railings by Samuel Yellin, stands 205 ft (62 m) high. Marble bridges cross a surrounding moat to allow access to it.

Single tax, proposed reform that tax on land value should be a government's sole revenue, stated by Henry George in *Progress and Poverty* (1879). He argued that economic rent of land results from the growth of an economy, not from an individual's effort; therefore, governments are justified in approaching all economic rents, thus eliminating the need for other taxes. The proposal was never enacted in the United States.

Sing Sing, state prison in the city of Ossining, N.Y. Built in 1925 under a program that employed inmates as laborers, the prison has been expanded with the addition of later buildings.
See also: Prison.

Sinhalese, also Singhalese or Sinhala, Indo-Aryan language derived from Sanskrit, spoken by the majority of the people of Sri Lanka. Most other Sri Lankans (or Sinhalese) speak Tamil.

Sinn Féin (Irish, "we, ourselves"), Irish nationalist movement formed by Arthur Griffith in 1905. It secured wide support in 1916, when most of the leaders of the Easter Rebellion against English suppression were martyred. Led by Eamon De Valera, the Sinn Féin set up a separate Irish Parliament, the Dáil Éireann, which declared Irish independence (1918). Sinn Féin guerrilla activity was countered by British Black and Tans military terrorists (1920), but Irish resolve strengthened to the point of war. Britain negotiated a peace treaty with De Valera, and the result was the establishment of the Irish Free State in 1922. The treaty split the Sinn Féin into factions; civil war ensued. Eventually the majority of the Irish backed De Valera's party, the Fainna Fáil, and he became president of the Irish Free State in 1932. With independence, the Sinn Féin movement ended—except for that faction called the Irish Republican Army, which was outlawed. In April 1998 Sinn Féin participated in the peace talks which led to a peace agreement.
See also: De Valera, Eamon.

Sintering, process by which powdered metal is used to form solid objects. The particles of the powdered metal are heated until they adhere one to the other to form solid objects.

Sinus, body cavity, usually containing air or blood. Generally, this term refers to the large air space connected with the nose that may become infected and obstructed after upper respiratory infection and cause facial pain and fever (sinusitis). The major nasal sinuses are maxillary, frontal, ethmoid, and sphenoid.

Sioux, or Dakota, confederation of Native American peoples in the North American plains. There were 7 main Sioux tribes, including the Santee, or Dakota, of what is now Minnesota, and the Lakota, or Teton, of the western Dakotas and Nebraska. There were about 30,000 Sioux; 15,000 of these were Lakota, of whom 3,000 were Oglala. The Sioux lived in tepees, and their principal activities were buffalo hunting and raiding. Their most famous ceremony was the sun dance. First noted in the Great Lakes region, the Sioux slowly moved westward after the introduction of the horse in the 17th century, and by the 18th century they roamed the plains of the upper Midwest. They fought on the side of the British in both the American Revolution and the War of 1812. In 1862 a serious revolt of the Sioux led by Little Crow occurred in Minnesota, and 800 European-Americans were massacred, but by 1867 the Sioux had given up their lands and moved to reservations in the Black Hills. The discovery of gold there brought an influx of prospectors and further trouble erupted, resulting in the Sioux's famous defeat of Gen. George Custer and his troops in the Battle of Little Bighorn (1876). After repeated revolts against European-American misrule and treachery, the Sioux were finally defeated at Wounded Knee, S.D. (1890). About 40,000 Sioux now live on reservations in Minnesota, Nebraska, the Dakotas, and Montana.

Sioux City (pop. 115,018), city in western Iowa, on the Missouri River near where the borders of Iowa, Nebraska, and South Dakota meet. Settled in 1854 by John K. Cook, Sioux City was incorporated in 1857. It is the market, meat-packing, and major distribution center for the surrounding agricultural area, which includes parts of the 3 states. The city's industries also produce automobile parts, farm machinery, and clothing.
See also: Iowa.

Sioux Falls (pop. 123,809), largest city in South Dakota, on the Big Sioux River in the southeastern corner of the state. Incorporated as a city in 1883 it is the seat of Minnehaha County. Sioux Falls is the livestock and poultry center for the surrounding area. Its chief industries are meat packing, food processing, and the manufacture of metal and wood products.
See also: South Dakota.

Siphon, device, usually consisting of a bent tube with 2 legs of unequal length, that utilizes atmospheric pressure to transfer liquid over the edge of one container into another at a lower level. The flowing action depends on the difference in the pressures acting on the 2 liquid surfaces and stops when these coincide.

Siple, Paul Allman (1908-68), U.S. geographer and explorer of Antarctica. He was a member of 2 expeditions led by Richard E. Byrd (1928, 1933-35), heading the biology department for the later one. He also served as geographer for the 1939-41 U.S. expedition. He continued his exploration of Antarctica from 1946 to 1957, serving as scientific leader of the South Polar Station 1956-67.
See also: Antarctica.

Siren, device used to create loud, shrill warning signals. Foghorns are sirens that warn of low visibility due to foggy weather conditions. Electronic

devices are now often used as sirens. Older ones worked mechanically, one cylinder or disk rotating within another punctured with air holes. The motion created the sound waves.
See also: Civil defense.

Sirenian, or sea cow, any of an order (Sirenia) of aquatic mammals. These large, shy animals feed on plant life in shallow tropical seas. The manatee of Florida, a sirenian, is an endangered species. The name comes from the sirens, sea creatures of Greek mythology.

Sirens, in Greek mythology, sea nymphs whose irresistible singing lured sailors to their deaths on rocky coasts. Sirens appear in ancient stories, including Homer's *Odyssey*, whose hero, Odysseus, had himself tied to a mast and his men's ears plugged as they sailed past the sirens' coast in order to resist.
See also: Mythology.

Sirius, Alpha Canis Majoris (Dog Star), brightest star in the night sky. About 8.8 light years distant from the earth, it is 20 times more luminous than the sun and has an absolute magnitude of +1.4. A double star, its major component is twice the size of the sun; its major component (the Pup), the first white-dwarf star to be discovered, has a diameter only 50% greater than that of the earth but is extremely dense, its mass being just less than that of the sun.
See also: Binary star.

Sirocco, in southern Europe, warm, humid wind from the south or southeast, originating as a dry wind over the Sahara and gaining humidity from passage over the Mediterranean.

Sisal, any of various plants of the agave family, genus *Agave*. Two types of sisal, *A. sisalana*, found in eastern Africa and Brazil, and *A. fourcroydes*, found in Mexico, El Salvador, and Cuba, contain long fibers used to manufacture twine and hemp.

Sisley, Alfred (1839-99), Anglo-French painter, a founder of impressionism. His fine landscapes and snow scenes, painted in the 1870s, often show London and Paris neighborhoods; for example, *Effet de neige* (1874). His work achieved wide recognition only after his death.
See also: Impressionism.

Sistine Chapel, papal chapel in the Vatican Palace, Rome, renowned for its magnificent frescoes by Michelangelo and other Renaissance artists like Perugino, Botticelli, and Ghirlandaio. It is named for Pope Sixtus IV, who began its construction in 1473, and is used by the College of Cardinals when it meets to elect a new pope.

Sisyphus, in Greek mythology, founder and king of the ancient city-state of Corinth. Zeus, the head of the gods, was angered at Sisyphus and condemned him to push a heavy rock to the top of a hill. When it reached the top, it rolled back down, and Sisyphus was compelled to repeat the task for all eternity.
See also: Mythology.

Sitar, Indian stringed instrument with a long neck and smallish, rounded soundbox. There are usually 7 strings—5 melody and 2 drone. These are plucked by a player seated on cushions or the floor. In 1957 the Indian sitar virtuoso Ravi Shankar made the first of several concert tours of the United States, spreading the popularity of the instrument, which was then used by several rock bands.

Sitka (pop. 7,803), city in southeastern Alaska, on Baranof Island, west of British Columbia. Sitka was a Russian settlement founded (1799) by the trader Alexander Baranof. With the U.S. purchase of Alaska, the city served as the territorial capital from 1884 to 1900. Today it is a center for fishing and lumber industries. The Sitka National Historical Park commemorates a battle (1804) between the Russians and the Tlingit tribe.
See also: Alaska.

Sitting Bull (c.1831-90), chief of the Teton Sioux who led the last major Native American resistance in the United States. Born in South Dakota, he became head of the Sioux nation and inspired the 1876 campaign that resulted in the massacre of Gen. George Custer and his troops at Little Bighorn. Escaping to Canada, he was pardoned and returned to the Standing Rock reservation, N.D. (1881). He continued to support his people's causes, including their practice of the messianic Ghost Dance religion. At a performance of it he was killed by Native American police who were attempting to arrest him.

Sitwell, Dame Edith (1887-1964), British poet and critic. A master technician of sound, rhythm, and symbol, she helped launch *Wheels* (1916), a magazine of experimental poetry, and wrote the satirical *Façade* (1922; music by William Walton).

Six, les, term coined in 1920 for a group of French composers: Georges Auric, Louis Durey, Arthur Honegger, Darius Milhaud, Francis Poulenc, and Germaine Tailleferre, inspired by the anti-impressionist work of Erik Satie. They also worked with the writer Jean Cocteau.

Sixtus, name of 5 popes. **Sixtus IV** (1414-84) succeeded in 1471 and built the Sistine Chapel. His reign was characterized by nepotism and simony. **Sixtus V** (1521-90) succeeded in 1585 and brought the Papal States to order and made the pope one of Europe's richest princes. His reforms of church administration were part of the Counter-Reformation.

Skagerrak, also spelled Skager-Rak and Skagerrack, arm of the North Sea that separates Denmark from Norway and Sweden. About 130 mi (209 km) long, the Skagerrak joins the North Sea and the Kattegat.
See also: North Sea.

Skate, any of various fish (genus *Raja*) similar to rays. A popular skate used for food is the little skate (*R. erinacea*), which measures up to 2 ft (61 cm) long and is caught along the U.S. and Canadian Atlantic coast. Along the Pacific coast, the big skate (*R. binoculata*), which can measure up to 8 ft (2.5 m) long, are found. The pectoral fins of skate look and act like underwater wings, spanning the length of the fish from head nearly to its rudderlike tail.

The wings move up and down to move the fish along. Skates generally feed on smaller animals, such as snails.

Skateboard, small board with plastic wheels, forming a kind of surfboard to be used on land. Professional and experienced skateboard riders can turn in circles on one wheel (endovers), travel on just 2 of the 4 wheels (wheelies), and jump over a multitude of objects during a ride.

Skeena River, river in British Columbia, Canada, rising in the Stikine mountains and flowing about 360 mi (580 k) to the Pacific Ocean. The river is known for the numerous salmon that are caught in its waters. Canneries are located near the mouth of this river, at Hecate Strait.

Skeet, sport in which the competitor shoots at clay disks mechanically thrown into the air. The disks are tossed to imitate the flight of certain birds. Shooters, using modified shotguns, stand at specific stations from which they shoot at the disks, which may be tossed individually or in pairs.

Skeleton, in vertebrates, framework of bones that supports and protects the soft tissues and organs of the body. It acts as an attachment for the muscles, especially those producing movement, and protects vital organs such as the brain, heart, and lungs. It is also a store of calcium, magnesium, sodium, phosphorous, and proteins, while its bone marrow is the site of red blood corpuscle formation. In the adult human body there are about 206 bones, to which more than 600 muscles are attached.
The skeleton consists of the axial skeleton (the skull, backbone, and ribcage) and the appendicular skeleton (limbs). The function of the *axial skeleton* is mainly protective. The skull consists of 29 bones, 8 being fused to form the cranium, protecting the brain. The *vertebral column*, or backbone, consists of 33 small bones (or vertebrae). The upper 25 are joined by ligaments and thick cartilaginous disks, and the lower 9 are fused. It supports the upper body and protects the spinal cord, which runs through it. The *ribcage* consists of 12 pairs of ribs forming a protective cage around the heart and lungs, and assists in breathing. The *appendicular skeleton* is primarily concerned with locomotion and consists of the arms and pectoral girdle and the legs and pelvic girdle. The limbs articulate with their girdles in ball-and-socket joints that permit the shoulder and hip great freedom of movement but that are prone to dislocation. In contrast, the elbows and knees are hinge joints that permit movement in one plane only but that are very strong.

Skepticism, philosophical attitude of doubting all claims to knowledge, chiefly on the ground that the adequacy of any proposed criterion is itself questionable. Examples of thoroughgoing skeptics, wary of dogmatism in whatever guise, were Pyrrho of Elis (*Pyrrhonism* and *skepticism* are virtual synonyms) and David Hume. Other thinkers—among them St. Augustine, Desiderius Erasmus, Michel de Montaigne, Blaise Pascal, Pierre Bayle, and Sören Kierkegaard—sought to defend faith and religion by directing skeptical arguments against the epistemological claims of rationalism and empiricism. Pragmatism and Immanuel Kant's critical philosophy represent two influential attempts to resolve skeptical dilemmas.
See also: Carneades; Pyrrho of Elis.

Skew line, in geometry, line that neither intersects nor runs parallel to another line in the same plane; in statistics, a line, as on a graph, indicating that the measured quantity departs from a normal distribution to the right or left of the curve.
See also: Geometry.

Skidmore, Louis (1897-1962), U.S. architect and cofounder of the firm of Skidmore, Owings and Merrill (1936), which designed such government and corporate projects as Oak Ridge, Tenn. (1943-45), the U.S. Air Force Academy in Colorado Springs (1954-62), and the Sears Tower in Chicago (1971-73).
See also: Architecture.

Skiing, sport of gliding over snow on long, thin runners called skis. It began some 5,000 years ago in northern Europe as a form of transport and became a sport in the 19th century. In 1924 the Fédération Internationale de Ski was formed and the first Winter Olympics held. It has increased enormously in popularity, either for pleasure or through participation in such Olympic-style activities as Alpine downhill slaloms, giant slalom obstacle races, Nordic cross-country skiing, or ski-jumping. Skis are generally made of laminated wood, fiberglass, plastic, metal, or a combination of these. They have safety bindings attaching the specially made boot firmly to the ski; ski poles are used for balance.

Skimmer, seabird whose lower half of its bill is longer than the upper half. It flies low over the water with its bill cutting through the water to catch fish. Skimmers are found mainly along tropical coasts, but the black skimmer comes up the western Atlantic as far as Massachusetts. They live in flocks, and their calls sound like a pack of hounds.

Skin, tissue that forms a sensitive, elastic, protective, and waterproof covering of the body, together with its specializations (e.g., nails, hair). In the adult human it weighs 6.1 lb (2.75 kg), covers 18.3 sq ft (1.7 sq m), and varies in thickness from .04 in (1mm) in the eyelids to .12 in (3 mm) in the palms and soles. It consists of 2 layers: the outer, epidermis, and the inner, dermis, or true skin. The outermost part of the epidermis, the stratum corneum, contains a tough protein called keratin. Consequently, it provides protection against mechanical trauma, a barrier against microorganisms, and waterproofing. The epidermis also contains cells that produce the melanin responsible for skin pigmentation and that provide protection against the sun's ultraviolet rays. The unique pattern of skin folding on the soles and palms provides a gripping surface and is the basis of identification by fingerprints. The dermis is usually thicker than the epidermis and contains blood vessels, nerves, and sensory receptors, sweat glands, sebaceous glands, hair follicles, fat cells, and fibers. Temperature regulation of the body is aided by the evaporative cooling of sweat, regulation of the skin blood flow, and the erection of hairs that trap an insulating layer of air next to the skin. The rich nerve supply of the dermis is responsible for the reception of touch, pressure, pain, and temperature stimuli. Leading into the hair follicles are sebaceous glands that produce the antibacterial sebum, a fluid that keeps the hairs oiled and the skin moist. The action of sunlight on the skin initiates the formation of vitamin D, which helps prevent rickets.

Skin diving, underwater swimming and diving with or without selfcontained underwater breathing apparatus (SCUBA). The simplest apparatus is the snorkel, generally used with goggles, or mask, and flippers. An aqualung consists of compressed-air cylinders with an automatic demand regulator that supplies air at the correct pressure according to the diver's depth. "Closed-circuit" SCUBA contains a chemical that absorbs carbon dioxide from exhaled air.

Skin grafting, application of portions of skin, either the outer layers or the full thickness, to a raw surface to promote healing or to replace a defect. *See also:* Plastic surgery.

Skink, slender lizard found in many of the warmer parts of the world. Skinks are abundant in Africa and 50 species live in the Americas. Some have rough scales, but the rest have very flat scales, sometimes so small that they are hard to see. Skinks may be aquatic or tree dwellers, and many have taken up burrowing, like the Florida sand skink. The largest skink is the 2-ft (0.61-m) giant zebra skink of the Solomon Islands, which has a prehensile tail. Skinks eat plants or small animals. Most lay eggs that are guarded by the mother; others bear live young. Young skinks often have blue tails that break off when they are attacked.

Skinner, B.F. (1904-90), U.S. psychologist and author whose advocacy of behaviorism helped it gain acceptance in 20th-century psychology. His best-known books are *Science and Human Behavior* (1953); *Walden Two* (1961), a Utopian novel based on behaviorism; and *Beyond Freedom and Dignity* (1971).

Sklodowska, Marie *See:* Curie, Marie Sklodowska.

Skryabin, Alexander *See:* Scriabin, Alexander.

Skua, any of various sea birds (genus *Stercorarius*) known for stealing food from other sea birds, such as gulls, terns, petrels, and penguins. The skua lives in arctic and antarctic regions. Similar in looks to a sea gull, it is normally reddish to brown, with white patches on the wings. Skuas are strong fliers who harass weaker birds, causing them to drop their prey.

Skull, bony structure of the head and face situated at the top of the vertebral column. It forms a thick, bony protection of the brain, with small apertures for blood vessels, nerves, the spinal cord, and the thinner framework of facial structure.

Skunk, carnivorous mammal of the weasel family renowned for the foul stink it produces when threatened. There are 10 species distributed throughout the Americas. All are boldly patterned in black and white. Most are nocturnal and feed on insects, mice, and eggs. For defense, a skunk can expel fine jets of foul-smelling liquid from scent glands under the tail to a distance of 10 ft (3 m) with a remarkably accurate aim.

Skunk cabbage, either of two plant species (*Symplocarpus foetidus* or *Lysichitum americanum*), of temperate regions named for the foul smell that comes from the plant when the tissues are squeezed. Apart from the smell, the skunk cabbage is a welcome addition to the damp woods and fields of the eastern United States for its purple and green arum-type flower, which appears in late winter. The leaves appear after the flowers have died. A third species, *Veratrum californicum*, also called false hellebore or corn lily, grows in western North and Central America and is poisonous.

Sky *See:* Atmosphere.

Skydiving, popular name for sport parachuting. Skydivers reach speeds of up to 100 mph (160 kmph) after jumping out of planes at altitudes of up to 15,000 ft (4,600 m). The last 3,000 ft (920 m) or so of the fall is slowed by a parachute. Skydivers who aim for a ground target are called accuracy skydivers. Those that fall in formation with other divers are called relative work skydivers.

Skye terrier, breed of dog named after the Isle of Skye, Scotland, where it was first bred, in the 17th century. A work dog, good rat hunter, and pleasant companion, this terrier stands up to 10 in (25 cm) high at the shoulder and has a long body. Ears may be floppy or erect.

Skylab *See:* Space exploration.

Skyscraper, extremely tall building. In the mid-19th century the rising cost of land in big cities made building upward rather than outward worthwhile, and this became practicable with the development of safe electric elevators. The first skyscraper was the 130-ft (39.6 m) Equitable Life Assurance Society Building in New York (1870). A major design breakthrough was the use of a load-bearing skeletal iron frame, first used in the 10-story Home Insurance Building in Chicago (1883). The tallest skyscrapers are the Sears Tower in Chicago and the World Trade Center in New York City, with more than 110 stories.

Slag, residual material produced during the manufacture of pig iron and the smelting of metals, such as copper or lead. Slag is used in the making of concrete, road-building materials, and fertilizer. Its composition depends on the metallurgical process that produced it, though all slag contains silicates.

Slander, false statements intended to damage a person's reputation. A slanderous statement that is written or printed is called libel. The civil laws of the United States allow people to sue for libel.
See also: Libel.

Slang, informal and innovative use of language. Slang generally expresses new ideas or variations of old ones, most often in spoken speech. The particular words and expressions used tend not to remain popular for long, and slang often changes from region to region or from one ethnic or class group to the next.

Slate, fine-grained, low-grade metamorphic rock formed by the regional metamorphism of shale. The parallel orientation of platy minerals in the rock causes it to split evenly (slaty cleavage) in a plane that is perpendicular to the direction of the compressive metamorphic stress.

Slater, Samuel (1768-1835), British-born originator of the U.S. textile industry. As an employee of a company using the Richard Arkwright spinning machine, Slater learned about this revolutionary textile manufacturing process. Once in the United States, Slater reconstructed the Arkwright spinning machine from memory for Almy & Brown, a Rhode Island firm. Eventually he opened his own companies throughout New England, beginning with one in Rehoboth, Mass. (1798).
See also: Textile.

Slavery, practice found at different times in most parts of the world, now condemned in the UN's Universal Declaration of Human Rights. Slavery generally means enforced servitude, along with society's recognition that the master has ownership rights over the slave and his or her labor. Some elements of slavery can be found in serfdom, as practiced during the Middle Ages and in Russia up to 1861; in debt bondage and peonage, both forms of enforced labor for the payment of debts; and in forced labor itself, exacted for punishment or for political or military reasons (examples being the "slave" labor used by the Nazis in World War II and the Soviet labor camps). In some places a form of slavery, or bondage, is still practiced today, under the guise of exacting a bride price, or the "adoption" of poor children by wealthier families for labor purposes. While peonage is still rampant in South America, actual slavery is reputed to exist in Africa, the Arabian Peninsula, Tibet, and elsewhere. Slavery in Saudi Arabia was officially abolished only in 1962.
Warfare was the main source of slaves in ancient times, along with enslavement for debt or as punishment and the selling of children. But there was not necessarily a distinction in race or color between master and slave. Manumission (the granting of freedom) was commonplace, and in Greece and Rome many slaves or freedmen rose to influential posts. A slave dynasty, the Mamelukes, ruled Egypt (1250-1517). Germans enslaved many Slavic people (hence *slave*) in the Dark Ages. By the 13th century feudal serfdom was widespread in Europe. Slavery increased when the Portuguese, exploring the coast of Africa, began to import slaves in 1433. With the European discovery of the Americas and the development of plantations, the need for cheap, abundant labor encouraged slave trade. The British abolished its own slave trade in 1807 and slavery in 1833. By constitutional provision, the U.S. slave trade ended in 1808, but not the practice. The abolition issue ignited the U.S. Civil War in 1861. President Lincoln's Emancipation Proclamation (1863) took full effect with the end of the war in 1865.

Slavonic, 3 groups of Indo-European languages spoken by about 440 million people in central and eastern Europe and Siberia. The groups are West Slavonic (Polish, Czech, Slovak), South Slavonic (Slovene, Serbo-Croatian, Macedonian, Bulgarian), and East Slavonic (Russian, Ukrainian, Byelorussian). Byzantine missionaries in the 9th century first developed written Slavic, using a modified Greek alphabet known as Cyrillic. Today Slavs converted by the Orthodox church use Cyrillic characters, and Slavs converted by the Roman church use the Latin alphabet.

Slavs, largest European ethnic group, living today in central and eastern Europe and Siberia, all speaking Slavic languages.
About 4,000 years ago they migrated to land north of the Black Sea and later split into 3 groups: the East Slavs (Byelorussians, Russians, and Ukrainians), the West Slavs (Czechs, Poles, Slovaks, and Sorbs (Wends), and the South Slavs (Bulgarians, Macedonians, Serbs, Croats, and Slovens). By the 9th century Slavic nations were formed, but almost all were overwhelmed by Turkish or Mongol invaders. In the 15th century Russia gained national independence, but other Slavic nations did not regain their national identities until World War I.

Slayton, Donald Kent (1924-), U.S. astronaut. In a cooperative venture between the United States and the USSR (Apollo-Soyuz Test Project, 1975), Slayton and his Apollo crew (Thomas P. Stafford and Vance D. Brand) orbited the earth while docked with a Soviet spacecraft and its crew. Slayton was later director of flight crew operations for the NASA.
See also: Astronaut.

Sled, transportation vehicle that moves over ice and snow on runners. Early sleds were made from joined logs. Some Native American tribes developed toboggans—sleds shaped like canoes. Today in Alaska and other ice-covered regions, sleds with thin, parallel runners pulled by dogs help to transport people and goods. Bobsleds are fiberglass-and-steel sleds ridden on special courses for speed.

Sleep, state of relative unconsciousness and inactivity. The need for sleep recurs periodically in all animals. If deprived of sleep, humans initially experience hallucinations and acute anxiety and become highly suggestible. Eventually coma and sometimes death result. During sleep, the body is relaxed and most bodily activity is reduced. Cortical, or higher, brain activity, is measured by the electroencephalograph; blood pressure, body temperature, and rate of heartbeat and breathing are decreased. However, certain activities, such as gastric and alimentary activity, are increased. Sleep tends to occur in daily cycles that exhibit up to 5 or 6 periods of deepness—alternating with periods of paradoxical, or rapid-eye-movement (REM), sleep, characterized by restlessness and jerky movements of the eyes. Paradoxical sleep occurs only when we are dreaming and occupies about 20% of total sleeping time. Sleepwalking (somnambulism) occurs only during orthodox sleep, when we are not dreaming. Sleeptalking occurs mostly in orthodox sleep. Many theories have been proposed to explain sleep. Separate sleeping and waking centers in the hypothalamus cooperate with other parts of the brain in controlling sleep. Sleep as a whole—and particularly paradoxical sleep, when dreaming occurs—is essential to health and life. Consequently, the key to why animals sleep may reside in a need to dream.

Sleeping sickness, serious disease caused by protozoan parasites and transmitted by the bite of the tsetse fly. Sleeping sickness is common in many areas of Africa. Symptoms include fever, headache, skin rash, swollen lymph nodes, and lethargy. The disease is named after the comalike state that may eventually result. Early diagnosis and drug treatment can lessen the sometimes fatal effects.

Sleepwalking (somnambulism), condition in which a partly awakened sleeper performs physical activities during a period of tension or worry. It occurs during deep sleep, early in the night. Most sleepwalkers do not remember their activities upon awakening. Sleepwalking is generally harmless, although injury can occur.

Sleet, partially frozen, transparent bits of ice, falling initially as rain or melted snowflakes and freezing as they travel through parts of the atmosphere below 32°F (0°C).

Slime mold, organism classified as a fungus but that resembles an animal in its ability to move. A slime mold is a yellowish mass, like the raw white of an egg, that is found in damp, dark woods, where it oozes over rotten logs and decayed leaves. It moves like an amoeba, sweeping up particles of dead leaves and bacteria as it goes.

Sling, device used to hurl stones or other objects. In ancient slings, a stone was placed on a strap and spun quickly above the head before being let loose to fly through the air with great force. The biblical hero David killed Goliath with a stone from a sling. Soldiers from the armies of ancient Egypt through those of medieval Europe used slings in combat. Another form of sling, the bola, is tossed along with the stone. Thrown at an animal, it will entangle its legs as well as forcefully hit it.

Slipperwort, or slipper flower, any of a group of 300-400 evergreen plants belonging to the figwort family found in Mexico and South America. Its name derives from the slipperlike shape of its flowers, which are variously colored.

Sloan, Alfred P. (1875-1966), U.S. industrialist, president (1923-37) and chairman of the board (1937-56) of General Motors. His Sloan Foundation (1934) finances social and medical research, particularly through the Sloan-Kettering Institute for Cancer Research in New York City.

Sloan, John (1871-1951), U.S. painter, member of the Ashcan School and influential in the development of modern art. He is noted for his paintings of nudes and of urban scenes, such as *McSorley's Bar* (1912) and *Wake of the Ferry* (1907).
See also: Ashcan School.

Sloe, or blackthorn, spiny shrub (*Prunus spinosa*) of the rose family found in some parts of North America, Asia, and Europe. Its plumlike fruits are used to make a variety of products, such as dyes, jellies, and wine.

Sloth, slow, tree-dwelling, toothless mammal. There are 2 genera of modern tree sloths; 2-toed sloths (*Choloepus*) and 3-toed sloths, or ai (*Bradypus*), descending from the giant ground sloths (*Megatherium*) of the Pleistocene epoch. The arms and legs are long and the digits are bound together by tissue and terminate in long, strong claws. With these the sloth can suspend its body from branches. All sloths are South American in origin and vegetarian, feeding on fruits, shoots, and leaves.

Slovakia

Capital:	Bratislava
Area:	18,933 sq mi (49,036 sq km)
Population:	5,393,000
Language:	Slowak
Government:	Republic
Independent:	1993
Head of gov.:	Prime minister
Per capita:	U.S. $2,950
Mon. unit:	1 Koruna = 100 halierov

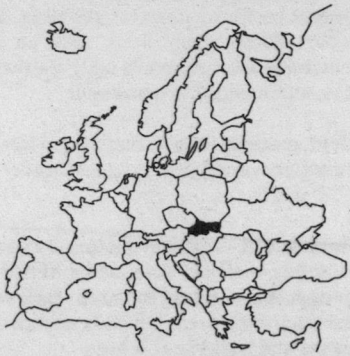

Sloth bear, or honey bear, slow-moving mammal of the bear family found in the warm forest regions of India and Sri Lanka. Although its sense of smell is highly developed, the sloth bear has poor vision and hearing. A staple of its diet is insects, which it ferrets out with its long claws and snout, then sucks in through spaces between the teeth. It is also known to like honey. A sloth bear stands about 5 ft (1.5 m) tall and can weigh up to 250 lb (113 kg). Unlike some other bears, it does not hibernate during the winter months.

Slot machine, mechanized gambling device first developed in 1899. Coins are inserted through a slot, a handle is pulled, and a series of reels, visible through a window, spin for a while before coming to a halt. The player wins if the reels show a certain number of identical symbols.

Slovakia, or Slovak Republic, independent country in central Europe, bordered on the north by Poland, on the east by Ukraine, on the west by Austria, and on the northwest by the Czech republic. The capital is Bratislava.
Land and climate. Slovakia is mostly mountainous, but the heights slope down to plains and the Danube River in the south and southwest. The climate is continental with warm summers and cold winters.
People. The population consists mainly of Slovaks (68%), minorities are Hungarians (11%) and gypsies. The official language is Slovak. About 60% of the population is Roman Catholic.
Economy. Slovakia has rich farmlands and mineral deposits; shipbuilding and metal processing are leading industries. The capital is a prominent Danube port.
History. Slovakia was principally under Hungarian rule from the early 10th century to 1918. Slovakia then became part of Czechoslovakia until its independence in 1993. In 1997 Slovakia tightened its ties with Russia. For the moment, it can not join NATO or the EU, due to a lack of democratic relations within the country.
See also: Czechoslovakia.

Slovaks, Slavic people who settled in central Europe during the 5th and 6th centuries. Slovakia was dominated by Hungary from about 900 until the 1800s, when the Slovaks began a struggle for autonomy. Together with the

Slovenia

Capital:	Ljubljana
Area:	7,820 sq mi (20,253 sq km)
Population:	1,972,000
Language:	Slovene
Government:	Republic
Independent:	1991
Head of gov.:	Prime minister
Per capita:	U.S. $8,200
Mon. unit:	1 Tolar = 100 storins

more numerous Czechs, they formed the independent nation of Czechoslavakia in 1918.
See also: Slavs.

Slovenia (Republic of), independent country in central Eastern Europe, bounded by the Adriatic Sea and Italy in the west, Austria in the north, Hungary in the northeast, and Croatia in the south. Its capital is Ljubljana.
Land and climate. This small country (7,819 sq mi; 20,251 sq km) is mostly mountainous, with a narrow coastal strip. The largest part has a continental climate, with an alpine climate in the mountainous north and a Mediterranean climate along the coast.
People. The population consists of Slovenes (88%), with minorities of Croats, Serbs, and Muslims. The official language is Slovene. The majority is Roman Catholic (84%)
Economy. Industries currently include chemicals, textiles, and and active tourist trade. As a Yugoslav republic Slovenia used to be the most prosperous one. In the 1990s prosperity diminished, but the outlook is not unfavourable.
History. From the 13th century until the end of World War I Slovenia was ruled by Austria. In 1918, it became part of Yugoslavia. In recent years Slovenia sought increasing independence from Yugoslavia and finally declared its own sovereignty in 1991. After that, its foreign policy was focused on entry into the western organisations.
See also: Yugoslavia.

Slug, mollusk best described as a snail without a shell or with a tiny shell inside the body. An exception is the roundback slug, which has an outside shell. Behind the head, with its 4 tentacles, is an oval shield containing a pore that leads to the lungs. Slugs creep over the ground like snails and leave a trail of slime. As they have no shell to retire into, they have to live in moist places to escape drying up. Some slugs eat fungi, others eat green plants and are garden pests.

Small Business Administration, independent agency of the U.S. government that furnishes small businesses with practical advice and low-cost loans. The agency also helps small businesses obtain government contracts and aids minority-owned firms.

Small-claims court, U.S. court set up to resolve lawsuits involving claims of less than $ 5000. First begun in 1913 in Cleveland, Ohio, small-claims courts now exist in every state. Cases frequently pertain to unpaid bills or debts, inferior product performance, or poorly provided services.

Smallpox, acute, highly contagious viral disease, initiated by sudden severe constitutional symptoms and characterized by a progressive skin eruption that often results in permanent pits and scars. The disease is of historical interest only, for the World Health Organization declared the world free of smallpox in 1980.
See also: Jenner, Edward.

Smartweed, weed belonging to the buckwheat family and found in the lowlands and marshes of North America. It can grow up to 5 ft (1.5 m) tall. It is recognized by its small white, pink, or green flowers. The name derives from its sharp, bitter taste.

Smell, sense that enables humans and animals to perceive and identify odors. The organ of smell is the nose. Respiratory air is drawn into the nostrils and passes across a specialized receptor surface—the olfactory epithelium. Receptor cells detect the tiny concentrations of odors in the airstream and stimulate nerve impulses that pass to olfactory centers in the brain for coding and perception. It is not possible to classify odors in the same way as the primary colors in vision, and it is probable that pattern recognition is more important. Certain animals depend mainly on the sense of smell, while humans are predominantly visual animals. But with training, humans can achieve sensitive detection and discrimination of odors.

Smelling salts, chemical stimulant used to alleviate faintness. It consists of a mixture of ammonium carbonate, alcohol, and fragrance. When fumes are inhaled, nasal membranes are irritated and breathing becomes more rapid, resulting in a feeling of clear-headedness.
See also: Ammonia.

Smelt, small, silvery fish that lives in large shoals in the colder waters of the Northern Hemisphere. Smelts range from 3 to 12 in (7.6 to 30.5 cm) and are an important food for other fishes. Like the related salmon and trout, they have a fleshy fin on the back. The American smelt is caught in large numbers as it ascends Atlantic Coast rivers to spawn. Pacific smelt are not often eaten because of their oily flesh.

Smelting, in metallurgy, process of extracting a metal from its ore by heating the ore in a blast furnace or reverberatory furnace (one in which a shallow hearth is heated by radiation from a low roof heated by flames from the burning fuel). A reducing agent, usually a coke, is used, and a flux is added to remove impurities.
See also: Metallurgy.

Smetana, Bedrich (1824-84), Czech composer. Many of Smetana's compositions reflect his ardent Bohemian nationalism; best known are the comic opera *The Bartered Bride* (1866) and the symphonic poem *Má Vlast* (*My Fatherland*; 1874-79), which contains *Vltava* (*The Moldau*).

Smilax, any of many species of woody vines (genus *Smilax*) found in temperate or tropical areas. There are about 300 different species, including the common greenbrier. Smilax typically have prickly stems, veined leaves, white or yellow-green flowers, and bluish-black or red berries.

Smith, Adam (1723-90), Scottish economist and philosopher. The free-market system he advocated in *Inquiry into the Nature and Causes of the Wealth of Nations* (1776) came to be regarded as the classic system of economics. Smith drew on the ideas of his friends D. Hume, A. R. Turgot, F. Quesnay, and C. Montesquieu, and argued that if market forces were allowed to operate without state intervention "an invisible hand" would guide self-interest for the well-being of all. His concept of the division of labor and the belief that value derives from productive labor were major insights. An earlier work, *Theory of Moral Sentiments* (1759), contrasts with *The Wealth of Nations* in its emphasis upon sympathy rather than self-interest as a basic force in human nature.
See also: Economics.

Smith, Alfred Emanuel (1873-1944), U.S. politician elected governor of New York 4 times (1918, 1922-26). He was a Tammany Hall politician and a leading Democrat. Although supported by Franklin D. Roosevelt, Smith, the first Roman Catholic to run for the presidency, failed to be nominated in 1924 and was beaten by Herbert Hoover in 1928. When Roosevelt became president, Smith opposed the New Deal.

Smith, Bessie (1894-1937), U.S. jazz singer. "The Empress of the Blues" came from a poor Tennessee home and first recorded in 1923; later she performed with many leading musicians, including Louis Armstrong and Benny Goodman.

Smith Act (1940), federal U.S. law making it a criminal offense to advocate the violent overthrow of the government or to belong to any group advocating this. Used to convict Communist Party leaders, the act also required registration and fingerprinting of aliens.

Smith, David (1906-65), influential U.S. sculptor, famous for his constructions of wrought iron and cut steel. His late works, like *Cubi XVIII* (1964), comprised burnished or painted cubic forms dramatically welded together.

Smith, Edmund Kirby (1824-93), U.S. general who served in the Confederate army during the Civil War, having previously fought in the Mexican War. He is known as the last Southern general to surrender to the North at the end of the war.
See also: Civil War, U.S.

Smith, Ian Douglas (1919-), Rhodesian prime minister (1964-79). As leader of a white minority government, he declared unilateral independence from Great Britain and made Rhodesia a republic in 1970. Civil strife ensued. In 1978 Smith and 3 black leaders agreed to share control until power was transferred to the black majority, but guerrilla nationalists rejected the plan. A British cease-fire was accepted in 1979, and complete independence came in 1980 with the formation of a black regime in Rhodesia, renamed Zimbabwe. Under the black majority rule Smith remained active in politics until 1987.

Smith, James (1719?-1806), Irish-born U.S. lawyer and legislator and one of the signers of the Declaration of Independence. He was a member of the Continental Congress from 1776 to 1778.

Smith, Jedediah Strong (1799-1831), U.S. pioneer who led fur-trapping expeditions to the Missouri and Wind rivers and in 1824 discovered the South Pass route across the Rocky Mountains to the far West. Smith was the first white man to cross the Sierra Nevada and the Great Salt Desert and to explore the California-Oregon coast by land. He was killed by Comanches.
See also: Pioneer life in America.

Smith, John (1580?-1631), English soldier who helped found the first successful English colony in America, in 1607. As president of the colony—Jamestown, Va.—Smith enforced organization and discipline among the settlers. His harsh treatment of Native Americans, however, contributed to hostilities between the groups. Late in life, he wrote several books about his experiences, one of which was the source of the story of his capture by Powhatan and last-minute rescue by Pocahontas.

Smith, Joseph (1805-44), founder of the Church of Jesus Christ of Latter-Day Saints in Fayette, N.Y., in 1830. Its doctrine and organization are derived from several texts, principally the *Book of Mormon* (1830), which is based on golden tablets inscribed with sacred writings that Smith claimed to have found and translated with miraculous help. Community opposition caused him to move his colony to the Midwest, where it flourished despite schisms. But when Smith announced his candidacy for the US presidency in 1844, non-Mormons arrested both him and his brother, Hyrum, for conspiracy and treason. Taken from jail at Carthage, Ill., by a mob, they were shot.
See also: Mormons.

Smith, Kate (Kathryn Elizabeth Smith; 1909-86), singer and radio and television personality. Although she appeared on the New York stage, she made her reputation on radio in the 1930s. She is associated with Irving Berlin's song "God Bless America," to which she had exclusive radio rights. Smith entertained during World War II, selling war bonds and appearing for the troops. She appeared regularly on television from 1950 to 1956.

Smith, Margaret Chase (1897-), U.S. legislator, first woman to serve in both the House of Representatives and the Senate. She was named to replace her husband (a representative from Maine) when he died in office in 1940, and was later elected for 4 full terms. As a senator, she was one of the first opponents of Senator Joseph McCarthy. In 1964 she became the first woman from a major party to campaign for the presidency.

Smith, Walter Bedell (1895-1961), U.S. Army chief of staff in Europe in World War II. He negotiated the surrenders of Italy (1943) and Germany (1945), was ambassador to the USSR (1946-49), CIA director (1950-53), and undersecretary of state (1953-54).
See also: World War II.

Smith-Hughes Act, congressional act adopted in 1917 providing eligible states with funds for job-training programs. State proposals must be submitted and approved prior to the allocation of funds.

Smithson, James (1765-1829), British chemist and mineralogist. Though he never visited the United States, he bequeathed to it his entire fortune of over £100,000 (then about $500,000) to found the Smithsonian Institution in Washington, D.C.

Smithsonian Institution, world's largest museum complex, known as the "nation's attic," comprising 14 U.S. government-sponsored museums and the National Zoo. All of these are in Washington, D.C., except for the Cooper-Hewitt Museum in New York City, and hold perhaps 100 million artifacts illustrating both scientific and artistic culture. Founded with a bequest from James Smithson, the institution was established by Congress in 1846. The Smithsonian undertakes considerable scientific research, but is popularly known for its National Air and Space Museum, National Museum of Natural History, National Gallery of Art, National Portrait Gallery, and National Museum of American Art. The institution is governed by a board of regents comprising the U.S. vice president and chief justice, 3 senators, 3 representatives, and 9 private citizens appointed by Congress.
See also: Smithson, James.

Smog, term first used in 1905 to describe the combination of smoke and thick fog that hung over London and other cities in Great Britain. London-type fog occurs when moisture in the air condenses on smoke particles produced by burning coal. Sulfur dioxide, the dangerous part of London-type smog, attacks the lungs. Petrochemical smog results from the action of sunlight on hydrocarbons and nitrogen oxides in the air that are formed by burning gasoline and petroleum products. It can irritate the eyes, nose, throat, and lungs. Smog is poisonous in heavy concentrations and can be fatal. It also destroys plant life and deteriorates building materials.
See also: Air pollution.

Smoke, vapor consisting of fine carbonaceous particles suspended in a gas, produced by the burning of fuel. Smoke can harm the lungs as well as cause damage to property and vegetation. It is used commercially in agriculture and in the preservation of meats.
See also: Air pollution.

Smoke detector, or smoke alarm, device placed in a room or floor of a building to signal the presence of smoke or fire. When smoke passes through the device, a loud, high-pitched sound is triggered. The 2 basic types are photoelectric detectors and ionization detectors.

Smoking, habit of inhaling the smoke of dried tobacco or other leaves from a pipe or a cigarette. Smoking has been practiced for centuries in various communities, often using plants with hallucinogenic or other mood-altering properties. The modern habit of smoking began in America and spread to Europe in the 16th century. Mass production of cigarettes began in the 19th century.

Researchers have noted an uneqivocal association between smoking and such life-threatening diseases as lung cancer, chronic arthritis, emphysema, and diseases of the arteries and heart. Smoking appears to play a part in other forms of cancer and peptic ulcers, and is responsible for 2-2.5 million deaths each year. It is not yet clear what part of the smoke is responsible for promoting disease. Nonsmokers may be affected by environmental smoke; passive smokers are perhaps 3 times more likely to die of lung cancer than they would be otherwise. Smoking causes both physical and psychological addiction.

The health hazards resulting from the practice of smoking have generally been recognized by the public. Filter cigarettes and then low-tar and low-nicotine cigarettes have gained popular acceptance. Behavioral scientists have devoted much attention to helping people stop smoking. Although many people have successfully quit, many others have had great difficulty ending the habit. Efforts to educate the public have concentrated on presenting negative images of smoking, regulating the advertising of cigarettes, limiting the public spaces in which smoking is permitted, and increasing the cost of cigarettes by taxation. Some controversy exists between those who believe smoking is an individual choice and those who believe society has the right to act on its own behalf.

Smuggling, unlawful conveyance of goods or individuals across a border. Legitimate goods are often smuggled to avoid payment of a duty; illegal goods—such as drugs—are smuggled. Nations have varying laws regulating the importation of goods, and penalties vary as well. In the United States, proof of intent is a necessary precondition for conviction.

Smut, fungi named for the masses of sooty spores formed on the surface of the host plant. Within the plant the smut develops a network of threads that take nutrients from it and cause stunting. Smuts attack wheat, corn, and other cereals, onions, sunflowers, and a few other plants. Smuts are hard to control because their spores can survive in the ground over the winter.

Smuts, Jan Christiaan (1870-1950), Afrikaaner soldier and politician, prime minister of South Africa (1919-24 and 1939-48). A general in the South African War against the British, Smuts later cooperated with them to found the Union of South Africa (1910). He was made a field marshal during World War II and participated in the British military leadership.
See also: South Africa.

Snail, herbivorous gastropod mollusk with, typically, a spirally coiled shell, found on land, in fresh water, or in the sea. The shell is secreted by the underlying mantle and houses the internal organs. The internal structure is similar in all groups, though land snails (pulmonates) have air-breathing lungs instead of gills. Nonpulmonate snails are mostly unisexual, while pulmonates are typically hermaphrodite.

Snake, legless reptile related to the lizards. There are about 2,700 species, most of which live in tropical countries, though a few survive in nearly arctic conditions. Snakes do not have legs, although the boas and pythons have the remains of a hind pair of legs. It is thought that they evolved from burrowing, legless lizards. Snakes, unlike lizards, do not have eardrums and are deaf to airborne sounds (they cannot hear the snake charmer's flute), but they can sense sounds coming through the ground by their vibrations. Locomotion is achieved by several methods. In the common serpentine movement, the body is pushed forward in S-shaped waves. In concertina movement the body is thrown forward in loops. Large snakes can push themselves along by movements of the belly scales. The sidewinder and the horned viper move over loose sand by throwing the body into S-shaped waves in side-winding locomotion.

Snakes feed on live animals or eggs. They kill their prey by constriction—preventing it from breathing but not crushing it—or by biting. Poisonous snakes inject venom through grooved or hollow fangs from modified saliva glands. Hematoxic venoms attack the blood and nervous system; and neurotoxic venoms attack the nerves. The young hatch from eggs or are born alive. The mother may look after the eggs; otherwise they are left in a nest in soil or under a log. Snakes grow throughout their lives and shed their skins every year or so.

Snakebird *See:* Anhinga; Wryneck.

Snakebite, bite of a snake that, when poisonous, can be fatal. Sometimes it may be necessary to cut and suction the wound, and many first-aid kits contain a syringe for this purpose.

Snake charming, folk art originating in northern Africa and southern Asia in which a charmer uses rhythmic body movements to encourage similar swaying movements by a snake, usually a cobra. Although snakes cannot hear, the charmer typically plays a flute while swaying.

Snake dance, religious ceremony of the Hopi tribe of Native Americans in the Southwest. It is part of a larger ceremony held every year to ensure peace, health, and good crops. At the climax of the snake dance, which lasts 9 days, the men hold live rattlesnakes in their mouths as they dance.

Snake killer *See:* Roadrunner.

Snake River, large branch of the Columbia River in the Pacific Northwest, made up of the Upper, Middle, and Lower Snake rivers. Each one has many tributaries. The river has great importance as a generator of hydroelectric power, and its tributaries are used for irrigation. Streams of the Upper Snake River sink beneath the ground to form a huge subterranean reservoir. The river is navigable and is used as a trade link between the Pacific Ocean and inland areas.

Snakeroot, any of a group of unrelated plants found in the prairies and wooded areas of North America and believed to be useful in curing snakebite. Black snakeroot, Virginia snakeroot, and button snakeroot were used to treat a variety of ailments. Texas snakeroot was used as an anesthetic and stimulant.

Snapdragon, plant (genus *Antirrhinum*) of the figwort family whose flowers have the upper and lower petals pressed together like an animal's jaws. Only strong insects, such as bumblebees, can force their way inside the petals to pollinate the flower, but butterflies can insert their tubular tongues between the "lips" to suck nectar. Snapdragons came from the Mediterranean and are a favorite garden flower.

Snapper, large-headed fish with a long dorsal fin and a deep body. There are over 250 warm water species. They live in shoals and feed on almost anything edible. Many have red bodies, and several kinds are marketed as red snapper. The fish is good to eat, and some of the inshore species are caught by anglers. Snappers get their name from a habit of suddenly shutting their mouths when dying—which can be painful for someone who has a finger in the way, for they have sharp teeth.

SNCC *See:* Student Nonviolent Coordinating Committee.

Snead, Sam (1912-), U.S. golfer. Known for his strong drives and fluent swing, "Slamming Sammy" won a record 84 Professional Golfers' Association (PGA) tournaments between 1936 and 1965. His achievements include winning the PGA championship (1942, 1949, 1951), the Masters Tournament (1949, 1952, 1954) and the British Open (1946).

Sneeze, explosive expiration through the nose and mouth stimulated by irritation or inflammation in the nasal epithelium. It is a reflex attempt to remove the source of irritation.

Sneezewort (*Achillea ptarmica*), perennial plant of Europe and Asia, a species of yarrow, whose leaves are used to make sneezing powder.

Snipe, long-billed bird of the family Scolopacidae with flexible bill tips that can be opened below ground to grasp food items. Active mainly at dawn and dusk, snipes are birds of marshy areas or open moorland with large eyes set far back on the head. Extraordinarily well camouflaged, they rise sharply if disturbed at close quarters and escape with an erratic zigzag flight. In courtship many species produce loud whistling or drumming noises by vibration of the primaries or tail coverts in rapid dives.

Sniperscope, device developed during World War II to enable soldiers to aim rifles accurately at night. The scope emits invisible infrared rays whose reflection off objects the shooter can see by looking through the scope. It had limited effectiveness and has since been replaced by the starlight scope.

Snooker *See:* Billiards.

Snoring, rough, hoarse respiration of certain persons during sleep; the noise is caused by vibration of the soft palate. It is predisposed to by the shape of the pharynx and by the sleeping position.

Snow, precipitation consisting of flakes or clumps of ice crystals. The crystals are plane hexagonal, showing an infinite variety of beautiful, branched forms; needles, columns, and irregular forms are also found. Snow forms by direct vapor-to-ice condensation from humid air below 32°F (0°C). On reaching the ground, snow crystals lose their structure and become granular. Fresh snow is very light (specific gravity about 0.1) and is a good insulator, protecting underlying plants from severe cold. In time, pressure, sublimation, melting, and refreezing lead to compaction into névé.

Snow, C(harles) P(ercy) (1905-80), English physicist, government official, and author, many of whose works deal with the widening gap between art and technology. He is best known for his *Strangers and Brothers* series: 11 novels (1940-70) about the English professional classes.

Snow, Edgar (1905-72), U.S. journalist and author. The first Westerner to visit the Chinese Communists in their remote headquarters in Yanan (1936), he wrote a sympathetic account of their programs and idealism in *Red Star over China* (1937). A personal friend of Mao Zedong and Zhou Enlai, he was one of the few U.S. citizens to visit China regularly after the 1949 revolution, about which he wrote *The Other Side of the River* (1962) and *The Long Revolution* (1972).

Snowball, or European cranberry bush, any of various berry-producing shrubs (genus *Viburnum*) of the honeysuckle family native to Gelderland province, the Netherlands. They have clusters of large white flowers. When cultivated, they do not bear fruit and can grow as high as 12 ft (3.7 m).

Snow blindness, temporary loss of vision with severe pain, tears, and swelling due to excessive ultraviolet light reflected from snow. Permanent damage is rare; protective polarized glasses helps prevent snow blindness.

Snow bunting, or snowflake, bird of the finch family found in Arctic regions. It resembles a sparrow except that it has a white head and breast in winter. During the coldest months, it migrates south into Canada and occasionally the United States.

Snowdrop, flowering herb (*Galanthus nivalis*) of the amaryllis family found predominantly in Eurasia. Each plant consists of a leaved stalk topped by a drooping, fragile-looking white flower resembling a snowdrop. A hardy and attractive plant, it is popular with gardeners.

Snowflake *See:* Snow; Snow bunting.

Snow leopard, or ounce, large mammal (*Felis uncia*) of the cat family found in central Asia. During the warmer months it lives high in the Tibetan plateau; in winter, it moves south into the valley. Its pale gray fur, which serves as camouflage in the snow, has been much valued by hunters and traders, and the snow leopard is now an endangered species.

Snow line, uneven line along mountain slopes marking areas of permanent snow. Since its position depends on many factors, it varies greatly from place to place. Snow lines can be used to evaluate global climatic shifts.

Snowmobile, engine-driven sled used for transport over large areas of ice and snow. An early, more cumbersome form of the vehicle was used in the

1920s. Today snowmobiling is a popular sport in many parts of North America and northern Europe. The snowmobile is also used by hunters, fishers, rescue workers, forest rangers, and power companies. In some areas its use has been restricted because of criticisms from environmentalists.

Snow-on-the-mountain, annual plant (*Euphorbia marginata*) of the spurge family found predominantly in the central plains of the United States. Popular with gardeners and florists, it grows to about 2 ft (61 cm) in height and has small, white flowers.

Snowshoe, oval-shaped wooden frame with crosspieces strung with thongs, attached to the foot to distribute body weight so as to make it easier to walk on snow without sinking. Snowshoes were invented by Native Americans. Today they are used by loggers, hunters, and farmers. They are made of light wood and leather, and are at least 3 ft (91 cm) long and 1-1.5 ft (30-46 cm) wide.

Snowshoe hare, or varying hare, North American mammal of the rabbit family. A hare of medium size, it is recognized by its large, thickly furred hind feet, which allow it to hop effortlessly over snow. It sheds its brown coat in winter and grows a white one. It is prey for the lynx, snowy owls, and hunters.

Snowy egret *See:* Egret.

Snuff, pulverized, fermented tobacco leaves ground into a powder and inhaled, chewed, or placed in the mouth. The taking of snuff was popular in the 18th century, and decorated snuffboxes were commonly worn as jewelry. Today the practice is believed to pose substantial health risks.

Soapberry, species of trees and shrubs belonging to the soapberry family, grown in tropical and subtropical areas of the Americas and Asia, as well as on Pacific islands. When rubbed in water, the leaves and leathery fruits, which contain saponin, produce a soapy lather.

Soap Box Derby, downhill coasting race for small racing cars without motors or pedals, open to young people from 9 to 16 years. Using homebuilt cars that must comply to rules for size, weight, and cost, contestants first race in local competitions. Winners are eligible to compete in the All-American Soap Box Derby held annually in August in Akron, Ohio.

Soap plant, herb (*Chlorogalum pomeridianum*) of the lily family, native to California. It can grow to a height of 8 ft (2.4 m). The soap plant's small, white flowers open in late afternoon or evening and close in the morning. It grows from a large bulb, which was once used by Native Americans as soap and roasted for food.

Soap sculpture, raised design or figure sculpted from a bar of soap. The design, traced in carbon on the soap, may be cut with a sharp knife and smoothed with a nail file. It may be lacquered or painted with acrylic or poster paints.

Soapstone, or steatite, metamorphic rock consisting largely of compacted talc with some serpentine and carbonates, formed by alteration of peridotite. Soft and soapy to the touch, soapstone has been used from prehistoric times for carvings and vessels. When fired it becomes hard and is used for insulators. The chief deposits are in the United States, Canada, and Norway. *See also:* Talc.

Soares, Mário Alberto Nobre Lopes (1924-), Portuguese politician, premier (1976-78 and 1983-85) and president (1986-96). An opponent of dictator António Salazar, he was repeatedly imprisoned and exiled. Under Soares, Portugal entered the European Community (EC) in 1986.

Sobieski, John *See:* John III Sobieski.

Soccer, national sport of most European and Latin American countries, and rapidly increasing in popularity in the United States. It is played with an inflated leather ball 27-28 in (68.6-71.1 m in circumference) on a field measuring 115 yd by 75 yd (105.2 m by 68.6 m); the goal is 8 yd (7.3 m) wide and 8 ft (2.4 m) high. Two 45-min halves make a game, supervised by 1 referee and 2 lines officials. The aim of each 11-player team is to score by kicking or heading the ball into the opponent's goal. To advance the ball, a player may dribble it (repeatedly kick it while running with it) or kick it to a teammate. The ball may not be touched with the hand or arm, except by the goalkeeper in the penalty area in front of the goal. Modern professional soccer began in the United Kingdom in 1885, in the United States in 1967. The major international competition is the World Cup, held every 4 years.

Social class, group of people with a similar social standing based on factors such as wealth, ancestry, or occupation. The different social classes recognized by members of a society form a hierarchy. This hierarchy may be an informal one, such as exists in democracies like the United States, or it may be rigidly delineated, as is the case of the caste system in India. In the United States, social class is popularly determined by income; people are grouped into upper, middle, and lower classes, with subdivisions of each main category.

Social contract, in political philosophy, concept of the formation of society in which people agree to surrender part of their "natural" freedom to enjoy the security of the organized state. The idea, though of ancient origin, was first fully formulated in the 17th and 18th centuries by Thomas Hobbes (in *Leviathan*, 1651), John Locke, and Jean Jacques Rousseau, and was then controversial because it suggested that heads of state ruled only by their subjects' consent.

Social Credit Party, Canadian party formed (1935) by William Aberhart. It aimed to implement Clifford Douglas's policy of avoiding economic depression by distributing surplus money as a "social dividend" to increase purchasing power. It failed in this but governed Alberta (1935-71) and British Columbia (1952-72). The party failed to win seats in the 1980 federal parliamentary elections.

Social Darwinism, late-19th-century school of thought that held that society evolved on Darwin's biological model. Social inequalities were explained (and made to seem natural and inevitable) by the principle of "survival of the fittest." Its chief theorist was Herbert Spencer.
See also: Darwin, Charles Robert; Spencer, Herbert.

Socialism, economic philosophy and political movement that aims to achieve a just, classless society through the collective or governmental ownership of all property and means of manufacture and distribution of goods. Socialism was born out of the hardships of capitalism and the Industrial Revolution (late 18th-early 19th centuries). The ideas of class war, first put forth by F.N. Babeuf (and rejected by Utopian socialists such as Robert Owen and Charles Fourier), were later elaborated upon by Karl Marx and Friedrich Engels in their *Communist Manifesto* (1848). They suggested that revolution, led by the workers of the world, was inevitable. The first workers' party had already been founded by this time—in Germany in 1863 by Ferdinand Lasalle. This example was soon followed throughout Europe (1870s). Disagreement between gradualists and revolutionists soon emerged and was highlighted in 20th-century Russian socialism, eventually resulting in a split from which Bolshevism and Menshevism emerged. This was the forerunner to the worldwide break that occurred between socialism and communism after the Russian Revolution (1917). Socialism today, as well as its established place in the electoral politics of Europe, is especially active in the Third World, where its focus is on land reform and centralized economic planning.

Socialist realism, compulsory artistic doctrine since the early 1930s and until recently the dominant philosophy and style in most Communist countries. The doctrine holds that, in order to serve the people and the revolution, artistic and literary works should be realistic (representational), yet portray, with "positive" heros, the workers' progress toward socialism.
See also: Communism.

Socialization, in psychology and sociology, process by which individuals are indoctrinated by parents, teachers, and peers into accepting and following the written and unwritten rules of conduct of a particular society.

Socialized medicine *See:* Health Insurance, National.

Social psychology, branch of psychology concerned with group processes and interactions among individuals. Subjects studied by social psychologists include conformity, altruism, interpersonal attraction, and the development of values.
See also: Psychology.

Social sciences, group of studies concerned with humanity in relation to its cultural, social, and physical environment; 1 of the 3 main divisions of human knowledge, the others being the natural sciences and the humanities. The social sciences usually include anthropology, archeology, demography, economics, political science, psychology, and sociology. Social scientists model their disciplines on the natural sciences in order to achieve a similar level of consensus, but can be frustrated by conceptual tools that are limited in relation to the complexity of their subject matter and by controlled experiments of limited scope.

Social security, government programs for protecting people from hardship due to loss of income through old age, disability, unemployment, injury, sickness, etc. State social security systems developed in Europe after 1883, when Germany started a compulsory health insurance scheme. In 1911 Great Britain adopted an unemployment insurance program. In the United States in the Depression, the Social Security Act (1935) established a federal program of old-age insurance and a federal-state program of unemployment insurance. It also provided federal grants for public assistance, public health, and child welfare services. The federal plan has become compulsory, except for railway and government workers, who have their own schemes, and special types of workers who are not regularly employed.

The plan is financed by equal employer and employee contributions. Old-age and survivor benefits are paid to retired workers and their dependents or to survivors of workers who have died. The amount people receive is related to their average monthly earnings over a number of years. The aging of the U.S. population has recently threatened the solvency of this system. The social security tax has become a heavy burden for workers as the ratio of retirees to taxpayers has increased in favor of the former.

In the early 1980s the Reagan administration considered alternatives for reforming the system: reducing benefits, raising the retirement age, or funding the social security program from general revenues.

Disability benefits are paid to workers and dependents in the event of disability lasting over a year. Health insurance for the aged was added in 1965. Those over 65 are automatically helped with payment for hospital and post-hospital care; a supplementary medical insurance scheme, at an extra voluntary premium, covers 80% of doctors' and some other bills.

A claimant of unemployment insurance is usually eligible for about half his earnings. Public assistance, which in some states predates 1935, differs in being financed through federal grants (largely) and state revenues, rather than individual contributions. It goes to the care of the elderly, disabled, the blind, and their dependents. Workmen's compensation, dating from the early 1990s and varying widely between states, aids those employees injured at work or with industrial disease. A few states administer sickness insurance plans. Government social insurance schemes are more comprehensive in most western European and Communist countries. In the United States private insurance companies play a more prominent role.

Social studies, elementary and secondary educational course designed to give students a knowledge of how people and institutions function in different societies and to promote understanding of both Western and non-Western cultures. The course typically is a combination of several disciplines, including history, economics, and geography.

Social work, activity of trained social workers that has as its aim the alleviation of social problems. Casework, group work, and community organization are employed. Casework involves close cooperation with individuals or families who are under mental, physical, or social handicaps. Group work developed from that in early social settlements and involves group education and recreational activities. Community organization involves the identification of community problems and the coordination of local welfare services, both public and private, in solving them. A social worker's training may include psychology, sociology, law, medicine, and criminology. The person might specialize in family service, child welfare, or medical, psychiatric, or correctional social work.

Society for the Prevention of Cruelty to Animals (SPCA), organizations promoting humane treatment of animals. These various societies aim to educate the public, introduce legislation, and assure the enforcement of laws that protect animals. Many societies maintain animal shelters and provide adoption and neutering services. There are about 1,000 local anti-cruelty societies in the United States today.

Society Islands, southern Pacific islands covering about 650 sq mi (1,684 sq km) in western French Polynesia, comprising the Windward and Leeward archipelagoes. Discovered in 1607 by the Portuguese but named for Britain's Royal Society, which explored the mountainous, volcanic, and coral islands in 1768, the 450-mi (724-km)-long chain has been France's since 1843. Most of the Polynesian population (about 100,000) live on the largest island, Tahiti, in the Windwards. Copra, sugar, and tourism are important industries.

Society of Friends *See:* Quakers.

Society of Jesus *See:* Jesuits.

Sociobiology, controversial theory that attempts to prove the influence of natural selection on human and animal behavior. The theory postulates that genes can influence behavior as well as physiology and that behavior may therefore be as subject to the laws of evolution as is the physical development of the species.

Sociology, systematic study that seeks to describe and explain collective human behavior—as manifested in cultures, societies, communities, and subgroups—by exploring the institutional relationships that hold between individuals and so sustain this behavior. Sociology shares its subject matter with anthropology, which traditionally focuses on small, relatively isolated societies, and social psychology, where the emphasis is on the study of subgroup behavior. The main emphasis in contemporary sociology is on the study of social structures and institutions and on the causes and effects of social change. Some current areas of inquiry are the family, religion, work, politics, urban life, and science.

Sociologists attempt to model their investigations on those of the physical sciences. Mainly because of the complexity of its subject matter and the political implications of social change, questions as to its proper aims and methods remain far from settled. There is little doubt, however, that sociological concepts such as internalization—the processes by which the values and norms of a particular society are learned by its members—and institutionalization—the processes by which norms are incorporated in a culture as binding rules of behavior—do often illuminate important social problems. The 2 great pioneers of modern sociology were Émile Durkheim and Max Weber. Leading U.S. sociologists include the pioneers William Sumner and George Mead, and Talcott Parsons and Daniel Bell.

Socrates (469-399 B.C.), Greek philosopher and mentor of Plato. Born in Athens and the son of a sculptor, Sophroniscus, Socrates became a self-appointed guide to the improvement of the intellectual and moral lives of the Athenians. His search for wisdom about right conduct used the method of discussing virtue, justice, and piety with his many listeners. He wrote nothing, but much of his life and thought is vividly recorded in the dialogues of Plato. The exact extent of Plato's indebtedness to Socrates is uncertain—e.g., it is still disputed whether the doctrine of the forms is Socratic or Platonic; but Socrates made at least 2 fundamental contributions to Western philosophy: by shifting the focus of Greek philosophy from cosmology to ethics, and by developing the "Socratic method" of inquiry. He argued that the good life is the life illuminated by reason and strove to clarify the ideas of his interlocutors by leading them to detect the inconsistencies in their beliefs. His doctrines are the basis of idealistic philosophy. Socrates' passion for self-consistency was evident even in his death. Ultimately condemned for "impiety," he decided to accept the lawful sentence—and so remain true to his principles—rather than make good an easy escape. In prison, surrounded by disciples, he drank hemlock.
See also: Philosophy.

Soda, any of a group of sodium compounds derived from common salt (NaCl). This group contains sodium carbonate (Na_2C0_3), or sal soda, a crystalline or powdered product with strong, acid-neutralizing, alkaline properties used in the production of paper and glass; sodium bicarbonate ($NaHCO_3$), or baking soda, which is used in cooking and for the relief of stomach distress; and sodium hydroxide (NaOH), or caustic soda, which is used in the manufacture of chemicals, soap, aluminum, and paper.

Soddy, Frederick (1877-1956), British chemist awarded the 1921 Nobel Prize in chemistry for his research in radioactive decay and particularly for his formulation (1913) of the theory of isotopes. His many scientific books range from *The Interpretation of Radium* (1922) to *Atomic Transmutation* (1953), and his views on technocracy and the social credit movement are found in *Money versus Man* (1933), among others.
See also: Chemistry; Isotope.

Sod house, ancient northern European type of house made from strips of turf that were used like bricks, the roof being reinforced with wood. Sod houses were also built by early settlers on the Great Plains of the United States and in western Canada.

Sodium, chemical element, symbol Na; for physical constants see Periodic Table. Sodium is the sixth most abundant element on earth. The free element was obtained by Sir Humphry Davy in 1807 by electrolysis of caustic soda (sodium hydroxide). It is found most commonly as common salt, but it occurs in many other minerals. It is obtained commercially by the electrolysis of dry fused sodium chloride. Sodium is a silvery-white, reactive metal, the most abundant of the alkali metal group. It is essential in human and animal nutrition. Sodium and its compounds are used in the paper, glass, soap, textile, petroleum, chemical, and metal industries. It is the cheapest of all metals.

Sodium chloride *See:* Salt.

Sodium hydroxide *See:* Lye; Soda.

Sodium nitrate *See:* Saltpeter.

Sodium nitrite *See:* Nitrite.

Sodium pentothal *See:* Thiopental.

Sodom and Gomorrah, in Old Testament history, cities probably in the southern region of the Dead Sea. According to Genesis, these 2 of the 5 cities on the Jordan plain were destroyed by God for their carnal wickedness. Only Lot and his family were spared, although Lot's wife turned into a pillar of salt.
See also: Old Testament.

Soeharto *See:* Suharto.

Soekarno *See:* Sukarno.

Sofia (pop. 1,220,900), capital, largest city and commercial center of Bulgaria, in west-central Bulgaria between the Balkan Mountains in the north and the Vitosa Mountains in the south. Its industry includes machinery, textiles, and electrical equipment. Landmarks include the former royal palace, the parliament building, old mosques, churches, and synagogues. Sofia was settled by the Thracians; between the 1st and 4th centuries, Rome, Byzantium, and the first and second Bulgarian kingdoms were the ruling powers. In 1832 Turkish rule took hold until Russian's ascendance in 1878. Bulgaria achieved independence in 1879, with Sofia as its capital. Occupied by the Germans in World War II, it was taken by Soviet troops in 1944, and a Communist government was established and ruled until 1991.

Softball, type of baseball played with a softer, larger ball (12 in/30.5 cm in circumference) and a modified bat. The bases are 60 ft (18.3 m) apart and the pitcher stands 46 ft (14 m) from the home plate (40 ft/12 m in women's games). The ball is pitched underhand, and a game lasts 7 innings. Softball was developed in Chicago in 1888 by G. W. Hancock as an indoor form of baseball. Many countries, particularly in the Americas, now compete in the annual amateur world championships.
See also: Baseball.

Soft-coated wheaten terrier, sporting dog of Irish origin, used for hunting, herding, and as a guard dog. This terrier has a strong, compact body about 19 in (48 cm) high, weighs about 40 lb (30 kg), and has a shaggy coat of soft, wavy hair.

Soft drink, nonalcoholic beverage generally containing fruit acids, sweetening agents, and natural or artificial flavorings and colorings. In the early 19th century carbonated water (soda water) was developed in imitation of effervescent spa, or mineral, water; this was the antecedent of carbonated soft drinks, made by absorption of carbon dioxide under pressure. The dissolved gas gives a pleasant, slightly acid taste and acts as a preservative. Soft drinks without carbon dioxide are frozen or subjected to pasteurization.

Softwood *See:* Wood.

Soil, uppermost surface layer of the earth, in which plants grow and on which, directly or indirectly, all life on earth depends. Soil consists, in the uppermost layers, of organic material mixed with inorganic matter resultant from weathering. Soil depth (where soil exists) may reach to many meters. Between the soil and the bedrock is a layer called the subsoil. Mature (or zonal) soil may be described in terms of 4 soil horizons. The uppermost layer, containing organic components, is a continuous stream to which is added an "active" component produced by bursts of activity on the sun's surface.

Solanum, group of herbs, shrubs, and trees belonging to the nightshade family. Solanum grows worldwide, particularly in the temperate regions of South and North America. Many of the members of this family are important for food and medicinal purposes, although all contain some amounts of poisonous alkaloids such as atropine, nicotine, and solanin. Included in this group are the potato, tomato, eggplant, tobacco, bittersweet, common nightshade, and horse nettle. The fruit may be either capsulated (tobacco) or in berry form (potato and eggplant).

Solar eclipse *See:* Eclipse.

Solar energy, power derived from the sun. Because the earth's supplies of coal, petroleum, and other fossil fuels will eventually be exhausted, while the sun's energy will not, several methods of using solar energy have been developed. One is the solar furnace, basically a huge parabolic mirror that focuses the sun's heat onto a small area. Temperatures of more than 7,232°F (4,000°C) may be produced by this method. The heat can be used to raise steam and generate electricity, or for scientific research. In the Soviet Union a solar power station has been built with a system of 1,300 moving mirrors covering an area of 5 acres (about 2 hectares). It produces 2 1/2 million kilowatt-hours of electricity annually.
Solar energy is used increasingly for domestic heating. Heat is collected by exposing a large, darkened metal plate, covered with 1 or more layers of glass, to the sun. Water or air is passed through tubes attached to the plate and either circulated through the building or stored. Hot water is stored in insulated tanks. Hot air is passed through a tank full of rocks, which hold the heat until it is required to warm up air for circulation around the house.
Sunlight can also be converted directly into electricity in a solar cell, and there is research into the possibility of using sunlight to produce chemical energy by the same sort of reaction as photosynthesis in plants.
See also: Radiation.

Solar plexus, ganglion of nerve cells and fibers situated at the back of the abdomen that subserve the autonomic nervous system function for much of the gastrointestinal tract. A sharp blow on the abdomen over the plexus causes visceral pain and the sensation that all the "wind" has been knocked out of the lungs.
See also: Nervous system.

Solar System, the sun and all the objects orbiting it, including the planets, asteroids, comets, and meteors. There are 9 known planets in the Solar System. Mercury, Venus, Earth, Mars, and Pluto make up the terrestrial (Earthlike) planets. Jupiter, Saturn, Uranus, and Neptune are giants largely made of gas. All but 3 planets have their own moons orbiting them. There are at least 66 known moons in the Solar System. Astronomers estimate that the Solar System contains at least 100,000 asteroids and about 100 billion comets. But the combined mass of all these bodies is little more than 1/1000th the mass of the Sun.

The Solar System is vast. Pluto, usually the outermost planet (sometimes Neptune is), moves as far as 4 1/2 billion mi (7.2 billion km) from the Sun, while comets move even farther than this.

Origin of the Solar System. From the dating of meteorites (pieces of rock from the Solar System that have hit the earth), scientists believe that the Solar System formed about 4 1/2 billion years ago. No one knows exactly how the planets originated. The first scientific theories were developed in the 18th century by the philosopher Immanuel Kant and the mathematician Pierre Simon Laplace. They believed that the Sun and planets formed together from a cloud of gas or dust. Early in the 20th century a rival theory gained favor. This suggested that a star passed close to the Sun and pulled out some of its material. Part of this material fell into orbit around the Sun, forming planets. Modern theories have returned to Laplace's idea. Astronomers now believe that stars form when giant, diffuse clouds of gas condense. As the cloud contracts, a star forms at its center. Around the rapidly spinning star is a disk of material that slowly spirals away. Most of the disk is lost into space, but at certain points the material of the disk starts to collide and build into lumps. These lumps sweep up more of the surrounding material, eventually forming planets.

Other Solar Systems. The above theory suggests that Solar Systems form naturally around most stars. Although planets are far too faint to be seen going around other stars, they will exert a slight gravitational tug on those stars. By looking at the slight movements of nearby stars, observers have found that some stars have dark companions revolving around them. Astronomers now think that Solar Systems are common in the universe and that perhaps half the stars in the sky have planets orbiting them.

Solar wind, gases in the Sun's corona that escape from its gravitational field. Made of electrically charged particles, particularly ions, and expanding under the high temperatures of the corona, about 4,000,000°F (2,200,000°C), the solar wind accelerates to a velocity of about 310 m/s (500 km/s), a speed that allows escape from the solar gravitational field. The solar wind causes deflection of the tail of Earth's magnetosphere and comet's tails away from the sun. A shock wave results when the solar wind encounters the Earth's magnetic field. The portions of the solar wind that do not encounter either the Earth or other obstacles continue to travel at supersonic velocities until they eventually lose their supersonic characteristics and pour out into galactic space.

Soldering, joining metal objects using a low-melting-point alloy, solder, as the adhesive. Soft solder, commonly used in electronics to join wires and other components, is an alloy of mainly lead and tin. The parts to be joined are cleaned and then heated by applying a hot soldering iron (usually having a copper bit). A flux is used to dissolve oxides, protect the surfaces, and enable the solder to flow freely. The solder melts when applied, solidifying again to form a strong joint when the iron is withdrawn. Solder is often applied as wire with a core of noncorrosive rosin flux. Soldering at higher temperatures is termed *brazing*.

Sole, any of several species (family Soleidae) of flatfishes found in temperate seas and fresh water. Soles are commonly brown with dark patches, have flattened bodies about 10-25 in (25-66 cm) long, weigh about 1 lb (0.5 kg), and have both eyes on the right side of the head. Sole is a valued food fish, particularly the European or Dover sole and the American hogchoker.

Solenodon (genus *Solenodon*), rare, nocturnal, insect-eating mammal of Cuba and Haiti. It looks like a long-nosed rat, measuring about 2 ft (61 cm) long and 2 lb (1 kg), with long claws, a stiff tail, and short, coarse hair. Its saliva is poisonous.

Soleri, Paolo (1919-), Italian-born U.S. architect. A visionary planner and once an apprentice of Frank Lloyd Wright, Soleri published in *Sketchbooks* (1971) his designs for Mesa City, a solar-powered desert metropolis. He began work on Arcosanti, a scaled-down version of it near Scottsdale, Ariz., in 1970. His buildings include Domed Desert House (1951) near Cave Creek, Ariz., and the Solimene Ceramics factory in Vietri sul Mare, Italy, near Salerno.
See also: Architecture.

Solid, one of 3 states of matter possessing the property of excluding all other bodies from the space occupied by itself; it has a definite volume and definite shape. As a result of heating, the molecules of a solid begin to vibrate more rapidly, eventually breaking out of their fixed positions (at the melting point) and becoming a liquid.

Solidarity *See:* Walesa, Lech.

Solid-state physics, branch of physics concerned with the nature and properties of solid materials, many of which arise from the association and regular arrangements of atoms or molecules in crystalline solids. The term is applied particularly to studies of semiconductors and solid-state electronic devices.
See also: Quantum mechanics.

Solitaire, or Patience, any of several card games played by 1 person. Solitaire has countless varieties, but all are played with 1 or 2 decks of 52 cards, a portion of which are laid out, some face-up, others face-down, to form a foundation (tableau) of cards, upon which the game is played. Play resumes when one card is played out onto another in a prescribed manner. The purpose of the game is to play each card out, thus successfully completing the foundations.Canfield, Klondike, Accordion, Napoleon at St. Helena, Spider, and Pyramid are a few of the games of solitaire.

Solomon (d.922 B.C.), second son of David and Bathsheba. He ruled ancient Israel c.970-933 B.C. at the height of its prosperity, and gained a reputation for great wisdom. His success in establishing lucrative foreign trade and his

Solomon Islands

Capital:	Honiara
Area:	10,639 sq mi (27,556 sq km)
Population:	441,000
Language:	English
Government:	Parliamentary monarchy
Independent:	1978
Head of gov.:	Prime minister
Per capita:	U.S. $910
Mon. unit:	1 Solomon Islands dollar = 100 cents

introduction at home of taxation and forced labor enabled him to finance a massive building program that included a temple and royal palaces on an unprecedented scale of opulence. His story is told in I Kings 1-11 and II Chronicles 1-9 of the Old Testament. Biblical writings later attributed to him include Proverbs, Ecclesiastes, and the Song of Solomon.
See also: Old Testament.

Solomon Islands, independent democracy in the British Commonwealth, extending across an ocean area of over 232,000 sq mi (600,880 sq km) in the southwestern Pacific. The land area of the islands is approximately 10,639 sq mi (27,556 sq km).
Land and climate. The mountainous Solomon Island archipelago, composed of 21 large islands and many islets, is of volcanic origin; 4 volcanoes are intermittently active. The highest peak, Mt. Makarakombou (8,028 ft/2,447 m) is on Guadalcanal, the largest island, where Honiara, the capital, is located. The Solomons are well watered and covered with dense tropical rain forests, with grasslands on the northern plains of Guadalcanal. The climate is equatorial, and temperatures vary little during the year; rainfall, averaging 120 in (305 cm) annually, is concentrated from Nov. to Apr.
People and economy. The population is 95% Melanesian, with Polynesian, Micronesian, European, and Chinese minorities. Most follow tradition, living in small villages, fishing, and growing coconuts, taro, yams, and cassava. Exports, formerly exclusively copra, now also include fish and timber. Tourism is increasingly important.
History. In 1568 a Peruvian expedition sighted the Solomons but they were ignored by Europeans until the 19th century, when islanders were forcibly recruited to labor overseas. By 1900 Great Britain had established a protectorate over the islands. Invaded by the Japanese in 1942, the Solomons were recaptured by U.S. forces only after heavy fighting in 1943. Since independence in 1978, the Solomons have been plagued by regional disputes.

Solomon Islands, island chain in the South Pacific Ocean. The islands are divided into 2 countries, one at the southern end and one at the northern end of the group. The southern portion, including Choiseul, Guadalcanal, Malaita, New Georgia, San Cristobal, Santa Isabel, and numerous smaller

islands, is part of the nation of the Solomon Islands. The northern portion, including Bougainville, Buka, and various smaller islands, is part of Papua New Guinea. Together they cover a land area of about 15,700 sq mi (40,663 sq km). The Solomon Islands were the scene, during World War II (1942-44), of numerous battles between the Japanese and the Allied forces.
See also: Papua New Guinea.

Solomon's seal, perennial plant that grows in woods and thickets. The rootstock, used for medicinal purposes, makes a good poultice for bruises, inflammations, and wounds; in a wash, it helps heal skin blemishes and counteracts the effects of poison ivy.

Solon (c.640-559 B.C.), Athenian politician and poet, and one of the Seven Wise Men of Greece (Seven Sages). Solon gained fame in 612 B.C. with his poems, which compelled the Athenians to recover the Island of Salamis. He was elected leader (archon) of the government in 594 B.C. During his leadership many political and economic reforms were initiated. They included the abolition of unfair debt laws, the institution of habeas corpus, emancipation of slaves, and reforms in the representation of the common citizens in the assembly and in courts of law.
See also: Athens; Greece, Ancient.

Solow, Robert Merton (1924-), U.S. economist. Senior economist (1961-68) on the Council of Economic Advisors and president (1975-80) of the Boston Federal Reserve Bank, he won the 1987 Nobel Prize in economics for work he did in the 1950s, particularly on the importance of technology in economic growth. He was an outspoken critic of "Reagonomics," President Ronald Reagan's economic policies.
See also: Economics.

Solstice, two times each year when the sun is on the points of the ecliptic farthest from the equator. At the summer solstice, in late June (about June 22), the sun is directly overhead at noon on the Tropic of Cancer; at winter solstice, in late December (about Dec. 22), it is overhead at noon on the Tropic of Capricorn. In the Northern Hemisphere these celestial events are used as the traditional commencement of summer and winter. They are also the days of the longest and shortest daylight hours.
See also: Equinox.

Solti, Sir Georg (1912-97), Hungarian-born British conductor. He is noted for his recordings of works by Richard Wagner and Richard Strauss, and performances he led, usually as musical director, at London's Covent Garden (1961-71), the Paris Opera (from 1973), the London Philharmonic (1979-83), and the Chicago Symphony (1969-91).

Solution, in chemistry, homogeneous molecular mixtures of 2 or more substances (solid, liquid, gas), commonly of a solid and a liquid, though solid/solid solutions also exist. The liquid component is usually termed the *solvent*; the other component (solid, liquid, or gas), which is dissolved in it, the *solute*. The solubility of a solute in a given solvent at a particular temperature is usually stated as the mass that will dissolve in 3.53 oz (100 g) of the solvent to give a saturated solution. Solubility generally increases

Somalia

Capital:	Mogadishu
Area:	246,091 sq mi (637,541 sq km)
Population:	8,842,000
Language:	Somali
Government:	Republic
Independent:	1960
Head of gov.:	Prime minister
Per capita:	U.S. $765
Mon. unit:	1 Somali shilling = 100 cents

with temperature. Two common examples of solutions include vinegar (a solution of a liquid, acetic acid, in water) and syrup (a solution of a solid, sugar, dissolved in water).

Solvent, liquid capable of dissolving a substance to form a solution. Generally "like dissolves like"; thus a nonpolar covalent solid such as naphthalene dissolves well in a hydrocarbon solvent. Overall, the best solvents are those with polar molecules and high dielectric constant; water is the most effective known.

Solzhenitsyn, Alexander Isayevich (1918-), Russian writer. His own experience of Stalin's labor camps was described in *One Day in the Life of Ivan Denisovich* (1962), acclaimed in the USSR and abroad. But *First Circle* and *Cancer Ward* (both 1968) were officially condemned. He accepted the 1970 Nobel Prize in literature by letter. His expulsion from the USSR to West Germany in 1974 and his warnings on the moral and political fate of the West drew worldwide publicity. He has resided in the United States since 1976. Solzhenitsyn's work includes *August 1914* (1971), *The Gulag Archipelago* (1973-75), and *October 1916* (1985).

Somalia, or Somali Democratic Republic, republic occupying the horn, or northeastern tip, of Africa. The capital is Mogadishu.
Land and climate. Covering 246,091 sq mi (637,541 sq km), Somalia is bounded on the north by the Gulf of Aden, on the west and southwest by Ethiopia and Kenya, on the east by the Indian Ocean, and on the northwest by Djibouti. In the north, a narrow, barren coastal plain is hemmed in by mountains rising to more than 8,000 ft (2,438 m) with high plateaus and dry savannas extending inland. Plateaus, plains, and valleys extend westward from a wider coastal plain bordering the Indian Ocean. Flowing southeastward from the Ethiopian highlands are Somalia's only two permanent rivers, the Wabe Shebele and the Juba. The prevailing climate is hot.
People. The population consists mainly of Somalis belonging to northern nomadic or southern farming clans. Somali, the national language, lacks a written form; Arabic, Italian, and English are the chief written languages. Sunni Islam is the country's official religion.

Economy. Most Somalis are nomadic pastoralists moving from place to place with their herds and portable wood-frame huts. Agriculture accounts for the economy's major revenues, with bananas and sugar-cane the cash crops. There is a small mining and oil-producing sector of the economy.
History. The British, French, and Italians colonized Somalia in the late 1800s, with the British establishing a protectorate in the region in 1887 and the Italians in 1889. Independent since 1960, Somalia was heavily dependent upon foreign aid. In 1969 Pres. Shermarke was assassinated, and a revolutionary council headed by Maj. Gen. Muhammad Siyad Barre took control, declaring the Somali Democratic Republic a Socialist state. Armed conflict erupted with Ethiopia in 1963-64 and again in 1977-78 over the disputed territory of the Ogaden. As a result, hundreds of thousands of refugees streamed into Somalia, straining the country's meager resources. After Siyad Barre was disposed in 1991 a power struggle between rivaling factions developed. In 1992 US troops launched a military operation, which was set up to improve the food situation, but proved to be inadequate. The operation was taken over by the UN, but was terminated in 1995 without a political agreement having been reached.

Somaliland *See:* Djibouti.

Somerset, Edward Seymour, 1st duke of (1500-52), protector of England (1547-49) on the death of Henry VIII and accession of Edward VI. He used his great power to repeal heresy and treason laws and with Thomas Cranmer introduced the first *Book of Common Prayer* for the Church of England. Falsely accused of treason by his rivals, he was executed.
See also: England.

Somme River, river rising in northern France near Saint-Quentin, flowing west about 152 mi (245 km) to the English Channel. The Somme was the scene of major fighting with heavy casualties in World War I (1939-45). The Somme's upper valley has canals to the Oise and Escaut rivers.

Somnambulism *See:* Sleepwalking.

Somoza, Nicaraguan political family, 3 members of which controlled Nicaragua from 1936 to 1979. In 1936 **Anastasio Somoza Garcia** (1896-1956) deposed his uncle, President Juan Sacasa, and became president in a nepotistic dictatorship (1937-47; 1950-56) ending in assassination. He was succeeded by his son **Luis Somoza Debayle** (1922-67), who held formal office until 1963. In 1967 Anastasio's second son, **Anastasio Somoza Debayle** (1925-80), was elected president. Replaced by a puppet triumvirate in 1972, he retained control of the army and was reelected president in 1974. His corrupt rule led to a revolt in 1977 by leftist Sandinista guerrillas, who gradually gained broad support and forced him to flee into exile in Paraguay in 1979. A year later he was assassinated in Asunción.
See also: Nicaragua.

Sonar, acronym for Sound Navigation and Ranging, technique used at sea for detecting and determining the position of underwater objects (e.g., submarines, shoals of fish) and for finding the depth of water under a ship's keel. Sonar works on the principle of echolocation. High-frequency sound pulses are beamed from the ship, and the direction of and time taken for any returning echoes are measured to give the direction and range of the reflecting objects.

Sonata, in music, term used in the 17th and early 18th centuries to describe works for various small groups of instruments, as opposed to the cantata, originally for voices only. Since the late 18th century the term has been restricted to works for piano or other solo instruments (the latter usually with keyboard accompaniment), generally in 3 movements.

Sondheim, Stephen (1930-), U.S. composer and lyricist, whose work is characterized by sophisticated lyrics and intricate music that enriches a storyline. Sondheim began his career as the lyricist for *West Side Story* (1959). He was awarded the Pulitzer Prize in drama in 1985 for *Sunday in the Park with George*. Other works include *Gypsy* (1959), *A Funny Thing Happened on the Way to the Forum* (1962), *Do I Hear a Waltz?* (1965), and *A Little Night Music* (1973).

Song, musical setting of words, usually a short poem, often with instrumental accompaniment. There are 2 basic kinds: songs in which each verse repeats the same tune, and songs with a continuous thematic development. The origins of the song are lost in the history of folk music and poetry (poetry was originally sung); it became a mature art in Western cultures in opera arias, German *Lieder*—those of Schubert are supreme examples—and the French *chanson*. The song forms that have most influenced 20th-century popular music are probably the ballad and the blues.

Song dynasty (960-1279), period of Chinese rule and cultural advancement, founded by Zhao Kuangyin, who became the first emperor. The dynasty encompassed most of China. During this era of enlightenment trade, education, sculpture, painting, and literature flourished; a humane welfare system was instituted; and Confucian philosophy was organized into a cohesive doctrine. The Song dynasty was ended when it was conquered by the Mongols in 1279.
See also: China.

Songhai Empire, West African trading state created by the Songhai people of the Middle Niger. Founded in the 700s and flourishing in the 1400s, Songhai was a powerful and wealthy empire in control of trans-Saharan trade. At the height of power, during the reign of Sunni Ali (1464-92) and that of Askia Muhammad (1493-1528), the Songhai Empire extended west to the Atlantic Ocean and encompassed roughly what is now Mali, Nigeria, and portions of Senegal. Gao, on the Niger River, was the capital. Most of the Songhai people farmed, fished, or were traders. Askia Muhammad was deposed by his 3 sons and by 1591 the empire was defeated by Moroccans at the Battle of Tondibi.

Song of Roland *See:* Roland.

Song of Solomon, or Song of Songs, book of love poems in the Old Testament of the Bible. Although spoken between a man and a woman and

sensual in content, the poems are usually interpreted as allegorical and dramatic descriptions of God's love for the Hebrew people.
See also: Old Testament.

Sonic boom, loud noise generated in the form of a shock-wave cone when an airplane traveling faster than the speed of sound overtakes the pressure waves it produces. Because of sonic-boom damage, supersonic planes are confined to closely defined flight paths.

Sonnet, lyric poem of 14 lines with traditional rules of structure and rhyme scheme. There are two traditional types of sonnets: The Petrarchan is comprised of an octave and sestet (rhyming scheme *abbaabba cdecde*) and the Shakespearean comprising three quatrains and a couplet (rhyming scheme *abab cdcd efef gg*). Devised in 13th-century Italy and perfected by Petrarch, it entered English literature in the 16th century and was adopted by such poets as William Shakespeare, John Milton, John Keats, and William Wordsworth as a vehicle for concentrated thought and feeling, very often of love.

Sons of the American Revolution, patriotic organization for male descendants of Revolutionary War veterans or of those who furthered independence in other ways. This group, founded in 1889, seeks to preserve patriotic ideals and American traditions, and to protect the U.S. Constitution. Members also encourage historical research and the conservation of documents and artifacts of the Revolutionary period. The organization is headquartered in Washington, D.C.
See also: Revolutionary War in America.

Sontag, Susan (1933-), U.S. novelist, short-story writer, filmmaker, and essayist. Her best-known books include *Against Interpretation* (1966), *On Photography* (1977), *Illness as Metaphor* (1978) coupled with *AIDS and Its Metaphors* (1989), and *Under the Sign of Saturn* (1980).

Soo Canals, or Sault Sainte Marie Canals, waterways on the U.S.-Canada border linking Lake Superior and Lake Huron. The U.S. canal has 2 channels and 4 locks, the Canadian canal has 1 lock. About 85 million short tons (77 million metric tons) of cargo are shipped through the canals annually. Cargo is comprised mainly of iron ore, coal, oil, stone, and grain. By using these canals, which are icebound during the winter months, ships may bypass the dangerous rapids on St. Mary's River.

Sooners, Oklahoma homesteaders who entered the Indian Territory in advance of the date of the first official "run" for property: Apr. 22, 1889. Oklahoma is still familiarly known as the Sooner State.
See also: Oklahoma.

Soong Ching-ling (1892-1981), deputy head of state of the Chinese Communist government (1949-75). She also headed the Sino Soviet Friendship Association, and was awarded the Stalin Peace Prize in 1951. Soong Ching-ling was the wife of the left-wing revolutionary leader Sun Yat-sen. When he died in 1925, she continued his work in the Kuomintang (Nationalist Party). In 1927 when Chiang Kai-Shek, then president of the Chinese

Nationalist government, broke with the Chinese Communists, she went into self-exile, living in Moscow until 1937. During the Sino-Japanese War, having returned to China, Soong was the organizer of the China Defense League.

Sophist (Greek, "wise men"), name given to certain teachers in Greece in the 5th and 4th centuries B.C., the most famous of whom were Gorgias and Protagoras. They taught rhetoric and the qualities needed for success in political life. Plato attacked them for taking fees; for teaching skepticism about law, morality, and knowledge; and for concentrating on how to win arguments regardless of truth—attacks still reflected in the modern word *sophistry*.
See also: Greece, Ancient.

Sophocles (c.496-406 B.C.), great Athenian dramatist (also, priest and general), who, together with contemporaries Aeschylus and Euripides, was one of the founders of Greek tragedy. Only 7 of about 123 plays survive, the best known being *Oedipus Rex*, *Oedipus at Colonus*, *Antigone*, and *Electra*. Sophocles, who won many dramatic competitions, introduced scene painting to the stage, expanded the size of the chorus, and added a third actor. He also chose to focus on self-contained tragedy, as opposed to the popular trilogies of his day. His plays dwell on tragic ironies of human existence, and the fate of his characters are determined more by their faults than by the gods.

Sorbonne, college founded in Paris in 1253 (named 1257) by Robert de Sorbon (1201-74). A noted medieval theological center, it was rebuilt in the 17th century by Richelieu and, after being closed in the French Revolution, was reestablished in 1808. Its name is often used to refer to the University of Paris, into which it was incorporated in the 19th century.

Sorghum, widely cultivated cereal crop (*Sorghum vulgare*), the most important grown in Africa. It grows best in warm conditions and it is vital as a drought-resistant crop. For human food, the grain is first ground into a meal and then made into porridge, bread, or cakes. Some varieties yield molasses from the cane's juice. The grain is also used as a cattle feed and the whole plants as forage. Many types are in cultivation, including durra and kaffir.

Sorokin, Pitirim Alexandrovich (1889-1968), Russian-U.S. sociologist. He distinguished between sensate (empirical, scientific) and ideational (mystical, authoritarian) societies and wrote *Social and Cultural Dynamics* (1937-41).
See also: Sociology.

Sorrel, plant (genus *Rumex*) of the buckwheat family. This herbaceous perennial has sour, succulent, arrow-shaped leaves and stems that are used in soups and salads. The common American sorrel (sheep sorrel or red sorrel) grows in acid soil.

Sound, sensation produced by stimulation of the organ of hearing; instrument for insertion into a cavity to detect a foreign body or stricture; or noise, normal or abnormal, heard within the body.

Sound, in geography, any of several types of waterways, most commonly a long arm of ocean, larger than a strait or channel, that runs parallel to a mainland coast. A sound may rest between the mainland and an island or peninsula, connect an ocean and a sea, or be a fjord or lagoon.

Sour gum *See:* Tupelo.

Sourwood, or sorrel tree, ornamental deciduous tree (*Oxydendrum arboreum*) of the heath family. The sourwood is native to the United States and grows in the woods of the southern states and in Pennsylvania, Indiana, and Ohio. The trees grow to about 75 ft (23 m) in height, have small, fragrant, white flowers, and oval, sour-tasting leaves that turn bright red in the autumn.

Sousa, John Philip (1854-1932), U.S. bandmaster and composer. He wrote many light operas but is best remembered for his military marches, including "The Stars and Stripes Forever" and "The Washington Post." Sousa was leader of the U.S. Marine Band (1880-92) before forming a world tour band of his own.

Souter, David Hackett (1939-), associate justice of the Supreme Court of the United States (1990-). He was appointed by President George Bush as a replacement for Justice William J. Brennan, Jr., who retired. His judicial approach is considered conservative.
See also: Supreme Court of the United States.

South Africa, independent republic occupying most of the southern tip of the African continent.
Land and climate. South Africa covers 471,320 sq mi (1,221,037 sq km). It is bordered by the Atlantic Ocean on the west, the Indian Ocean on the east and south, Namibia to the northwest, Botswana and Zimbabwe to the north, and Mozambique and Swaziland to the northeast. Geographically, South Africa is a vast system of plateaus separated from narrow coastal plains by the ranges of the Great Escarpment. The plateaus are mostly flat and undulating, their monotony occasionally varied by kopjes (low, flat-topped hills) and low ridges. From the southwestern coastal plain in Cape Province the land rises in a series of steps to the dry valleys of the Little Karroo and the plateau of the Great Karroo, bounded by the ranges of the Great Escarpment. Among these ranges are the lofty Drakensberg Mountains. Beyond the Great Escarpment is the Northern Karroo, or High Veld, the highest and most fertile of the plateaus. The westward flowing Orange River rises in the Drakensberg Mountains and drains most of the interior plateau. The South African climate is mainly subtropical with dry, sunny winters and hot summers. The country is divided into nine provinces: Eastern Cape, Western Cape, Northern Cape, Northwest, Pretoria-Witwatersrand-Vereeniging, Northern Transvaal, Eastern Transvaal, Kwazulu Natal and Orange Free State. Its principal cities are Pretoria, the administrative capital; Cape Town, the legislative capital; Bloemfontein, the judicial capital; and Johannesburg and Durban.
People. The population of South Africa is about 70% black African, principally Zulu and Xhosa peoples, about 14% white, 9% of mixed white and African descent, and 3% Asiatics. Some two-thirds of whites are Afrikaners, descendants of Dutch settlers. Until 1993 South Africa's government and

South Africa

Capital:	Pretoria/Cape Town
Area:	471,320 sq mi (1,221,037 sq km)
Population:	42,835,000
Language:	Afrikaans, English, 9 African languages
Government:	Presidential republic
Independent:	1931
Head of gov.:	State president
Per capita:	U.S. $3,160
Mon. unit:	1 Rand = 100 cents

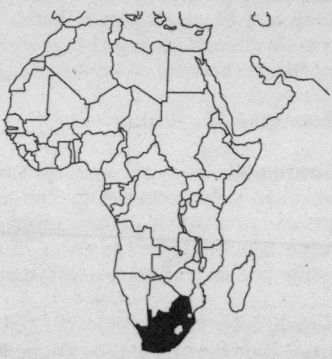

economy were dominated by whites. Blacks were excluded from the franchise, and the government ruthlessly and efficiently pursued a rigorous policy of racial segregation and systematic subjugation of black Africans known officially as apartheid. Christianity is the dominant religion, with the majority of whites adhering to the Dutch Reformed Church. There are also Hindus and Jews. The official languages are Afrikaans, English and nine African languages. The most important African languages are Xhosa, Zulu and Sesotho. Literacy among whites is 95% and among blacks 30%.

Economy. South Africa produces most of the world's gem diamonds and gold, has large coal reserves, and is also rich in uranium, iron ore, asbestos, copper, manganese, nickel, chrome, titanium, and phosphates. Mining contributes the major share of export earnings, but accounts for only 10% of the gross domestic product. The largest contribution is from manufacturing, which includes food processing, iron, steel, and oil from coal production, engineering, and textiles. South Africa is self-sufficient in food production and is a major exporter of food to neighboring countries. Nonwhites comprise more than 75% of South Africa's work force.

History. South Africa was already inhabited by San (Bushmen), Khoikhoi, and Bantu peoples from the north when white settlement began in 1652 with the establishment of a Dutch colony at Cape Town. The British came to the area in 1795, and from 1835 to 1843 the Boers, descendants of Dutch settlers, moved inland on the Great Trek to escape British dominance. They founded the Boer republics and eventually fought the British in the Boer War (1899-1902). The bitter contest was eventually won by the British, and in 1910 the Union of South Africa was formed. During World War I, South West Africa (Namibia) was wrested from the Germans and placed under a mandate. In 1931 South Africa became independent. Since 1948 it has been ruled by the Afrikaner-led National Party and committed to the policy of apartheid. In 1961 under H.F. Verwoerd, South Africa became a republic and left the Commonwealth largely because of differences over apartheid. Succeeding governments under B.J. Vorster (1966-78) and P.W. Botha (1978-89) continued to enforce apartheid, and in the 1980s, met with increasingly determined and often violent resistance internally, engaged in armed conflicts in Namibia and Angola, and were subject to greater and greater international pressure and censure. As a result, the government, headed by Willem de Klerk, gradually took steps toward ending apartheid, a change of policy signalled by the release from prison of Nelson Mandela in 1990. Mandela's release triggered the democratization proces and in 1994 the white minority government was replaced by a democratically chosen black government headed by president Mandela. In 1997 Thabo Mbeki was chosen to be Mandela's successor when the latter retires in 1999.

South America, southern of the 2 continents comprising the Western Hemisphere. South America is separated from North America at the Isthmus of Panama. Covering an area of 6,880,000 sq mi (17,819,000 sq km), South America contains the 12 independent republics of Argentina, Bolivia, Brazil, Chile, Colombia, Ecuador, Guyana, Paraguay, Peru, Suriname, Uruguay, and Venezuela. There also remains one European possession on the continent, French Guiana.
Land and climate. Roughly triangular in shape, South America extends some 4,750 mi (7,640 km) north to south and, at its widest, is 3,300 mi (5,300 km) east to west. It is surrounded by the Caribbean Sea on the north, the Atlantic Ocean on the east, Drake Passage on the south, and the Pacific Ocean on the west. The continent contains 3 main river basins, the Amazon, Paraná, and Orinoco. The Amazon, the world's most voluminous river, forms a basin containing the world's largest tropical rain forest. The Andes Mountains run in a nearly continuous chain from north to south. Other major topographical features include the grasslands of the pampas, the Gran Chaco, and the Patagonian plateau. The climate ranges from extreme cold in the high Andes to tropical heat and humidity in the lowlands and rain forests at the equator.
Economy. South America is rich in unique varieties of plant and animal life as well as mineral resources, including oil, iron ore, copper, tin, lead, zinc, manganese, gold, nitrate, and bauxite. Much of South America's natural wealth remains to be fully developed. The continent has very little coal, but considerable hydroelectric potential.
People. The peoples of South America are divisible into 4 main groups. These are Native Americans, the original inhabitants of the continent; descendants of Europeans, mostly Spanish and Portuguese; Africans, originally taken to South America as slaves; and peoples of mixed ancestry, usually divided into mestizos, a mixture of European and Native American, or mulattoes, a mixture of African and European. The total population of the continent is about 448 million with about one-third of that number in Brazil. The chief official languages are Spanish and Portuguese, the latter spoken in Brazil. In Guyana, Suriname, and French Guiana, the official languages are, respectively, English, Dutch, and French. The most widely spoken of the Native American languages are Guaraní in Paraguay; Quechua in Peru, Bolivia, and Ecuador; and Aymará in Bolivia. About 90% of South Americans are at least nominally Roman Catholic.

Southampton (pop. 208,100), English seaport city, on the River Test, near the English Channel. The city is England's chief passenger port. Founded as a Roman settlement by A.D. 43, Southampton's modern industries include ship building and repair, construction, harbor services, and tobacco processing. Of interest to visitors are various medieval structures, including Bar Gate, a portion of wall from the Middle Ages, and the priory of St. Denys (1124).
See also: England.

South Arabia, Federation of, previously an English protectorate of the crown colony of Aden and several Arab states including Alawi, Aqrabi, Audhali, Upper and Lower Aulaqi, Fadhli, Haushabi, Lahej, Mufhahi, Shaibi, Wahidi, and Lower Yafa. At the southern point of the Arabian peninsula, the federation covered about 60,000 sq mi (160,000 sq km) and was controlled economically and politically by England. On Nov. 30, 1967, the alliance gained independence and with the islands of Kamaran, Perim, and Socotra, became the Republic of South Yemen.

South Australia, state in south-central Australia, with an area of 380,070 sq mi (984,381 sq km). Wheat, barley, wool, and wine are produced in the fertile southeast. Minerals include iron ore, opals, salt, gypsum, and coal. Major industries, centered in Adelaide, the capital and chief port, include smelting, chemicals, fertilizers, engineering, and automobiles.
See also: Australia.

South Bend (pop. 247,052), city in northern Indiana, seat of St. Joseph County. Founded as a fur trading post on the St. Joseph River at the site of a Miami Native American village in the early 1820s, South Bend is now a center for commerce and education. It is the seat of the University of Notre Dame, Indiana University-South Bend Campus, and St. Mary's College. Industries include the production of automotive parts, plastics, and machinery.
See also: Indiana.

South Carolina, state in the southeastern United States; bordered by North Carolina to the north, the Atlantic Ocean to the southeast, and Georgia to the southwest.
Land and climate. South Carolina has 3 main land regions. The Blue Ridge, a narrow region in the state's northwestern corner, is part of the Blue Ridge Mountains, which extend into the state. The Piedmont covers most of northwestern South Carolina. This region's rolling land slopes from high in the northwest to low in the southeast, making for swift-flowing rivers and streams. The Atlantic Coastal Plain, in the southeastern two-thirds of the state, has long, sandy beaches in the north; southward, it becomes increasingly swampy, with salt marshes, pine barrens, bays, and tidal rivers.
South Carolina has many large rivers, the main ones being the Santee, Pee Dee, and Savannah. There are many rapids and waterfalls, but no large natural lakes. Forests cover nearly two-thirds of the state. South Carolina has a warm climate, with hot summers and mild winters. Principal cities are Columbia, Charleston, and North Charleston.
Economy. South Carolina's economy is led by manufacturing, followed by various service industries, including tourism. Chief manufactured goods are textiles, chemicals, machinery, and apparel. Agriculture and mining account for minor shares of the economy. Chief farm products are tobacco, soybeans, corn, cotton, and peaches; chief livestock products are eggs, milk, and beef cattle. Chief mining products are granite, limestone, crushed stone, and cement.
Government. South Carolina's present constitution was adopted in 1895. The governor serves a 4-year term. The state's legislature, called the General Assembly, consists of 46 senators serving 4-year terms and 124 representatives serving 2-year terms. In the U.S. Congress, South Carolina is represented by 2 senators and 6 representatives.

South Carolina

Capital:	Columbia
Statehood:	May 23, 1788 (8th state)
Familiar name:	Palmetto State
Area:	31,113 sq mi (80,582 sq km); ranks 40th
Population:	3,760,000 (1997); ranks 25th
Elevation:	Highest—3,560 ft (1,085 m), Sassaras Mountain; Lowest—sea level, along the Atlantic coast
Mottoes:	Animis Opibusque Parati (Prepared in Mind and Resources); Dum Spiro Spero (While I Breathe, I Hope)
Flower:	Carolina jessamine
Bird:	Carolina wren
Tree:	Palmetto
Song:	"Carolina"

History. Many Native American tribes were living in the area when the first Europeans—Spanish explorers—arrived in 1521. In 1670 the first permanent non-native settlement was established near present-day Charleston by English colonists. In 1719 the settlers revolted against the colony's proprietors; the province became a royal colony in 1729. South Carolina was one of the 13 British colonies that broke from Britain and fought the American Revolution; in 1788 it became the eighth state. In 1861 South Carolina—a strong proponent of states' rights, free trade, and slavery—became the first state to secede from the Union; the war's first shots were fired at Fort Sumter. Much of the state was damaged during the Civil War. During Reconstruction, federal troops occupied the state, which suffered agricultural depression and political corruption. South Carolina was readmitted to the Union in 1868. In the late 1800s and early 1900s, industrial growth aided recovery. The widespread unemployment of the Great Depression (1930s) was alleviated by World War II, and industry expanded in the 1950s and 1960s. In the 1960s and 1970s, the state's black majority, disenfranchised during Reconstruction, began voting in larger numbers, and integration, which met strong resistance at first, began taking hold. Today South Carolina seeks new industries as its key tobacco industry faces growing opposition to smoking.

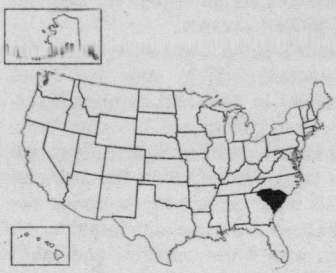

South Dakota, midwestern state in north-central United States; bordered by North Dakota to the north, Minnesota and the Big Sioux River (with Iowa on the other side) to the east, the Missouri River and Nebraska to the south, and Wyoming and Montana to the west.

South Dakota

Capital:	Pierre
Statehood:	Nov. 2, 1889 (40th state)
Familiar names:	Sunshine State, Coyote State
Area:	77,116 sq mi (119,730 sq km); ranks 16th
Population:	738,000 (1997); ranks 45th
Elevation:	Highest—7,242 ft (2,207 m), Harney Peak; Lowest—962 ft (293 m), Big Stone Lake
Motto:	Under God the People Rule
Flower:	American pasqueflower
Bird:	Ring-necked pheasant
Tree:	Black Hills spruce
Song:	"Hail, South Dakota"

Land and climate. The geographic center of the United States is in South Dakota, near Castle Rock. South Dakota has 4 main land regions. The Black Hills, a small region on the state's west-central border, is mountainous, with deep canyons and huge rock formations. The Great Plains, covering most of the state's western two-thirds, has rolling, grassy plains and rugged canyons and buttes. The Drift Prairie, in eastern South Dakota, is a low-lying region of rolling hills. The Dissected Till Plains, in the state's southeastern corner, is rolling land cut by glacial streams.

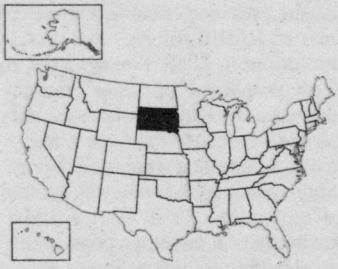

South Dakota's main rivers are the Missouri, which cuts the state roughly in half, and its branches—the Grand, Moreau, Cheyenne, White, James, and Big Sioux. There are no large natural lakes, but artificial ones were created by damming the Missouri. Forests cover less than 4% of the state. South Dakota's climate is dry, with warm summers and cold winters. Principal cities are Sioux Falls and Rapid City.

Economy. Wholesale and retail trade lead South Dakota's economy, followed by other service industries, agriculture, manufacturing, and mining. Tourists visit the scenic Black Hills and Mount Rushmore, into which huge heads of Presidents Washington, Jefferson, Lincoln, and Theodore Roosevelt were carved. Beef cattle, hogs, sheep, and wool lead the agricultural share of the economy. Chief crops are corn, wheat, sunflower seeds, rye, flaxseed, and soybeans. Chief manufactured goods are processed foods, machinery, surgical instruments, and electrical equipment. Chief mining products are gold, petroleum, and crushed stone.

Government. South Dakota's constitution was adopted in 1889. The governor serves a 4-year term. The state legislature consists of 35 senators and 70 representatives; all serve 2-year terms. In the U.S. Congress, South Dakota is represented by 2 senators and 1 representative.

History. Until both gained statehood in 1889, South Dakota shared much of its history with North Dakota. Cheyenne and Arikara peoples lived in the area before the first Europeans, French explorers, arrived about 1743. The area had been claimed for France by explorer Robert La Salle in 1682. France ceded it to Spain in 1762, regained it in 1800, then sold it to the United States under the Louisiana Purchase (1803). The Lewis and Clark expedition explored the area from 1804 to 1806. European-American settlement, at first by fur traders, was dominated by farmers by the 1850s. In 1861 Congress created the Dakota Territory. During the 1860s wars with Native Americans led to the Laramie Treaty (1868), which created the Great Sioux Reservation. In the 1870s a gold rush to the Black Hills violated the treaty, sparking new Native American resistance that ended only with the 1890 massacre of the Sioux at Wounded Knee Creek. Railroads brought rapid settlement to South Dakota, which became the 40th state in 1889. During the Great Depression (1930s), farmers suffered; World War II brought higher farm prices, but mechanized farming put many farmers out of work. Although South Dakota has since broadened its economic base, it was hard hit by the farm crisis of the 1980s.

Southeast Asia, region of Asia south of the southernmost boundaries of China and India, including Brunei, Burma, Cambodia, Indonesia, Laos, Malaysia, the Philippines, Singapore, Thailand, and Vietnam. The area covers about 1,740,000 sq mi (4,506,600 sq km) and is comprised mostly of areas of rich agricultural lands that produce rubber, rice, tea, coffee, tobacco, pepper, and coconut oil. There are also abundant teak forests, petroleum deposits, tin and gem mines, and fish. Southeast Asia is a land of diverse cultural backgrounds influenced in part by Europeans, who as early as the 16th century were drawn by the area's resources. Cities include Bangkok, Thailand; Ho Chi Minh City, Vietnam; Jakarta, Indonesia; Manila, the Philippines; and Singapore.
See also: Asia.

Southeast Asia Treaty Organization (SEATO), defense treaty signed by Australia, France, Great Britain, New Zealand, Pakistan, the Philippines, Thailand, and United States after France withdrew from Indochina in 1954. Headquarters were at Bangkok, Thailand. Although there were no standing forces, its aim was to prevent Communist expansion. The treaty was invoked by the United States in the Vietnam War (1964-73). Pakistan withdrew in 1972. SEATO dissolved in 1977.

Southern Baptist Convention, largest Baptist association. The organization was established in Georgia (1845) by Baptists in the southern states who differed in opinion with northern Baptists on the question of slavery. Theologically more conservative than other Baptist conventions, and more centralized, the Southern Baptist Convention, in part to maintain that conservatism, developed extensive missions, schools, colleges, seminaries, hospitals, and specialized homes of its own. The convention now has over 37,000 churches, and is headquartered in Nashville, Tenn.
See also: Baptists.

Southern Christian Leadership Conference (SCLC), U.S. civil rights organization. The group was established (1957) by the Rev. Martin Luther

King, Jr., and his co-workers to coordinate localized groups working for equal rights for African Americans and other minorities. Adhering to King's doctrine of nonviolent civil protest, the SCLC organized numerous marches and voter-registration drives that, in the early 1960s, led to passage of the Civil Rights Act of 1964 and the Voting Rights Act of 1965. Rev. King led the group until his assassination in 1968. Headquarters are in Atlanta, Ga.
See also: King, Martin Luther, Jr.

Southern Cross, or Crux, constellation visible in the Southern Hemisphere, defined by 4 stars in the shape of a cross. In ancient Babylonia and Greece it was part of the constellation Centaurus.
See also: Constellation.

South Island *See:* New Zealand.

South Korea *See:* Korea.

South Pole, point in Antarctica through which passes the earth's axis of rotation. It does not coincide with the earth's south magnetic pole. It was first reached by Roald Amundsen in 1911.
See also: Antarctica.

South Vietnam *See:* Vietnam.

South West Africa *See:* Namibia.

South Yemen *See:* Yemen.

Sovereignty, ultimate political power in a state. In political theory, debates on sovereignty center on the role of the sovereign and on the nature of supreme power—by what rights, and by whom, it should be wielded. A sovereign state is one that is independent of control by other states. The modern theory of sovereignty was developed by Jean Bodin and Thomas Hobbes (1756), who studied the sovereignty of monarchs. The extension of their thought has been applied to the modern state.

Soviet (from Russian *sovet*, "council"), the fundamental political unit of the former USSR. The soviets, ranging in importance from rural councils to the Supreme Soviet, the major legislative body of the Soviet Union, are elected policy-making and administrative units. The first soviets were the strike committees set up during the 1905 revolution and others developed during the 1917 revolution. Lenin institutionalized the soviet with the Bolshevik victory.

Soviet Union *See:* Union of Soviet Socialist Republics.

Sow bug *See:* Wood louse.

Soybean (*Glycine soja* or *Glycine max*), annual legume that is one of the best sources of complete protein, as well as being a good source of calcium, phosphorus, magnesium, and virtually all other minerals, plus vitamins A, B, and C and lecithin. Most of the world's soybeans are grown in China and the United States. In Asia, the soybean seed is sometimes ground into a meal, fermented, or dried, and used as a substitute for meat. In the United States, soybeans are generally made into oil or ground for animal feed; soybeans are also used in adhesives and for waterproofing and in many industrial products.

Soyer brothers, family name of 2 U.S. artists. Twins **Raphael** (1899-1987) and **Moses** (1899-1974) emigrated from Russia in 1912. They were impressed by U.S. realist artists and began to paint scenes of everyday life and of common people. Raphael, whose works include *Mission* (1935), *Office Workers* (1936), and *Avenue of the Americas* (1970), was called the "dean of American realism." Moses painted with a more vigorous style, using sharp contrasts and vibrant colors. His works include *Out of Work* (1937) and *Ballet Studio* (1955).

Soyinka, Wole (1934-), Nigerian writer, first African to win a Nobel Prize in literature (1986). His works include the novel *The Interpreters* (1965) and the memoir *Ake: The Years of Childhood* (1981). He has been president of the International Theater Institute since 1985. Soyinka has been jailed for his activities on behalf of black political freedom. In 1997, the Nigerian military regime accused Soyinka—who lives in the U.S.—of high treason.

Spaak, Paul Henri (1899-1972), Belgium's first Socialist premier (1938-39, 1946, 1947-50), and deputy premier (1961-65). He was the first president of the UN General Assembly (1946). He was influential in setting up the European Economic Community and was secretary-general of the North Atlantic Treaty Organization (NATO; 1957-61).

Spaatz, Carl (1891-1974), U.S. Army commander, first chief of staff of the United States Air Force. He led the U.S. Strategic Air Forces in Europe for the final attack on Germany (1944-45) during World War II.
See also: World War II.

Space *See:* Space exploration.

Spacecraft *See:* Space exploration.

Space exploration, investigation of planets, stars, and space through the use of satellites, spacecraft, and probes built by human beings. At 10:56 P.M. (E.D.T.) on July 20, 1969, Neil Armstrong stepped off Apollo 11 and became the first human to set foot on the moon. This was the climax of an intensive U.S. space program sparked by the successful launch of the Soviet artificial satellite Sputnik 1 in 1957 and accelerated by Yuri Gagarin's flight in Vostok 1, the first spacecraft flown by a human, in 1961. Later that year Alan Shepard piloted the first U.S. spacecraft, and President John F. Kennedy set the goal, to be realized within the decade, of landing astronauts on the moon and returning them safely to earth.
On Feb. 20, 1962, John Glenn orbited the earth 3 times in the first Mercury craft to be boosted by an Atlas rocket. The next Soviet mission, in June 1963, involved 2 craft. Piloting Vostok 5, Valery Bykovsky set the 1-person endurance record with a 5-day mission; and piloting Vostok 6, Valentina Tereshkova became the first woman cosmonaut. Aleksei Leonov completed

the first space walk in Mar. 1965. But then it was the turn of the Gemini missions to break all records. Both countries lost men, on the ground and in space: among them Virgil Grissom, Edward White, and Roger Chaffee (in a fire on board Apollo during ground tests in 1967) and the crew of Soyuz 11, killed during reentry in 1971. Earlier Soyuz missions had docked successfully with the first space station and set new records.

Meanwhile unpiloted probes—such as Orbiter, Ranger, and Surveyor—were searching out Apollo moon-landing sites; teams preparing the Soviet Luna and Lunokhod craft were also studying the moon. In 1968 Apollo 7 carried out an 11-day earth-orbit flight, and at Christmas Apollo 8 made 10 lunar orbits. The lunar landing craft was tested on the Apollo 9 and Apollo 10 missions, opening the way for the triumphant success of Apollo 11.

Apollo 12 was equally victorious, landing only 600 yards from the lunar probe Surveyor 3, but Apollo 13's aborted mission in 1970 was a near disaster. An explosion damaged the craft on its way to the moon, and reentry was achieved only with great difficulty. Apollo 14 had no such problems in 1971, visiting the moon's Fra Mauro area and collecting a wide range of lunar samples. Apollo 16 brought back 213 lb (96.6 kg) of moon rock, and in Dec. 1972 Apollo 17 made the last lunar landing, remaining on the moon for a record 75 hours.

In 1973 the United States launched the Skylab space station, a kind of satellite designed so that astronauts can live and work in orbit for several weeks. The station serves as a laboratory and as a base for other spacecraft.

Exploration of the planets has been carried out by unmanned probes: the Mariner series to Mars, Venus, and Mercury, and the Pioneer missions to the outer planets. There have been a number of Soviet contributions, such as the Venera soft-landing missions to Venus, the Zond bypass probe, and the Mars soft-landing craft. Results from the 2 U.S. Viking probes that soft-landed in Mars in 1976 did not show conclusively existence of life there. Voyagers 1 and 2 (1977) revealed a wealth of new information about Jupiter and Saturn.The United States launched the first reusable manned space vehicle, the space shuttle Columbia, in 1981. In 1983 Sally K. Ride, one of five crew members aboard the space shuttle Challenger, became the first U.S. woman in space. In the 25th space shuttle mission (1986), the shuttle Challenger exploded immediately after its launch, killing all seven crew members. A commission appointed by President Ronald Reagan to investigate the accident criticized NASA's decision to launch the shuttle and made several recommendations regarding safety measures to be used in future missions.The United States' Magellan space probe (launched 1989) reached Venus in 1990 and relayed to the earth clear images of Venus's surface. The Ulysses probe, launched by the United States in 1990, reaced the sun's south pole in 1994 and the north pole in 1995.

Space shuttle *See:* Space exploration.

Space station *See:* Space exploration.

Space telescope *See:* Hubble Space Telescope.

Space-time, concept of the physical universe arising from Einstein's special theory of relativity. Space and time are considered as a single 4-dimensional continuum rather than as a 3-dimensional space with a separate, infinite,

1-dimensional time. Time thus becomes the 4th dimension. Events in space-time are analogous to points in space and invariant space-time intervals to distances in space.
See also: Relativity.

Spahn, Warren (1921-), U.S. baseball player. Considered one of the greatest pitchers of all time, Spahn's achievements include winning the Cy Young award (1957) and setting a record for left-handed pitching in victories (363) and shutouts (63). He played in the major leagues for the Boston (Milwaukee) Braves (1942-64), New York Mets (1965), and San Francisco Giants (1965). Spahn was inducted to the National Baseball Hall of Fame in 1973.

Spaight, Richard Dobbs (1758-1802), North Carolina legislator and a signer of the U.S. Constitution. After the ratification of the Constitution he was governor of North Carolina (1792-95) and served in the U.S. House of Representatives (1798-1801).

Spain, country occupying about four-fifths of the Iberian Peninsula south of the Pyrenees in southwestern Europe.
Land and climate. Including the Balearic and Canary islands, Spain covers 194,898 sq mi (504,783 sq km). Peninsular Spain is bounded on the north by the Bay of Biscay. On the northeast, the Pyrenees mark the borders with France and Andorra. On the west, Spain is bounded by Portugal and the Atlantic Ocean, and to the east and south, by the Mediterranean Sea and the Strait of Gibraltar.
About three-quarters of Spain is the great interior plateau called the Meseta, extending from the Cantabrian Mountains and the Ebro River in the north to the Sierra Morena and the Guadalquivir River in the south. In the west the plateau continues into Portugal; in the east low ranges separate it from the coastal plain. The Meseta is higher in the north than in the south, the dividing line being the central cordillera. It is traversed by the Douro, Tagus, and Guadiana rivers, which flow into the Atlantic. Except for irrigated areas and fertile valleys, the Meseta is mostly arid and large areas are barren. In the southeast, beyond the Guadalquivir River, are the Andalusian Mountains, which contain Spain's highest mountain range, the Sierra Nevada. Spain's coastal plains are mostly narrow, becoming broadest along the Gulf of Cádiz in the south. The north and northwest coasts, hemmed in by mountains, have rocky cliffs and long inlets providing good harbors and some fine beaches. The Mediterranean coast is also rocky but there are fine sand beaches north of Barcelona along the famed Costa Brava. Spain is mainly a dry country with hot summers and cool winters. But great extremes occur on the Meseta. The climate of northern Spain is more equable. Along the south and east coasts, winters are mild and summers hot.
People. The Spanish people are in many ways homogeneous, but certain traditional and ethnic differences distinguish several groups. The Basques are an ethnically distinct people and, together with the Catalonians and Galicians, have preserved their own languages. The official language is Castilian Spanish. The capital of the country is Madrid and Roman Catholicism is the established religion.
Economy. Tourism makes the most important contribution to Spain's income, followed by industry and agriculture. Mineral wealth includes mercury, iron ore, coal, pyrites, potash, and salt. Oil was found near Borgos in 1964.

Spain

Capital:	Madrid
Area:	194,898 sq mi (504,783 sq km)
Population:	39,134,000
Language:	Spanish, Castilian, Galician, Basque
Government:	Parliamentary monarchy
Independent:	1492
Head of gov.:	Prime minister
Per capita:	U.S. $13,580
Mon. unit:	1 Peseta = 100 céntimos

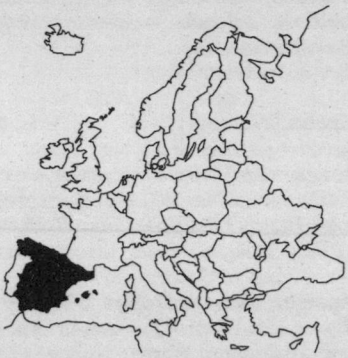

Manufacturing includes textiles, chemicals, iron and steel, paper, explosives, and armaments. Agriculture is about equally divided between crops and livestock. Oranges, olive oil, wine, and cork are exported. Fishing is also important.

History. Present-day Spain was settled successively from prehistoric times to the 3rd century B.C. by Celts, Phoenicians, Greeks, and Carthaginians. A more enduring influence was that of the Romans, who conquered Spain in the Second Punic War in the 2nd century B.C. and remained dominant until the Vandals and Visigoths invaded in the 5th century A.D. The last invaders were the Moors, who advanced in A.D. 711. The Christian kingdoms that remained, all in the north, undertook the gradual reconquest of the peninsula, which was not completed until 1492 with the fall of Granada in the reign of Ferdinand V (Ferdinand II of Aragon) and Isabella of Castile (1474-1504). The same monarchs financed the voyages of Columbus, expelled the Jews from Spain, and sponsored the Inquisition. Within a brief period, Spain acquired a vast empire in the New World and North Africa and became rich, particularly in gold and silver from the Americas. Spain's new holdings were augmented by Habsburg lands when Charles I (1516-56) was elected Holy Roman Emperor as Charles V. Under his son and successor, Philip II (1556-98), Spain was at the height of its political and cultural power, as evidenced in the works of Cervantes, Lope da Vega, Velásquez, and El Greco. But Philip's reign also saw the onset of Spain's decline. The Netherlands revolted in 1568, and the Armada was defeated by the English in 1588. The War of the Spanish Succession at the beginning of the 18th century resulted in huge losses for Spain. The French, under Napoleon, invaded in 1808 and were driven out in the Peninsular War, but with revolutions in the Latin American colonies and defeat in the Spanish-American War (1898), the empire was finished. Political division in the early 20th century culminated in the Spanish Civil War (1936-39) between leftists and Fascists, which was won by the right wing under General Francisco Franco, who subsequently became dictator. After Franco's death in 1975, Juan Carlos de Bourbon restored the Spanish monarchy and also encouraged parliamentary democracy. In 1982 socialists won the elections to lead the first leftist government in Spain since the Civil War. In 1996 the socialists were defeated by José Aznar's Partido Popular.

Spaniel, one of a large family of sporting dogs, probably descended from a Spanish dog, hence the name. Spaniels make good pets and companions as well as good hunters. Most spaniels have silky coats, long ears, and sturdy bodies and legs. The American Kennel Club recognizes these 10 breeds of spaniels: American water, clumber, cocker, English cocker, English springer, field, Irish water, Sussex, Welsh springer, and Brittany.

Spanish, Romance language spoken by about 341 million people, primarily in Spain and Latin America. Modern Spanish arose from the Castilian dialect centered in the town of Burgos, in north-central Spain.

Spanish-American War (1898), fought between the United States and Spain, initially over the conduct of Spanish colonial authorities in Cuba. Strong anti-Spanish feeling was fomented in the United States by stories of the cruel treatment meted out to Cuban rebels and the hardships suffered by U.S. business interests. Though President Grover Cleveland took no action, his successor, President William McKinley, had promised to recognize Cuban independence. He succeeded in obtaining limited self-government for the Cubans, but an explosion aboard the U.S. battleship *Maine* (1898), from which 260 died, was blamed on the Spanish. McKinley sent an ultimatum, some of whose terms were actually being implemented when Congress declared war on Apr. 25 (Spain had declared war the previous day). On May 1 Admiral George Dewey destroyed the Spanish fleet in Manila harbor. What remained was trapped in the harbor at Santiago, Cuba, and destroyed on July 3 by U.S. forces that had already shattered Spanish land forces in several battles, including the Battle of San Juan Hill (July 1), famed for the charge of the Rough Riders, led by Theodore Roosevelt, up Kettle Hill. Santiago surrendered on July 17. General Nelson A. Miles occupied Puerto Rico, and on Aug. 13 troops occupied Manila. The Treaty of Paris (Dec. 10, 1898) ended Spanish rule in Cuba. The United States gained the islands of Guam, Puerto Rico, and the Philippines, thus acquiring an overseas empire with accompanying world military power and responsibilities.

Spanish Armada, naval fleet from Spain that attacked England in 1588. At that time the Catholic monarchy of Spain, under King Philip II, wielded great power through its wealthy colonies in the Americas and its control over Portugal and the Netherlands in Europe. Philip wanted to invade and control England, a Protestant country under the rule of Queen Elizabeth I. Sir Francis Drake, encouraged by the Queen, successfully raided Spain and Spanish holdings, which provoked Philip II to attack England from the English Channel. The smaller, swifter ships of the English navy drove the larger Spanish boats away from the coast, sunk 2 Spanish vessels, and damaged many others. Bad weather conditions also wrecked many ships of the Armada as they fled the English coast. Only about half the ships of the Spanish Armada returned to Spain.

Spanish bayonet, plant in the agave family, of the genus *Yucca*. The Spanish bayonet *(Y. aloifolia)* is about 25 ft (8 m) in height. Its name refers to the shape of its leaves, which are like slender, pointed bayonets. This plant can be found in the United States, the West Indies in the Caribbean, and Mexico.

Spanish Civil War (1936-39), one of the most violent and bloody conflicts in Spanish history, between the liberal second republic and conservative forces in Spain. After the bloodless overthrow of the monarchy in 1931, the democratic republican government proposed far-reaching reforms that alienated conservatives. On the election (1936) of the Popular Front, a left-wing coalition, the rightists under Gen. Francisco Franco resorted to force. Supported by Hitler and Mussolini, Franco was on the verge of shattering the republicans when the Soviet Union began to send them aid. Madrid and Barcelona fell to Franco in 1939. Over 600,000 died in the war, many of them foreign volunteers, and the country suffered massive damage. Franco's dictatorship remained in power until his death in 1975. The Luftwaffe's systematic destruction of the Basque town of Guernica, a preview of Hitler's blitzkrieg, shocked the world.

Spanish fly, beetle found mainly in southern Europe. It is the source of cantharidin, which causes blistering and bleeding of the skin and was a fashionable remedy for many diseases in the 19th century. It was also alleged to be an aphrodisiac. When taken by mouth, it is poisonous.

Spanish Inquisition *See:* Inquisition; Torquemada, Tomás de.

Spanish literature, European literature containing elements of the Western traditions of Europe and the Eastern traditions of North Africa. The heritage left behind when the Romans occupied the Spanish peninsula was the vernacular Latin, the foundation for the Romance languages, three of which became the most common Spanish dialects—Castilian, Galician-Portuguese, and Catalan. The long struggle from the A.D. 700s to 1400s between the Christians and the Muslim Moors created a religious patriotism that inspired some of the finest poetry and prose.

The Middle Ages. The first lyric poems, called *jarchas*, appeared in the A.D. 900s, expressing themes of longing for love. The epic work, *Poem of the Cid*, relates the adventures of Castilian hero, Rodrigo Díaz de Vivar. Early Spanish prose was promoted by the Castilian king Alfonso X. Two histories, *General Chronicle of Spain* and *General History*, appeared under his direction. Prose fiction first appeared about 1100 in a series of moral tales written by Pedro Alfonso entitled *Scholar's Guide*. The first distinctive prose writing was that of Don Juan Manuel who wrote on a variety of subjects; his *Count Lucanor* (1335) is a collection of moral tales. The three great poets of the 1400s were Iñigo López de Mendoza, Juan de Mena, and Jorge Manrique. López de Mendoza wrote elaborate pastoral poems called *serranillas*. Mena's allegorical work, *The Labyrinth of Fate* (1444), was inspired by Dante. Manrique eulogized his father in the *Coplas* (1476).

Printing was introduced to Spain c. 1473. The first book to set forth the rules of a European language, *Castilian Grammar*, by Antonio de Nebrija, was published in 1492. Other prose works such as Diego de San Pedro's *The Prison of Love* (1492) and a book of chivalry, *Tirant lo Blanch* (1490) appeared at this time. A novel about chivalry, *Amadís of Gaul*, was the masterpiece of the period. *La Celestina*, appeared as an anonymous novel in the late 1400s; it combines medieval theology with Renaissance concern for life and love. The story, probably written by Fernando de Rojas, features a witch, Celestina, who unites two lovers, Calisto and Melibea.

The Golden Age. The two main schools of poetry were the Castilian school of Salamanca and the Andalusian school of Seville, both of which followed the style of the Italian poet Petrarch. Writers of the Salamanca school adopted a cautious use of metaphor, while the poets of the Seville school developed a formal use of language that led to the Baroque style of the 1600s. The mystic poets wrote lyrically of a union with God, while the epic poets glorified people and events in long works. The pastoral novel, glorifying the simple life, became popular during the Renaissance. The picaresque novel presented life in satiric fashion through the eyes of a rogue.

Playwriting developed more slowly during the 1500s. The actor-playwright Lope de Rueda created short, farce works called *pasos* that ridiculed the everyday life of his time.

In the 1600s the picaresque novel quickly became a tradition. Mateo Alemán's *Guzmán de Alfarache* presents a bitter, pessimistic view of life in which neither human nature nor the conditions of life can be changed. Francisco López de Beda created a female rogue in *La pícara Justina* (1605).

In contrast to the picaresque novel, Cervantes's masterpiece novel, *Don Quixote*, contrasts the ideal and the practical. His characters present universal themes and qualities that extend to all humanity.

Lope de Vega was the leading dramatist of the Golden Age, presenting love and honor as sources of conflict, especially in his two greatest dramas, *Fuenteovejuna* (1619) and *Justice Without Revenge* (1634).

Two literary examples of the Baroque (ornamental) style of writing of the 1600s were *conceptismo* and *culteranismo*. Conceptismo writers used metaphors to create complicated, original views of life. Culteranismos such as Pedro Soto de Rojas created lyric poetry in full color and imagery.

In drama, Pedro Calderon de la Barca's brilliant work *Life Is a Dream* (1635) was written in the Baroque style. He used symbolism to express in verse philosophical explorations of life and death, original sin, and free will.

Neoclassicism, romanticism, and realism. Neoclassicism, stressing the ideas of reason, proper behavior, and moral sense, became the important literary trend of the 1700s. A Benedictine monk, Benito Jerónimo Feijoo, covered almost every branch of learning in the 9-volume *Universal Theatre of Criticism* (1726-40) and the 5-volume *Erudite and Interesting Letters* (1742-60). In the 1800s the most accomplished writer of neoclassical comedy was Leandro Fernández de Moratín, whose most famous play was *The Maiden's Consent* (1806).

Romantic literary forms intensified after the death of King Ferdinand VII in 1833. Ángel de Saavedra's drama *Don lvaro or The Force of Destiny* (1835) was a successful romantic tragedy. Antonio García Gutiérrez's historical tragedy *The Troubadour* (1836) was a triumph. Francisco Martínez de la Rosa and Juan Eugenio Hartzenbusch wrote plays reflecting rebellion, melancholy, and the passion of Spanish romanticism. José de Espronseda's poems *The Student from Salamanca* (1836-39) and *Devil World*, unfinished, are rich expressions of Spanish romantic anguish and social protest. Gustavo Adolfo Bécquer's light, airy poetry contains elements of romanticism, and he is often considered the most sensitive poet of the 1800s.

Short prose sketches, called *costumbrismo*, led to the development of the realistic Spanish novel in the mid-1800s. José María de Pereda's *The Upper Cliffs* (1895) was a costumbrista novel describing life on Spain's northern coast. Emilia Pardo Bazán's *The Ulloa Estate* (1886) narrated local traditions and politics in the interior of Galicia. Vicente Blasco Ibáñez's novel *The Cabin* (1898) described life in Valencia. Ibáñez gained international popularity for his novel about the terror of World War I, *The Four Horsemen of the Apocalypse* (1916).

The 1900s. The loss of the last remnants of Spain's empire during the Spanish-American War (1898) led to a resurgence of creative genius that dominated Spanish letters in the early 1900s. Miguel de Unamuno's essay *The Tragic Sense of Life* (1913) was an expression of romantic and philosophical grief. He is often considered the forerunner of the existential movement. Antonio Machado's poetry expresses the severe spirit and landscape of Castile. Ramón María del Valle-Inclán's *Bohemian Lights* (1924) was a picture of Spain as a grotesque distortion of normalcy. Scholars also rediscovered Spain's literary past, and interpreted, edited, and published works at the Center of Historical Studies in Madrid.

The short-lived age of modernism was represented by Manuel Machado and Gregorio Martínez Sierra. It inspired poetry of unequaled quality and intensity in Spanish literature. In Spanish drama, the best-known works are the comedy *The Bonds of Interest* (1907) and the domestic tragedy *The Passion Flower* (1913), by Jacinto Benavente.

The poets of the Generation of 1927 turned to the traditional ballad for inspiration. Their members included Pedro Salinas, Jorge Guillén, León Felipe, Gerardo Diego, Federico García Lorca, and others.

The Spanish Civil War (1936-39) caused a disruption in Spanish literature. Some writers were killed, and others continued to work in exile. The dark novel *The Family of Pascual Duarte* (1942) by Camilo José Cela was followed by Carmen Laforet's existential novel *Nothing* (1944).

Major novels since the mid-1950s have included *The Jarama River* (1956) by Rafael Sanchez Ferlioso, *Time of Silence* (1962) by Luis Martín Santos, and *Soldiers Cry at Night* by Ana María Matute.

Playwrights wrote in a variety of styles. Miguel Mihura wrote farces about everyday life. Antonio Bueno Vallejo promoted interest in serious drama with *History of a Staircase* (1949). The poets who wrote after 1939 used simpler forms of expression than the Generation of 1927. Some, including Claudio Rodríguez and Carlos Bousoño, were less interested in social realism. The newest generation of poets, called *novisimos*, reject social concerns and show interest in more personal, intimate, and intellectual concerns.

Spanish Main, former name of the north Caribbean coast of South America, from Panama to the Orinoco River in Venezuela. It was the hunting ground of the English pirates and buccaneers who attacked the Spanish treasure fleets.

Spanish moss, or Florida moss, epiphyte (*Tillandsia usneoides*) that can be found festooning trees, such as oaks and cypresses, and even telephone poles and wires in the southeastern United States. It is not a true moss. It absorbs water through scaly hairs on the leaves and stem, and is used as a substitute for horsehair stuffing and for insulation.

Spanish Succession, War of the (1701-14), conflict between France and the Grand Alliance of England, the Netherlands, Austria, and the smaller states of the Holy Roman Empire over control of the Spanish Empire. The childless Charles II of Spain willed his kingdom and its empire to France on his deathbed. The alliance sought to prevent France from becoming the dominant European power. Though the decisive battles were fought in Europe, there were also engagements overseas, including North America.

The duke of Marlborough and Prince Eugene of Savoy won remarkable victories at Blenheim (1704), Ramillies (1706), and Malplaquet (1709), but Louis XIV fought on. The accession of Charles VI as the new Holy Roman emperor removed obstacles to the recognition of Philip of Anjou as Philip V of Spain. England made a separate peace in 1712, and a general settlement of differences in the Peace of Utrecht followed in 1713.

Spark, Muriel (1918-), Scottish writer best known for her witty, often satirical novels, including *Memento Mori* (1959), *The Prime of Miss Jean Brodie* (1961; later a play and film), *The Mandelbaum Gate* (1965), *Loitering with Intent* (1981), *Curiculum Vitae* (1992), and *Reality and Dreams* (1996).

Sparks, Jared (1789-1866), U.S. historian best known for *Writings of George Washington* (12 vols., 1834-37). He edited the *North American Review* (1824-30) and was president of Harvard University (1849-53).

Sparrow, gregarious, seed-eating bird of the subfamily Passerinae of the weaver-bird family. There are 8 genera: 5 confined to Africa, the other 3—the true sparrows, rock sparrows, and snow finches—are also found in the Palearctic. Of the true sparrows, one species, the house sparrow (*Passer domesticus*), has been successfully introduced to the Americas. Closely associated with human habitation, it is the only bird not known to occur in a "natural" habitat but always with human beings. In the United states some small finches are called sparrows (song sparrow, tree sparrow, field sparrow, etc.).

Sparrowhawk, name for small birds of prey (genus *Accipiter*). They eat insects and small birds and mammals and often hunt by hovering. Upper feathers range from gray to rusty brown. In the United States the kestrel, a small falcon, is called the sparrow hawk.

Sparta, or Lacedaemon, city of ancient Greece, capital of Laconia in the Peloponnesus, on the Eurotas River. A center for culture and wealth, its society was divided into 3 classes: the helots (serfs bound to the land); the free perioeci (freemen allowed to take part in commerce and crafts); and the Spartiates, citizens with legal and civil rights, whose rigorous military training led to the word *Spartan*. There were 2 hereditary kings, though real power resided with the 5 annually elected ephors (magistrates). Founded in the 13th century B.C., Sparta dominated the Peloponnesus by 550 B.C. Despite alliance with Athens in the Persian Wars, Sparta fought and won the Peloponnesian War against Athens (431-404 B.C.), but a series of revolts and defeats destroyed Spartan power, and in 146 B.C. the city became subject to Roman rule. It prospered under the Romans but was destroyed by the Goths in A.D. 395.
See also: Greece, Ancient.

Spartacus (d.71 B.C.), leader of the Gladiators' War, a slave revolt against ancient Rome (73-71 B.C.). With an army of runaway slaves, Spartacus heavily defeated forces sent against him and gained control of southern Italy, but after his death in battle the revolt was quickly crushed and 6,000 slaves were crucified along the Appian Way.
See also: Rome, Ancient.

Spastic paralysis, form of paralysis due to disease of the brain (e.g., stroke) or spinal cord (e.g., multiple sclerosis), in which the affected muscles are in a state of constantly increased tone (or resting contraction). Spasticity is a segmental motor phenomenon where muscle contractions occur without voluntary control.
See also: Cerebral palsy.

Speaker, in U.S. government, officer presiding in the U.S. House of Representatives. Formally elected by the whole House, the speaker is in fact selected from the majority party by its members and holds powers of recognition, referral of bills to committee, and control of debates. Other, wider powers were stripped from the speaker after the term of Joseph G. Cannon (Rep., Illinois; 1903-11). During the long service of Sam Rayburn (Dem., Texas) as speaker (1940-47, 1949-53, 1955-61), he effectively advanced party programs by maintaining firm discipline. Thomas S. Foley (Dem., Washington) became speaker in 1989.
See also: House of Representatives.

Speaker, Tristram E. (1888-1958), U.S. baseball player. Known for his outstanding defense and speed, Speaker holds the American League record for putouts by an outfielder (6,794 career). He compiled a lifetime batting average of .344 and set a major league record for doubles (793). Speaker played for the Boston Red Sox (1907-15) and Cleveland Indians (1916-26), managing the Indians as well (1919-26). He was inducted into the National Baseball Hall of Fame in 1937.

Spear, weapon on which a point tops a long shank. Spears have been constructed and used by humans since primitive times. The points of spears have evolved from the earliest ones made of wood to those crafted from bones, stones, bronze, and iron. Whether used in hunting or warfare, spears may be thrown toward their targets or used by their owners to stab the intended targets. In the 17th century, the bayonet took over the popular role of the spear in combat.
See also: Javelin.

Spearfishing, sport in which fish are caught underwater with the use of spears. An underwater slingshot device called a Hawaiian sling, a simple spear with a metal tip called a pole spear, and various kinds of spearguns are used to catch the fish. People spear fish from the surface or dive underwater, using breathing equipment, such as snorkels or scuba gear. In official meets, divers must breathe on their own underwater. After a fish is caught, the diver must gain control of it, with the help of a line that connects the spear to the spearing apparatus.

Spearmint, herb in the mint family. Spearmint (*Mentha spicata*), originally from Europe and Asia, is plentiful in North America. It grows to about 2 ft (61 cm) high and displays white to light purple flowers. The leaves, when dried, are used for cooking, baking, and flavoring beverages. Oil extracted from the leaves is used in perfume.

Special education, instruction designed for the special needs of certain students, both gifted and handicapped. Mainstreaming refers to the time spent by these exceptional students in a regular classroom; special instruction takes place in "resource rooms." Over 10% of U.S. schoolchildren need special education programs (approximately 8% are handicapped, including physical and mental impairments; 3-5% are considered gifted). Students of both average and above-average intelligence may need special education, due to learning disabilities from minor disorders. Hyperactive children also participate in special education programs. The Education for All Handicapped Children Act (1975) provides for their education.

Special effects, in cinema, technique developed to enhance visual illusion, especially important in "disaster movies" and ambitious science fiction films, such as *Star Wars*. Most effects are produced in special studios and are added to the film after it is shot. A great many techniques are employed, including animation, the use of miniature models, and slow-speed or fast-speed photography. An important and increasingly sophisticated technique is the creation of a composite picture—using several different images superimposed within a single frame—often with the aid of electronic memories and timers to match perspectives, light, and camera angles.

Special Olympics, international sporting program designed for participation by mentally retarded people. This program is active in summer and winter sports year round through communities and schools. Like the Olympics, an international winter and summer Special Olympic event takes place every 4 years. The program develops events according to the age and ability of its participants. Headquartered in Washington, D.C., the Special Olympics were founded (1968) and are sponsored by the Joseph P. Kennedy, Jr., Foundation.

Species *See:* Classification.

Specific heat, warmth required to raise the temperature of 1 kg (2.2 lb) of a substance through 1 kelvin; measured by calorimetry. The concept was introduced in 1760 by Joseph Black (1728-99). Subsequently, P. L. Dulong and A. T. Petit evolved a law in 1819 showing that the specific heat of elements is inversely proportional to their atomic weights, which could thus be roughly determined, and the product of the atomic weight and the specific heat is a constant for all solid elements.
See also: Black, Joseph.

Spectrometer, tool that analyzes an object through a spectrum of light. This device can be used to examine evidence at crime scenes, to determine the composition of celestial bodies, and to detect pollution in the sky or water. Spectroscopes allow a scientist to view the light spectrum of an object, which for every object is different. Sometimes photographs of the light spectrum are taken by a spectrograph. The brightness of light in an object may be determined through a spectrophotometer.

Spectrum, array of light in the form of different colors produced when a ray of plain white light passes through a prism by a process known as dispersion. The different colors of light are created by different wavelengths, which are forms of electromagnetic radiation. The short-wave lengths (low frequency) create indigo and violet on one end of the spectrum; the long-wave lengths (high frequency) produce red, orange, and yellow on the other end of the spectrum.

Speculation, practice of entering into business transactions in order to make a quick profit from an anticipated substantial price fluctuation. Speculation is also applied to investment in any undertaking when the risks and the potential profit are both high. Most speculation, however, involves the buying of commodities or stocks and bonds.
See also: Stock exchange.

Speech and speech disorders, communication through spoken words and the impairments of this ability. Speech can be subdivided into conception, or formulation, and production, or phonation and articulation. Speech development in children starts with associating sounds with persons and objects, comprehension usually predating vocalization by some months. Nouns are developed first, often with 1 or 2 syllables only; later acquisition of verbs, adjectives, etc., allows the construction of phrases and sentences. A phase of babbling speech, where the child toys with sounds resembling speech, is probably essential for development.
Reading is closely related to speech development and involves the association of auditory and visual symbols. Speech involves coordination of many aspects of brain function (hearing, vision, etc.), but 3 areas particularly concerned with aspects of speech are located in the dominant hemisphere of right-handed persons and in either hemisphere of left-handed people.
Disease of these parts of the brain leads to characteristic forms of dysphasia or aphasia alexia, etc. Development dyslexia is a childhood defect of visual pattern recognition. Stammering or stuttering, with repetition and hesitation over certain syllables, is a common disorder, in some cases representing frustrated left-handedness. Dysarthria is disordered voice production and is due to disease of the neuromuscular control of voice. In speech therapy, attempts are made to overcome or circumvent speech difficulties, which is particularly important to address in children.

Speech therapy, detection and correction of speech problems. Speech-language pathologists work with people who, for various reasons, cannot speak at all (asphasiacs), cannot speak clearly or easily, stutter or have a problem with voice pitch or volume. The most common problem dealt with in speech therapy is that of articulation, the way in which sounds are produced. Speech problems may be physical, environmental, or emotional in origin. Many speech-language professionals belong to The American Speech and Hearing Association (founded 1925).

Speed *See:* Methamphetamine.

Speedometer, instrument for indicating the speed of a motor vehicle. The common type works by magnetic induction. A circular, permanent magnet is rotated by a flexible cable geared to the transmission. The rotating magnetic field induces a magnetic field in an aluminum cup, thus tending to turn it in the same direction as the magnet. This torque, proportional to the speed of rotation, is opposed by a spiral spring. The angle through which the cup turns against the spring measures the speed. The speedometer is usually coupled with an odometer, a counting device geared to the magnet, that registers the distance traveled.

Speed reading, mastery of reading material in terms of both speed and comprehension. Mental training helps quicken the reading pace more than do exercises that improve visual focus, according to experts in this field. A combination of complete concentration, attention to a specific reading purpose (pleasure, fact-finding), and continual reading without pause (regardless of multisyllabic vocabulary or total speed comfort) often yield increased comprehension simultaneously with increased speed.

Speedwriting, writing method that uses the letters of the alphabet in a shortened form. Each letter corresponds with a sound, which in longhand often is made up of a cluster of letters. For example, the letter *a* is pronounced like the word *ate*; therefore, *fa* would stand for *fate*, *stra* would stand for *straight*, etc. Because of fewer (though familiar) letter and sound relationships employed, a person may write what is dictated quickly. Emma B. Dearborn invented this trademarked method of shorthand writing in 1923.
See also: Shorthand.

Speer, Albert (1905-81), German architect and Nazi leader. For his organization of slave labor for Germany during World War II, the international tribunal at Nuremberg sentenced him to 20 years' imprisonment in Spandau. After his release he wrote revealingly of the inner workings of the Nazi regime in *Inside the Third Reich* (1972).
See also: Nazism; World War II.

Speleology, scientific study of caves. The world's first speleological society was founded in France in 1895, and interest soon became worldwide. The U.S. National Speleological Society was founded in 1939. Nonacademic cave exploration is called *spelunking*.
See also: Cave.

Spelling, often referred to as orthography, manner in which letters represent words in writing. Orthographers study sound and letter relationships, base words and affixes (which include prefixes and suffixes), preferred spellings of words, spelling rules and exceptions, homophones, and word pronunciation. Individuals devise their own methods for correct spelling, which may include word visualization, spoken pronunciation, syllabic division of words, repeat writing of the word, and using the word in context.

Spencer, Anna Garlin (1851-1931), U.S. religious and political leader, educator, and author, especially in the field of women's rights. She was the first woman in Rhode Island to become a minister (1891), at the Bell Street Chapel in Providence. She taught sociology in universities and was a leader in the New York School of Philanthropy. She supported woman suffrage, prohibition, world peace, and family unity. Her vision of equal rights for women was expressed in her book *Woman's Share in Social Culture* (1913).
See also: Woman suffrage.

Spencer, Herbert (1820-1903), English philosopher, social theorist, and early evolutionist. In his multivolume *System of Synthetic Philosophy* (1855-

93) he expounded a world view based on a close study of physical, biological, and social phenomena, arguing that species evolve by a process of differentiation from the simple to the complex. Spencer coined the phrase "survival of the fittest." His political individualism deeply influenced the growth of Social Darwinism, and, in general, U.S. social thinking.
See also: Social Darwinism.

Spender, Sir Stephen Harold (1909-95), English poet and critic, coeditor of the literary magazine *Encounter* (1953-65). His poetry collections include *Poems* (1933), *Ruins and Visions* (1941), and *Generous Days* (1971).

Spenser, Edmund (1552?-99), English poet. His most famous poem, *The Faerie Queene* (1590, 1596), considered a classic in English literature, is an allegory—a story in which people or personified things represent qualities and virtues in addition to their human character. Spenser projected that his masterpiece would contain 12 sections, or books, but at the time of his death only 6 of those books were completed. He lived in the Elizabethan age, under the reign of Queen Elizabeth I. Through her, monies and political position (sheriff of Cork, in Ireland, 1598) were granted to Spenser. Some of his other poems include *The Shepheardes Calendar* (1579), *Colin Clouts Come Home Againe* (1595), and *Amoretti* (1595)—a collection of sonnets that includes a famous poem about marriage, "Epithalamion." Although born and educated in England, Spenser lived his adult life in Ireland.

Sperm *See:* Reproduction.

Sperm whale, family of toothed whales, with 2 species: the cachalot (*Physeter catodon*) and pigmy sperm whale (*Kogia breviceps*). They are among the best known of all whales because of their enormous, squared heads. The front of the head contains a huge reservoir of spermaceti oil, perhaps used as a lens to focus the sounds produced by the whales in echolocation. Spermaceti solidifies in cool air to form a wax once used for candles and cosmetics. Sperm whales are also the source of ambergris, a secretion in the gut produced in response to irritation by the beaks of squids, an important prey. Ambergris is used as a fixative in perfumes. Sperm whales are found in all oceans, migrating from the poles into warmer waters during the breeding season. They are deep-water whales, capable of diving to 1,650 ft (503 m) or more. Female and young form large schools of up to several hundred animals. Males tend to travel alone or in small groups.

Sperry, Elmer Ambrose (1860-1930), U.S. inventor and manufacturer. Although he began his career with inventions in the field of lighting (in particular, arc lamps and searchlights), he is known mainly for his invention of and work with the gyroscope (1911)—a device that always points to the true north. His gyrocompass enabled steel ships to navigate without interference from magnetic fields. He further developed devices based on the gyroscope that stabilized ships and allowed planes to fly on automatic pilot. The gyroscope also made possible advanced weaponry used in World War II, such as naval gunsights and the aerial torpedo. The Sperry Gyroscope Company (1910) was founded and is still located outside New York City.
See also: Gyroscope.

Sphagnum moss *See:* Peat moss.

Sphalerite, also called zinc blende, zinc ore and sulfur ore. It is the major mineral ore of zinc. Sphalerite appears in a variety of colors—brown, red, black, yellow—but is always opaque and dark. When it is abraded by a sharp metal object, an orange flash appears in this ore. The sulfur content may release the scent of rotten eggs. Sphalerite is found in the United States, Mexico, northern Europe, and northern Africa.
See also: Zinc.

Sphere, surface produced by the rotation of a circle through 180° about one of its diameters. The intersection of a sphere and any plane is circular; should the plane pass through the center, the intersection is a great circle. The surface area of a sphere is $4\pi r^2$, where r is the radius; its volume $4/3\pi r^3$. If mutually perpendicular x-, y-, and z- axes are constructed such that they intersect at the center, the sphere's equation is $x^2 + y^2 + z^2 = r^2$.

Sphinx, mythical monster of the ancient Middle East, in Egypt portrayed as a lion with a human head and used as a symbol of the pharaoh. In Greek mythology the sphinx propounded a riddle to travelers on the road to Thebes: When Oedipus answered correctly the sphinx threw herself from her rocky perch.
See also: Mythology.

Sphinx moth *See:* Hawk moth.

Spice, one of a large number of aromatic plant products that have a distinctive flavor or aroma and are used to season food. Most spices are obtained from tropical plants and were once highly valued as a means of making poor-quality food more palatable.

Spider, any of an order (*Araneida*) of arachnids, with a body of 2 main parts, 4 pairs of legs, and 4 pairs of eyes. Unlike insects, spiders have no antennae and no larval or pupal stages. Their abdominal spinnerets produce silk thread that is used to make cocoons for their eggs and nests, to capture their prey, and as a means of travel. They are a diverse group of some 26,000 species, including jumping spiders, wolf spiders, and trapdoor spiders. They paralyze their prey with poison, which in several species (e.g., black widows) is dangerous to humans.

Spider monkey, slender, pot-bellied monkey found in the forests of central and northern South America. It has a prehensile tail with a naked patch at the end that is ridged like a fingerprint. Spider monkeys swing through the trees by their long forearms and tails. The 2 species, the common and the woolly spider monkeys, live in small groups and feed solely on fruit.

Spiderwort, or Job's tears, family of plants found in the tropical and temperate Americas and cultivated as house plants. Spiderworts have hairy stems that exude a sticky substance that can be drawn into a thread as fine as a spider's web. The leaves are grasslike, and the clusters of 3-petaled flowers open in the morning and die in the afternoon. Spiderwort can be found wild in woods across the country. As house plants they are usually known by their scientific name of *Tradescantia*. Wandering Jew, a house plant from Mexico, belongs to the same family.

Spielberg, Steven (1947-), U.S. film director, writer, and producer. Many of his films have been box office hits, such as *Jaws* (1975), *Close Encounters of the Third Kind* (1977), *Raiders of the Lost Ark* (1981), *E.T.: The Extra-Terrestrial* (1982), and *The Color Purple* (1985). Brilliant technical special effects plus a romantic and heroic quality are signature characteristics of his films.

Spikenard, flowering plant in the Valerianaeceae family (*Nardostachys jatamansi*) or in the ginseng family (*Aralia racemosa*). The oriental, or "true" spikenard, from India, has a thick stem and a root shaped like an ear of corn; it is valued for its perfume. The American spikenard, or Indian root, is an herb often used in place of sarsaparilla for flavor.

Spina bifida, congenital deformity in which a fissure in the lower part of the spine allows the spinal membranes to protrude. The condition leads to a variable degree of leg paralysis and loss of urine and feces sphincter control; it may be associated with other malformation, particularly hydrocephalus. Mild cases can be treated by surgical closure of the defect, and orthopedic procedures can be applied to balance muscle power.

Spinach (*Spinacia oleracea*), leafy annual plant widely cultivated as an edible vegetable. Spinach leaves have a relatively high content of iron and vitamins A and C.

Spinal cord and spinal nerves, that part of the central nervous system contained within the spinal column and extending from the skull to the level of the first or second lumbar vertebra; the nerve structures and nerve pathways within the vertebral canal, extending from the skull opening to the second lumbar vertebra. These nerves carry sensory information from the body to the brain, and then return with commands from the brain to the rest of the body.
See also: Nervous system; Spine.

Spinal tap, or lumbar puncture, procedure to remove cerebrospinal fluid (CSF) from the lumbar spinal canal using a fine needle. It is used in diagnosis of meningitis, encephalitis, multiple sclerosis, and tumors. In neurology it may be used in treatment, by reducing CSF pressure or allowing insertion of drugs.

Spine, spinal column or vertebral cord, vertical structure of bone, nerves and nerve fibers, ligaments, and cartilage that act as a skeletal support and transmission center for the nervous system in vertebrate animals. Vertebrae are the flexible, bony joints that make up the spinal column; they number 33 in humans. The spinal cord, where bundles of nerve fibers are found, is encased in the spinal column. The human spine extends from the brainstem to the tailbone region, or coccyx. Sensory impulses travel up the spinal column to the brain; in turn, the brain sends its commands down the spinal column to voluntary muscles used for motion and balance. Paralysis occurs when an injury to the spine interrupts the transmission of these messages between the brain and limbs.
See also: Skeleton.

Spinning, craft of twisting together fibers from a mass to form strong, continuous thread suitable for weaving. The earliest method was merely to roll the fibers between hand and thigh. Later 2 sticks were used: the distaff to hold the bundle of fibers, and a spindle to twist and wind the yarn. Mechanization began with the spinning wheel, which was invented in India and spread to Europe by the 14th century. Improved weaving methods in the Industrial Revolution caused increased demand, which in turn provoked several inventions. The spinning jenny, invented by James Hargreaves (1767), spun as many as 16 threads at once. Richard Arkwright's "water frame" (1769), so-called from being water-powered, produced strong thread. Then Samuel Crompton produced (1779) a hybrid of the two—his "mule," which had a movable carriage. One modern spinning machine is the ring-spinning frame (1828) in which the strands, drawn out by rollers, are twisted by a "traveler" that revolves on a ring around the bobbin on which they are wound.

Spinoza, Baruch, or **Benedict de** (1632-77), Dutch philosopher who held that God is nature or all that is, an interpretation that brought him expulsion from the Amsterdam Jewish community. He claimed that matter and mind are attributes of the one substance: God. His most famous work, *Ethics* (1677), contains the development of his pantheism, which is both rationalist and mystical.
See also: Philosophy.

Spiny anteater *See:* Echidna.

Spiraea, any of several shrubs with tall clusters of pink or white flowers. They grow wild in the Northern Hemisphere, and several are grown in gardens. Meadowsweet, staplebush, and queen-of-the-meadow are wild American species. The cultivated forms, of which bridal wreath is the most popular, come mainly from the Far East.

Spirit of '76, popular image of the American Revolution, depicted in a painting by Archibald M. Willard. Willard, a U.S. artist, created this image originally as a cartoon (c.1875). Later it was painted and displayed in the Philadelphia Centennial Exhibition (1876). The image of a fife player and 2 drummers leading troops of the American army was modeled by acquaintances and relatives of the artist.
See also: Revolutionary War in America.

Spiritual, form of emotional, often sorrowful, religious folk song using syncopation, a variety of rhythms, and the pentatonic scale (5 whole tones). It usually consists of a number of verses for solo voice, often with biblical text, and a rhythmic choral refrain. Originally though to have been developed solely by African-American slaves and their descendants in the southern United States, it is now believed to be a form that combined African musical systems with those of 19th-century white Southerners (i.e., revival meeting songs).

Spiritualism, belief in the survival of the human personality after death and its ability to communicate with those left behind, usually through a medium.

Spitz, family of dogs, distinguished by their thick, long coats, curly tails, and pointed ears. Breeds in the spitz family include small dogs, such as the

Pomeranian; medium-size dogs, such as the Samoyed and chow chow; and large dogs, such as the Alaskan malamute and Akita. Spitz dogs are native to northern climates in the Americas, Europe, and Asia.

Spleen, spongy vascular organ between the stomach and diaphragm on the left side of the abdomen. It eliminates foreign organisms and worn-out red blood cells, recycling their iron. Most of its functions are duplicated by other organs.

Split (pop. 189,400), city in Croatia, in the southwestern region of Dalmatia on the Adriatic Sea; known as Spalato in Italian. The remains of the palace of the Roman emperor Diocletian (A.D. 245-313) are central to this modern port city. The tomb of the emperor, within the palace walls, became the Cathedral of Split (A.D. 653). Many have ruled this city, including the Byzantine Empire (mid-4th century to early 12th century), Venice (1420-1797), and Austria (1797-1918). It was part of Yugoslavia from 1918-91. Today it supports many industries, including chemicals, plastics, aluminum, and shipbuilding.

Spock, Benjamin McLane (1903-98), known as "Dr. Spock," U.S. pediatrician and pacifist noted for his best-selling *Common Sense Book of Baby and Child Care* (1946) and *Bringing Up Children in a Difficult Time* (1974). He ran for president in 1972 as candidate of the People's Party.
See also: Pediatrics.

Spode, British family of potters. **Josiah Spode I** (1733-97) founded the Spode works at Stoke-on-Trent and introduced transfer decoration and oriental motifs. His son, **Josiah Spode II** (1754-1827), developed stone china, porcelain, and bone china. He popularized the willow pattern and gained royal patronage.
See also: Pottery and porcelain.

Spoils system, use of appointments to public offices to reward supporters of a victorious political party. With the growth of a 2-party system in the United States, political patronage increased. It was Pres. Andrew Jackson's friend, Sen. William L. Marcy, who said in 1832 that "to the victor belong the spoils," and the system soon operated on every political level. Reforms began with the creation of the Civil Service Commission in 1871, and the Pendleton Act of 1883, introducing competitive entrance examinations for public employees, marked the gradual introduction of a merit system.

Spokane (pop. 173,000), city in Washington state, located on the Spokane River, about 15 mi (24 km) west of the Idaho border. The town site, originally known as Spokane Falls, was first settled in the 1870s and prospered with the advent of the railroad and the growth of local mining industries. The economy of the modern city is diversified. Numerous factories and mills make aluminum products, foodstuffs, paper and other wood products, and cement. The cultural and industrial center of a large, 2-state area, the city is the home of Gonzaga University and Whitworth College.

Sponge, primitive animal of both marine and fresh water. Sponges are true animals, although they have only a simple body wall and no specialized organ or tissue system. They may be solitary or live in colonies. They are filter-feeders, straining tiny food particles out of water drawn in through pores all over the body surface and expelled through one or more vents. The body wall is strengthened by spicules of calcite or silica, or by a meshwork of protein fibers called spongin. Sponges with spongin skeletons are fished for use as bath sponges.

Spontaneous combustion, or spontaneous ignition, phenomenon in which material suddenly bursts into flame without apparent cause but resulting from a slow build-up of heat. The chemical process of oxidation naturally produces heat. If that heat is trapped, oxidation becomes more rapid, and heat builds up quickly. A critical temperature may be reached, causing ignition.

Spontaneous generation, or abiogenesis, theory that living creatures can arise from nonliving matter. Dating from the writings of Aristotle, the idea remained current even after it had become clear that higher orders of life could not be created in this way. It was only with the work of Francesco Redi (1626-97), showing that maggots did not appear in decaying meat protected from flies, and Louis Pasteur (1822-95), who proved that the equivalent was true of microorganisms (i.e., bacteria), that the theory was finally discarded.

Spoonbill, bird in the ibis family. The Roseate spoonbill *(Ajaia ajaja)* lives in warm locations in the Americas. The spoonbill can grow to 32 in (80 cm) long, with rose to red coloring on its body and white on and around its head. The bill is dipped and then moved through water in search for water insects, crabs, and fish. Other kinds of spoonbills are found in southern regions on all continents.

Spore, minute single- or multicelled body produced during the process of reproduction of many plants, particularly bacteria, algae and fungi, and some protozoa. Their structures vary greatly and depend upon the means of dissemination from the parent. Some, such as the zoospores of algae, are capable of movement.

Sports, organized athletic events in which people are either participants or spectators. Some sporting activities include team playing, such as baseball, football, and basketball; others engage one participant in competition against another, such as tennis and ping-pong. Other sports may not necessarily be competitive, such as jogging, swimming, and horseback riding. There are organized amateur sporting competitions, such as the Olympics, and professional leagues and associations, such as the National Football League (NFL) and the National Basketball Association (NBA).

Sports medicine, area of medical practice based on the effects of sports on the human body. Physicians who practice sports medicine develop preventive treatments, exercises, and mechanical devices for individual athletes and specific activities, as well as treatment for specific injuries. Coaches work with sports medicine professionals to maximize the output of athletes, while minimizing the physical stress experienced by those participating in sports. Sports medicine grew as a separate branch of medicine beginning in the 1970s, through the work of doctors attached to professional teams.

Spot, fish in the croaker family. The spot *(Leiostomus xanthurus)* inhabits the coastal waters of the Atlantic Ocean and the Gulf of Mexico. It is caught for sport and has a commercial value because it is edible. A dark spot at the pectoral fin, or shoulder, of this fish is its most prominent characteristic. It is 6-10 in (15-25 cm) long and weighs about 0.5 lb (0.2 kg).

Spotted fever, Rocky Mountain, *see:* Rocky Mountain spotted fever.

Spotted Tail (Sioux: *Sinte-galeshka*; 1823?-81), Brulé Sioux leader. Unlike his nephew Crazy Horse or such contemporaries as Red Cloud and Sitting Bull, Spotted Tail worked hard for peaceful solutions to Sioux conflicts with the settlers and the U.S. government. He had a reputation when a young man as a warrior, but he believed compromise would best serve his people, who he knew could not win against the U.S. government. Spotted Tail kept his people out of the war with the U.S. Army resulting from the 1874 gold rush in the Black Hills, where the Sioux lived. This war included the famous battle of the Little Big Horn. In order to keep peace, Spotted Tail signed treaties with the U.S. government that forced the Sioux onto the Rosebud reservation in South Dakota. Spotted Tail was killed by a Sioux assassin, possibly in an effort to further weaken branches of the Sioux nation.
See also: Sioux.

Sprague, Frank Julian (1857-1934), U.S. inventor and engineer of the high-speed electric elevator and the electric railroad system, including that now used in the New York City subway.
See also: Elevator; Railroad.

Sprain, injury to a ligament (which connects bone to bone in a joint). The symptoms are rapid swelling and inflammation and some initial pain and stiffness around a joint. Swelling and pain seem worse 24 to 48 hours after injury occurs. Discoloration and limitation in motion and function may also take place.
A ligament is like a rope that, when stretched beyond resting length, is susceptible to injury, and with a severe enough force it may be torn apart. This usually occurs when turning and twisting are involved, especially very quick, sudden motions that twist the joint. The disability depends on the degree of damage. It can be as minor as swelling and inflammation only, causing minimal discomfort, or as severe as a rupture of the ligament(s).
Treatment is with cold compresses (not heat) after the injury occurs and elevation of the injured joint, if possible. The joint should be immobilized and a compression wrap used. If quite painful, inflamed, or swollen, a doctor should be consulted. Some sprains resolve themselves with rest and immobility, while others require splinting, casting, or bracing. With very serious sprains, surgical repair may be required.
See also: Ligament.

Sprat (*Clupea sprattus*), small marine food fish of the herring family native to coastal waters of Europe. Sprats have a flat body and grow to 8 in (20 cm). Canned sprats are sometimes known as brisling sardines.

Spring, mechanical device that exhibits elasticity according to Hooke's Law. Most springs are made of steel, brass, or bronze. The most common type is

the *helical spring*, a coil of stiff wire, loose wound if to be compressed, tight wound if to be extended under tension. Helical springs have many uses, including closing valves, spring balances, and accelerometers. The *spiral spring* is a wire or strip coiled in one plane, responding to torque applied to its inner end, and used to store energy, notably in clocks and watches. The *leaf spring*, used in vehicle suspension systems, consists of several steel strips of different lengths clamped on top of each other at one end. When deformed, springs store potential energy, and exert a restoring force. Hydraulic and air springs work by compression of a fluid in a cylinder.
See also: Hooke, Robert.

Spring, in geology, naturally occurring flow of water from the ground. Some are outflows from underground streams, but most often a spring occurs when an aquifer (a layer of water-bearing porous rock or sediment) intersects with the earth's surface. Such an aquifer may travel for hundreds of kilometers underground before emerging to the surface. Spring water is generally fairly clean, since it has been filtered through permeable rocks, but all spring water contains some dissolved minerals.

Spring beauty, wild flowers in the purslane family. This North American wild flower grows in forests. It has white to pink blooms and slender, lengthy leaves on stems up to 12 in (30 cm) high. The Virginia spring beauty (*Claytonia virginica*)—sometimes called the Mayflower—and the Carolina (*C. caroliniana*) are found from Canada through Georgia in the east and Texas in the west.

Springbok, animal in the cattle family, also called springbuck. The springbok *(Antidorcas marsupialis)* inhabit the plains of South Africa, for which area they are considered an emblem. They are a kind of antelope, unusual because of their ability to spring into the air 6.5-11.5 ft (2-3.5 m) as a defensive action to detract predators, such as cheetahs. These red to brown slim-legged animals stand about 32 in (80 cm) at the shoulder and weigh 73-95 lb (33-43 k). Males and females have curved horns. Their once-enormous herds were greatly reduced by hunters.

Springer spaniel *See:* Spaniel.

Springfield (pop. 189,550), capital of Illinois. It lies near the Sangamon River in the central part of the state, c.100 mi (160 km) northeast of St. Louis, Mo. The economy of the city is based upon government, a variety of manufactures, and the marketing and processing of regional agricultural products. Springfield was founded in 1818, and in 1837 it became the capital of Illinois. Abraham Lincoln had come to Springfield that year, and he made the city his home until he became president in 1861. Lincoln, his wife, and 3 of their children are buried in the Lincoln Tomb State Memorial in Springfield, and the only house Lincoln ever owned is also preserved there as a memorial. Other Springfield landmarks include the old state capitol (1837-53), the new statehouse (1868-88), and the Centennial Building (1918-23) with its collection of Lincoln artifacts.
See also: Illinois.

Springfield (pop. 529,519), city in Massachusetts. Located on the east bank of the Connecticut River, near the Connecticut state line, it is a commercial

and industrial center. Springfield is basically a manufacturing city; its factories turn out machinery, chemicals, electrical equipment, and a wide variety of other goods. It has long been a center of firearms manufacture. Springfield was first settled in the 1630s. It is the home of the Basketball Hall of Fame and of Springfield College, American International College, and Western New England College.
See also: Massachusetts.

Springfield (pop. 240,593), city in southwestern Missouri, the seat of Greene County. Located at the edge of the Ozark Mountains, the city is the principal distribution and processing center for the Ozark region's mines, orchards, farmland, and timber resources, and produces a variety of related manufactures. The town was first settled in 1829.
See also: Missouri.

Springfield (pop. 70,487), city in west-central Ohio, on the Mad River about 45 mi (72.5 km) west of Columbus. The city serves as a marketing and processing center for the surrounding agricultural region and also produces a wide variety of machinery and other manufactured products. First settled in 1799, Springfield is the home of Wittenberg University (chartered 1845) and the seat of Clark County.
See also: Ohio.

Springhare, or springhaas (*Pedetes capensis*), small, nocturnal, herbivorous rodent of eastern and southern Africa, resembling a rabbit with a long tail but belonging to the family Pedetidae. Springhares grow to a body length of 17 in (43 cm) and a weight of 9 lb (4 kg). Their large hind legs enable them to jump up to 10 ft (3 m). They live singly or in small families in burrows and feed on roots and bulbs.

Springsteen, Bruce (1949-), U.S. rock singer, songwriter, and guitarist, known as "The Boss." He has performed with his E Street Band since the early 1970s, recording such albums as *Born to Run* (1975, *Born in the U.S.A.* (1984), which sold 15 million copies, *Human Touch* (1992), and *The Ghost of Tom Joad* (1995). His lyrics are often topical and idealistic.

Spruance, Raymond Ames (1886-1969), U.S. naval officer known for victories in the Pacific theater during World War II under the command of Admiral Chester W. Nimitz. His first notable victory took place at Midway Island (1942), after which he became Nimitz's chief of staff. From 1943-44 he won victories in islands throughout the central Pacific, including the Gilbert Islands, the Marshall Islands, the island of Truk in Micronesia, Guam, Saipan, and the battle of the Philippines. Spruance also led the victory at Okinawa (1945). He was promoted to commander in chief of the U.S. Pacific Fleet (1945). He took over the presidency of the Naval War College (1946) and served as the U.S. ambassador to the Philippines (1952-55).
See also: World War II.

Spruce, evergreen coniferous tree of the genus *Picea*, with a conical form. There are some 40 species, all of which grow in the cooler regions of the Northern Hemisphere. Among the species found in the United States are the black (*P. mariana*), blue (*P. pungens*), and white (*P. glauca*) spruces.

Spruce budworm, destructive insect in the Tortricidae family. This insect *(Choristoneura fumiferana)* lives in the northern United States and Canada. It destroys evergreen trees—particularly the spruce—by feeding on the needles and pollen each spring for 3-6 years while in the caterpillar stage. Each summer the small moths that display dark markings lay their eggs in the trees, which in turn spin cocoons. Methods of forest management and other biological controls check the spread of these insects more effectively than do pesticides. In the past devastating outbreaks of these pests have occurred approximately once every half century.

Spurge family, group of plants that include herbs, shrubs, and trees that grow mainly in tropical climates throughout the world. These plants provide castor oil, cassava, and rubber; some are poinsettias. Commercial applications for waterproofing, polishes, candle waxes, and other products are derived from a species of the spurge family (*Euphorbia antisyphilitica*) native to Mexico.

Sputnik, series of unmanned satellites launched by the Soviet Union. The first was launched on Oct. 4, 1957. It circled the earth once about every 95 minutes at a speed of 18,000 mph (29,000 kmph) until it fell to earth on Jan. 4, 1958. Nine more Sputnik missions were carried out from 1957 to 1961.
See also: Space exploration.

Squanto (d.1622), Native American of the Pawtuxet tribe, who befriended the newly arrived settlers of the Plymouth colony, acting as their interpreter in dealing with the powerful chief Massasoit and teaching them how to grown corn.

Square dancing, popular, lively U.S. folk dance in which 4 couples formed in a square carry out steps and formations under the direction of a caller. It dates back to the quadrille dances of 15th-century Europe.

Square Deal, policy of Theodore Roosevelt when, as presidential candidate (1912), he sought to reconcile the demands of both workers and industrialists.
See also: Roosevelt, Theodore.

Squash, any of several edible plants in the Cucurbitaceae family. These vegetables, related to the pumpkin, are eaten cooked or raw. Different species both look and taste different from one another; they have in common a 5-pointed leaf that grows from either a bush or vine. Summer squash (zucchini, crookneck, pattypan) are harvested when immature, about 2 months after planting. Winter squash (Hubbard, acorn, butternut) are harvested when mature, up to 4 months after planting, and can be stored. Squash, popular with home gardeners and truck farmers, were introduced to settlers by Native Americans.

Squash, game played on a 4-walled court with a small, hard-rubber ball and 27-in (68-cm) rackets. Singles squash is played on an indoor court that measures 18.5 ft x 32 ft (5.6 m x 9.75 m); doubles squash requires a larger court. The ball may be hit against any of the 4 walls as long as it bounces on the front wall before striking the floor. The opponent must then hit the ball before it touches the floor twice.

Squeteague *See:* Weakfish.

Squid, shell-less cephalopod mollusk, order Teuthoidea. Although a few species live in coastal waters, the majority inhabit the open ocean. The squid is a streamlined animal with 10 arms around the head, facing forward. The mantle at the rear of the body houses the gills and the openings of the excretory, sex, and digestive organs. Sudden contraction of the mantle cavity produces a blast of water that can be directed forward or backward, providing the main means of propulsion. All squid can swim very rapidly and are active predators of fish, shooting out their long arms, provided with suckers and hooks, to grab their prey.

Squill, plant in the lily family. The sea onion *(Urginea maritima)*, like other squill, is a plant with a bulb root; it is used as medicine. Other species of squill ornament gardens with their clusters of tiny white to blue leafless flowers *(Scilla peruviana)*.

Squire *See:* Knights and knighthood.

Squirrel, member of one of the largest families, Sciuridae, of rodents. The name commonly refers only to tree squirrels, found in most forested parts of the world. Typically they have long, bushy tails and short muzzles. They are diurnal and feed on seeds, nuts, and leaf buds, with some insect and other animal food. A number of temperate species, while not true hibernators, store food for the winter and enter deep torpor. The family includes the chipmunk, woodchuck, and prairie dog.

Squirrel monkey, primate of the New World monkey family, Cebidae. They live in the rain forests in Central and South America. Small in size, no longer than 1 ft (30 cm), they weigh no more than 2 lb (0.9 kg). They use their dark-tipped tail for balance as they travel in large groups, single file behind a leader, on paths through the forest trees. Squirrel monkeys have white fur on their undersides and faces, dark facial features, and large eyes. Their fur color ranges from black to gray or reddish brown and olive green to yellow. They are used as laboratory animals and make good pets when kept with other squirrel monkeys.

Sri Lanka, formerly Ceylon, officially the Democratic Socialist Republic of Sri Lanka, independent island republic in the Indian Ocean.
Land and climate. Sri Lanka is separated from southeastern India by the Gulf of Mannar, Palk Strait, and Adam's Bridge, a 30-mi (48-km)-chain of shoals. With an area of 24,879 sq mi (64,454 sq km), Sri Lanka extends 270 mi (435 km) north to south and 140 mi (225 km) east to west. The south-central area of the island is mountainous and its major rivers, including the Mahaweli Ganga, rise in this region, which is dominated by Mt. Pidurutalagala (8,281 ft/2,524 m) and Adam's Peak (7,360 ft/2,243 m). Around the mountains extends a coastal plain up to 100 mi (161 km) wide in the north. Originally dense with tropical forest, much of the plain has been cleared for agriculture. The climate is tropical, but due to its situation the island enjoys more equable temperatures than those prevailing in southernmost India.
People. Buddhist Sinhalese make up 75% of the population. The Hindu Tamils, people of South Indian origin living mainly in the north and east, are the principal minority, but there are also Veddas, probably the island's

Sri Lanka

Capital:	Colombo
Area:	24,879 sq mi (64,454 sq km)
Population:	18,934,000
Language:	Sinhala, Tamil, English
Government:	Socialist presidential republic
Independent:	1948
Head of gov.:	Prime minister
Per capita:	U.S. $700
Mon. unit:	1 Sri Lanka rupee = 100 cents

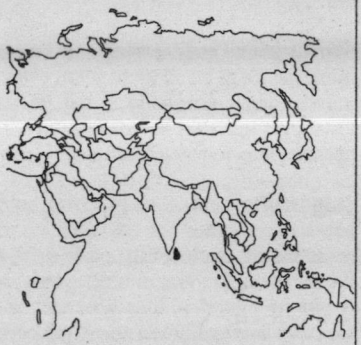

original inhabitants, and Burghero, Christian descendants of Dutch-Sinhalese forebears. The capital of Sri Lanka is Colombo and Sinhala (Sinhalese) is the official language, though English and Tamil are also widely spoken.
Economy. Sri Lanka produces a large proportion of the world's tea and over 100,000 tons of rubber a year. Coconuts are commercially grown for their oil, but rice, the main food crop, often has to be supplemented by imports. The country is the world's chief producer of high-grade graphite.
History. The island was settled around 550 B.C. by the Sinhalese, a people from the Indian subcontinent, who built Anuradhapura and made the island a center of Buddhist thought after the religion was introduced there in the 3rd century B.C. The Tamil people held the northern part of the island from the 12th to the 16th centuries. Lured by the spice trade, Europeans began arriving in the 16th century. They called the island Ceylon, and it was held successively by the Portuguese, who landed in 1505, the Dutch, who came after 1658, and finally the British, who came in 1796. Ceylon gained its independence in 1948, and it became a republic in 1956. In 1972 a new constitution was adopted and Ceylon was given the Sinhalese name Sri Lanka. In the late 1970s and early 1980s violence flared up between the Sinhalese and Tamil separatists. The conflict remains unresolved and has been accompanied by charges that India has secretly financed and armed separatist forces. In 1997 a new constitution was adopted, which amongst other things had to meet the Tamil demand for sovereignty in the north and in the east.

Staël, Madame de (Anne Louise Germaine Necker; 1766-1817), French-Swiss novelist and critic, celebrated personality, and liberal opponent of Napoleon I's regime. A noted interpreter of German Romanticism, she maintained brilliant salons in Paris until her exile to Geneva. Her major work, *On Germany* (1810), influenced European culture. She also wrote the novels *Delphine* (1802) and *Corinne* (1807). Her memoirs, *Ten Years of Exile* (1818), is a fascinating account of her times. She had liaisons with Talleyrand and the writer Benjamin Constant.

Stafford, Jean (1915-79), U.S. author noted for her sensitive, well-crafted novels and short stories. Her *Collected Stories* (1969) won a Pulitzer Prize.

Her novels include *Boston Adventure* (1944) and *The Catherine Wheel* (1952).

Staffordshire bull terrier, also known as pit bull terrier, breed of dog. These muscular dogs stand up to 19 in (48 cm) and weigh up to 50 lb (23 k). They may be any color, solid in patches, or brindled. They are named after the town in which they were bred in early 19th-century England. Their original purpose was to fight other dogs—usually in pits—or bears.

Stag beetle, also called pinching bug, beetle in the Lucanidae family. These beetles are named for the jaws, or mandibles, of the males, which greatly resemble the horns of the male deer, or stag. These mandibles may be from half to the entire length of the body, which ranges from 1.5-2 in (3.8-5 cm). A bite by a toothed mandible can cause bleeding. Stag beetles feed on tree sap, and live and breed among decomposing trees.

Stained glass, pieces of colored glass held in place by a framework usually of lead strips, to form patterns or pictures in a window. The earliest Western windows date from the 5th century, but the art reached its highest development in the period of Gothic architecture (1150-1500): The series of windows made (1200-40) for the cathedral at Chartres is a well-known example. Huge circular windows became common during this period. These windows, because of their flowerlike shape, were known as rose windows. Interest revived in the 19th and 20th centuries with the work of Edward Burne-Jones, Louis Comfort Tiffany, and John La Farge. Later masters of stained glass were the painters Henri Matisse, Fernand Léger, Georges Rouault, and Marc Chagall. The glass is colored during manufacture by mixing it with metallic oxides, then cut according to full-scale cartoons. Details may be painted onto the glass with colored enamels, which fuse to the surface when it is heated.

Stainless steel, corrosion-resistant steel containing more than 10% chromium, little carbon, and often nickel and other metals. There are 4 main types: ferritic, martensitic, austenitic, and precipitation-hardening. Stainless steel is used for cutlery and many industrial components.

Stalactite, and **stalagmite**, rocky structures found in limestone caves. Rainwater (containing atmospheric carbon dioxide) percolates through the rocks above limestone caves, dissolving some calcium carbonate, a major component of limestone. Upon reaching the cave, some of the water that drips from the roof evaporates, leaving a little of the calcium carbonate as calcite on the roof; repetition of this process forms a stalactite. The water that continues to drip to the floor leaves a small amount of calcium carbonate (as calcite) on the floor; repetition of this process forms a stalagmite. The two structures often meet to form pillars.

Stalin, Joseph (Josif Vissarionovich Dzhugashvili; 1879-1953), ruler of the Soviet Union from 1924 until his death. A Georgian village shoemaker's son intended for the priesthood, he joined the Georgian Social Democratic Party in 1901. In 1912 V. I. Lenin placed him on the Bolshevik central committee. (Around this time he took the name Stalin, "man of steel.") After the Russian Revolution (1917) he advanced rapidly. In 1922 he was elected general secretary of the Russian Communist Party. In the struggle for the leadership

after Lenin's death (1924), he eliminated all opposition and established himself as virtual dictator. In 1928 he launched a vast development and industrialization program that involved the forced collectivization of agriculture and intensive industrialization.
Stalin sought to "Russianize" the Soviet Union, attempting to eradicate by force the separate identities of minorities. Dissent was met with a powerful secret police, informers, mass deportations, executions, and show trials. In 1935 he initiated the first of the great "purges," which spared neither his family nor former political associates. Equally ruthless in foreign affairs, he partitioned Poland with Germany (1939) and imposed Communist rule on the Baltic states (1940). The reversal of German fortunes on the eastern front during World War II strengthened his hand. In 1945 at Yalta he sealed the postwar fate of Eastern Europe to his satisfaction. Thereafter, he pursued Cold War policies abroad and supported rapid industrial recovery at home until his death from a brain hemorrhage. Almost immediately a process of "destalinization" began, culminating in Nikita Khrushchev's 1956 attack on the Stalinist terror and personality cult.
See also: Union of Soviet Socialist Republics.

Stalingrad *See:* Volgograd.

Stalingrad, Battle of, decisive engagement in World War II, fought in the vicinity of Stalingrad (since 1961, Volgograd) from Aug. 1942 to Feb. 1943. The 500,000-man German 6th army surrounded the city on Sept. 14, 1942, but was itself encircled early in 1943 by a Russian army, and forced to surrender. The battle wrested the psychological initiative from the Nazis for the remainder of the war.
See also: World War II.

Stalino *See:* Donetsk.

Stamford (pop. 102,466), U.S. city in Connecticut. Located on the Long Island Sound, Stamford is considered a suburb of New York City, a short distance away. It also is an active city in its own right, with many corporate headquarters located in the new buildings that were constructed as part of an urban renewal project begun in the 1960s. Settlers founded the city in 1641 and named it after an English counterpart. It was incorporated in 1893.
See also: Connecticut.

Stamp Act (1765), first direct tax imposed by the English Parliament on the 13 North American colonies. All legal and commercial documents, pamphlets, playing cards, and newspapers were to carry revenue stamps, which would help finance the British army quartered in America. The colonists balked at the idea of "taxation without representation," and delegates from 9 colonies met in the Stamp Act Congress held in New York to protest the law. A boycott of British goods finally led Parliament to repeal the act in Mar. 1766.
See also: Taxation.

Stamp collecting, or philately, popular worldwide hobby. The first postage stamps were issued in England on May 1, 1840. The first in the United States appeared in 1847, and by 1860 most countries had adopted the prepaid postage stamp system. Today stamp catalogs list more than 200,000 items. Serious collectors, who generally specialize in particular countries, periods, or themes, make a close study of each stamp's paper, ink, printing method, perforations, cancellation, design, information content, and historical occasion. Stamps can also be a good investment; large sums of money have been paid for rare specimens.

Stamp weed *See:* Indian mallow.

Standard of living, statistical measure that attempts to rate the quality of life in a nation or a group in terms of its level of consumption of food, clothing, and other basic goods and services, including transportation, education, and medical care.

Standard schnauzer, breed of dog originally from Bavaria, Germany, in the 15th century. These dogs stand up to 19.5 in (50 cm) at the shoulder and weigh up to 40 lb (18 kg). They have short, gray to black, wiry coats, short docked ears and tail, shaggy whiskers, and bushy eyebrows. They were originally used as herders and rodent killers. Later, in the 18th century they were used as carriage and guard dogs for stables. Today they are kept as pets.

Standard time, time kept in the time zones of the world. In the United States the zones are called Eastern, Central, Mountain, and Pacific. The standard time in each zone lags Greenwich mean time (GMT) by 5, 6, 7, and 8 hours respectively. Standard time in Hawaii and Alaska is 10 hours behind GMT. The zones depend on the fact that the earth takes an hour to rotate 15°. Therefore the sun rises an hour later for every 15° west. Each time zone is roughly centered on a meridian (line of longitude) 15° farther west than its predecessor.
See also: Fleming, Sir Sandford.

Standard & Poor's indexes, U.S. stock market statistics prepared by the Standard & Poor's Corporation. These averages are calculated each business day at 5-min. intervals. They are based on the price-per-share of 500 companies (industrial firms, public utilities, financial institutions, and transportation companies) in comparison to price per share information from the years 1941-43, considered the base period for the U.S. stock market. This information helps investors make decisions in both the buying and selling of stocks. In addition, *The Outlook,* a weekly publication, presents statistics on 100 companies and is used as an overview for the stock market.
See also: Dow Jones Industrial Average.

Standish, Miles (1584?-1656), English passenger on the *Mayflower* and colonist. Unlike most of his fellow travelers from England in 1620, Standish was not a Puritan and did not come to the New World as a religious exile. He led successful military operations for the Plymouth Colony against hostile Native American tribes. He took over ownership of stock from a London-based investment group that financed the Plymouth Colony (1627). Standish participated in the colonial government as assistant governor (beginning in either 1624 or 1633) and treasurer (1652-55). He helped found Auxbury, Mass., where he went to live (c.1632). Although his courtship is the subject of a famous poem by Henry Wadsworth Longfellow, the details are not based in fact.

Stanford-Binet test, adaptation of the Stanford Revision of the Binet-Simon Intelligence Tests introduced by Lewis Madison Terman (1916; 2d revision, 1937), and used primarily to determine the Intelligence Quotient (IQ) of children.
See also: Intelligence quotient.

Stanford University, leading U.S. educational and research center. Stanford was founded by Leland and Jane Lathrop Stanford in 1885 as a memorial to their son who died of typhoid fever. Located in Stanford, Calif., Stanford is a private, coeducational university that offers both undergraduate and graduate courses of study.

Stanislavski, Konstantin (Konstantin Sergeyevich Alekseyev; 1863-1938), Russian-born stage director, teacher, and author. Stanislavski and Vladmir Nemirovich-Danchencko founded the Moscow Art Theater (1898); they used a new acting technique called the *method*, in which actors drew upon personal experiences to bring out the emotions of the characters they portrayed. This technique, outlined in Stanislavski's book *An Actor Prepares* (1926), is often used by actors today.

Stanley and Livingstone, British explorers in Afica. David Livingstone (1813-73) traveled to southern Africa as a missionary and remained on the continent for the rest of his life. His interest in geography ignited a coast-to-coast journey in which he followed the Zambezi River (1853-56). Victoria Falls was named by him, the first European to see it (1855). He met Henry Morton Stanley (1841-1904) while on Lake Tanganyika (1871). Stanley was a reporter employed by the *New York Herald* (1869) to find Livingstone, believed lost in the interior of Africa. Upon discovering Livingstone, Stanley, instead of returning with him to New York, joined Livingstone in a search for the source of the Nile River. After Livingstone's death, Stanley explored the Congo River (1874-77) in a grueling journey that ended up on the Atlantic coast. He helped found the Free Congo State for the king of Belgium, recognized in 1885. He described his African experience in 2 books, *In Darkest Africa* (1890) and *Through South Africa* (1898). He served in the British Parliament (1895-1900) and was knighted (1899).

Stanley brothers, U.S. inventors and twins; **Francis Edgar Stanley** (1849-1918) and **Freeland Oscar Stanley** (1849-1940). Their first company manufactured their inventions related to the field of photography and was eventually sold to Eastman Kodak Company (1904). Their experimentation with steam engines led to building the Stanley Steamer (1897). Their Stanley Motor Carriage Company (1901) produced a steam engine that traveled 128 mph (206 km), breaking the existing speed record (1906). With the manufacture of gasoline-engine automobiles, Stanley Steamers became far less popular; they were discontinued in 1924.

Stanley Cup, trophy presented annually to the winner of the National Hockey League (NHL) postseason playoffs. Lord Stanley, governor general of Canada (1888-1893), first presented the award to the Canadian amateur hockey champion in 1893. From 1918-26, the NHL competed with the Pacific Coast Hockey Association (PCHA) for the Stanley Cup. Since 1926, when the PCHA disbanded, the trophy has been identified solely with the NHL.

Stanton, Edwin McMasters (1814-69), U.S. politician, secretary of war during the Civil War (1862-68), and important ally of the Radical Republicans during Reconstruction. As U.S. attorney general in the last months of President James Buchanan's cabinet, he stood against Southern secession. He resigned following President Andrew Johnson's narrow escape from impeachment (1868). Stanton was appointed to the Supreme Court but died prior to assuming the post.

Stanton, Elizabeth Cady (1815-1902), U.S. abolitionist and feminist. With Lucretia Mott, she organized the first women's rights convention in the United States (1848). She founded the National Woman Suffrage Association with Susan B. Anthony (1869).
See also: Mott, Lucretia Coffin; Woman suffrage.

Staphylococcus, bacterium responsible for numerous skin, soft tissue, and bone infections, less often causing septicemia, pneumonia, bacterial endocarditis, and enterocolitis. Boils, carbuncles, impetigo, and osteomyelitis are commonly caused by staphylococci. Treatment usually requires antibiotics and drainage of pus from abscesses.

Star, large incandescent ball of gases held together by its own gravity. The sun is a fairly normal star in its composition, parameters, and color. It is believed that stars originate as condensations out of interstellar matter. In certain circumstances a protostar will form, slowly contracting under its own gravity, part of the energy from this contraction being radiated, the remainder heating up the core; this stage may last several million years. At last the core becomes hot enough for thermonuclear reactions to be sustained and stops contracting. Eventually the star as a whole ceases contracting and radiates entirely by the thermonuclear conversion of hydrogen into helium; it is then said to be on the main sequence. When all the hydrogen in the core has been converted into helium, the now purely helium core begins to contract while the outer layers continue to "burn" hydrogen; this contraction heats up the core and forces the outer layers outward, so that the star as a whole expands for some 100-200 million years until it becomes a red giant star. Although the outer layers are comparatively cool, the core has become far hotter than before, and thermonuclear conversions of helium into carbon begin. The star contracts once more (though some expand still further to become supergiants) and ends its life as a white dwarf star. It is thought that more massive stars become neutron stars, whose matter is so dense that its protons and electrons are packed together to form neutrons; were the sun to become a neutron star, it would have a radius of less than 12.5 mi (20 km). Finally, when the star can no longer radiate through thermonuclear or gravitational means, it ceases to shine. At this stage some stars may undergo ultimate gravitational collapse to form black holes.

Starbuck Island, South Pacific island. This coral island, covering about 1 sq mi (2.6 sq km), claims no human population. Guano, a natural material

used in fertilizer, was mined off this island until the resource was depleted (1870-1920). Starbuck Island is located 2,000 mi (3,000 km) south of Hawaii. Now part of the country of Kiribati (1979), it was formally discovered (1823) and appropriated (1866) by Britain.
See also: Kiribati.

Starch, white, odorless carbohydrate powder, essential to both plants and animals as a source of energy (it is converted to glucose when needed). It is made naturally in green plants during photosynthesis; commercially, it is made chiefly from potatoes and corn. Cornstarch is used to make corn syrup and corn sugar, both of which are used to sweeten food products. Starch is also used to size paper and textiles and to stiffen shirts and other laundered items.

Star Chamber, in early English history, meeting room for the King's advisors. The room was located in Westminster Palace, London, and derives its name from the stars which decorated the ceiling of the chamber. During the 1400s these advisors evolved into a powerful council that assumed courtlike powers. It was officially set up in 1487. Operating outside common law, with no jury, it was speedy and efficient but also arbitrary and cruel, particularly under James I and Charles I. It was abolished by the Long Parliament (1641) for its abuses.
See also: United Kingdom.

Starfish, member of a class, Asteroidea, of star-shaped marine echinoderms, with 5-fold symmetry. A starfish consists of a central disk surrounded by 5 or more radiating arms. There is a dermal skeleton of calcite plates, and a water-vascular system gives rise to rows of tube feet on the lower surface by which the animal moves about. The mouth is on the lower surface. Most species are carnivorous or omnivorous scavengers. Starfishes can regenerate lost or damaged parts.

Stark, Johannes (1874-1957), German physicist who received the Nobel Prize (1919) for his discovery that light was uniquely affected by an electrical field, in that the field would cause spectral lines to split. Stark also discovered the laboratory basis (as opposed to celestial observation) of the Doppler effect in optics, in which the light frequencies of moving atoms dispensed in a gas-charged tube changed. Stark was a professor of physics at the Universities of Greifswald (1917-20) and Wurzburg (1920-22). He served as president of Reich Physical-Technical Institute (1933-39). He served 4 years in a labor camp, beginning in 1947, for his Nazi participation.
See also: Relativity.

Stark, John (1728-1822), American Revolutionary soldier. After distinguishing himself at the battles of Bunker Hill and Trenton, he was made a brigadier general of the New Hampshire militia. Stark won a crucial battle at Bennington, Vt., and was instrumental in forcing the surrender at Saratoga. He was made a major general in 1783.
See also. Revolutionary War in America.

Starling, member of a family, Sturnidae, of more than 100 species of songbirds. They have slender bills, an upright stance, and smooth, glossy plumage. Found worldwide, they feed on insects, invertebrates, and seeds. They flock for feeding and roosting, with communal roosts of up to 500,000 birds.

Star-of-Bethlehem, flower in the lily family. This flower (*Ornithogalum umbellatum*) assumes a star shape with 6 white petals. It grows from a bulb, which is poisonous. Star-of-Bethlehem flowers have green stripes on their undersides, while the green leaves have white stripes. They bloom in May and June, often in home gardens or window boxes.

Star of David, known also as Shield of David, symbol of Judaism and the state of Israel. This star is comprised of 2 triangles, one inverted and superimposed over the other. The Hebrew title *Magen David* originates from the late A.D. 200s. Its first recorded appearance is from as long ago as 960 B.C.
See also: Judaism.

Starr, Belle (1848-89), U.S. outlaw. Legend has it that Starr started her career as a horse and cattle thief called Bandit Queen. She served 9 months in prison (1883) for stealing horses. She was killed by a gunman while her companion, Bill July, was being tried in court.

Starr, Ringo *See:* Beatles.

Star-spangled Banner, U.S. national anthem, officially adopted by an act of Congress in 1931. Francis Scott Key wrote the words in 1814, near the end of the so-called War of 1812, and they were later set to the tune of an old English drinking song.
See also: Key, Francis Scott.

Starter, device that causes the crankshaft in an engine to turn and operate. Different kinds of engines require different kinds of starters. For example, the starter in an automobile receives electric current from the battery, which, in turn, starts the starter motor: This rotates the crankshaft and ignites the spark plugs in the engine. Diesel-powered engines, including those found on many railroad cars, sometimes inject compressed air into cylinders that start the engine. The air turbine starters or jet turbine starters on airplanes use high-pressure air to start the engine; a separate device on the aircraft or ground—the auxiliary power unit (APU)—ignites the starter.
See also: Kettering, Charles Franklin.

Star Wars *See:* Strategic Defense Initiative.

State, U.S. Department of, oldest executive department of the U.S. government. Originally in charge of domestic as well as foreign affairs, it now conducts U.S. foreign policy. It collects and analyzes information from abroad, gives policy advice to the president, and negotiates treaties and agreements. The Department of State is in charge of the U.S. Foreign Service, which maintains some 280 diplomatic and consular offices. The secretary of state is a senior member of the president's cabinet.

State government, body that administers laws and regulations within a state. Under the U.S. federal system, each state government has its own constitution and consists of an executive branch headed by a governor, a legislative branch, and a judicial branch. State governments have powers that are independent from those of the federal government and can set policy as long as there is no breach of constitutional law. Powers overlap in some areas, however, and it becomes necessary for the state and federal governments to work closely together.

Staten Island, in New York Harbor, 5 mi (8 km) southwest of the Battery tip of Manhattan Island. Staten Island, with an area of more than 60 sq mi (155 sq km), comprises the whole borough and county of Richmond, one of the 5 boroughs of New York City. The island is connected with Manhattan by ferry, with Brooklyn by the Verrazano-Narrows Bridge, and with New Jersey by several bridges. The first permanent settlements on Staten Island were established in the 1660s. It is now a residential suburb and industrial area.

State press, system of publishing owned and controlled by a government or dominant political party. The opposite of a free press, a state press is common in dictatorships, and is used by the state to shape popular opinion and to conceal or manipulate the flow of information to the public.

States' rights, power allowed by the U.S. Constitution to individual states, other than those rights vested in the federal government.

Static, interference in a radio or television signal caused by disturbance in the electrical charge of the receiver. The motion of charged dust particles or drops of water can result in static. More serious static may occur in the event of such natural disasters as earthquakes, volcanoes, and tornadoes.
See also: Frequency modulation.

Statics, branch of mechanics dealing with systems in equilibrium, i.e., those in which all forces are balanced and there is no motion.

Statistics, branch of mathematics that collects, tabulates, and analyzes data by a numerical system which, in turn, is used to make predictions and projections about situations that are uncertain. The process usually involves the acquisition of data from a small group that is used to make predictions about the behavior of a larger group. For example, in a presidential campaign most candidates take polls indicating their level of popularity. These polls do not survey every person in the country, but are based on a sample from a much smaller number of people. Essential to such calculations is the theory of probability, which is utilized to judge the soundness of the numerical assumptions. Statistics plays a significant role in many areas, including scientific research, business (insurance), and politics.

Statuary Hall, domed chamber in the U.S. Capitol building in Washington, D.C., in which statues of important Americans are displayed. Created in 1870, the hall contains at least 1 statue from each of the 50 states. Because of space, some of the statues have been placed in other areas of the Capitol. Statuary Hall is the former site of the House of Representatives.

Statue of Liberty, colossal bronze female figure rising more than 300 ft (91 m) above the sea, on Liberty Island in New York Harbor. She bears in one

hand a tablet marked "July 4, 1776" and in the other a torch. Designed by the sculptor Frédéric Bartholdi, the statue was given to the United States by France on the 100th anniversary of U.S. independence. The U.S poet Emma Lazarus epitomized the statue's meaning in an inscription on its base, which reads in part:
"Give me your tired, your poor,
Your huddled masses yearning to breathe free,
The wretched refuse of your teeming shore.
Send these, the homeless, tempest-tost to me,
I lift my lamp beside the golden door!"

Statue of Liberty National Monument, on New York City's Ellis and Liberty islands, 58-acre (23 ha) monument. It includes the Statue of Liberty on Liberty Island, a massive copper work given to the United States by the people of France on July 4, 1884. It was created by the sculptor Frédéric-Auguste Bartholdi to commemorate the friendship between the 2 nations. Ellis Island, an immigration station until 1954, was made part of the national monument in 1965; from 1892 to 1943 it was the chief entry station for thousands of immigrants seeking a new life in the United States.
See also: Ellis Island.

Statute of limitations, law that prevents suits from being filed after a certain period has elapsed. Time limits differ according to the type of claim. Statutes of limitations vary from state to state. The U.S. federal government has its own set of statutes. Crimes such as murder are not affected by these laws.

STD *See:* Venereal disease.

Steamboat, any steam-powered sailing vessel. The term is commonly used to identify the kind of riverboat used in the United States in the 1800s, particularly along the Mississippi. The steamboat was a primary means of transportation before the advent of the railroad. The most famous of the U.S. steamboats was the *Clermont,* which sailed along the Hudson River from New York to Albany in about 30 hours in 1807.
See also: Fulton, Robert.

Steam engine, first important heat engine, supplying the power that made the Industrial Revolution possible. It was the principal power source for industry and transport (notably railroad locomotives and steamships) until the 20th-century advent of steam turbines and internal-combustion engines. The steam engine is an external-combustion engine, the steam being raised in a boiler heated by a furnace. The first working example was that of Thomas Newcomen (1712). Steam was admitted to a cylinder as a piston moved up and was condensed by a water spray inside the cylinder, whereupon the air pressure outside forced the piston down again. James Watt radically improved Newcomen's engine (1769) by condensing the steam outside the cylinder (thus no longer having to reheat the cylinder at each stroke) and by using the steam pressure to force the piston up. Watt also invented the double-action principle—both strokes being powered by applying the steam alternately to each end of the piston—and devices for converting the piston's linear motion to rotary motion. The compound engine (1781) made more efficient use of the steam by using the exhaust steam from one cylinder to

drive the piston of a second cylinder. Later developments included the use of high-pressure steam.
See also: Newcomen, Thomas; Watt, James.

Stearic acid, or octadecanoic acid, common fatty acid derived from animal or vegetable fats. A waxy, colorless solid, it has a wide variety of industrial uses, including the manufacture of soap, cosmetics, and pharmaceuticals.

Steatite *See:* Soapstone.

Steel, alloy of iron and up to 1.7% carbon, with small amounts of manganese, phosphorous, sulfur, and silicon. These are termed carbon steels; those with other metals are termed alloy steels—low-alloy steels if they have less than 5% of the alloying metal, high-alloy steels if more than 5%. Carbon steels are far stronger than iron, and their properties can be tailored to their uses by adjusting composition and treatment. Alloy steels—including stainless steels—are used for their special properties. Steel was first mass-produced in the mid-19th century and is now basic to all industrial economies. The United States, the former USSR, and Japan are the major producers. All steelmaking processes remove the impurities in the raw materials—pig iron, scrap steel, and reduced iron ore—by oxidizing them with an air or oxygen blast. Thus most of the carbon, silicon, manganese, phosphorus, and sulfur are converted to their oxides and, together with added flux and other waste matter present, form slag. The main processes are the Bessemer process; the Linz-Donawitz, or basic oxygen, process, and the similar electric-arc process, used for highest-quality steel; and the open-hearth process. When the impurities have been removed, desired elements are added in calculated proportions. The molten steel is cast as ingots that are shaped while still red-hot in rolling mills, or it may be cast as a continuous bar (strand casting). The properties of carbon steels may be greatly improved by heat treatment: annealing, casehardening, and tempering.

Steele, Sir Richard (1672-1729), Irish-born English essayist, playwright, and poet. His first play was *The Funeral* (1701) and his last, *The Conscious Lovers* (1722). He founded a periodical *The Tatler* (1709-11) and soon began collaborating with Joseph Addison. Together they founded the *Spectator* (1711-12). *The Tatler* and the *Spectator* contained their essays on theater, literature, and family life.

Steelworkers of America, United (USWA), large U.S. labor union affiliated with the American Federation of Labor and Congress of Industrial Organizations (AFL-CIO) and consisting mainly of workers in the steel, iron, metal, aluminum, and chemical industries. Founded in 1936, the USWA has since merged with 4 other unions. It has its headquarters in Pittsburgh, Pa., with local chapters throughout the United States and Canada.
See also: Labor movement.

Steen, Jan (c.1626-79), Dutch painter, a master of color and facial expressions. His almost 900 surviving works include jovial scenes of eating, drinking, and revelry, such as *St. Nicholas' Feast* and *As the Old Sing, the Young Pipe*; portraits; landscapes, such as *The Game of Skittles*; and classical and biblical scenes.

Steenbok, or steinbok, small African antelope belonging to the family Bovidae. It lives alone in wooded areas. A distinctive feature is its ability to obtain all the water it needs from the plants it eats. It stands about 21 in (53 cm) high and is reddish in color; the male has small, pointed horns.

Steeplechasing, horse-racing over a course with such obstacles as fences, hedges, and water. It originated in England as a race from one church steeple to another. The world's most famous steeplechase is the Grand National, first run in 1839 and held annually near Liverpool, England. U.S. steeplechases are normally held at racing tracks or hunts.

Steffens, Lincoln (1866-1936), U.S. writer, lecturer, and political critic. Identified with a group of journalists called muckrakers, he worked to expose the corrupt connection between government and private self-interest. He later developed an interest in revolutionary politics. He wrote numerous magazine articles for *McClure's Magazine, American Magazine,* and *Everybody's Magazine,* as well as his *Autobiography* (1931).
See also: Muckraker.

Stegosaurus *See:* Dinosaur.

Steichen, Edward (1879-1973), U.S. photographer known for his sharp, realistic portraits. He was a member of the Photo-Secession Group, founded (1902) by Alfred Steiglitz to advance the cause of photography as a fine art. An air force photographer during World War I (1914-18), he later became known for his fashion work and celebrity portraits. He directed the photography department of the Museum of Modern Art (1947-62) in New York City. For its popular 1955 exhibit "The Family of Man," he selected and assembled photographs of people from around the world.

Stein, Gertrude (1874-1946), U.S. writer who lived in Paris from 1903. Author of short stories, long narratives, critical essays, "cubist" poetry, and operas, her first important work was *Three Lives* (1909). Stein is best known for her experimental syntax and her influence on such figures as Pablo Picasso, Ernest Hemingway, Henri Matisse, and André Gide. These friendships are described in Stein's *The Autobiography of Alice B. Toklas* (1933).

Steinbeck, John (1902-68), U.S. author who came to the fore in the 1930s with his novels about poverty and social injustice. *The Grapes of Wrath* (1939), about Depression-era farm workers migrating from the Midwest's Dust Bowl to California, won a Pulitzer Prize. Other works include *Tortilla Flat* (1935), *Of Mice and Men* (1937), *Cannery Row* (1945), *East of Eden* (1952), and *The Winter of Our Discontent* (1961). He was awarded the 1962 Nobel Prize in literature.

Steinberger, Jack (1921-), U.S. physicist. Steinberger, Leon Lederman, and Melvin Schwartz won the 1988 Nobel Prize in physics for their work on the use of the subatomic particles known as neutrinos to study other subatomic particles, and their discovery of the muon neutrino. He worked at the University of California, Berkeley (1948-50), Columbia University (1950-71), and the European Laboratory for Particle Physics (1968-).
See also: Neutrino.

Steinbok *See:* Steenbok.

Steinem, Gloria (1934-), U.S feminist and writer. A founding editor of *New York* magazine and cofounder (1971) of the National Women's Political Caucus, she also founded (1972) and edited *Ms.* magazine. *Outrageous Acts and Everyday Rebellions* is a collection of her writings.

Steiner, Rudolf (1861-1925), Austrian founder of anthroposophy, an attempt to recapture spiritual realities ignored by modern man. He founded the Waldorf School movement and stressed music and drama as aids to self-discovery. Works include *The Philosophy of Spiritual Activity* (1922).

Steinmetz, Charles Proteus (1865-1923), German-born U.S. mathematician, electrical engineer, and politician. He is best known for his calculation of hysteresis loss (loss of efficiency from certain magnetic effects in alternating current). A Socialist, Steinmetz was forced to emigrate to the United States in 1889. He began his career as a researcher for General Electric Company in 1892. He also held U.S. political office as a Socialist.

Steinway, U.S. family of piano manufacturers. **Henry Engelhard Steinweg** (1797-1871), who changed his name to Steinway after emigrating from Germany to the United States in 1851, founded Steinway & Sons in 1853 in New York City. It was carried on by his sons, notably **Christian Friedrich Theodore** (1825-89) and **William** (1835-96).

Stella, Frank (1936-), U.S. painter. Stella developed the abstract style called minimalism in the 1960s, and he began using 3-dimensional canvases in the 1980s. His paintings are usually large with angular or curved shapes. Often the canvases themselves are irregularly shaped to conform to the shape of the image in the painting.

Stem, part of a plant from which the leaves and flowers sprout. Formed by the growing tip as it emerges from the seed after germination, it may divide repeatedly to produce branches and twigs. A stem may be very short, as in low-growing plants in which the leaves appear to sprout directly from the roots. In trees the stem is represented by the trunk, which may be over 100 ft (30 m) high. Stems are responsible for support and contain strengthening tissues, such as wood. They also carry food and water between the leaves and roots. Green stems carry out photosynthesis; modified stems, such as the tuber, act as food stores.

Stendhal (Marie Henri Beyle; 1783-1842), French pioneer of the psychological novel. *The Red and the Black* (1831) and *The Charterhouse of Parma* (1839) explore the search for happiness through love and political power, with minute analysis of the heroes' feelings. His treatment of the figure of the "outsider," his social criticism, and brilliant ironic prose style make him one of the greatest and most "modern" of French novelists.

Stengel, Casey (c.1890-1975), U.S. baseball manager. A popular and garrulous figure, he managed the Brooklyn Dodgers (1934-36), Boston Braves (1938-43), New York Yankees (1949-60), and New York Mets (1962-65).

Stengel led the Yankees to 7 World Series championships (1949-53, 56, 58) and was inducted to the National Baseball Hall of Fame in 1966.

Stephen, name of 9 popes. **Stephen I** (reigned 254-57), who died during Emperor Valerian's persecutions, defended the validity of the baptism of heretics, a stance St. Cyprian of Carthage denounced. **Stephen II** (reigned 752-57) was supported by Pepin the Short in his defeat of the Lombards. The Papal States were founded with land gifts from Pepin. Controversy over papal elections dominated the reign (768-72) of **Stephen III**. **Stephen IV** (reigned 816-17) crowned Louis I emperor (establishing a prerogative of the papacy) and strengthened links with the Franks. **Stephen VI** (reigned 896-97) declared void the reign of his predecessor, Formosus, but was himself imprisoned and strangled. His rule marked the papacy's lowest point. **Stephen IX** (b.1000; reigned 1057-58) continued the reforms of Leo IX, enforcing priestly celibacy and attacking simony. But he failed to stop the rift between the Eastern and Western churches.

Stephen (c.1097-1154), king of England (1135-54). A nephew of Henry I, he was briefly supplanted (1141) by Matilda, Henry's daughter. Though a just and generous ruler, he was not strong enough to govern the warring factions of his realm.

Stephens, Alexander Hamilton (1812-83), vice president of the Confederate States of America (1861-65). A representative from Georgia (1843-59), he opposed secession but stayed loyal to his state in the Civil War. He served in Congress (1873-82) and as governor of Georgia (1882-83).
See also: United Kingdom.

Stephenson, British family of inventors and railroad engineers. **George** (1781-1848) first worked on stationary steam engines. His first locomotive, the Blucher, took to the rails in 1814; it traveled at 4 mph (6.5 kmph). In 1825 his Locomotion carried 450 people at a rate of 15 mph (25 kmph), and the modern railroad was born. In 1829 the Rocket ran the 40 mi (65 km) of his new Manchester-Liverpool line at speeds up to 30 mph (48 kmph). His only son, **Robert** (1803-59), is best known as a bridge builder, notably for the tubular bridges over the Menai Straits, North Wales (1850), and the St. Lawrence River at Montreal, Canada (1859).

Steppe, extensive temperate grasslands of Europe and Asia (equivalent to the North American prairies and South American pampas). They extend from southwest Siberia to the lower reaches of the Danube River.

Stereoscope, optical instrument that stimulates binocular vision by presenting slightly different pictures to the 2 eyes so that an apparently 3-dimensional image is produced.

Stereotyping, in printing, process in which a metal plate is made from a mold of typeface or art. The same plate is then used to print many pages. Use of this method speeds up the printing process and lowers its cost. Although largely replaced in the United States by offset lithography, stereotyping is still used in other parts of the world.
See also: Printing.

Sterility, condition of being incapable of producing offspring; freedom from germs. In human beings, the inability to reproduce can have several causes, including defects in the reproductive organs, hormonal imbalance, and surgical sterilization.

Sterilization, surgical procedure designed to prevent conception. In females, the fallopian tubes are cut and tied to prevent eggs reaching the womb, thus providing permanent contraception. The procedure is essentially irreversible. In males, sterilization may be achieved by vasectomy, an operation in which the vas deferens on each side is tied off and cut to prevent sperm from reaching the seminal vesicles. Sterilization is also the name of the process of treating medical equipment to ensure that it is not contaminated by bacteria and other microorganisms. Metal and linen objects are often sterilized by heat. Chemical disinfection is also used, and plastic equipment is exposed to gamma rays.

Stern, Isaac (1920-), U.S. violinist. A child prodigy born in the USSR, he came to the United States as a baby, where he studied and made his debut in 1931 in San Francisco. A noted virtuoso, he has recorded extensively and concertized worldwide.

Sternberg, Joseph von (1891-1969), Austrian-born German-U.S. film director. He is most famous for the films he made with Marlene Dietrich, notably *The Blue Angel* (1930), *Morocco* (1930), and *Shanghai Express* (1932).

Sterne, Laurence (1713-68), British clergyman who became known as a novelist, largely because of the popularity of his book *The Life and Opinions of Tristram Shandy, Gentleman* (1760-67). In it, Sterne was thought to anticipate the work of post-Freudian stream-of-consciousness writers. Sterne drew on the ideas of philosopher John Locke to give form to this impressionistic, unconventionally structured novel about life as seen through the eyes of a young boy. Sterne also wrote a work of satire and a book about his experiences and reflections while traveling.

Steroid, hormone produced in the body from cholesterol, mainly by the adrenal glands. Cortisol is the main glucocorticoid (steroids that regulate glucose metabolism) and aldosterone, the main mineralocorticoid (regulating salt, potassium, and water balance). Increased amounts of cortisol are secreted during times of stress, such as shock, surgery, and severe infection. Sterols, mainly of the glucocorticoid type, are also given in doses above normal hormone levels to obtain other effects, e.g., the suppression of inflammation, allergy, and immunity. High-dose systemic steroids may have adverse effects if used for long periods; they may cause acne, osteoporosis, hypertension, fluid retention, altered facial appearance, and growth retardation in children.
See also: Hormone.

Stethoscope, instrument devised (1819) by René T. H. Laënnec (1781-1826) for listening to sounds within the body, especially those from the heart, lungs, abdomen, and blood vessels.

Stettin *See:* Szczecin.

Stettinius, Edward Riley, Jr. (1900-49), U.S. businessperson and politician. By age 35, he was chairman (1935-39) of the finance committee of the U.S. Steel Corp. and president at 39 (1939). In government he was lend-lease administrator (1941-43), undersecretary and then secretary of state (1943-45), and a founder-delegate and U.S. representative to the UN (1945-46).

Steuben, Friedrich Wilhelm Augustin, Baron von (1730-94), Prussian soldier who helped train the Continental army. Arriving in America in 1777 with an introduction from Benjamin Franklin, he was appointed inspector general of the army by Congress in 1778. He organized Washington's troops at Valley Forge into an effective fighting force, which was apparent at the Battle of Monmouth (1778) and siege of Yorktown (1780).
See also: Revolutionary War in America.

Stevens, U.S. family of inventors and engineers. **John** (1749-1838) built the first steamboat with a screw propeller (1802) and the first seagoing steamboat (1809). He also built the first U.S. steam locomotive (1825). His son **Robert Livingston** (1787-1856) invented the inverted T-rail still used in modern railroads (1830). Another son, **Edwin Augustus** (1795-1868), also made contributions to railroad technology.
See also: Railroad.

Stevens, John Paul (1920-), U.S. jurist. He served on the U.S. Court of Appeals and then, by appointment of President Gerald Ford, on the U.S. Supreme Court as an associate justice (1975-).
See also: Supreme Court of the United States.

Stevens, Thaddeus (1792-1868), militant member of the U.S. House of Representatives (1849-53, 1859-68) from Pennsylvania, and an aggressive opponent of slavery. After the Civil War he supported radical measures, such as the confiscation and redistribution of Southern planters' lands, and proposed the Fourteenth Amendment, guaranteeing civil rights. In 1867 he headed the committee to impeach President Andrew Johnson.

Stevens, Wallace (1879-1955), U.S. poet. Working for a Connecticut insurance company, he achieved wide literary recognition with the 1955 Pulitzer Prize for his *Collected Poems*. Rich in imagery and vocabulary, his verse explores the use of imagination to give meaning to life.

Stevenson, family of U.S. Democratic politicians. **Adlai Ewing** (1835-1914) was elected U.S. vice president (1893-97). His grandson **Adlai Ewing** (1900-65) was elected governor of Illinois (1949-53). He was chosen as his party's presidential candidate in 1952 and 1956 but lost to Dwight D. Eisenhower. His positions on halting the arms race and promoting the economies of Africa and Asia were unpopular. He lost the 1960 nomination to John F. Kennedy. From 1961 until his death he was U.S. ambassador to the UN. His son **Adlai Ewing III** (1930-) was elected from Illinois to the U.S. Senate (1970-81) and ran unsuccessfully for governor in 1982 and 1986.

Stevenson, Robert Louis (1850-94), Scottish author, essayist, and poet who was one of the most successful writers of his day. Critically acclaimed for his exceptional ability as a prose stylist, his novels of adventure and romance—among them *Treasure Island* (1883) and *The Strange Case of Dr. Jekyll and Mr. Hyde* (1886)—are known worldwide. He also wrote a popular book of children's poems, *A Child's Garden of Verses* (1885).

Steward, Julian Haynes (1902-72), U.S. anthropologist. A major exponent of cultural evolution, he was among the first anthropologists to emphasize ecology as a determinant of culture. He edited the *Handbook of South American Indians* (7 vol., 1946-59) and wrote *The Theory of Culture Change* (1955).
See also: Anthropology.

Stewart, James (1908-97), U.S. popular screen actor acclaimed for his sympathetic portrayals of the American common man. He was known for his lanky build, midwestern drawl, and folksy charm. Stewart starred in several films directed by such cinematic pioneers as Frank Capra and Alfred Hitchcock. Among his most well-known films are *It's a Wonderful Life* (1946) and *Rear Window* (1954). In 1985 he received an Academy Award for his complete works.

Stewart, Potter (1915-85), associate justice of the U.S. Supreme Court (1958-81). Appointed by President Dwight D. Eisenhower, he held a moderate point of view and often cast a "swing" vote.
See also: Supreme Court of the United States.

Stibnite *See:* Antimony.

Stickleback, small fish with spines on its back that lives in fresh and salt waters of the Northern Hemisphere. There are sticklebacks with 3, 4, and 10 spines and the marine stickleback has 15. Sticklebacks are very abundant. They feed on small animals. The male builds a nest of waterweed and entices several females to lay their eggs in it. He stays with the young and drives away enemies.

Stickseed, North American wild plant belonging to the borage family. Its name derives from the stickiness of its fruit, which adheres to clothing and animal fur. It has small white, lavender, or blue flowers.

Stieglitz, Alfred (1864-1946), U.S. photographer and founder of Photo-Secession (1902), an organization dedicated to the promotion of photography as a fine art. His magazine *Camera Work* (first published in 1903) as well as his gallery "291" helped introduce the work of many avante-garde artists, critics, and photographers. His wife was the painter Georgia O'Keeffe, a frequent subject of his photographic compositions.
See also: Photography.

Still, Clyfford (1904-80), one of the first abstract expressionist painters in the United States, known for his dramatic use of color. He abandoned his landscape paintings in the late 1940s and began experimenting with large jagged shapes and abstract themes. Still significantly influenced the work of younger abstract painters.
See also: Abstract expressionism.

Stillwater (pop. 12,290), historic city in Minnesota, located on the boundary between Minnesota and Wisconsin and known as the "birthplace of Minne-

sota." Founded in 1839, it was one of the earliest settlements in the state and the site of a convention that led to the formation of Minnesota territory. Once a major lumbering center, its chief industries are dairy processing and manufacturing.
See also: Minnesota.

Stilt, bird belonging to the stilt and avocet family, commonly found in warm pond areas throughout the world. It is known for its long, thin legs and bill. It measures from 14-18 in (35-45 cm) and usually has black and white feathers and pink legs. It wades in the water and feeds on the small creatures it finds there.

Stilwell, Joseph Warren (1883-1946), U.S. commander of the Allied forces in the Far East in World War II, sometimes referred to as "Vinegar Joe" because of his acerbic comments. Driven back to India by the Japanese in 1942, he rebuilt his forces and counterattacked through Burma to China (1943-4). He was recalled in 1944 after disagreeing with Chiang Kai-shek, under whom he was serving. An excellent history of his era is recounted in *Stilwell and the American Experience in China* (1971) by the historian Barbara Tuchman.
See also: World War II.

Stimson, Henry Lewis (1867-1950), U.S. politician, author of the Stimson Doctrine. As secretary of state (1929-33), he declared at the time of Japan's invasion of Manchuria that the United States would not recognize any territorial changes that impaired U.S. treaty rights or were brought about by force. As secretary of war (1940-45), he advocated development and use of the atomic bomb.

Stimulant, drug that stimulates an organ. Nervous system stimulants range from amphetamines and hallucinogenic drugs to drugs liable to induce convulsions. Cardiac stimulants such as digitalis and adrenaline are used in cardiac failure and resuscitation, respectively. Bowel stimulants have a laxative effect. Womb stimulants (oxytocin and ergometrine) are used in obstetrics to induce labor and prevent postpartum hemorrhage.
See also: Drug.

Stingray, one of 100 species of flat, disk-shaped fish belonging to the family Dasyatidae. On its tail are poisonous spines that can cause serious injury to swimmers. Although some varieties can be found in rivers, most live in saltwater. Stingrays vary in size; the largest can measure up to 14 ft (4 m).

Stink bug, shield-shaped insect belonging to the stink bug family, known for the unpleasant odor it emits when disturbed. It feeds on plants and insects. Some varieties are pests that destroy cabbage and rice crops and cause damage to certain kinds of garden plants.

Stirling engine, type of external-combustion engine invented in Scotland by the Rev. Robert Stirling in 1816. Long in disuse, the Stirling engine has recently been reinvestigated as a possible substitute for the gasoline engine, but so far has not proved practical. Different versions of the Stirling engine exist, but all involve a gas (usually air) circulating in a closed system of cylinders and pistons and deriving energy from an external source of heat.

Stoat *See:* Ermine.

Stock, group of about 50 varieties of fragrant garden flowers belonging to the family Cruciferae. Common types are the Virginia stock, the Grecian stock, and the Brampton, or common, stock. They are variously red, white, lilac, or yellow in color.

Stock, capital, ownership in a corporation. A corporation allows stockholders to purchase stock certificates to represent shares of the corporation they own. Stocks can be sold by the stockholders, often for a profit. The value of the stock fluctuates according to such factors as the success of the corporation or the general state of the economy. There are various kinds of stock; a newly formed corporation decides which kinds of stock will be issued.

Stock exchange, auction for the sale and exchange of stock, which is a certificate of ownership in a corporation. Stock markets exist in all major industrial states; stock market proceedings are published in most large daily newspapers. The price of each stock is determined each hour of the trading day, according to the laws of supply and demand. Factors that influence stock prices include the state of the economy, the public confidence in the economy, the amount of profit a company has made or is predicted to make, the rate of a company's growth or decline, and the market for a particular product.

Stocks bought and sold most actively are usually listed on the New York Stock Exchange (NYSE) in New York City. This market, established in 1792, is the leading exchange in the United States. Housed in a large building on Wall Street, the NYSE trades more than 22,000 common and preferred stocks and has a membership of 1,567, most of whom represent brokerage houses. The exchange serves as a place where such brokers can buy and sell stock for their clients, who pay them a commission. Information on stock market transactions and prices are transmitted by computer to every brokerage office in the nation.

In addition to the NYSE there are 12 other exchanges in the United States. The second largest is the American Stock Exchange (AMEX), also in New York City. Other important exchanges include the Midwest Stock Exchange in Chicago and the Pacific Exchange in San Francisco and Los Angeles. The largest securities market in the world is the over-the-counter (OTC) market, which exists primarily as a communications network. It is subject to the rules and regulations of the National Association of Security Dealers, Inc., which has the power to expel dishonest companies or dealers, or corporations that are insolvent.

Stockhausen, Karlheinz (1928-), German composer and theorist. An experimenter with a variety of avant-garde musical techniques, including electronic, 12-tone, and aleatory music, he studied with Frank Martin, Olivier Messiaen, and Darius Milhaud, and was much influenced by Anton Webern. He has produced works like *Gruppen* (1959), in which 3 orchestras play "groups" of sounds against each other, and the electronic *Kontakte* (1959-60).

Stockholm (pop. 693,100), capital of Sweden, located on a network of islands on the country's eastern coast. It is Sweden's major commercial, industrial, cultural, and financial center, and an important port. Chief industries are machinery, paper and print, shipbuilding, chemicals, and foodstuffs. Founded in the 13th century, it was long dominated by the Hanseatic League. It became the capital in 1634.
See also: Sweden.

Stock market crash of 1929 *See:* Great Depression.

Stock ticker, teletype device for recording the buying and selling of stock. The machine prints transactions on a continuous strip of tape, with symbols to refer to the names of the corporations. First used by the New York Stock Exchange in 1867, the stock ticker became widely used during the early 20th century. It is now almost obsolete, having been largely replaced by electronic devices.

Stockton, Richard (1730-81), member of the Continental Congress and one of the signers of the Declaration of Independence. A lawyer from New Jersey, he was appointed chief justice of his state's Supreme Court in 1776. Soon after, he was captured and imprisoned by the British.

Stoicism, ancient Greek school of philosophy founded by Zeno of Citium, who taught in a stoa (portico) in Athens c.300 B.C. The Stoics believed that man should live rationally and in harmony with nature, and that virtue is the only good. In performing his duty the virtuous man should be indifferent to pleasure and misfortune, thus rising above the effects of chance and achieving spiritual freedom and conformity with the divine reason controlling all nature. Famous Stoics include Seneca, Epictetus, and Marcus Aurelius.
See also: Zeno of Citium.

Stoke-on-Trent (pop. 252,900), city in England known for its pottery, located on the River Trent. Created in 1910 by the confederation of 5 ceramic-producing towns called The Potteries, it achieved status as a city in 1925. It still exists as the pottery center of England. Its other industries include coal mining and steel and iron production.

Stoker, Bram (1847-1912), British author who won notoriety for his book *Dracula* (1897), a tale of horror about a Transylvanian vampire with supernatural abilities. He wrote a sequel, *Dracula's Guest* (1927), as well as other novels. Stoker spent many years as the manager and companion of actor Sir Henry Irving.

Stokes, Carl Burton (1927-), mayor of Cleveland (1967-71) and first African-American mayor of a large U.S. city. He became a lawyer in 1957 and served for 3 terms in the Ohio House of Representatives. After running unsuccessfully as an Independent, he won the mayoral election as a Democrat in 1967. Stokes was reelected in 1969.

Stokowski, Leopold (Boleslawowicz Stanislaw Antoni; 1882-1977), U.S. conductor. He gained his early reputation as musical director of the Philadelphia Orchestra (1912-36), which he conducted in recording the soundtrack for Walt Disney's *Fantasia* (1940). He was noted for innovative orchestrations and championing modern music in his repertoire.

Stol *See:* V/STOL.

Stomach, large organ of the digestive system. It receives food from the esophagus and mixes it with hydrochloric acid and the stomach enzymes; fats are partially emulsified. After some time, the pyloric sphincter relaxes and food enters the duodenum and the rest of the gastrointestinal tract.
See also: Digestive system.

Stone, Edward Durell (1902-78), U.S. architect whose works include the U.S. pavilion for the Brussels World's Fair (1958), the U.S. Embassy in Delhi (1958), and the Kennedy Center for the Performing Arts in Washington, D.C. (1971).
See also: Architecture.

Stone Age, stage of earliest human cultural development, preceding the Bronze Age and Iron Age. It is characterized by the nearly exclusive use of stone tools and weapons and is divided into 3 periods. The Paleolithic period, or Old Stone Age, began with the emergence of *Homo sapiens*. These nomadic hunters and gatherers lived in caves, used fire, and made tools of chipped stone (some relics have been dated at 2.5 million years old). By the end of this period, known as the Upper Paleolithic, it is believed hunting was communal, shelter was manmade, and belief in the supernatural, or magic, had been born. The Mesolithic period, or Middle Stone Age, was confined exclusively to northeastern Europe where, between 10,000 B.C. and 3000 B.C., various peoples enjoyed a culture that showed similarities with those of both the Paleolithic and Neolithic periods. There were the beginnings of settled communities and domesticated plants and animals; hunting was expanded to include use of the bow; and the making of pottery was introduced. The Neolithic, or New Stone Age, began in Asia c.8000 B.C. and spread through Europe between 6000 B.C. and 2000 B.C.; it was signaled by the development of agriculture, with a consequent increase in the stability of the population and hence elaboration of the social structure. The tools of this period were of polished stone. In addition to farming, men also worked mines. The Neolithic period merged slowly into the Early Bronze Age.

Stone, Harlan Fiske (1872-1946), U.S. jurist. Appointed attorney general (1924) to restore confidence in the scandal-ridden Justice Department, he became associate justice (1925-41) and chief justice (1941-46) of the U.S. Supreme Court. He was noted for his dissenting opinions, many supporting New Deal legislation.
See also: Supreme Court of the United States.

Stone, Lucy (1818-93), U.S. reformer and feminist. A fervent abolitionist, she helped to found the American Woman Suffrage Association (1869) and edited its magazine, *Woman's Journal* (1870-93).
See also: Woman suffrage.

Stone, Oliver (1946-), U.S. film director and screenwriter. He won an Academy Award for direction of *Platoon* (1987), for which he also wrote the screenplay, based on his own experiences serving in the Vietnam war. He also directed *Wall Street* (1987), *Born on the Fourth of July* (1989), *JFK* (1991), *The Doors* (1991), *Heaven and Earth* (1993), *Natural Born Killers* (1994), and *Nixon* (1995).

Stone, Thomas (1743-87), Maryland lawyer and one of the signers of the Declaration of Independence. Although an advocate of colonial independence, he favored a peaceful settlement to America's conflicts with Britain. He died during his third term in the Maryland Senate.

Stonechat (*Saxicola torquata*), small bird of the thrush subfamily native to the Eastern Hemisphere, named for the percussive sound of its call. The male is black and chestnut in color, the female somewhat duller. The bird nests on the ground and feeds on insects and seeds.

Stonefly, any of approximately 1,550 species of insects of the order Plecoptera. Stoneflies range in length from 0.25 in (6 mm) to 2.5 in (60 mm). Their gray, black, or brown coloration blends with their environment. Although they have 2 pairs of wings, they do not fly well, and are often found on rocks close to the water. Females drop their eggs—up to 6,000 at a time—into small bodies of water. Fish eat many of them before they have a chance to develop into stonefly nymphs, which have gills and live in the water for 1 to 4 years before becoming adults and developing wings.

Stonehenge, ruins of a megalithic monument, dating from the Stone Age and early Bronze Age, on Salisbury Plain, in southern England. Its most noticeable features are concentric rings of stones surrounding a horseshoe of upright stones, and a solitary vertical stone, the Heel Stone, to the northeast. Stonehenge was built between 1900 B.C. and 1400 B.C. in 3 distinct phases. It appears to have been both a religious center and an astronomical observatory.

Stone Mountain, granite dome, 650 ft (198 m), near Atlanta, Ga. A portion of the north face has been sculpted as a memorial to the heroes of the Confederacy. It is part of Stone Mountain Memorial Park.

Stoneware, durable kind of pottery with a variety of industrial and aesthetic applications. Because it is nonporous, it is used to store food and chemicals and to create art objects, such as statues. It is produced by subjecting a mixture of clays to temperatures as high as 2,200°F (1,200°C). The art of making stoneware was developed in China in the 5th century. The technique achieved popularity throughout Europe and was widely used by the early American colonists.
See also: Pottery and porcelain.

Stoppard, Tom (1937-), English playwright best known for *Rosencrantz and Guildenstern Are Dead* (1966), an existentialist drama centering on 2 minor characters from Shakespeare's *Hamlet*. Critics admire his scintillating dialogue in plays such as *Travesties* (1974) and *Hapgood* (1988).

Storey, David (1933-), English playwright and novelist. *This Sporting Life*, his novel (1960) and film (1963), and the play *The Changing Room*

(1971), his best-known works, are based on his years as a professional rugby player.

Stork, large, heavily built bird, family Ciconiiodae, with long legs and neck, a long, stout bill, and usually black-and-white plumage. The stork's long legs and slightly webbed feet are adaptations for wading in shallow water, where it feeds on freshwater animals and large insects. Storks tend to be gregarious. They mainly live in the tropics, though some spend part of the year in temperate zones.

Story, Joseph (1779-1845), associate Supreme Court justice (1812-45). He was the author of an extensive series of essays that significantly influenced legal thought in the United States and in other parts of the world. He worked with Chief Justice John Marshall to extend the powers of the federal government under the Constitution.
See also: Marshall, John; Supreme Court of the United States.

Storytelling, folk art practiced throughout the ages whose forms include the reciting of folk tales, myths, legends, epics, and fables. Some stories are handed down through the generations; others are created by an author. Storytelling has been used to transmit information about culture and history, explain the nature of existence, expand the imagination, entertain, and reinforce moral values. The earliest forms of storytelling combined narrative, music, and dance. Since the 1970s there has been a resurgence of interest in the art of storytelling.

Stoss, Veit (1440?-1533), influential German sculptor and wood carver who created dramatic, detailed religious statues in the late Gothic style. His most ambitious work, a carved and painted altar depicting the life of Mary, is located in the Church of St. Mary's in Krakow, Poland; it measures over 42 ft (13 m) high and 36 ft (11 m) wide.

Stowe, Harriet Beecher (1811-96), U.S. writer, author of the antislavery novel *Uncle Tom's Cabin* (1852). From her home in Cincinnati, Ohio, she learned about slavery in nearby Kentucky. Her other books include the documentary *Key to Uncle Tom's Cabin* (1853) and the novels *Dred: A Tale of the Great Dismal Swamp* (1856) and *The Minister's Wooing* (1859). She was also committed to the temperance and woman suffrage movements.
See also: Abolitionism.

Strabismus, condition in which the 2 eyes do not see the identical image simultaneously; usually one eye is directed in a slightly different direction from the other. Most often this condition is the result of an eye muscle weakness (eye movement is controlled by 6 different muscles); it can also come from brain and nerve involvement. Forms of strabismus include heterotropia (squinting); esotropia (cross-eyes), where one or both eyes look inward; exotropia (walleyes), where one eye looks outward; and diplopia (double vision).

Strabo (63 B.C.?-A.D. 24?), ancient Greek geographer and historian known for his massive *Geographical Sketches*, a detailed description of the geography of the known world of his day. His work is a chief source of ancient

knowledge on people and places in Europe, Asia, and Africa. He also wrote a 47-volume work, *Historical Sketches,* which has not been recovered.
See also: Geography.

Strachey, Lytton (1880-1932), English critic and biographer who belonged to the famed circle of artists and intellectuals known as the Bloomsbury group in London. He revolutionized biographical writing with his imaginative, irreverent, and psychologically astute sketches of famous Victorian figures. He is best known for his biographies *Eminent Victorians* (1918) and *Queen Victoria* (1921).
See also: Bloomsbury group.

Stradivari, or **Stradivarius, Antonio** (1644-1737), Italian violin maker, most famous of a group of fine craftspeople who worked in Cremona. Stradivarius violins, violas, and cellos are highly prized.

Strait, narrow water channel that joins 2 larger bodies of water, such as an ocean or a sea. Major straits include the Bosporous Strait, the Strait of Magellan, and the Strait of Gibraltar. Considered strategically advantageous, they have been the focus of many of history's great battles.

Strand, Paul (1890-1976), U.S. photographer whose work helped raise photography to an art. He was best known for his photographs of modern machinery and of scenes of life in Manhattan. Later on in his life, Strand took nature photographs and worked a motion pictures.
See also: Photography.

Strasbourg (pop. 255,900), commercial and industrial city in northeastern France, famed for its Gothic cathedral. A major river port linked with the Rhine and the Rhône, it has metallurgical, petroleum, heavy-machinery, and food-processing industries. Seat of the Council of Europe, it was a free imperial city until the French seized it in 1681. Strasbourg was under German rule from 1871 to 1919.

Strassmann, Fritz (1902-), German physical chemist who, with Otto Hahn, split the uranium atom (1938). He briefly joined the staff at the Kaiser Wilhelm Institute for Chemistry, taught inorganic and nuclear chemistry at the University of Mainz, and became the head of the Max Planck Institute for Chemistry. In 1966 the U.S. Atomic Energy Commission presented him, Hahn, and Lise Meitner with the Fermi Award.
See also: Chemistry; Uranium.

Strategic Air Command (SAC), main U.S. nuclear striking force, containing U.S. land-based ballistic missiles and long-range bombers. SAC is linked to U.S. warning systems and is a specified command under the Defense Department.
See also: Nuclear weapon.

Strategic Arms Limitation Talks (SALT), negotiations between the United States and the USSR aimed at preventing the expansion of strategic weapons in both countries. Salt I (1969-72) achieved an antiballistic missile treaty and an interim agreement on some offensive nuclear weapons. Salt II was initiated in 1972. A treaty was signed in 1979, but ratification by the U.S. Senate was shelved (1980) after the USSR invaded Afghanistan. In 1982 the United States and USSR initiated a new series of negotiations called the Strategic Arms Reduction Talks (START). A treaty to eliminate intermediate-range nuclear weapons was signed in 1987 by Pres. Ronald Reagan and Soviet Premier Mikhail Gorbachev. The treaty was ratified by the U.S. Senate and the Soviet Presidium in 1988.

Strategic Defense Initiative (SDI), controversial program developed by the U.S. government in 1983 to develop a space-based shield against nuclear missile attack. Commonly called "Star Wars," the program was to rely on satellites and lasers to destroy incoming missiles. Its opponents argued that it was impractical and costly. Funding for research on the project continues, although at a reduced rate. Part of the program has been replaced by GPALS, Global Protection Against Limited Strikes.

Strategic Services, Office of (OSS), U.S. government organization founded during World War II (1942) to gather intelligence. It was headed by William J. Donovan, working under the authority of the Joint Chiefs of Staff. With the end of the war the agency was dismantled, its tasks being distributed to the War Department and the Department of State. In 1947 the Central Intelligence Agency (CIA) became the successor to the OSS.
See also: Central Intelligence Agency (CIA).

Stratemeyer, Edward (1862-1930), U.S. writer of popular children's literature. His Stratemeyer Syndicate was established in New York City in 1906 with a large staff of writers to develop new productions. The author of more than 160 books (many published under other names), Stratemeyer commonly invented teenage heroes and heroines in adventure-filled tales, including the stories of the Hardy Boys ("Franklin W. Dixon") and the Nancy Drew books ("Carolyn Keene").

Stratford-upon-Avon (pop. 104,600), market town in west-central England, home of William Shakespeare. A tourist mecca, it contains his birthplace (now a museum), his tomb, and the riverside theater where the Royal Shakespeare Company performs.
See also: England.

Stratosphere, layer of the atmosphere that extends upward from the tropopause (upper level of the troposphere) to approximately 18 mi (29 km) above the earth's surface. Its upper level is called the stratopause, which includes the ozone layer.
See also: Atmosphere.

Stratus *See:* Cloud.

Straus, Oscar (1870-1954), Austrian composer of about 50 operettas, notably *A Waltz Dream* (1907; film, 1926) and *The Chocolate Soldier* (1908; film, 1941), performed internationally. In the 1930s he wrote a half-dozen Hollywood film scores.

Strauss, Viennese composers, father and son. **Johann, the Elder** (1804-49), achieved immense popularity and established the distinctive light style of the Viennese waltz. His son, **Johann, the Younger** (1825-99), wrote many favorites, including the waltzes *The Blue Danube* (1866) and *Tales from the Vienna Woods* (1868), and the operetta *Die Fledermaus* (1873).

Strauss, Levi (1829-1902), German-born U.S. clothing manufacturer, founder of Levi Strauss & Co. (1853). The company began making denim work clothes in 1874, and was the world's first manufacturer of denim jeans.

Strauss, Richard (1864-1949), German composer and conductor, the last of the great Romantic composers. He leapt to fame with the tone poem *Don Juan* (1888). Other symphonic poems include *Till Eulenspiegel's Merry Pranks* (1895), *Thus Spake Zarathustra* (1896), *Don Quixote* (1898), and *A Hero's Life* (1898). After 1900 he concentrated on vocal music, and with Hugo von Hofmannsthal as librettist, produced brilliantly scored and popular operas, including *Salome* (1905), *Elektra* (1909), *Der Rosenkavalier* (1911), and *Die Frau ohne Schatten* (1919).

Stravinsky, Igor (1882-1971), Russian-born U.S. composer. He caused a sensation with his scores for the ballets *The Firebird* (1910), *Petrouchka* (1911), and *The Rite of Spring* (1913). Living in France from 1920, he adopted an austere neoclassical style, as in *Symphonies of Wind Instruments* (1920), the opera *Oedipus Rex* (1927), and *Symphony of Psalms* (1930). As a U.S. resident after 1939, he wrote many works, including *Symphony in Three Movements* (1945) and the opera *The Rakes' Progress* (1951). He adopted 12-tone composition for such late pieces as *Agon* (1957) and *Threni* (1958).

Straw, dried stalks of several kinds of grain, including wheat, barley, oats, rye, and buckwheat. Straw is employed on farms for litter or bedding. It can also be used as livestock feed although it is inferior to hay in feeding value. Straw forms an important ingredient of farmyard manure and garden composts. In some parts of the world, houses are still thatched with straw.

Strawberry, fruit-bearing plant of the genus *Fragaria*, native to the Americas, Europe, and Asia. Strawberries have been cultivated locally for many centuries; most modern varieties originated in crosses between New World species.

Strawflower, any of various tall annual plants, originally grown in Australia, particularly the *Helichrysum bracteatum*, which measures up to 3 ft (91 cm). This plant produces a variously colored, paperlike flower that is commonly dried and used in winter bouquets.

Streamlining, process of contouring a body to minimize its drag as it travels through a fluid, whether liquid or gas. At subsonic speeds turbulent flow is minimized by using a rounded shape in the front of the body and tapering to a point in the rear. At supersonic speeds a different shape is needed, thin and pointed at both ends.
See also: Aerodynamics.

Stream of consciousness, literary technique in which a character's thoughts are presented in the jumbled, nonsequential manner of real life, apparently without the author imposing any order on them. Its best-known exponents are Marcel Proust, James Joyce, and Virginia Woolf.

Streep, Meryl (Mary Louise Streep; 1949-), U.S. actress. Streep made her New York stage debut in 1975. She has appeared in many successful films, including *The Deer Hunter* (1978), *Kramer vs. Kramer* (1979; Academy Award, best supporting actress), *Sophie's Choice* (1982; Academy Award, best actress), *Silkwood* (1983), *Out of Africa* (1985), *A Cry in the Dark* (1988), *House of the Spirits* (1992), *The River Wild* (1994), and *The Bridges of Madison County* (1995).

Street, public road in a town or city. A street within an urban area usually has a sidewalk and buildings on one or both sides. Streets are part of a network of thoroughfares that include roads, highways, and expressways connecting communities and cities. Most modern streets are paved with tar or asphalt mixed with sand and crushed stone, although some may be paved with cobblestones, bricks, or concrete.

Streetcar, passenger vehicle that rides on rails laid in the pavements of city streets. Horse-drawn streetcars (horsecars) were first used in New York City in 1852. Electrified streetcars (trolley cars), developed in 1888, drew power from overhead lines by means of a trolley, a device consisting of a pole attached to a wheel that ran along the lines. Although internal combustion buses replaced U.S. streetcars during the mid-1900s, the use of streetcars may be on the increase because they are more energy-efficient and less polluting.

Strep throat, infection affecting the throat and tonsils. Its symptoms include fever and a reddening and swelling of the tonsils. The infection is caused by bacteria called *streptococci*, treatable with penicillin. Left untreated, the bacteria may spread from the throat to other parts of the body, such as the lungs, nose, and ears, causing greater health problems.

Streptococcus, any of a genus of bacteria responsible for many common infections, including sore throat, tonsilitis, scarlet fever, and other ailments. Penicillin is the antibiotic of choice.

Streptomycin, strong antibiotic acquired from a fungus that lives in soil. Streptomycin has the ability to hinder bacteria's protein-creating process. Its discovery in 1943 led to its widespread use to treat infectious diseases, such as tuberculosis, pneumonia, typhoid fever, and spinal meningitis. However, it was found that with continued use, streptomycin loses its effectiveness and some bacteria become resistant to it. Streptomycin today has been replaced by more powerful antibiotics.
See also: Antibiotic; Waksman, Selman Abraham.

Stress, in medicine, physical, chemical, or emotional factor that causes tension, whether physical or mental, and may result in disease or malfunction.

Strike, cessation of work by a group of employees to achieve certain goals. Reasons for a strike may include demands for higher wages, better working conditions, shorter work hours, and more benefits. Trade unions may play a role in strikes. Workers may strike to force the employer to recognize a certain union as their bargaining representative. Strikes are intended to create a financial loss for the company in goods produced or services rendered, thus prompting earnest negotiations. The first nationwide strike in the United States occurred in 1877, by railroad workers. As organized labor grew stronger in the late 19th century and strikes occurred more frequently, employers sometimes responded with harassment, engaging police or armed guards to disperse striking workers or to protect strike breakers. In Europe strikes involving all the workers of a nation or region are common.

Strindberg, Johan August (1849-1912), Swedish playwright and novelist, widely considered the leading author in the Swedish language. His biting, pessimistic plays, such as *Master Olof* (1873), *The Father* (1887), and *Miss Julie* (1888), have made a deep mark on modern drama. His novel *The Red Room* (1879), about injustice and hypocrisy, won international acclaim. Later plays, such as *The Ghost Sonata* (1907), combine dream sequences with Swedenborgian religious mysticism.

Stringed instruments, musical instruments whose sound is produced by vibrating strings or wires, the pitch being controlled by their length and tension. In the balalaika, banjo, guitar, harp, lute, mandolin, sitar, ukulele, and zither, the vibration is produced by plucking with the fingers or a plectrum. The strings of the dulcimer are struck with 2 small, light hammers. In the keyboard instruments—clavichord, harpsichord, piano, spinet, virginal—the strings are either plucked or struck by hammers operated by depressing the keys. The violin, viola, cello, and bass are played with a horsehair bow, which is drawn across the strings, or the strings are plucked.

Strip mining, technique used where ore deposits, such as coal, lie close enough to the surface to be uncovered merely by removal of the overlying material.

Stroessner, Alfredo (1912-), president of Paraguay (1954-89). An army commander, he took power in a coup and established a totalitarian dictatorship that proved one of Latin America's most stable. He was ousted in a coup in 1989 during his eighth term as president.

Stroheim, Erich von (1885-1957), German-born U.S. film director. Working under D. W. Griffith, Stroheim became known for his realism, careful construction, and attention to detail, as in *Greed* (1924) and *The Wedding March* (1928), in which he also acted. Other distinguished screen performances were in *Grand Illusion* (1937) and *Sunset Boulevard* (1950).

Stroke, or cerebrovascular accident (CVA), sudden loss of some aspect of brain function due to lack of blood supply to a given area. Stroke may result from embolism, arteriosclerosis and thrombosis, or hemorrhage (in which case it is termed apoplexy). Areas with permanent loss of blood supply do not recover, but other areas may take over their function.

Stromboli, Italian island located in the Tyrrhenian Sea, off northeastern Sicily. It has an area of approximately 5 sq mi (13 sq km) and contains an active volcano, which is 3,031 ft (924 m) high. The volcano produces a continuous flow of lava that pours into the sea. Its volcano, as well as its climate and beaches, make Stromboli a popular tourist attraction.

Strontium, chemical element, symbol Sr; for physical constants see Periodic Table. Strontium was discovered by Adair Crawford in 1790. In nature it is found as celestite and strontianite. Strontium is prepared by electrolysis of its fused chloride mixed with potassium chloride. Strontium is a silvery-white, soft, reactive metal, a member of the alkaline earth metals. It reacts with water more vigorously than calcium, and quickly oxides in air. Strontium-90, present in nuclear fallout, is a strong, long-lived beta emitter and is of potential use in nuclear-electric power devices. Strontium and its compounds are used in fireworks, flares, glass for color television picture tubes, and optical materials.

Struve, Otto (1897-1963), U.S. astronomer. Struve studied the wavelengths of the light emitted from stars to help him draw conclusions about the stars—such as their size, and gases and elements in or surrounding them. Struve was born in the Soviet Union and came to the United States in 1921. He became the director of the Yerkes Observatory in 1932. In 1939 he founded the McDonald Observatory at the University of Texas. Struve subsequently held various important posts at other observatories throughout the United States, and wrote *Stellar Evolution* (1950) and *The Universe* (1962).
See also: Astronomy; Star.

Strychnine, poisonous alkaloid produced from the seeds of the *Strychnos nux vomica* tree, which grows in India, Sri Lanka, and Australia. It can cause violant spinal convulsions and asphyxia, which can be fatal if not treated swiftly with barbiturate sedatives.

Stuart, Charles Edward (1720-88), pretender to the throne of England. The grandson of James II, he was known as the Young Pretender and, in Scotland, as Bonnie Prince Charlie. After the French refused to support his cause, he rallied the Highland clans to invade England, but was defeated at Culloden Moor in 1746.
See also: United Kingdom.

Stuart, Gilbert Charles (1755-1828), U.S. portrait painter, best known for the portrait of George Washington (1796) reproduced on the one-dollar bill. Praised for his use of color, technique, and psychological insight, he painted nearly 1,000 portraits and created a distinctive U.S. portrait style.

Stuart, House of, royal family of Scotland (1371-1714) and England (1603-1714). The first Stuart king, Robert II (r. 1371-90) was a hereditary steward of Scotland whose father had married a daughter of Robert the Bruce. A descendant, James IV (r. 1488-1513), married Margaret, daughter of Henry VII of England (r. 1567-1625). Their grandson, James VI (r. 1603-25), became James I of England. Between 1603 and 1714, six Stuarts ruled: James I, his son Charles I (r. 1625-49), Charles II (r. 1660-85), James II (deposed 1688), Mary II, wife of William III (r. 1689-94), and Anne (1702-14).
See also: Scotland.

Stuart, James Ewell Brown 'Jeb' (1833-64), Confederate cavalry officer. Upon resigning from the U.S. Army, he won command of a Confederate brigade after the first Battle of Bull Run (1861) and began his famous cavalry raids in 1862. Promoted to command all the cavalry in the North Virginia army, he led the cavalry force at Gettysburg (1863). He was killed in the Wilderness campaign.

Studebaker, family name of 5 brothers (Clement, Harry, John Mohler, Peter Everst, and Jacob Franklin) whose company was the largest producer of horse-drawn wagons in the United States and was also a leading manufacturer of automobiles and trucks. Originally a blacksmith and wagon shop (1852) in South Bend, Ind., the company subsequently expanded (becoming the Studebaker Brothers Manufacturing Co., 1868) as a result of the growing demand for wagons created by the agricultural development of the Midwest. Near the end of the 19th century, the company began developing automobiles, creating an electric vehicle in 1902 and producing gasoline-powered cars in 1904. After chganging its name to the Studebaker Corporation (1911), it eventually produced only cars and trucks and merged with Packard Motors, Inc. in 1954. In 1966 it discontinued production of automobiles, and in 1967 it became part of Studebaker-Worthington, Inc.
See also: Automobile.

Student Nonviolent Coordinating Committee (SNCC), U.S. civil rights organization in the 1960s. It originally consisted of both black and white college students who demonstrated to end segregation in the South. In 1966 Stokely Carmichael became the leader of SNCC. Carmichael, frustrated with the slow progress that SNCC's nonviolent approach was having, began his Black Power campaign and rejected most of SNCC's white support.
See also: Civil rights.

Students for a Democratic Society (SDS), left-wing U.S. student organization founded in 1960 as the youth group of the Social Democratic organization of the League for Industrial Democracy. As SDS became more radical, it broke from its parent organization and began championing the ideas that came to be considered characteristic of the New Left. The influence of SDS spread widely through U.S. universities, and it helped launch the movement against the Vietnam War (1965), as well as providing support for the civil rights movement. In 1969 it split into many competing factions.

Sturgeon, fish of the north temperate zone whose eggs are eaten as caviar. Sturgeon have a row of bony plates down the side of the body and sharklike tailfins; toothless, they suck their food (mostly crayfish) from the water bottom. Most of the 2 dozen or so species are marine but breed in fresh water. The largest is the Russian sturgeon, or belluga (*Acipenser huso*), which grows to 13 ft (4 m) and can weigh 2,000 lb (908 kg). This species, which lives entirely in fresh water, provides half the world's caviar. The white sturgeon of the U.S. Pacific Northwest has been overfished and is now much reduced in number.

Sturges, Preston (1898-1959), U.S. playwright, screenwriter, and film director. His films, many of them witty satires of U.S. life and values, include

The Great McGinty (1940), *Sullivan's Travels* (1941), and *The Miracle of Morgan's Creek* (1944).

Sturm und Drang (German, "storm and stress"), name given to a period of literary ferment in Germany (1770-84). Influenced by Jean Jacques Rousseau, its leading figures—Johann Gottfried von Herder, Johann Wolfgang von Goethe, and Friedrich von Schiller—espoused an antirationalist and rebellious individualism in opposition to the prevailing classicism.

Stuttering, speech impairment characterized by repeated attempts to pronounce a syllable or word.

Stuttgart (pop. 583,700), capital of Baden-Württemberg, a state in southwest Germany. Stuttgart is a major governing, industrial, and cultural center in West Germany. Once the capital of the Württemberg kingdom, Stuttgart is situated on the Neckar River, in a rich farm and vineyard region. Besides producing wines and fruits, Stuttgart manufactures automobiles, machines, precision instruments, tools, computers, musical instruments, beer, and paper. It has more than 200 publishing houses. A powerful manufacturing center, Stuttgart was severely bombed by the Allies during World War II; it has since been rebuilt. Some of the many historic buildings in Stuttgart are notable for their fine architecture. Two examples are the Old Palace, which was built in the Renaissance style, and the New Palace, which was built in the baroque and rococo styles; both were the homes of rulers of Württemberg. Stuttgart is culturally active with museums and an opera house, as well as schools for art, architecture, and music.
See also: Germany.

Stuyvesant, Peter (c.1610-72), Dutch director-general (1647-64) of New Netherland, Holland's North American colony, which included the city of New Amsterdam, later renamed New York. Autocratic and unpopular, he lost Dutch territory to Connecticut in 1650, conquered and annexed New Sweden in 1655, and finally surrendered New Netherland to England in 1664, after his citizens failed to support him against a surprise English attack. He retired to his farm, "the Bouwerie," now New York's Bowery.

Sty, infection in an eyelash follicle or in a gland in the eyelid. A sty is usually caused by staphylococcus bacteria. Sties are treated with antibiotics and, in some cases, with surgery.

Styron, William (1925-), U.S. novelist and winner of the 1968 Pulitzer Prize for *The Confessions of Nat Turner* (1967), a first-person novelization of an 1831 slave rebellion. Other novels include *Lie Down in Darkness* (1951), *Sophie's Choice* (1979), *Darkness Visible: a Memoir of Madness* (1990), and *A Tidewater Morning* (1993).

Styx, in Greek mythology, river of the underworld. The souls of the dead had to cross the Styx to reach Hades, the underworld. For payment, the boatman Charon would ferry them across. *Styx* in Greek means "hateful." The Greeks abhorred death. According to the Greek poet Homer, the gods made their most important oaths in the name of the Styx. If a god lied, he or she would be punished severely by being banished to a deep pit in the

underworld for nine years. The Styx was thought to begin at a waterfall in Arcadia, an ancient Greek region.
See also: Mythology.

Suárez, Francisco (1548-1617), Spanish Jesuit philosopher who represented a late flowering of Scholasticism. He was an influential political and legal theorist, attacking the divine right of kings and arguing that international law was based on custom, not natural law.
See also: Scholasticism.

Sublimation, in chemistry, act of changing a solid into a gas, or a gas into a solid, without going through a liquid stage. Some substances when heated vaporize and become a gas, without melting into a liquid first. When the gas is cooled, the substance returns directly to a solid state. Examples of such substances are dry ice and iodine crystals. Sublimation is used to purify substances: When the solid is heated, only the substance that is pure becomes a gas—the impurities remain solid. When the impurities are removed the substance becomes refined.

Submarine, ship capable of sustained underwater operation. The first working craft, built by the Dutch inventor Cornelis Drebbel (1620), was a wooden rowboat covered with greased leather that could remain submerged for as long as 15 hours. The first submarine used in warfare, designed by David Bushnell of the United States (1776), was a one-man, hand-powered, screw-driven vessel designed to attach mines to enemy ships. In the Civil War the Confederate states produced several submarines. Later (late 1800s and early 1900s) John P. Holland and his rival Simon Lake designed vessels powered by gasoline engines on the surface and by electric motors when submerged. The forerunners of modern submarines, they were armed with torpedoes and guns. Great advances were made during World War I and World War II. German U-boats introduced snorkels to hinder detection while recharging batteries. The first nuclear-powered submarine was the USS *Nautilus* (1955), which made the first voyage under the polar ice-cap (1958). Modern submarines are streamlined vessels, generally with a double hull, the inner one a pressure hull separated from the outer one by fuel and ballast tanks. The submarine submerges by flooding the ballast tanks to displace its own weight of water. It uses hydrofoil diving planes. Besides their military applications, submarines are used for oceanographic research and exploration, salvage, and rescue.

Suburb, community that lies on the outskirts of a city. Suburbs can be residential or industrial, or a combination of both. A city may have any number of suburbs surrounding it. A suburb may be self-governing, or be governed by the city near it, or by the county in which it lies. Suburbs began in the late 19th century when railroad expansion enabled people to work in a city and commute to homes outside of it. Suburbs blossomed further with the development of automobiles and roads. Now, more people live in suburbs than in cities.

Subway, underground railroad system designed for urban and suburban passenger transport. The first subway, known as the Underground, was built in London (1860-63) and used steam trains. From 1886 to 1890 a 3-mile

section of the London subway was built using a large, cylindrical steel tube (developed by J.H. Greathead) that was forced forward through the earth by hydraulic jacks; tunnel walls were then built around it. This technique made deep tunnels possible without surface disturbance. The London "tube" thus constructed was the first to use electrically-powered trains, which soon replaced steam trains everywhere. Many cities throughout the world then followed London's lead, notably Paris (begun 1898) and New York (begun 1900). The New York subway, using multiple-unit trains developed by Frank Sprague, is now the largest in the world. The Moscow subway (begun 1931) is noted for its palatial marble stations. Many cities have extended, improved, and automated their subway systems to reduce surface congestion. Some, such as Montreal, have introduced quieter rubber-tired trains that run on concrete guideways.
See also: Railroad.

Succession wars, conflicts that result from disagreements about who should inherit a throne, or who should succeed a monarch. These disputes usually arise when a monarch has no child, or son, to whom to pass the throne. Europe has experienced 4 succession wars, all during the 18th century. They were the War of Spanish Succession (1701-14), the War of Polish Succession (1733-38), the War of Austrian Succession (1740-48), and the War of Bavarian Succession (1778-79).

Succot *See:* Sukkot.

Succulent, category of plants whose leaves or stems are covered with a waxy substance that reduces water loss and enables them to live in arid regions. Cacti are the most familiar, but aloes and yuccas are other examples. Many succulents have attractive foliage and colorful flowers.

Sucker, any of various freshwater fishes (family Catostomidae) related to the minnows. Most suckers live in North America, but there are a few in Asia. They have thick lips and feed by sucking food from the bottoms of lakes and rivers. Some suck up mud and eject inedible matter, while others turn over pebbles and suck the animals attached to the underside. A few have hard lips for scraping rocks.

Suckling, Sir John (1609-42), poet and playwright. Suckling belonged to a troup known as the Cavalier poets, associated with the court of the British king Charles I. Born into a wealthy family in Middlesex, he was knighted at the age of 21 and became a familiar figure at court, where he was a colorful, witty, gallant character. Suckling was a friend of the king, whom he accompanied in the war against the Scots in 1639. In 1641 Suckling fled to Paris when he was suspected of taking part in a scheme to free the earl of Strafford from prison. He died shortly thereafter, perhaps by suicide. Suckling's works include the plays *Aglaura* (1637), a tragedy, and *The Goblins* (1638), a comedy. He also wrote *A Session of Poets* (1637), an entertaining verse about famous poets much admired by his contemporaries.
See also: Navy.

Sucre (pop. 88,800), city in central Bolivia, founded as La Plata in 1538 and renamed for Antonio José de Sucre in 1839. A commercial and agricultural

center and the seat of the national university and the Supreme Court, Sucre is the judicial capital of Bolivia. It is 250 mi (400 km) southeast of La Paz, which is the administrative capital of the country.
See also: Bolivia.

Sucre, Antonio José de (1795-1830), important leader in Latin American wars against Spanish rule and first president of Bolivia (1826-28). Born in Venezuela, he joined the revolutionary army at age 15 and soon displayed great military skills. He gained the respect of the Venezuelan leader of the Latin American revolution, Simón Bolívar, who made him a general. In the course of several battles, Sucre successfully drove the Spanish from Ecuador and Bolivia. Bolívar appointed Sucre lifetime president of Bolivia (1826). Sucre agreed to serve 2 years, after which time he wanted to retire to Ecuador. Although he was a skillful executive, his attempts to set up a strong Bolivian government were thwarted by other political groups. He resigned his office in 1828 and withdrew to Ecuador when the Peruvian army invaded Bolivia. The next year he returned to drive away the Peruvian invaders. Sucre was assassinated the following year by what were believed to be opponents of Simón Bolívar. He is considered a Latin American hero. The capital of Bolivia is named after him.
See also: Bolivia.

Sucrose, white, crystalline disaccharide carbohydrate ($C_{12}H_{22}O_{11}$) commercially obtained from sugar beet, sugarcane, and sweet sorghum. Common table sugar, sucrose is composed of a glucose unit joined to a fructose unit. Sucrose is produced from juice or sap, which is evaporated to form molasses. Additional evaporation yields brown-colored sugar, which is whitened through further refining.
See also: Sugar.

Sudan, Republic of the Sudan, largest country in Africa, located in the northeast of the continent.
Land and climate. Sudan occupies 967,494 sq mi (2,505,813 sq km) and is bounded on the north by Egypt; on the west by Libya, Chad, the Central African Republic, and Zaire; on the south by Uganda and Kenya; and on the east by Ethiopia and Eritrea. It has a 400-mi (644-km) coastline on the Red Sea. Sudan may be divided into two main regions: the barren desert region north of Khartoum, comprising about one-third of the country, and the well-watered region of the south. The Nile River enters Sudan from Uganda in the south and crosses the entire length of the country on its way to Egypt and the Mediterranean. In the far south is a region of tropical forest and to the southeast wooded grassland. Further north is the Sudd region, a great marshy area where the river is congested with floating vegetation. Between the Sudd and Khartoum, the central area of the Sudan is grasslands. At Khartoum the White Nile is joined by the Blue Nile, both branches of the Nile flowing north to form a triangle of land between them whose apex is at Khartoum, where the rivers meet. The land between them is the Gezira plain, the most fertile part of the Sudan. Beyond Khartoum to the north, the Nile flows through the Libyan and Nubian deserts. In the northeast there are mountain ranges bordering the Red Sea coastal plain. The prevailing climate of the Sudan is hot with rainfall increasing in frequency toward the south. The capital is Khartoum.

Sudan

Capital:	Khartoum
Area:	966,472 sq mi (2,503,813 sq km)
Population:	33,551,000
Language:	Arabic
Government:	Islamic republic
Independent:	1956
Head of gov.:	President
Per capita:	U.S. $765
Mon. unit:	1 Sudanese dinar = 10 pound = 100 piastres

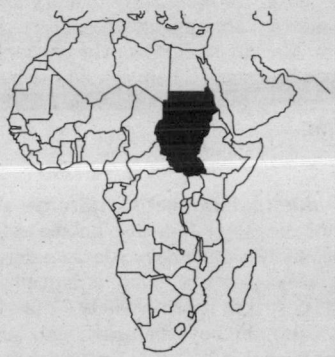

People. The people are divided into Arab-speaking Muslims in the north and black African and Nilotic peoples of the south and west. The Muslims are 80% of the population and profess Islam. The black Africans are mainly animists.
Economy. The Sudan is basically agricultural, and most people live by subsistence farming. The chief cash crops are cotton, gum arabic, and peanuts. Domestic crops include millet, sorghum, wheat, and sugar cane. Livestock are raised in large numbers. Manufacturing is limited and there is a small mining industry. The only port is Port Sudan on the Red Sea.
History. Called Nubia in ancient times, North Sudan was colonized by Egypt in 2000 B.C. By 800 B.C. it had come under the Cush kingdom, which by A.D. 600 had given way to independent Coptic Christian states. In the 13th to 15th centuries they collapsed under Muslim expansion, and the Muslim Funj state was established, lasting until Egypt invaded the Sudan in 1821. The nationalist Mahdi led a revolt in 1881, after which a series of campaigns resulted in joint Anglo-Egyptian rule in 1899. Since independence in 1956, the country has been racked by civil war pitting southerners fearful of Muslim dominance against northerners. By 1972 1.5 million southerners had died in the fighting but some autonomy had been achieved for the south. Hostilities have continued and Sudan has been additionally burdened in recent years by an influx of nearly half a million refugees fleeing war and famine in neighboring countries. In 1997 the US decided to impose harsh sanctions against Sudan due to Sudan's supposed support of international terrorism. The continuing hostilities have resulted in a famine (1998).

Sudan grass (*Sorghum vulgare*, variety *sudanese*), hay plant in the grass family. Native to Sudan, in northeastern Africa, this grass was brought to the United States in 1909 to be planted in dry areas because it needs very little water to grow. Farmers grow it to feed their livestock. Sudan grass, first grown in the South and Southwest, now is found throughout the United States.

Sudbury (pop. 88,700), city in Ontario, Canada. In 1883 rich deposits of copper and nickel were discovered there by workers building the Canadian Pacific Railway. Since the early 1900s, Sudbury has been a major producer

of nickel for the world. Sudbury also produces most of the copper used in Ontario. Other metals mined there include gold, silver, platinum, and iron ore. The city suffers from heavy concentration of air pollution created by the metal plants. To help spread the pollution over a greater area, one mining company built a smokestack 1,250 ft (381 m) high—the tallest one in the world.
See also: Ontario.

Sudden infant death syndrome, sudden, unexpected death of an apparently healthy infant, also known as SIDS, crib death, or cot death. It usually occurs while the baby is asleep during the night. Victims' ages range from 2 weeks to 1 year. More crib deaths occur during cold than warm weather. SIDS strikes approximately 1 out of every 350 babies in the United States. It kills more boys than girls, and claims more children born prematurely and those born in poverty. The causes for crib death are difficult and sometimes impossible to determine. A baby dying of SIDS will first turn blue and then stop breathing. Investigation of cases has led to the belief that victims of SIDS may have a slightly defective nervous system that stops their breathing and heart.

Sudetenland, region in the north of the Czech Republic. Originally designated as the area of the Sudetes Mountains on the Bohemia-Silesia border, it came to apply to all the German-speaking Bohemian and Moravian borderlands incorporated into Czechoslovakia in 1919. The Sudetenland was ceded to Nazi Germany by the Munich Pact in 1938 and restored to Czechoslovakia in 1945.
See also: Czech Republic.

Suez (pop. 376,000), city in Egypt located at the top of the Gulf of Suez. The southern entranceway into the Suez Canal, it is an important Egyptian port and major industrial center. Railways and roads connect it to Cairo, 80 mi (130 km) west. Its major industries are oil refinement and the manufacture of artificial fertilizer. Suez has been a port since ancient times. Its economy and industries blossomed with the opening of the Suez Canal in 1869. Suez's industries suffered much destruction during the Arab-Israeli War, causing the canal to be closed. Since then, the industries have been rebuilt, and the canal was reopened in 1975.
See also: Egypt.

Suez Canal, canal in Egypt linking the Gulf of Suez (an arm of the Red Sea) to the eastern Mediterranean. About 100 mi (160 km) long, the canal cut over 4,000 mi (6,400 km) from the route from Britain to India and has been a major commercial waterway since its opening in 1869. It has a minimum width of 179 ft (54 m), a dredged depth of almost 40 ft (12 m), and no locks. Work began in 1859 under Ferdinand de Lesseps. In 1875 Britain acquired the canal from the Ottoman ruler of Egypt. In 1956 it was nationalized by President Gamal Abdel Nasser, prompting an invasion by Britain, France, and Israel. After UN intervention, the canal reopened in 1957 under Egyptian control. It was closed again by the Arab-Israeli War of 1967, but cleared of wreckage in 1974 and reopened in 1975. The canal was deepened (1976-80) to permit the passage of oil tankers up to 500,000 tons (453,600 metric tons) and 53 ft (16 m) in draft.

Suffrage *See:* Woman suffrage.

Sufism, Muslim mystical philosophical and literary movement dating from the 10th and 11th centuries. Stressing personal communion with God through ascetic practices or quietism, it has spread throughout Islam in a variety of forms, most apparently in Persia. Al-Ghazali was Sufism's greatest philosophical exponent, and among its great literary exponents are the poets Omar Khayyam and Hafiz.
See also: Omar Khayyam.

Sugar, sweet, soluble compound of carbon, hydrogen, and oxygen. There are 3 groups of sugars. Monosaccharides (such as fructose and glucose) are called simple because they contain a single chain of carbon atoms. Disaccharides (such as lactose and sucrose) contain 2 monosaccharide units joined by an oxygen bridge. Their chemical and physical properties are similar to those of monosaccharides. Trisaccharides (such as raffinose) are composed of 3 monosaccharide units.

Sugar beet, plant (*Beta vulgaris*) whose swollen root provides almost half the world's sugar. It was first extensively grown in Europe to replace cane sugar from the West Indies, supplies of which were cut off during the Napoleonic Wars. Sugar beet is grown in all temperate areas in which cool summers ensure good sugar formation.

Sugar cane (*Saccharum officinarum*), tall plant of the grass family. It grows in tropical and semitropical regions throughout the world. The plant is made up of a solid stalk with joints at regular intervals. Each joint has a single bud. Stalks grow to a height of 7-26 ft (2-8 m), with a diameter of 1.5-2 in (3.5-5 cm). The color of the stalk ranges from yellow to green, violet, or red, depending on the variety. Long, thin leaves grow from the stalk, which contains a juice from which sugar and syrup is made. It was grown as early as 8,000 years ago in the South Pacific. The leading producers of sugar cane are Brazil, India, and Cuba. Sugercane by-products include molasses, rum, alcohol, fuel, and livestock feed.

Sugar maple *See:* Maple.

Suharto (1921-), Indonesian statesman, president 1968-98. A general, he defeated an attempted Communist coup in 1965, in the process overthrowing the government of Sukarno and killing as many as 500,000 people. Popular unrest and an economic crisis forced him to resign in 1998.
See also: Indonesia.

Suicide, act of voluntarily taking one's own life. In some societies (notably Japan's) suicide is accepted or even expected in the face of disgrace. Judaism, Islam, and Christianity, however, condemn it. Until 1961 the United Kingdom sought to discourage it by making it a crime, and it is still illegal in some U.S. states. Suicide attempts are often considered by psychologists implicit pleas for help and may result from extreme depression.

Sui dynasty, dynasty (ruling family) that governed China from A.D. 581-618. Its first ruler, **Yang Jian**, united North and South China, which had been

involved in a lengthy civil war. After his death in 604, his son **Sui Yangdi** worked to strengthen the unified territory's government and economy. One of his most outstanding projects was the building of the Grand Canal, a waterway system over which products could be shipped between northern and southern China. Yangdi suffered military defeats, however, when he tried to overtake Korea and Manchuria, and when he fought Eastern Turks. He was overthrown and assassinated. The Sui dynasty ended with his death in 618. The T'ang dynasty, which began that same year, adopted many of the policies and systems established by the Sui dynasty.
See also: China.

Suite, musical form developed in Germany and France in the 17th and 18th centuries, originally inspired by dance. By the 19th century it had lost its connection to dance. The Baroque suite and its component movements—allemande, courante, sarabande, and gigue—is the more well-known suite form.

Sukarno (1901-70), first president of independent Indonesia (1945-65). A leader of the independence movement from 1927, he was instrumental in creating the republic in 1945. His flamboyant rule turned dictatorial in 1959 and in 1963 he proclaimed himself president for life. In 1965 an attempted coup by the Communist Party, which had been his ally, was crushed by Gen. Suharto who assumed de facto power from Sukarno, formally removing him from the presidency in 1966. Sukarno was placed under house arrest until his death.
See also: Indonesia.

Sukkot, or Feast of Tabernacles, 8-day autumn Jewish festival, during which meals are taken in a hut (sukkah) roofed with branches and fruits to symbolize the shelters used by the ancient Hebrews during their wanderings after the Exodus from Egypt.
See also: Simhat Torah.

Suleiman I, or **Sulayman** (1494-1566), sultan of Ottoman Empire from 1520-1566. He was also known as The Magnificent and The Lawgiver. His reign was marked by his numerous successful military campaigns and the legal, literary, and artistic achievements of his empire. He waged ground and naval wars in parts of Europe, Asia Minor, and Africa, enlarging his territory with each successive victory. During a brief period his navy dominated the Mediterranean Sea, the Red Sea, and the Persian Gulf. He did not succeed, however, in his naval warfare against Holy Roman Emperor Charles V and Venice. His court included lawyers, artists, writers and architects, whom he engaged to help him create his vision of a magnificent and sophisticated empire.
See also: Ottoman Empire.

Sulfa drug, any of various synthetic compounds derived from sulfanilimide that inhibit the multiplication of invading bacteria, thus allowing the body's cellular defense mechanisms to suppress infection. The first sulfa drug was synthesized in 1908 and used widely as a dye before Gerhard Domagk reported its effectiveness against streptococci (1938). In recent years many sulfa drugs have been replaced by antibiotics in the treatment of bacterial infections.

Sulfate, chemical mixture containing sulfur and oxygen. Sulfates are usually formed in crystals. Epsom salt and gypsum are two common sulfates. Most sulfates are water soluble, but some, such as lead sulfates, are not. Industrial uses for sulfates include fabric printing and dying and the manufacture of medicine and varnishes.

Sulfide, compound of sulfur and another element or elements. The element—made up of atoms that are alike and cannot be changed chemically—may be a metal, such as silver or gold, or a gas, such as oxygen or hydrogen. Sulfides have various industrial uses. When sulfur burns, it produces a poisonous gas. A mixture of carbon and sulfur is used as an insecticide. In small doses, it is used as an anesthetic. Some sulfides are used to create color in paints.

Sulfur, chemical element, symbol S; for physical constants see Periodic Table. Sulfur has been known and used for thousands of years. It is referred to in the bible as brimstone. As a mineral, it occurs in iron pyrites, galena, sphalerite, Epsom salts, barite, and many others. It occurs free in nature in the vicinity of volcanoes and hot springs. Sulfur is also found in the atmosphere of Venus and in meteorites and interstellar clouds. It is produced commercially using the Frasch process in which heated water is used to melt underground sulfur that is then brought to the surface. Sulfur is a yellow, brittle, low melting, reactive nonmetal. It readily forms sulfides with many elements. Hydrogen sulfide is poisonous and can cause death by respiratory paralysis. Sulfur forms several allotropes amorphous and crystalline. Sulfur is essential to human and animal life. Sulfur and its compounds are used in gunpowder, in the vulcanization of rubber, as a fungicide, in making sulfite paper, as a fumigant, and in bleaching dried fruits. It is used to produce sulfuric acid, the most important manufactured chemical.

Sulfur dioxide (SO_2), colorless, poisonous gas that has a sharp smell. It is released naturally in gases emitted during volcanic eruptions. Factories or refineries that burn oil or coal also release sulfur dioxide into the atmosphere, creating the potential for human health problems. Sulfur dioxide in the atmosphere may form acid rain when it dissolves in water droplets. Acid rain is damaging to the environment, killing animals and plants. For this reason, many nations are concerned about how much sulfur dioxide their industries should be allowed to release into the air.
See also: Acid rain.

Sulfuric acid, chemical compound (H_2SO_4) that is a colorless, oily liquid that corrodes materials. Exposure to it or its fumes can damage a person's nose, lungs, and skin. Sulfuric acid has been used since the 15th century. In the 19th century it was discovered that adding sulfuric acid to soil made the soil more fertile for plant growth; this discovery led to improved methods of manufacturing sulfuric acid. Besides being used in the manufacture of fertilizer, sulfuric acid is used in steel processing, petroleum refining, and the manufacture of other acids. Because it is so strong and potentially dangerous, great caution must be taken when handling sulfuric acid.

Sulgrave Manor, home of the ancestors of George Washington, first President of the United States. It is located in Sulgrave, a village in Northamptonshire, England. Built by Lawrence Washington, Sulgrave Manor remained in the family from 1539 to 1610. It is now a museum, furnished and restored to reflect the period when the Washingtons lived there.

Sulla, Lucius Cornelius (138-78 B.C.), Roman general and ruler. Sulla was born into the Roman upper class and entered politics as a praetor in 94 B.C. In 88 B.C., after fighting in the Social War, he became one of two consuls ruling Rome. As a military leader, he successfully fought armies of King Mithridates VI of Pontus that were attempting to overtake Roman territories (87-85 B.C.). After Mithridates surrendered, Sulla returned to Rome to confront his opponents, headed by Marius, who accused him of being an enemy of Rome (83 B.C.). He won the civil war against them the following year and became a dictator. Sulla initiated many reforms, such as restoring power to the Senate, but his reign was known for cruelty and illegality. He retired in 79 B.C.
See also: Marius, Gaius; Rome, Ancient.

Sullivan, Anne (1866-1936), U.S. teacher of Helen Keller. Partially blind herself, in 1887 she taught Keller to read and communicate through the touch alphabet and became her life-long companion.
See also: Keller, Helen Adams.

Sullivan, Harry Stack (1892-1949), U.S. psychiatrist and head of William Alanson White Institute and Washington School of Psychiatry, who contributed to the study of schizophrenia and originated the idea that psychiatry depends on study of culture and its influence on behavior.
See also: Psychiatry.

Sullivan, John L., U.S. boxing champion. Sullivan was the last bare-knuckle heavyweight champion, winning the title from Paddy Ryan in 1882 and defending it again in 1888 and 1889. He then boxed with gloves under the Queensbury Rules, losing his title to James J. Corbett in 1892.

Sullivan, Leon Howard (1922-), Baptist minister whose numerous projects have improved economic opportunities for African Americans. Acting on his belief that unemployment was a major reason for crime, he initiated a 1959 boycott of Philadelphia firms that did not hire African Americans. After 3 years, these companies made jobs available to African Americans. In 1964 Sullivan founded a center (Opportunities Industrialization Center) in Philadelphia at which members of minority groups could receive job training. The center was so successful that others were opened throughout the United States as well as in Africa. The following year Sullivan founded a corporation (Zion Investment Associates) that established several diverse African-American businesses. In 1971 Sullivan became a member of the board of directors of General Motors, the first African American ever to do so. In 1977 he initiated a plan for equal treatment of black Africans in South Africa. His Sullivan Principles urged firms there to ban segregation, provide greater opportunities for blacks, and pay blacks and whites equally for equal work. Although many U.S. companies operating in South Africa agreed to the principles, discrimination continued, causing Sullivan to conclude that U.S. firms should not remain in South Africa.

Sullivan, Louis Henri (1856-1924), U.S. architect whose office buildings pioneered modern design. In partnership with Dankmar Adler in Chicago (1881-95), he championed the view that a building's form should express its function. His works include the Auditorium (1889) and the Carson Pirie Scott building (1899-1904) in Chicago, and the Guaranty Building in Buffalo (1894-95). Frank Lloyd Wright was his pupil.
See also: Architecture.

Sullivan, Sir Arthur Seymour (1842-1900), English composer. He was born in London and studied at the Royal Academy of Music. He first met with success for the music he wrote for the Shakespeare play *The Tempest* (1862). Sullivan is perhaps best known for his collaborations with the playwright Sir William Gilbert in which he produced many operettas. Gilbert and Sullivan first became a team with *Thespis* (1871), an operetta that was not very successful. Their next work, *Trial by Jury* (1875), became an instant hit. Other successful collaborations include *The Pirates of Penzance* (1880), *The Mikado* (1885), and *The Gondoliers* (1889). Sullivan also collaborated with other writers and wrote several works alone, including classical music, operas, and hymns. One of his most famous songs is "Onward Christian Soldiers." Sullivan taught at and was later the principal of the Royal Academy of Music. He was also an organist and conductor.

Sully, Thomas (1783-1872), English-born U.S. portrait painter who studied briefly under Gilbert Stuart. Queen Victoria (1839) and several U.S. presidents sat for him, including Jefferson and Monroe. He also painted the well-known picture *Washington's Passage of the Delaware*.

Sully-Prudhomme, René François Armand (1839-1907), French Parnassian poet, winner of the first Nobel Prize in literature, in 1901. His philosophical poems include *Justice* (1878) and *Happiness* (1888).

Sulphur *See:* Sulfur.

Sulu Sea, also known as the Sea of Mindoro, sea located between Borneo and the Philippine Islands. It is bounded by many other islands as well, including the Sulu Islands and the Visaya Islands, and is used for trade among them. The sea has an area of approximately 100,000 sq mi (260,000 sq km). Narrow bodies of water connect the sea to the Pacific Ocean and the South China Sea.

Sulzberger, name of 2 publishers of The *New York Times*. **Arthur Hays Sulzberger** (1891-1968) was the publisher of the *Times* from 1935 to 1961. He printed more editorials than ever before in the paper's history and greatly increased circulation. **Arthur Ochs Sulzberger** (1926-) became publisher of the *Times* in 1963. He expanded coverage of business news and started printing national editions in several cities outside New York.

Sumac, common name for trees, shrubs, and vines (genus *Rhus*) with resinous, sometimes bitter sap. Members of the group include the staghorn sumac, used by Native Americans to make an acidic but pleasant drink, and the Sicilian sumac, whose bark is used for tanning leather. Sumacs, however, are often poisonous: poison oak, poison sumac, and poison ivy. They can be recognized by their white or gray berries.

Sumatra, second-largest island of Indonesia, about 183,000 sq mi (473,970 sq km) in area. Lying on the equator, with a hot, wet climate, Sumatra is heavily forested and rich in oil, bauxite, and coal; it produces 70% of Indonesia's export wealth. Crops include rubber, coffee, pepper, and tobacco. Medan and Palembang are the chief cities.
See also: Indonesia.

Sumer, southern region of ancient Mesopotamia (presently southern Iraq). From c.3000 B.C.-2400 B.C. it was dominated by several small kingdoms, the first civilizations in the world. The kingdoms had developed from cities founded in the fertile valley between the Tigris and Euphrates rivers, a setting ideal for farming and raising cattle. The Sumerians created an advanced civilization, building palaces and temples and constructing irrigation canals in their fields. Their craftspeople were skilled weavers, potters, jewelers, and stonecarvers. Sumerians traded their goods with regions surrounding the Persian Gulf and promoted the practice and study of medicine, astronomy, mathematics, economy, law, and politics. One of their most noteworthy achievements was the development of the first writing system, known as cuneiform, consisting of wedge-shaped characters pressed into clay tablets. Other civilizations that took control of Sumer absorbed the knowledge and skills developed by them.
See also: Mesopotamia.

Sumner, Charles (1811-74), U.S. political leader and opponent of slavery. He was a senator from Massachusetts from 1851 to 1874. As an active abolitionist, he denounced slavery and the South. In 1856 he made a speech in which he accused Senators Andrew P. Butler and Stephen A. Douglas of suppporting slavery. A few days later, Representative Preston S. Brooks, Butler's nephew, accused Sumner of slander and beat him with a cane, wounding him severely. After the Civil War, Sumner proposed stiff treatment of the South, demanding that Southern states could join the Union only after they allowed freed slaves voting rights. He was active in the impeachment of Andrew Johnson.

Sumter, Thomas (1734-1832), partisan of the American Revolution who formed a guerrilla band and harassed the British in the Carolina campaign (1780-81). He had notable successes at Hanging Rock, Fishdam Ford, and Blackstock. Later he was a South Carolina member of the House of Representatives (1789-93; 1797-1801) and Senate (1801-10). Fort Sumter in Charleston harbor was named for him.
See also: Revolutionary War in America.

Sun, star at the center of our Solar System, a luminous sphere of gas about 865,000 mi (1.4 million km) in diameter and 93 million mi (150 million km) from earth. The sun in 332,000 times as massive as earth, and its volume is 1.3 million times greater. The temperature in its center is about 15,000,000°K. The source of its energy is a series of nuclear fusion reactions

in which hydrogen is converted into helium—light, heat, and gamma rays being produced in the process. Light from the sun takes about 8 minutes to reach earth. Although the sun is entirely gaseous, its bright surface looks like a kind of skin. This outer layer is called the photosphere, whose temperature is about 6,000°K. Above the photosphere lies the chromosphere, an irregular layer of gases, sunspots, flares, and prominences visible to the naked eye only during eclipses. The corona is the sparse outer atmosphere.
See also: Solar System.

Sunbelt and Frostbelt, popular terms designating, respectively, the southern tier of states stretching from North Carolina to California and the states of the Northeast and Midwest. The Frostbelt states, besides their more rigorous climate, are characterized by aging industrial plants and urban infrastructures, unionized labor, high rates of unemployment and poverty, static or declining populations, and the severe fiscal problems these conditions impose on state and local governments. By contrast, the Sunbelt states are usually characterized by burgeoning economic development, expanding cities, rising populations (due to migration from the Frostbelt states), and increasing political importance.

Sunbird, any of approximately 115 species of songbirds in the sunbird family. Sunbirds are found in Africa, Southeast Asia, and the Pacific islands. They range in size from 3.5-6 in (9-15 cm). Their plumage may be yellow or gray. Breeding male birds have brilliantly colored feathers of various combinations of red, blue, purple, green, and yellow. Sunbirds resemble hummingbirds, but the two are not related. Like hummingbirds, sunbirds feed on nectar. But whereas a hummingbird hovers in the air as it extracts a flower's nectar, a sunbird perches on a flower or stalk while feeding.

Sunburn, burning effect on the skin caused by exposure to ultraviolet radiation from the sun. First-degree burns may occur, but usually only minor discomfort results, with skin sensitivity. Repeated sunburns may cause skin cancer, including melanoma, the most dangerous variety.

Sun dance, religious ceremony observed by a number of Plains tribes of Native Americans during the summer. It involves eight days of fasting, self-torture (as penance), and the seeking of visions. Common during the 19th century, the ceremonies were discouraged by the U.S. government and have almost died out.

Sunday, Billy (William Ashley Sunday; 1862-1935), U.S. revivalist preacher noted for his flamboyance and his vivid version of fundamentalist theology. He claimed to have saved over a million souls.

Sundew, any plant in the sundew family. Sundews have leaves that produce a sticky fluid enabling them to trap and digest insects. (This same fluid makes the leaves glisten like dew—hence their name.) Sundews are found throughout the world in regions with mild or tropical climates. The round-leaved sundew (genus *Drosera*) is the most common, thriving in wet marshy areas. Its thin, curving stem grows to a height of 4-10 in (10-25 cm) and has small white or pinkish flowers on top. The base of the stem has flat round leaves covered with gland-tipped hairs, which produce the sticky fluid that attracts insects. When an insect lands on the leaf, the tiny hairs curve around it and hold it while the fluid engulfs and suffocates it. Enzymes in the fluid digest the insect, after which the hairs unfold, ready to trap the next victim.

Sundial, ancient type of clock, consisting of a stylus (called a gnomon) parallel to the earth's axis that casts a shadow on a calibrated dial plate, which may be horizontal or vertical. Sundials usually show local time, but they may be calibrated to show standard time.

Sunfish, popular fresh water sports fish of the bass family, found in North America. The body is perchlike: deep and flattened, and with a long dorsal fin. Male sunfish dig nests in sand and guard the eggs. They feed on small animals and other fish and are active only during periods of sunshine. Ocean sunfish (*Mola mola*) are unrelated fish that live in the sea.

Sunflower, any of various tall plants (genus *Helianthus*) with large, disk-shaped yellow and brown flowers that twist to face the sun. Most of the 60 species are native to the United States. The common sunflower (*Helianthus annuus*) is cultivated in many parts of the world. The seeds yield an oil and the remainder becomes cattle feed.

Sunflower State *See:* Kansas.

Sung dynasty *See:* Song dynasty.

Sunni, followers of the majority branch of Islam, as distinct from the Shi'te. The term refers to the tradition (Sunna) of the prophet Muhammad. About 85% of the world's Muslims are Sunni, considered the orthodox or traditionalists. Within the Sunni currently, there are four recognized schools of Islamic law and ritual: Hamafi, Maliki, Shafi, and Hambali.
See also: Islam; Shi'te.

Sunset laws, U.S. laws that require regular periodic review of government agencies. The review determines whether the agency is to be restructured or discontinued. These laws were enacted to attempt to create greater efficiency in government agencies.
See also: Zero-base budgeting.

Sunshine laws, U.S. laws that require government agencies to permit the public to attend their meetings. These laws were enacted to prevent secrecy in government. In those cases where agencies need to discuss matters of security or sensitive issues, the law may permit a closed meeting to be held.
See also: Freedom of Information Act.

Sunshine State *See:* Florida; South Dakota.

Sunspot, apparent dark spot on the surface of the sun. Vortices of gas associated with strong electromagnetic activity, sunspots appear dark only by contrast with the surrounding photosphere. Single spots are known, but mostly they form in groups or pairs. They are never seen at the sun's poles

or equator. Their cause is not known, but they seem cyclical, reaching a maximum about every 11 years.
See also: Sun.

Sunstroke, or heatstroke, rise in body temperature and deficiency of sweating in hot climates, often following exertion. Delirium, coma, and convulsions may occur suddenly, and rapid cooling must then be effected.

Sun Valley, resort area in south-central Idaho, in the Sawtooth Mountains on the Big Wood River. The area was developed in 1936 by the Union Pacific Railroad because its climate, snowfall, and terrain were ideal for skiing and winter sports. There are numerous ski slopes and cross-country trails throughout the area. In the summer the recreations it offers are mainly golf and tennis.

Sun worship, reverence for the sun, as for a god or goddess. Sun worship was practiced by peoples throughout the world, especially in agricultural communities in which the sun was necessary for crop growth. Cultures in which sun worship was prevalent include those of ancient Egypt, Persia, India, and Rome. Native Americans and the Aztecs, Incas, and Mayas of Central and South America also considered the sun sacred.

Sun Yat-sen (1866-1925), Chinese political leader, regarded as the "father of modern China." Born in the Guangdong province, he spent most of his youth in Hawaii, where he learned about Western thought and politics. He then studied medicine in Hong Kong, becoming a doctor in 1892. In 1894 Sun founded a political group and attempted his first revolution against the Manchu dynasty. It failed and Sun left China in 1895. He traveled throughout Europe, the United States, and Japan, trying to gain support for his cause. In 1911, the Manchu dynasty was overthrown during a revolt, and Sun returned to China. He was elected temporary president and tried to unite China under a strong government. Some considered his ideas too extreme, however, and after 6 weeks he turned his presidency over to Yüan Shikai. Sun remained committed to his vision of a unified China. In 1923 he and his Kuomintang Party took control of China with assistance from the Soviet Union (Shih-kai had become increasingly dictatorial). He died 2 years later. The Communists and the Kuomintang, who eventually dissolved their partnership, both claimed his legacy to be their inheritance. *Three Principles of the People*, his writings in which he summarized his political doctrines, inspired and guided subsequent developments in China.
See also: China.

Superconductivity, complete disappearance of resistance to electricity in a wire or other electric circuit, which allows a current to continue without any driving voltage. Superconductivity was discovered in 1911 and was long thought to be possible only in certain metals at very low temperatures (close to absolute zero, a total absence of molecular movement). This severely limited the possible applications of superconductivity. In recent years, however, researchers have made considerable progress in inducing superconductivity in some materials at the relatively "high" temperature of about 125°K, or –243°F.
See also: Bardeen, John.

Superego, term coined by Sigmund Freud meaning the mostly subconscious dimension of personality that represents moral and cultural standards established by society. The superego (ego ideal and conscience) develops as a result of the child's identification with parental standards.
See also: Freud, Sigmund.

Superman *See:* Nietzsche, Friedrich.

Supernova, exploding star that may increase in brightness by as much as a billion times its original state in just a few days, after which it gradually fades back to less than its original brightness. It is thought that supernovas are caused by the gravitational collapse of extremely massive stars. Although many presumed remnants of supernovas have been detected, only four of these have been definitely matched to explosions that were seen and recorded in human history. These occurred in 1006, 1054, 1572, and 1604. In more recent times (since the 19th century) many supernovas have been observed by astronomers.
See also: Nova; Star.

Superstition, belief or practice that is not based on reason. Some superstitions involve the belief that an incident will have certain results, or foretell an event—for example, believing that walking under a ladder will bring bad luck. Other superstitions attribute qualities and powers to objects, such as a rabbit foot bringing luck. The origins of superstitions vary, but they have probably existed in every culture since ancient times. They arise out of uncertainty and fear and the desire to empower oneself somehow. Some superstitions are part of a cultural or religious tradition and are believed by a number of people, such as the belief that a groom should not see his bride before the ceremony on their wedding day. Other superstitions may be personal, such as having a lucky number.

Supply and demand, in economics, central concepts that explain changes in prices, production, and consumption of goods and services. Demand refers to the quantity of a product desired by consumers. Supply is the quantity available. Normally, if demand increases relative to supply, the price will rise. If supply rises relative to demand, the price will fall. Competition is the mechanism through which supply and demand tend to reach an equilibrium. In practice, however, such factors as monopolization, state interference, and other variables generally prevent this equilibrium from ever being reached.
See also: Economics.

Supply-side economics, theory of economic management that focuses on stimulating production through tax reduction, which is intended to inspire increased investment in business, leading to higher employment. The theory also calls for a cutback in government spending to achieve a balanced and much smaller budget, thus eliminating deficit spending, which causes inflation and drains funds from the private sector. Inspired by laissez-faire economic thought, the leading theorists of supply-side thinking include Milton Friedman, Arthur B. Lafter, Jack Kemp, and David Stockman. Supply-side economics dominated President Ronald Reagan's economic policies (1981-89).
See also: Economics.

Suprematism, art movement (1913-19) originated by the Russian-Polish painter Kasimir Malevich (1878-1935), establishing a system of nonrepresentational composition in terms of pure geometric shapes and patterns. The movement's influence on graphic design and typography has been significant.

Supreme Court of the United States, highest court of the United States, with the authority to adjudicate all cases arising under U.S. law, including treaties and constitutional matters. The number of justices is set by statute and so has varied; since 1869 the Court has comprised a chief justice and 8 associate justices, appointed for life by the president as vacancies arise. Nominees must be confirmed by majority vote of the Senate. Although theoretically above politics, the Court alone can determine the constitutionality of state and federal laws and interpret acts of Congress. Cases are brought before the Court by appeal (if, after being seen before the highest state court, there are questions concerning the constitutionality of the state's statutes) or by writ of certiorari (granted by discretion of the Court). The power of judicial review is not explicitly stated in the Constitution but is rather an operational precedent established by Chief Justice John Marshall in the case of *Marbury* v. *Madison* (1803). The Court may also overrule its own previous decisions, allowing it to change with the times. An example of this is the decision in *Brown* v. *Board of Education* (1954), which declared racial segregation in education unconstitutional, overturning *Plessy* v. *Ferguson* (1896). The Court of the 1950s and 1960s, under Chief Justice Earl Warren, was generally regarded as judicially liberal; it became more conservative under Chief Justice Warren Burger (1969-86). The first woman was appointed to the Court in 1981 by Pres. Ronald Reagan. Today's Court is headed by William Rehnquist (since 1986).

Surabaya, or Surakaja (pop. 2,473,300), city in Indonesia, located on the northeastern coast of Java at the mouth of the Mas River. Surabaya's port is the second busiest in Indonesia (Jakarta has the busiest). It exports Indonesian products, including sugar, coffee, tobacco, spices, oils,and petroleum. The port is also home to Indonesia's main naval base. Surabaya is a busy industrial center. Its industries include shipbuilding and repair, textiles, chemicals, rubber, and cigarettes. Surabaya's educational facilities include a large university and a naval college.
See also: Indonesia.

Surface tension, property that makes the surface of a liquid act as if it were an elastic film. The molecules in a liquid stay together because they are pulled towards each other equally. This force is called cohesion. The molecules at the surface of a liquid have no molecules above them to attract and pull them; these molecules are pulled only by those beside and below them. This continuous sideward and downward pull creates tension at the surface, making it act as if it were a resilient film. A razor blade placed flatly on the surface of water does not sink because the surface tension supports it. Because of surface tension some birds are able to stand on water.
See also: Capillarity; Cohesion.

Surfing, sport of riding a wooden or foam plastic surfboard on the incline of a wave. It requires balance, timing, and coordination. Surfing originated in

Suriname

Capital:	Paramaribo
Area:	63,251 sq mi (163,820 sq km)
Population:	428,000
Language:	Dutch
Government:	Presidential republic
Independent:	1975
Head of gov.:	Prime minister
Per capita:	U.S. $880
Mon. unit:	1 Suriname guilder = 100 cents

Hawaii and is the oldest sport in the United States. With worldwide competitions organized by the International Surfing Committee, surfing has gained widespread popularity, particularly in the United States, Australia, Brazil, France, Japan, Mexico, and Peru.

Surgeon general of the United States, chief medical adviser of the United States. The surgeon general commissions studies and research regarding health issues, informs the public about the findings, makes recommendations as to how health problems may be alleviated, and warns the public about health hazards.

Surgery, branch of medicine chiefly concerned with manual operations to remove or repair diseased, damaged, or deformed body tissues. The origins of surgery go back to ancient times, and there is evidence that the Egyptians, Greeks, and Romans achieved some impressive results. Infections and gangrene were major problems resulting from surgery during the Middle Ages in Europe, but this began to change in the 19th century. The development of techniques of sterilization and anesthetics allowed for the expansion of modern surgery under much safer conditions, and the invention of new diagnostic tools, such as X-rays and CAT scans, has made surgery more effective.

Suriname, republic on the northeastern coast of South America, bordered by Guyana on the west, Brazil on the south, and French Guiana on the east. The capital is Paramaribo.
Land and climate. The country consists largely of unexplored forested highlands and the flat Atlantic coast. The climate is tropical, with heavy rains.
People and economy. The population is about 34% East Indian, 35% Creole, and 16% Indonesian. Other groups include Europeans, Chinese, and Native Americans. The official language is Dutch, but most people speak the Creole Sranang Tongo. Hindi, Javanese, Chinese, English, French, and Spanish are also spoken. The most important product of the economy is bauxite. The main crops are rice, sugar, fruits, coffee, and bananas.
History. England ceded Suriname to the Dutch (1667) in exchange for New Amsterdam (now New York City), and the country was subsequently known

as Dutch Guiana. It became a self-governing part of the Netherlands in 1954 and gained full independence in 1975. The first years of independence were marked by an exodus of some 40,000 Surinamese to the Netherlands and by border disputes with French Guiana and Guyana. A bloodless military coup took place in 1980, but the country returned to democratic rule in 1988. The relationship with the Netherlands remained tensed. In 1998 there were massive demonstrations aimed at the country's financial policy and the increase in prices.

Surratt, Mary Eugenia (1820-65), boardinghouse keeper in Washington, D.C., unjustly hanged for complicity in the assassination of Abraham Lincoln. She was accused because of contact with the assassin John Wilkes Booth, who met in her house with his conspirators, including her son, John H. Subsequent revelations proved that her trial was flagrantly unjust and that she was innocent.

Surrealism, movement in literature and art that flourished between World War I and World War II, especially in Paris; influenced by Freudianism. Writers associated with surrealism include André Breton, Louis Aregon, and Jean Cocteau; surrealist artists include Salvador Dali, Joan Miró, René Magritte, Yves Tanguy, and Max Ernst. The movement was devoted to unleashing the imagination of the unconscious minds, free of the constraints of reason. In painting and films everyday objects were often placed in dreamlike settings; apparently unrelated objects were juxtaposed, and incongruous images were dominant.

Surrey, Earl of (1517?-47), English poet. Surrey was born into the English nobility and received a classical education in France. He was knighted in 1541 and was a member of the court of King Henry VIII.
Surrey's friendship with King Henry's illegitimate son, the duke of Richmond, created speculation that he was part of a treason plot against the king. This led to his arrest and beheading. Surrey's major achievement is his contribution of verse styles to English poetry. His translation of *The Aeneid* was the first English usage of blank verse. Together with Sir Thomas Wyatt (1503-42), Surrey introduced to English poetry the Petrarchan sonnet form used in Italy. Surrey and Wyatt's *The Book of Songs and Sonnets* was published in 1557. Many English poets and writers subsequently wrote in blank verse and the sonnet form, creating an age of high poetic achievement in England.

Surveying, process of measuring distances and features on the earth's surface for map preparation and locating boundary lines. Geodetic surveying, which covers large areas, takes the earth's curvature into account. After a base line of known length is established, the positions of other points are found by triangulation (measuring the angles of the point from each end of the base line) or by trilateration (measuring all the sides of the triangle formed by point and base line). Distances are measured by tape or by electronic means. Instruments for measuring angles are the theodolite and the alidade. Vertical elevations are determined by levels. Much modern surveying is done by photogrammetry, using the stereoscope to determine contours.

Susa (also called Shush), capital of the ancient Middle East country of Elam and later of the Persian Empire. Its ruins are located in southwestern Iran,

just north of the Persian Gulf. Susa was an active community as early as biblical times. Archeological digs in the region have unearthed remains of many civilizations. Elam reached the peak of its power after 1300 B.C., after overthrowing Babylonia.
See also: Persia, Ancient.

Suslov, Mikhail Andreyevich (1902-82), Communist Party official in the USSR. An orthodox Stalinist during Stalin's lifetime, Suslov rose steadily through the party ranks, helping to form the Cominform in 1947 and serving as editor of the party newspaper, *Pravda* (1949-50). A member of the ruling Politburo from 1955, he became one of its most rigid ideologues. With an instinct for survival, he at first supported Nikita Khrushchev and then helped overthrow him in 1964. He opposed any suggestion of relaxing party rule in the country.
See also: Union of Soviet Socialist Republics.

Suspension, in chemistry, mixture in which solid particles hang in a liquid or gas. The suspension is maintained by the continued movement of the molecules of the liquid or gas, which bump the molecules of the particles. Two examples of suspensions are dust (solid in a gas) and muddy water (solid in a liquid).
See also: Solution.

Suspension bridge *See:* Bridge.

Susquehanna River, river in the eastern United States, rising in Otsego Lake in central New York state and flowing southward 444 mi (715 km) across Pennsylvania and Maryland, emptying into Chesapeake Bay, Maryland. The Susquehanna's shallow, rapid water flow and many rock obstructions make it unsuitable as a shipping waterway, but it is an important source of waterpower. Several hydroelectric and other energy plants have been built along it.

Sussex spaniel, strong, short, stocky dog originally bred in Sussex, England. It weighs 35-45 lb (16-20 kg) and has a dark gold coat.

Sutherland, Dame Joan (1926-), Australian soprano, one of the foremost exponents of the art of bel canto. She made her debut in Sydney (1950), her U.S. debut in Dallas (1960), and her N.Y. Metropolitan debut (1961) in *Lucia di Lammermoor*. In 1990 she retired.
See also: Opera.

Suva (pop. 71,600), capital of Fiji, a country made up of more than 800 islands in the South Pacific. Suva is located on the southeast coast of Viti Levu, the fifth-largest Fijian island. Its harbor is the country's main port. It is also an educational center, with the University of Fiji and the Fiji School of Medicine located there.
See also: Fiji.

Suwannee River, river rising in the Okefenokee swamp of southeastern Georgia and flowing 250 mi (400 km) generally south through Florida to the Gulf of Mexico. It is the "Swannee River" of Stephen Foster's song, "The Old Folks at Home."

Suzuki method, style of musical instruction begun in the 1940s to teach very young children to play musical instruments. The method was initiated by Shinichi Suzuki, who believed that children could aquire musical skills as they do language, by listening and imitating. Parent involvement is an important component of the method.

Svalbard, or Spitsbergen, island group in the Arctic Ocean 400 mi (640 km) north of Norway and officially belonging to that country since 1920. The 5 main islands are Spitsbergen, North East Land, Edge Island, Barents Island, and Prince Charles Foreland. They were known to the Norwegians by the Middle Ages. Formerly of importance in the whaling and fur trading industries, since the 1890s they have been mined for coal, largely by companies of the former Soviet Union.

Svedberg, Theodor (1884-71), Swedish chemist awarded the 1926 Nobel Prize in chemistry for inventing the ultracentrifuge, important in studies of colloids and large molecules.
See also: Chemistry.

Sverdlovsk (nowadays Ekaterinburg; pop. 1,367,000), industrial city in the eastern Ural Mountains of Russia. The western terminus of the Trans-Siberian railroad, Sverdlovsk is a major industrial center, with over 200 factories producing machinery, turbines, diesels, and a variety of engineering products. The city was founded in 1721 and called Ekaterinburg, after Tsarina Catherine I. It was renamed in 1924 after Sverdlov, a Bolshevik leader. It was in Sverdlovsk that Tsar Nicholas II and his family were executed in 1918, during the Russian civil war. The city was renamed Ekaterinburg in 1991. The inhabitants of the area want more autonomy, but so far Yeltsin has refused.
See also: Union of Soviet Socialist Republics.

Swahili, Bantu language of East Africa, widely spoken in Kenya, Uganda, Tanzania, and parts of Zaire. Swahili is heavily influenced by Arabic in its vocabulary, the name of the language itself coming from the Arabic word for "coasts."

Swallow, common name for various small birds of the family Hirundinidae. There are at least 78 species; all have long, sickle-shaped wings and long, forked tails. The plumage is generally dark, often with a metallic sheen. Many species have lighter underparts. The legs and feet are small and weak. Swallows can perch on wires or tree branches but are adapted to spend most of their time on the wing, feeding on insects. Many species are migratory.

Swammerdam, Jan (1637-80), Dutch entomologist, zoologist, and anatomist, who made major contributions to research on insect metamorphosis, life cycles, and anatomy. He also studied red blood cells and the working nerves and muscles in animals, showing that muscles change their configuration but not their size when contracting. His written works include *A General History of Insects*, and the *Bible of Nature*.
See also: Entomology; Zoology

Swamp, area of poorly drained, low-lying land saturated with water. Swamps normally covered by water are called marshes. The obstruction of drainage that causes swamps to form may result from the flatness of the land, the presence of impermeable rock beneath the surface, or the growth of dense vegetation. Lakes that are filled in by sediment may develop into swamps. When drained, swamps usually make fertile farmland. Large swamps in the United States include the Everglades (Florida), the Dismal (North Carolina), and the Okefenokee (Georgia and Florida).

Swan, any of various large, long-necked aquatic birds related to ducks and geese. There are eight species, seven within the genus *Cygnus*. Five of these are found in the Northern Hemisphere; all are white in adult plumage but have different-colored bills. The two remaining species are the black swan of Australia and the black-necked swan of South America. Most feed on vegetation.

Swanscombe man, prehistoric human dating back to the Second Interglacial Period about 350,000 years ago. Three parts of a skull were discovered 3 consecutive years (1935, 1936, 1937) in Swanscombe, England at the River Thames. A better specimen, found in Steinheim, Germany, in 1933, dates back 375,000 years.
See also: Prehistoric people.

Swansea (pop. 188,000), industrial seaport in Wales, originally settled in the 1000s. Its 281 acres of waterfront docks on Swansea Bay export the products of nearby oil refineries, aluminum factories, nickel and zinc refineries, and coal mines. In the 1800s the city was a major copper trading center and produced great amounts of tin plate for cans.
See also: Wales.

Swastika, ancient symbol of well-being and prosperity employed by such diverse peoples as Greeks, Celts, Native Americans, and the Hindus of India, where it apparently arose. The word comes from the Sanskrit for "good fortune." In the 20th century the symbol became infamous as the emblem of Nazism.

Swaziland, country in southeastern Africa, bordered by Mozambique on the east and the Republic of South Africa on the other three sides. The capital is Mbabane.
Land and climate. There are three main regions: the mountainous High Veld in the west, the lower Middle Veld, and the Low Veld rising in the east to the narrow Lebombo range. The four major rivers, running west to east, are being developed for irrigation and could provide abundant hydroelectricity.
People and economy. Swazis and a smaller number of Zulus constitute 92% of the population. "Coloreds" (of mixed ancestry) and Europeans make up the rest. Agriculture, including forestry, is the largest single sector in the economy. Sugar, wood pulp, asbestos, fruits, iron ore, and canned meats are the main exports. Swaziland has close communication, economic, and trade links with South Africa.
History. Settled by the Swazis, a Bantu people, and unified as a kingdom in the 1800s, Swaziland was taken over by Britain in 1903 and later fell under South African influence. The country became self-governing in 1963 and fully independent in 1968 under King Sobhuza II. Mawati III has ruled since Sobhuza's death in 1982. At the beginning of the 1990s the king

Swaziland

Capitals:	Mbabane, Lobamba
Area:	6,704 sq mi (17,364 sq km)
Population:	966,000
Language:	Siswati, English
Government:	Monarchy
Independent:	1968
Head of gov.:	Prime minister
Per capita:	U.S. $1,170
Mon. unit:	1 Lilangeni = 100 cents

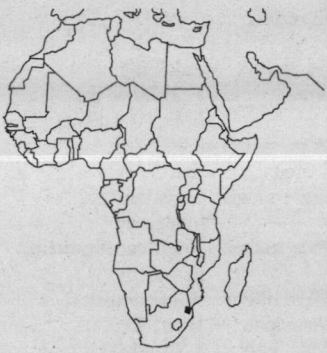

announced a reform or the electoral system. A blind eye was turned to the oppositional party PUDEMA (People's United Democratic Movement). However, at the 1993 parliamentary elections the existing political parties were not allowed to select candidates. As a result, in 1995 the king was asked to temporarily leave the country so as to allow the creation of a multi party system.

Sweat gland *See:* Perspiration.

Sweatshop, place of work with long hours, poor pay, and bad conditions. Such places often exploit those who find difficulty in obtaining employment, such as women, unskilled laborers, newly arrived immigrants, and children. Sweatshops have been curbed by the growth of organized labor.

Sweden, kingdom in northern Europe, occupying most of the eastern and southern portion of the Scandinavian peninsula.
Land and climate. Sweden has an area of 173,604 sq mi (449,750 sq km). It is bounded on the west and north by Norway; on the northeast by Finland; on the east and south by the Baltic Sea; and on the southwest by the Öresund, Kattegat, and Skagerrak, the narrows linking the Baltic with the North Sea. At its northernmost, it lies within the Arctic Circle and includes part of Lapland. Sweden may be divided into four main regions: Norrland, the northern two-thirds of the country; the central lowlands; southern Sweden; and Skåne. Barren heights, high lakes, peat bogs, and great forests of spruce, pine, and larch cover most of the thinly populated Norrland. Sweden's rivers and lakes make up nearly 10% of the country's area and some of the largest of its lakes are in the central lowlands. Most of the people live in this area and it is also the site of the country's two largest cities, Stockholm and Göteborg. Southern Sweden is a fertile, coastal lowland region, and Skåne is the low-lying agricultural region in the extreme south. Northern Sweden has long, cold winters and brief, cool summers. The south enjoys longer summers and milder winters. The capital of the country is Stockholm. ***People.*** The population is almost entirely Swedish, except for a minority of Lapps in the north. The official language is Swedish, and almost everyone is Lutheran.

Sweden

Capital:	Stockholm
Area:	173,604 sq mi (449,750 sq km)
Population:	8,887,000
Language:	Swedish
Government:	Constitutional monarchy
Independent:	1917 (constitutional monarchy)
Head of gov.:	Prime minister
Per capita:	U.S. $23,750
Mon. unit:	1 Swedish krona = 100 öre

Economy. Sweden has extensive forests, rich deposits of iron ore, abundant hydroelectric power, and enough good farmland to be nearly self-sufficient in food production. Main exports are machinery, iron, steel, paper, wood pulp, timber, and motor vehicles. Sweden enjoys one of the highest living standards in the world with relatively low unemployment and extensive social services, including free education, retirement pensions, and comprehensive medical care. An economic downturn in the 1970s, 1980s and 1990s partly eroded Swedish prosperity, slowing economic growth and leading to unemployment, inflation and the relinquishment of some social achievements.

History. Mention of the Swedes is first recorded by the Roman historian Tacitus in the 1st century A.D. In the 9th and 10th centuries A.D., Vikings from Sweden known as Varangians pioneered trade routes through Russia as far as the Black Sea. Throughout the Middle Ages, the history of the Swedes was tied to that of Norway and Denmark. The Danes, dominant in the Kalmar Union of Denmark, Norway, and Sweden, which was founded in 1397, were driven out of Sweden in 1523. In the 17th century, Gustavus II (Gustavus Adolphus) made Sweden a leading European power, but the rise of Russia in the 18th century checked Swedish ambitions. In 1809 the monarchy became constitutional; a new constitution took effect in 1975. Sweden took no part in World War I or World War II. The Social Democrats have been the predominant political party through much of Sweden's 20th-century history, architects of the country's social welfare system and its policy of neutrality. Sweden opposed the U.S. war in Vietnam and in 1969 recognized North Vietnam, thereby marking the high point of a period of strained relations with the United States. Swedish domestic politics have been free of violence with the sole exception being the assassination of Prime Minister Olof Palme (1986), a murder that remains unsolved. In 1995 Sweden joined the EU. At present the country does not wish to join the European Monetary Union.

Swedenborgians, followers of the religious ideas of the Swedish theologian Emanuel Swedenborg (1688-1772). A scientist and engineer, Swedenborg became a Christian mystic in 1747. He believed that the Second Coming of Christ occurred in 1757. After his death, his followers founded the Church of the New Jerusalem, first organized in London in 1787 and introduced in the United States in 1792.

Swedish, one of the North Germanic or Scandinavian languages, spoken by about 9 million people in Sweden, Finland, Estonia, the United States, and Canada. Old Swedish developed from Old Norse and gave place to modern Swedish (1500) with the onset of standardization.

Sweet alyssum, vigorous, low-growing perennial herb (*Lobularia maritima*) of the mustard family, originating in the Mediterranean area. It produces sweet, mostly white but sometimes lavender or pink flowers. Plants can grow to 9 in (23 cm) high.

Sweetbrier *See:* Eglantine.

Sweet flag, tall, straight, perennial marsh herb (*Acorus calamus*) of the arum family, growing in moist areas near streams and ponds. Its fat root is edible and is also used in medicines and perfumes. Flat leaves grow 2-6 ft (61-180 cm) high from the root rather than the stem.

Sweet gum, any of various tall shade trees (genus *Liquidambar*) of the hazel family named for the sweet-smelling gummy substance they produce, called storax. Sweet gums have star-shaped leaves that turn brilliant colors in the fall. Storax is used for perfumes, adhesives, and ointments. Brown, spiny seed balls are produced as fruit and remain on the tree most of the winter.

Sweet pea, fragrant, annual garden plant (*Lathyrus odoratus*) native to Italy and thriving in numerous temperate countries where there is rich soil and abundant sunshine. Flowers grow to 2 in (5 cm) across, either individually or in small clusters.

Sweet potato, trailing creeper plant (*Ipomoea batatas*) of the morning glory family, native to tropical America. It produces a tuberous root that is sweet-tasting when cooked. In the United States an orange variety is grown, with roots rich in carotene.

Sweet William, Eurasian pink biennial (*Dianthus barbatus*), also known as Newport pink. Originating in Europe and Asia, the plant produces thick clusters of white, pink, or purple ringed flowers.

Swift, any of several highly mobile, small, insect-eating lizards (genus *Sceloporus*) found in dry temperate regions of the United States, Mexico, and Central America. Most swifts reproduce by laying eggs, while others give birth to live young.

Swift, small, fast-flying insectivorous bird, similar to a swallow but classed with the hummingbirds in the order Apodiformes. Both swifts and hummingbirds have very small feet and extremely short arm bones, the major flight feathers being attached to the extended hand bones. Entirely aerial, most species feed and even sleep on the wing.

Swift, Gustavus Franklin (1839-1903), U.S. businessperson. The first to slaughter cattle in Chicago for shipment east (1875), he introduced refrigerated railroad cars, founded Swift & Co., and pioneered the manufacture of meat by-products.

Swift, Jonathan (1667-1745), Anglo-Irish writer, journalist, poet, and prose satirist. Two of his satires were published in 1704: *The Battle of the Books* and *The Tale of a Tub*. He became a Tory in 1710, taking over *The Examiner*, the Tory journal. From 1714 he lived in Ireland, as dean of St. Patrick's, Dublin. He deplored the plight of the Irish poor in the *Drapier's Letters* (1724). His masterpiece is *Gulliver's Travels* (1726), a political and social satire that has been adapted as a children's classic.
See also: Gulliver's Travels.

Swigert, John Leonard, Jr. (1931-82), U.S. astronaut who participated in the 1970 Apollo 13 moon mission, which was aborted in space after life-support systems failed. The astronauts returned to earth safely by relying on the lunar module's life systems. Swigert left the space program in 1977 and was elected to the U.S. House of Representatives.

Swimming and diving, popular water sports. Common swimming styles include the side stroke, a simple sidewise propulsion for distance swimming and lifesaving; the breaststroke, a froglike arm-and-leg thrust; backstroke, either overarm or, for distance endurance, an inverted breaststroke; and the crawl, the most common freestyle form, using an overarm pull and a flutter kick. The butterfly, a modified breaststroke that thrusts the head and arms up from the water and incorporates a dolphin kick, has become a popular competitive style. Distance swimming has produced many well-publicized attempts to cross the English Channel and other large bodies of water. Organized, artistic diving dates back to 17th century Sweden and Germany. Competitions include forward, backward, reverse, inward, twisting, and armstand dives in layout (extended), tuck (rolled in a ball), pike (bent at waist, legs straight), and free positions, from a platform or springboard. Various swimming and diving events are part of the Summer Olympic Games and other competitions.

Swinburne, Algernon Charles (1837-1909), English poet and literary critic. He established his reputation as a writer with the verse play *Atalanta in Calydon* (1865). Other important works were 2 volumes of *Poems and Ballads* (1866, 1878) and the long poem *Tristram of Lyonesse* (1882). His knowledge of literary works of classical Greece and Rome, Shakespeare and other Elizabethans, and French poetry informed his work. His own poetry is known both for its sensuality and its exploration of complex meters and rhyme schemes.

Swing *See:* Jazz.

Swiss chard, green leafy vegetable (*Beta vulgaris cicla*) similar to the beet but with an inedible root. Its large leaves, rich in vitamins A, B complex, and C, grow throughout the summer.

Swiss Family Robinson *See:* Wyss family.

Swiss Guard, member of the Swiss mercenary soldiers who served in various European armies from the 15th to the 19th centuries, most notably as bodyguards to the French monarch (1497-1792 and 1814-30). The colorfully uniformed Papal Swiss Guard at the Vatican Palace in Rome dates back to the late 1400s. It is the only surviving branch of the Guard.

Switzerland

Capital:	Bern
Area:	15,943 sq mi (41,293 sq km)
Population:	7,260,000
Language:	German, French, Italian
Government:	Federal republic
Independent:	1499
Head of gov.:	President (chosen each year by the Federal Council)
Per capita:	U.S. $40,630
Mon. unit:	1 Swiss franc = 100 rappen

Switzerland, officially the Swiss Confederation, federal republic situated in the Alps in central Europe.

Land and climate. Switzerland covers 15,943 sq mi (41,293 sq km). It is bounded by Germany on the north, Austria and Liechtenstein on the east, Italy on the south, and France on the west. Lying almost entirely within the western Alps, Switzerland has three main regions: the Jura Mountains of the western Alps, the Swiss Foreland or Plateau, and the Swiss Alps. The parallel ranges and narrow valleys of the Jura run southwest to northeast along the Swiss-French border from Lake Geneva to the Rhine River at Basel. The long, narrow Swiss Foreland or Plateau, between the Jura Mountains and the Swiss Alps, extends from Lake Geneva to Lake Constance. The plateau is Switzerland's major agricultural area. It contains most of Switzerland's large cities and important manufacturing centers, and is home to about 60% of the population. The outer ranges of the Swiss Alps stretch from Lake Geneva to Lake Thun. They are succeeded by much higher ranges culminating in the Perrine Alps in the south where Monte Rosa soars to 15,203 ft (4,634 m) and the Matterhorn rises to 14,701 ft (4,481 m). Covering more than half of Switzerland, the region contains less than 20% of the population. There are many lakes in the Alps, and both the Rhine and the Rhône have their sources in its mountains. There are great variations of climate in Switzerland, due mainly to differences in altitude. Much of the country has a typically Central European climate. Sheltered valleys in the south have hot summers and mild winters. Elsewhere winters are cold, with heavy snowfall. Among Switzerland's major cities are Zurich, Basel, and Geneva. The capital is Bern.

People. The four official language groups are German (74%), French (20%), Italian (5%), and Romansh, a Rhaeto-Roman dialect (1%). The Latin word for Switzerland, *Helvetia*, appears on Swiss currencies and postage stamps. The Swiss are divided almost equally between Protestant and Roman Catholic.

Economy. Highly industrialized and with plentiful hydroelectric power, Switzerland exports watches, jewelry, precision tools and instruments, textiles, and chemicals. Dairy cattle are raised. Cheese and chocolate are important exports, and tourism and international banking are major industries.

History. Rome conquered the Helvetii, the native Swiss, in 58 B.C. The area subsequently came under the Alemanni, the Burgundians, the Franks, and, in the 10th century, the Holy Roman Empire. Habsburg oppression led to the Perpetual Covenant among the cantons or states of Uri, Schwyz, and Unterwald in 1291, the traditional beginning of the Swiss Confederation. Wars against Austria resulted in virtual independence in 1499. During the Protestant Reformation, the country was divided by religious civil wars, but it remained neutral throughout the Thirty Years' War and its independence was formally recognized in the Peace of Westphalia of 1648. French revolutionary armies imposed a centralized Helvetic Republic from 1798 to 1803. In 1815 the Congress of Vienna restored the Confederation. After a three-week civil war, a federal democracy was established in 1848. Switzerland remained neutral in both world wars and is not a member of the UN. As presently constituted, the republic is a federation of 20 cantons and 6 semi-cantons, with Bern as the federal capital. Women have had the right to vote on federal matters since 1971. In 1997 Switzerland participated in NATO's Partnership for Peace. In 1998, a number of Swiss banks were forced to reimburse money to the next of kin of Jewish Holocaust victims.

Sword, ancient weapon consisting of a handle and a metal blade with a sharp point and one or two cutting edges. Leaf-shaped Bronze Age swords gave way to short, flat blades in Rome, and these to longer laminated iron (in Damascus) and tempered steel (notably in Toledo). Asian curved cutting blades (the Turkish scimitar) inspired the cavalry saber. The Japanese samurai used a longer, two-handed version. The thrust-and-parry rapier became the weapon of the duel and of fencing.

Swordfish, or broadbill, large, streamlined food and game fish (*Xiphias gladius*) of tropical seas, having a swordlike upper jaw. The maximum length is 16 ft (4.9 m); the maximum weight 1,500 lb (680 kg). Swordfish can swim extremely fast and, when hooked, will leap high out of the water. They eat fish that they kill with strokes of their swordlike jaw.

Sycamore, popular name for a number of deciduous trees. In North America the name is applied to a plane tree (*Platanus occidentalis*), the bark of which flakes off. In Europe the sycamore is a maple (*Acer pseudoplatanus*). The sycamore of ancient times is a fig (*Ficus occidentalis*) that is now seldom cultivated.

Sydenham, Thomas (1624-89), English physician, considered a founder of modern medicine. He pioneered the use of quinine for treating malaria and of laudanum as an anesthetic. He was the author of an important treatise on gout, and first described Sydenham's chorea (St. Vitus's Dance).

Sydney (pop. 3,656,500), oldest and largest city in Australia, capital of New South Wales, in southeastern Australia on the Port Jackson inlet of the Pacific Ocean. Famous for its natural harbor, Harbour Bridge, and opera house, Sydney was founded as a penal colony in 1788, and gold rushes of the 1850 spurred its growth. It is now a major commercial, industrial, shipping, cultural, and recreational center. Manufactures include ships, textiles, chemicals, and refined petroleum.
See also: Australia.

Syllogism, in logic, term for a form of argument consisting of 3 statements: 2 premises and a conclusion. The conclusion of a valid syllogism follows logically from the premises and is true if the premises are true. Aristotle first formulated the concept of syllogistic logic that has served as the basis for logical thought in the West for more than 2,000 years.

Sylvester II (940-1003), first Frenchman to serve as pope (999-1003), known for his learning, his close links to the Holy Roman emperor Otto III, and his support of the Christianization of Poland and Hungary. Before being elected pope, he was superior at the monastery of Bobbio, Italy, and archbishop of Reims, France.

Sylvester I, Saint (d.335), pope who reigned from 314 to 335. During his reign the Council of Nicaea declared Arius a heretic for arguing that the Son was unequal to God. Many legends associate Sylvester I with the Donation of Constantine, a document supposedly granting him control of church property. He is thought to be buried in the Cemetery of Saint Priscilla in Rome.
See also: Arianism.

Symbiosis, also called mutualism, relationship between 2 dependent organisms of different species in which mutual benefit is derived by both participants. Other types of symbiotic relationships are commensalism which denotes independence of the symbiotes; parasitism, which implies potential injury to the host organism, and helotism, which denotes a master-slave relationship.

Symbolism, in literature, movement begun by a group of French poets in the late 19th century in opposition to naturalism. Prominent poets associated with symbolism include Jules Laforgue, Stéphane Mallarmé, Paul Valéry, and Paul Verlaine. Influenced by Charles Baudelaire, the symbolists aimed to create poetic images, or symbols, that would be apprehended by the senses and reach into the preconscious world of the spirit. Though short-lived as a movement, symbolism influenced such major writers as James Joyce, Marcel Proust, R.M. Rilke, and W.B. Yeats.

Symphonic poem, or tone poem, form of orchestral music in one movement that describes a story or scene. Popular with composers c.1850-1900, the form was originated by Franz Liszt and perfected by Richard Strauss.

Symphony, major form of music for orchestra. Developed from the overture, by 1800 it had 4 movements: a fairly quick movement in sonata form; a slow movement; a minuet and trio; and a quick rondo. Haydn and Mozart played a central role in developing the classical symphony. Beethoven introduced the scherzo movement and a new range of emotion. Major symphonic composers include Schubert, Berlioz, Mendelssohn, Brahms, Bruckner, Dvorák, and Mahler in the 19th century, and Stravinsky, Prokofiev, Shostakovich, Vaughan Williams, Elgar, Sibelius, and Nielsen in the 20th century.
See also: Orchestra.

Synagogue (Greek, "house of assembly"), Jewish place of worship. The synagogue became the center of communal and religious life after the

destruction of the Temple in Jerusalem (A.D. 70) and dispersal of the Jews. Most synagogues have an ark containing the Torah, an "eternal light," 2 candelabra, pews, and a platform (bimah) for readings and conduct of services. Orthodox synagogues segregate women.
See also: Judaism.

Synchro-cyclotron, cylindrical-shaped particle accelerator designed to accelerate protons. A cylindrical magnet bends the particle beams into a circular path, as in a cyclotron, an electric field being applied to accelerate the protons each time they come around the circle. In the synchro-cyclotron the frequency of the electric field steadily decreases to compensate for the increasing mass acquired by the protons as they approach the speed of light.
See also: Lawrence, Ernest Orlando; Particle accelerator.

Synchrotron, type of particle accelerator in which a doughnut-shaped ring of magnets around a vacuum produces a magnetic field that rises in intensity as the accelerated protons rise in velocity. This keeps the particles moving in circular orbits whose radii remain constant. The design, which requires no magnet in the center, allows rings to be built of several miles in diameter.
See also: Particle accelerator.

Syndicalism (French: *syndicat*, "labor union"), revolutionary labor movement that aimed at seizing control of industry through strikes, sabotage, even violence, and, as its ultimate weapon, the general strike. It originated in late-19th-century France from the theories of Pierre Joseph Proudhon and Georges Sorel. Syndicalists agreed with Marxist class analysis but like anarchists rejected any state organization. Syndicalism was strong in France and Italy in the early 1900s and found U.S. expression in the industrial unionism of the Industrial Workers of the World. World War I and the advance of communism overtook the syndicalists; their influence lasted longest in Spain, where it was destroyed in the civil war (1936-39).
See also: Labor movement.

Synge, John Millington (1871-1909), Irish poet and playwright. His plays often portray rural Irish life of his times. Among his best-known and most-respected works are the tragedy *Riders to the Sea* (1904) and the comedy *Playboy of the Western World* (1907). Some of his plays were produced in the Abbey Theatre, Dublin, which he and W.B. Yeats helped to found (1904).

Synoptic Gospels, in the New Testament, comprehensive view of the life of Jesus according to Matthew, Mark, and Luke, which contain a high level of agreement on subject matter and phraseology. Modern scholars commonly regard Mark as having written his gospel first and suppose that Matthew and Luke also used *Q*, a now-lost source containing the non-Marcan material common to them.
See also: New Testament.

Synthesizer, electronic musical device able to produce and change the timbre, quality, and frequency of sounds generated. First developed in 1955 and increasingly complex since the advent of microprocessors, the instrument has enabled composers and entertainers to create new works using isolated sounds or various sound combinations.

Synthetic, substance created by chemical processing and used as a substitute for naturally occurring substances. Synthetic fibers such as acrylic and nylon are used as substitutes for silk, cotton, linen, and wool. Plastics, which are all synthetics, replace glass, wood, metal, and other materials. Synthetics are often produced from carbon, hydrogen, oxygen, and other elements by polymerization, which creates extremely large molecules. Rayon, a synthetic fiber, results from dissolving and extruding cellulose, which is one of the main components of wood. Properties of synthesized materials can be controlled to suit their intended form and function.

Synthetic fuels, combustible matter that can replace crude oil and natural gas. Sources for synthetic fuels include plant and animal matter, coal, oil shale, and bituminous sands.

Syphilis, highly contagious venereal disease, caused by a spirochete, *Treponema pallidum*, and characterized by a variety of lesions (chancres, mucous patches, and skin ulcers) at the point of infection. If untreated, syphilis can cause degeneration of the central nervous system resulting in death. It is most often transmitted by sexual contact, but can also be passed on by transfusions of infected blood. Once a widespread cause of death, syphilis is now relatively easily treatable with penicillin, if detected before major damage to the nervous system occurs.
See also: Venereal disease.

Syracuse (pop. 659,864), city in central New York, seat of Onondaga County, situated on Onondaga Lake. The original inhabitants of the area were the Onondaga, an Iroquois tribe. Although French explorers arrived in the 17th century, discovering its economically important salt springs, it was not until 1786 that Ephraim Webster established a permanent settlement. In 1825 the settlement was named for the ancient Greek city of Syracuse, which was also situated on salt springs. In addition to having saltworks, the city was a trade center along the Erie Canal (completed 1825) and a rail center. Manufactures now also include machinery, electronics, and chinaware. Syracuse is home to Syracuse University and the State of New York Upstate Medical Center, and hosts many conventions as well as the annual New York State Fair.

Syracuse, city in southeastern Sicily, on the Ionian Sea. Founded by Corinthians (734 B.C.), it became a brilliant center of Greek culture, notably under Hiero I (r.478-466 B.C.) and Dionysius the Elder (r.405-367 B.C.). Syracuse was defeated by Rome in 212 B.C. Later conquerors included the Arabs (878) and Normans (1085). The modern provincial capital, a port and tourist center, has many ancient monuments.
See also: Sicily.

Syria, Arab republic in southwest Asia.
Land and climate. Syria covers about 71,498 sq mi (185,180 sq km) and is bounded by Turkey on the north, Iraq on the east and southeast, Jordan and

Syria

Capital:	Damascus
Area:	71,498 sq mi (185,180 sq km)
Population:	16,673,000
Language:	Arabic
Government:	Presidential republic
Independent:	1946
Head of gov.:	Prime minister
Per capita:	U.S. $1,120
Mon. unit:	1 Syrian pound = 100 piastres

Israel on the south, and Lebanon and the Mediterranean Sea on the west. Syria has a 100-mi (161-km)-long coastline on the Mediterranean. The coastal plain is separated from the inland reaches by a coast range, the Jebel Ansariya, part of the Lebanon Mountains. In the southwest, the border with Lebanon is marked by the Anti-Lebanon Mountains and Syria's highest peak, Mt. Hermon (9,232 ft/2,814 m). The mountains fall away to the plains of Hawran, extending from the Jebel ed Druz Mountains to the Sea of Galilee and the Jordan River valley. To the east and southeast are the arid wastes of the Syrian Desert, dominating most of the country and extending through Jordan and Iraq into Saudi Arabia. Syria's largest river, the Euphrates, flows through the desert. The coastal region has a Mediterranean climate. In the inland plains and the desert, the climate is much harsher.

People. Over 70% of the Syrian people are Arab-speaking Sunnite Muslims, but there are also Kurdish, Turkish, Armenian, and Circassian minorities. Christian Orthodox churches claim some 1,000,000 members, and there are about 250,000 Druzes. The capital is Damascus.

Economy. About 25% of the people work in agriculture. Industry includes textiles, iron and steel, and assembly of transportation and electrical equipment. Exports include cotton, fruits and vegetables, and phosphates. Most oil revenues are derived from pipe lines crossing the country, but income from oil drilled in the northeast is increasing. The large Euphrates Dam power station, completed with aid from the Soviet Union, was opened in 1978.

History. Part of the Hittite Empire in the second millennium B.C., Syria was conquered in succeeding centuries by Assyrians, Babylonians, Persians, and Greeks. Under the Seleucids in the 4th century B.C., it was incorporated into the Roman Empire by Pompey in 63 B.C. Governed by the Byzantines from the 5th to the 7th centuries A.D., Syria was conquered by the Arabs in the 7th century A.D. and, in the centuries that followed, it was governed by the Umayyad caliphs, the Seljuk Turks, the Mongols, and the Mameluks. Part of the Ottoman Empire from 1516, Syria was mandated to the French after World War I and became fully independent in 1946. It joined with Egypt in the United Arab Republic from 1958 to 1961. The ruling Baathist Party, which assumed control of the government in 1963, favors socialism and pan-Arab nationalism. Its foreign policy aligns it with the Soviet Union and against the state of Israel. In the early 1980s, the Baathist regime under Hafez el-Assad faced a period of growing unrest and challenge to its authority from the fundamentalist Muslim Brotherhood. As a result of its participation against Israel in the Six-Day War of 1967, Syria lost control of the Golan Heights to an Israeli occupying force. In 1981 the Israelis annexed the area and tensions between the two countries increased. In 1976 Syrian troops intervened in the Lebanese civil war in support of Palestinians, and since then Syria has retained a force in Lebanon. Syrian forces suffered serious losses when Israel invaded Lebanon in 1982. Syria continued to maintain close ties with the Soviet Union and, although the regime has been linked to international terrorist organizations, its cooperation was sought by the United States in the Persian Gulf War (1990-91). Syrian troops were part of the international force created for the liberation of Kuwait. In the 1990s a process of economic and political liberalization took place. In 1996/97 peace negotiations with Israel were terminated due to the issue of returning the Golan Heights.

Syriac, Aramaic language of the northwestern Semitic group. It was used in early Christian writings but was largely superseded by Arabic after the spread of Islam. Closely related to Hebrew, Syriac is still spoken by a few groups in the Middle East.

Syrian Desert, triangular desert plateau covering much of the Arabian Peninsula, including portions of present-day Saudi Arabia, Jordan, Syria, and Iraq. Al-Hamad, the name of the western part of the desert, is sometimes used as a name for the entire expanse. The northern portion is a flat plain, while the southern portion is rocky, with a mountainous central region. The extreme aridity has made the desert nearly uninhabitable, although there are remains of ancient oasis towns, including the caravan city of Palmyra. The desert is now crossed by 2 highways and by oil pipelines from Iraqi oilfields.

Syringa *See:* Mock orange.

Systems analysis, method of studying the interactions of humans, machines, and other elements engaged in activity through the creation of mathematical models. The system is a particular environment of physical and social interaction (e.g., school, factory, economy) viewed as an abstraction so that it can be translated into mathematical statements describing its operation. These are then subject to logical analysis, which can be used to improve the efficient operation of the system. The field, developed in the 1930s, now makes extensive use of computers.

Systolic pressure *See:* Blood pressure.

Szczecin (German: *Stettin*; pop. 416,400), city in northwestern Poland, capital of Szczecin province, on the Baltic Sea at the mouth of the Oder River. It is the main port for Poland, and also an important shipping center for goods in and out of Czechoslovakia, Hungary, and Germany. Szczecin was a fishing settlement by the 8th century. Its status changed a number of times between the 10th century, when it was annexed to Poland, and 1720, when it came under Prussian control. It then remained in German hands until 1945, when it was made part of post-World War II Poland. In addition to shipping, its economy is based on shipbuilding and manufacturing.

Szell, George (1897-1970), Hungarian-born U.S. conductor. He established his reputation in Germany but emigrated to the United States when the Nazis rose to power. Szell's performances and recordings with the Cleveland Orchestra (1946-70) gained international acclaim.

Szent-Györgyi, Albert (1893-1966), Hungarian-born U.S. biochemist awarded the 1937 Nobel Prize in physiology or medicine for his work on biological oxidation processes and his discovery of ascorbic acid in the adrenal glands. He was also the first to isolate vitamin C.

Szilard, Leo (1898-1964), Hungarian-born U.S. physicist who helped pioneer the U.S. atomic bomb project. Along with Enrico Fermi, he designed the first self-sustaining uranium fission reactor. After 1945 he became a leader of the movement against using the bomb. Later he also made contributions in the field of molecular biology.

Szold, Henrietta (1860-1945), founder (1912) of the Women's Zionist Organization of America (Hadassah). She moved to Palestine in 1920 and directed medical and rehabilitation work, particularly for children.

T

T, 20th letter in the English alphabet, corresponding with the Semitic letter *taw*, meaning "mark," it is represented by an upright cross and is probably derived from an ancient Egyptian symbol for a check mark. The Greeks raised the horizontal cross-stroke to produce a capital *T*, which they called *tau*, and which became the 19th letter of the Roman alphabet. The small letter *t* developed from 6th century Roman script. *T* is used as an abbreviation for *testament*, *tablespoon*, and *township*, and *t* for words including *teaspoon*, *tempo*, *tense*, and *ton*.

Tabasco, southwestern state in Mexico on the Bay of Campeche of the Gulf of Mexico. The capital city is Villahermosa. Petroleum is the major resource of this flat, marshy region. Food crops, such as bananas and sugar cane, along with rubber, resins, and hardwoods constitute the important products of this state. Conflicts between native Mexicans (the Olmec) and the Spanish explorer Hernando Cortés took place here in the early 1500s.

Tabernacle, portable temple carried by the Israelis during their nomadic period. According to Exodus its design was given to Moses on Mt. Sinai. The inner chamber contained the Ark of the Covenant, which held the Ten Commandments.

Tabernacles, Feast of *See:* Sukkot.

Table tennis, or ping-pong, indoor game played with a ball, rackets ("paddles"), and a net, a miniature version of tennis. The 9-ft (3-m) table on which it is played is laid out like a tennis court, its 5-ft (150-cm) width spanned by a small net over which the players hit the hollow celluloid ball. The game is played by 2 players, one at either end, or by 4 players, as *doubles*. It originated in England in the late 19th century and is now popular in many countries, particularly in Asia.

Taboo, or **tabu**, prohibition linked to an object, place, or person by law or social custom. The word taboo comes from the Polynesian word *tapu*, meaning something sacred, dangerous, or unclean. In Polynesia, violation of a taboo requires a ritual purification and at times may even warrant the death of the offender (to save the community from suffering ill consequences). In most western societies incest is considered taboo. This taboo was established hundreds of years ago to promote genetic and cultural exchanges between members of clans and tribes by prohibiting the intermarriage of close family relations.

Tabriz (pop. 971,500), city in northwestern Iran, capital of East Azerbaijan province, on the Aji Chai (Talkheh) River. Once called Tauris, it was the capital of Armenia in the 3rd century A.D. It was also briefly the capital of Iran (16th century). Tabriz is surrounded by mountains and has been repeatedly damaged by earthquakes. It produces Persian rugs and other textiles, and is a resort and trade center.
See also: Iran.

Tabularium, library of ancient Rome, used to store records. Erected in 73 B.C, . tt was located on Capitoline Hill, the historic center of ancient Rome.

Taché, Sir Étienne-Paschal (1795-1865), Canadian politician. During Canada's pre-independence years, he served twice as prime minister (1856-57, 1864), an office held jointly with John A. Macdonald. In 1864 Taché presided over the Quebec Conference, which led to Canada's independence 3 years later.
See also: Macdonald, Sir John Alexander; Canada.

Tachometer, instrument that measures the speed at which a wheel or shaft spins. This measurement, usually given in terms of revolutions per minute (rpm), helps gauge the efficiency and power of an engine. Tachometers are used in automobiles, ships, and aircraft.

Tachycardia, abnormally fast heartrate. Generally, anything over 100 beats per minute is considered a tachycardia.
See also: Heart.

Tachyon, subatomic particles that in theory move faster than the speed of light. According to Albert Einstein's theory of relativity (1905), all matter moves slower than the speed of light (186,282 mi per sec/299,792 km per sec). Theoretically, tachyons gain energy as they slow down; it would take massive amounts of energy to slow them down to approximately the speed of light. Physicists today believe that the existence of tachyons fits into Einstein's theory, even though experiments have not as yet proved their existence.

Tacitus, Cornelius (c.A.D.55-120), Roman historian. His most famous works are critical studies of the 1st-century empire, the *Histories* and *Annals*. A son-in-law of Agricola, of whom he wrote a biography, he rose to consul

(97) and proconsul (112) of Asia. His *Germania* is the earliest study of the Germanic tribes.

Tacoma (pop. 158,501), port and industrial city of Washington State, on Puget Sound, about 25 mi (40 km) south of Seattle. It is the third-largest city of the state and the seat of Pierce County. The community developed in the 1850s and 1860s and became a terminus of the Northern Pacific Railway (1873). In 1884 two small towns were amalgamated to form Tacoma. Industries in Tacoma include shipbuilding, chemicals, clothing, and metal and wood products. The port can handle oceangoing ships. The University of Puget Sound and the Pacific Lutheran University are in Tacoma. Fort Lewis, an army post, lies 15 mi (24 km) to the south.
See also: Washington.

Taconite, rock containing about 30% iron ore, from which iron is made. The noniron-bearing part of taconite is called chert. Because taconite is very hard, it takes a number of steps to extract the iron ore material, which is speckled throughout the chert. After the rock is initially blasted or cracked, it is broken down further and crushed. Magnets then can attract the iron ore and separate it from the pulverized chert. A large deposit of taconite is found in the Mesabi Range in Minnesota. Taconite is named after the Taconic Mountains of southern New England, where taconite is also found.

Tadpole, or polliwog, larval amphibian hatched from transparent, jellylike eggs laid on the water. Tadpoles have the physical characteristics of fish (tail and gills). Through metamorphosis (a stage that can last from 10 days to 2 years, depending on the species) legs appear, the digestive system develops, the tail begins to shrink, and lungs develop as the gills disappear. In the adult frog or toad, the tail also disappears.

Tadzhikistan *See:* Tajikistan.

Taft, Robert Alphonso (1889-1953), U.S. senator from Ohio (1938-53). Eldest son of President William H. Taft, he studied law, served in the Ohio legislature, and became a leading conservative Republican. Taft was a fiscal conservative, an opponent of the New Deal, and an isolationist. His most famous congressional achievement was the Taft-Hartley Act.

Taft, William Howard (1909-13), 27th president of the United States. Taft was an imposing figure—he stood 6 ft tall and weighed more than 300 lbs. A good-natured, self-effacing man, he had the misfortune to follow the flamboyant Theodore Roosevelt in office—and suffered in the comparison. In his own time, Taft was judged one of the weakest of U.S. presidents, yet the achievements of his administration were substantial.
Early life. Taft's father, Alphonso Taft, was secretary of war and attorney general under President Ulysses S. Grant, then minister to Austria-Hungary and Russia. William graduated from Yale University in 1878 and, in 1880, earned his degree from the Cincinnati Law School and was admitted to the Ohio bar. In 1886, he married Helen (Nellie) Herron. They had three children.
Law and politics. Taft was appointed a state superior court judge (1887), U.S. solicitor general (1890), and a federal circuit judge (1892). He loved the law, but

William Howard Taft

27th president of the United States

Born:	Cincinnati, Ohio; Sept. 15, 1857
Term:	Mar. 1909-Mar. 1913
Vice president:	James S. Sherman (Mar. 1909-Oct. 1912; died in office)
Political party:	Republican
Spouse:	Helen (Nellie) Herron Taft
Children:	3
Died:	Washington, D.C.; Mar. 8, 1930

his father's influence in the Republican Party pushed him into politics. Taft served as the first civil governor of the Philippine Islands (1901-04), then as President Theodore Roosevelt's secretary of war. He became a valued troubleshooter, helping to reorganize the building of the Panama Canal, settle the Russo-Japanese War, and avert a revolution in Cuba.

Roosevelt, who chose not to run for reelection in 1908, pushed Taft as his successor—although Taft would have preferred an appointment to the U.S. Supreme Court. Taft easily defeated his opponent, William Jennings Bryan.

President. Taft resolved to carry on "the same old plan" of the Roosevelt administration: domestic reform, the curbing of big business, and conservation of the nation's resources. Taft's administration won twice as many antitrust suits against business monopolies as Roosevelt's. Taft believed that somewhat lower tariffs would help control trusts, but could get only limited tariff reduction passed. He greatly strengthened the powers of the Interstate Commerce Commission (ICC) in regulating transportation rates. He saved the government millions of dollars by instituting strict accounting, and laid the basis for a national budget. He also broadened the Civil Service, instituted the Dept. of Labor, pushed through a bill requiring disclosure of campaign expenses in federal elections, and drafted income-tax amendments. In foreign affairs, Taft was less successful. He and his secretary of state initiated "dollar diplomacy"—a policy of using trade and commerce to enhance the nation's influence abroad. It poisoned foreign relations, particularly with Latin America, for more than a generation. Taft's tariff and conservation policies put him at odds with Republican progressives. Theodore Roosevelt ran against him in 1912, splitting the Republican vote and allowing Democrat Woodrow Wilson to win the presidency.

Later life. Taft became a professor of constitutional law at Yale in 1913 and was co-chair of the National War Labor Board (1914-18). In 1921, President Warren G. Harding appointed him chief justice of the U.S. Supreme Court—the job Taft had always wanted. Taft served in that role until Feb. 1930, when ill health forced him to retire.

Taft-Hartley Act, the Labor-Management Relations Act of 1947, sponsored by Senator Robert A. Taft and Representative Fred Hartley. It was passed over the veto of President Harry S Truman and amended the Wagner Act. The act defined "unfair labor practices" and banned boycotts, sympathy strikes, and strikes in interunion disputes. A federal arbitration service was set up, and states were empowered to prohibit union shop agreements. A further controversial provision was presidential power to seek an 80-day injunction against a strike in cases of "national emergency."

Taglioni, Marie (1804-84), Swedish-born Italian ballerina. Trained from an early age by her father, Filippo Taglioni, she gained worldwide renown for her dancing in *La Sylphide* (1832) at the Paris Opéra. Taglioni was noted for her innovative style and was considered a major figure during ballet's romantic era, which lasted until the mid-1840s.
See also: Ballet.

Tagore, Sir Rabindranath (1861-1941), Bengali Indian writer, painter, musician, and mystic who founded what is now Visva-Bharati University to blend the best in Indian and Western culture. His literary work includes many songs, poems, plays, novels, short stories, and essays. He received the 1913 Nobel Prize for literature.

Tagus River, or Tajo River, river that runs 626 mi (1,007 km) from central eastern Spain west through Portugal to the Atlantic Ocean. The mouth of the river opens into the harbor at Lisbon, Portugal.

Tahiti, largest (400 sq mi/1,036 sq km) of the Society Islands in the South Pacific, the center of French Polynesia. The island is mountainous and rich in tropical vegetation. The people are mostly Polynesians, with some French and Chinese. Papeete is the capital. Tahiti, claimed for France by Bougainville in 1768, was visited by James Cook and William Bligh. Its beauty inspired the painter Paul Gauguin.

Taine, Hippolyte Adolphe (1828-93), French writer and intellectual concerned with aesthetics—the nature of art and artistic judgments. He approached his study of art as a scientist. Taine concluded that the artist's art was determined by influences such as the artist's heredity, environment, and aesthetic training. His belief in determinism supported the French philosophical movement of Positivism—a school of thought developed in 19th and 20th century Europe. It also influenced the artistic movement of naturalism in France, of which the 19th-century novels of Emile Zola are examples. Taine's books include *History of English Literature* (1863), *Philosophy of Art* (1865-69), and *Origins of Contemporary France* (1875-93). He was a professor at the École de Beaux-Arts in Paris (1864-83).
See also: Naturalism; Positivism.

Taipei (pop. 2,696,100), capital and largest city of Taiwan, lying to the north on the Tanshui River. A major industrial city, with steel plants, oil refineries and glass factories, Taipei is also the cultural and educational center of Taiwan. Founded in the early 1700s, it became capital of the Nationalist Chinese government in 1949.

Taiwan, formerly Formosa, island in the western Pacific Ocean, formally Republic of China. Together with the Pescadores, Quemoy, and Matsu groups, it is the official seat of the Republic of China government, which claims to be the legal ruler of all China. Taiwan is separated from mainland China by the Formosa Strait, about 90 mi (145 km) wide. The capital is Taipei.

Taiwan

Capital:	Taipei
Area:	13,900 sq mi (36,000 sq km)
Population:	21, 908,000
Language:	Mandarin Chinese
Government:	Republic
Independent:	1950
Head of gov.:	Prime minister
Per capita:	U.S. $11,600
Mon. unit:	1 New Taiwan dollar = 100 cents

Land and climate. With an area of 13,900 sq mi (36,000 sq km) the island of Taiwan is forested and mountainous, with extensive plains in the west. Its highest point is Yü Shan (13,113 ft/3,997 m). The monsoonal climate is tropical in the south, subtropical in the north, and makes possible 2 rice harvests a year.

People. Most of the people of Taiwan are Chinese and come largely from the Fukien province on the mainland. The major religions are Buddhism and Taoism. The official language is Chinese.

Economy. Once predominantly agricultural, Taiwan's economy has become heavily industrialized. Major industries include steel, aluminum, textiles, metals, machinery, and chemicals, but the mainstay of its manufacturing and exports is in electronics. Irrigation is vital for growing rice, sweet potatoes, soybeans, sugar, tea, fruits, and cotton; sugar and tea are exported. There are rich fisheries and the island has much timber. Its natural resources include coral, natural gas, some oil, gold, copper, and silver.

History. Named Formosa by the Portuguese, who arrived in 1590, the island came under the control of the Dutch in 1624. It subsequently fell to a Ming general in 1662 and then to the Manchus in 1683. Taiwan was ceded to Japan in 1895 as part of the settlement of the First Sino-Japanese War and remained in Japanese hands until the end of World War II. In 1949, it became a refuge and stronghold for Chiang Kai-shek's Nationalists after they were driven from the mainland by Communist forces under Mao Zedong. The Nationalists turned the island of Formosa into the Republic of China, and declared it the legitimate government of China under the presidency of Chiang Kai-shek. Between 1951 and 1965, Taiwan was supported with the help of substantial subsidies from the U.S. government. But eventually the United States decided to recognize Mao's government, and in 1971 Taiwan was expelled from the UN and its seat given to the government of the People's Republic of China. From 1954 to 1980, Taiwan was protected by the United States under the terms of the Mutual Defense Treaty of 1954, but in the years following U.S. recognition of the mainland government, Taiwan found itself increasingly isolated. The death of Chiang Kai-shek in 1975 dealt a further blow to Taiwan's political aspirations. Chiang was succeeded by his son, Chiang Ching-kuo, who died in 1988. From 1949 to 1987, Taiwan was under martial law, but with its suspension there arose opposition parties on the island in addition

Tajikistan

Capital:	Dushanbe
Area:	55,251 sq mi (143,100 sq km)
Population:	6,020,000
Language:	Tajik
Government:	Presidental republic
Independent:	1991
Head of gov.:	Prime minister
Per capita:	U.S. $340
Mon. unit:	1 Rouble = 100 kopeks

to the dominant Kuomintang of the Nationalists and their supporters. In 1990 Chiang Ching-kuo's successor, Lee Teng-hui, a native Taiwanese, was elected without opposition to a 6-year term. In 1991, the absolute power of the Kuomintang was terminated. In 1996 the first direct presidential elections were held, which were won by Lee. China regarded the elections as an illegal act, and tried to intimidate Taiwan by carrying out military drills and missile tests.

Tajikistan (Republic of), also Tadzhikistan, independent country in Central Asia, bordering China (east), Afghanistan (south), Kirghizstan (north), and Uzbekistan (west). Its capital is Dushanbe.
Land and climate. Tajikistan is the smallest of the five Central Asian republics (55,300 sq mi; 143,000 sq km). The country is very mountainous, and has a continental climate.
People. Most of its inhabitants are Tajiks (62%), a people related to Sunni Muslim Iranians. Uzbeks constitute the largest minority (24%). The official language is Tajik. The major religion is Sunni Islam.
Economy. Farming and mining are the region's chief industries. Cotton, barley, rice, and wheat are important crops. Major products from mining include fluorite, lead, uranium, zinc, and tungsten. During the civil war (after 1992) part of the infrastructure was destroyed.
History. In the past, the area was frequently occupied by other peoples: Macedonians (Alexander the Great), Persians, and Turks. In the seventh century the population was converted to Islam. After the Mongolian domination the country was conquered by Russia (19th century). One of the 15 constituent republics of the USSR (Soviet Union), Tajikistan became independent in 1991. The country is part of the Commonwealth of Independent States. Formerly one of the 15 constituent republics of the USSR, Tajikistan became independent in 1991.
See also: Union of Soviet Socialist Republics.

Taj Mahal, mausoleum built by the Mogul emperor Shah Jahan for his wife Mumtaz-i-Mahal at Agra in North India. Faced in white marble, the central domed tomb stands on a square block with a minaret at each corner, surrounded by water gardens, gateways, and walks. It took some 20,000 workers over 20 years to complete (1630-50).
See also: Shah Jahan.

Takeshita, Noboru (1924-), Japanese politician, prime minister 1987-89. He was elected to parliament in 1858, subsequently serving as chief cabinet secretary (1971-72, 1974), construction minister (1976), and finance minister (1979-80, 1982-86). He became head of the Liberal-Democratic Party in 1987. In a major upheaval, Takeshita and many other high officials of the Japanese government were implicated in a stocktrading scandal, and he resigned as prime minister in 1989.
See also: Japan.

Talbotype, or calotype, early photographic process invented by the English scientist W.H. Fox Talbot in the 1830s. Talbot first made the photographic paper light-sensitive by treating it with sodium chloride and silver nitrate solution. When he then placed the treated paper in a camera and exposed the paper to light, a negative image formed on it, which he then developed in gallo-nitrate of silver to produce the talbotype. Though this method did not produce pictures as clear as the daguerreotype, any number of prints could be made from the talbotype negative.
See also: Photography.

Talc, [$Mg_3Si_4O_{10}(OH)_2$], hydrous magnesium silicate mineral occurring in metamorphic rocks, chiefly in the United States, USSR, France, and Japan. It has a layer structure resembling that of mica, and is extremely soft. Talc is translucent but not transparent. It is used in ceramics, roof insulation, cosmetics, as an insecticide carrier, and as a filler in paints, paper, and rubber. Impure, massive talc is called soapstone.

Tallahassee (pop. 119,000), capital of Florida, located in the panhandle just south of the Georgia border. Tallahassee became the territorial capital in 1824 and the state capital when statehood was granted in 1845. The state government and 3 colleges are among the city's largest employers. The area, visited by the Spanish explorer Hernando DeSoto in 1539, was named for the Native American word for "old town." During the Civil War (1861-65) it was the only Confederate capital not to fall into Union hands. Today it is a seafood-processing, printing, and wood-product manufacturing center.
See also: Florida.

Tallchief, Maria (1925-), U.S. ballet dancer, of Native American and European ancestry. With her debut as a dancer for the Ballet Russe de Monte Carlo (1942), she became the first U.S. dancer of prominence in Europe—then the ballet center of the world. As a dancer with the New York City Ballet (1947-65), she performed the female lead in many of the ballets choreographed by George Balanchine. The ballet *Firebird* (1949) became her signature role. The Chicago City Ballet was established by her (1980), and for the first 7 years she was its artistic director.
See also: Ballet.

Talleyrand (Charles Maurice de Talleyrand-Périgord; 1754-1838), French politician. A member of the clergy, he represented them in the French parliament (States-General) in 1789 and became a moderate leader and influential spokesperson for the French Revolution in its early years. A fall from favor with the new leadership in 1792 led to a 4-year exile. Appointed an adviser by Napoleon I, Talleyrand rose to the rank of foreign minister

until mutual mistrust between the 2 men led to his resignation in 1807. After Napoleon's first exile (1814), Talleyrand helped restore the Bourbon monarchy and was a key negotiator at the Congress of Vienna (1815). In 1830 he helped lead the overthrow of the last Bourbon king, Charles X, and became the ambassador to England under King Louis Philippe. He helped steer the negotiations that resulted in the independence of Belgium (1830).
See also: France.

Tallinn (pop. 452,000), capital city of Estonia, on the Gulf of Finland, an arm of the Baltic Sea. Tallinn, which dates from the Middle Ages, was a member of the Hanseatic League from the late 1200s to the mid-1300s. Many churches, castles, and buildings survive from that time. From 1346 to 1710, control of Tallinn and the surrounding area passed from the Livonian Knights to Sweden and then Russia. In 1919 it became the capital of an independent Estonian republic, which was overrun in 1940 by the Soviet Union, along with the rest of Estonia and the other 2 Baltic republics, Latvia and Lithuania. Tallinn today is the capital of independent Estonia and is an important seaport and shipbuilding center.
See also: Estonia.

Tallowtree, any of several trees of the family Euphorbiaceae producing a waxy substance that can be used to produce tallow for candles. The Chinese tallowtree (*Sapium sebiferum*) has also been planted as a shade tree in the southeastern United States.

Talmud (Hebrew, "teaching"), compilation of Jewish oral law and rabbinical teachings begun in the 5th century A.D. It has two parts: the Mishnah (oral law), written between A.D. 70 and 200, and the Gemara (commentary on the Mishnah), written between 200 and 500. In addition to commentary and debates on the details of Jewish law, the Gemara contains many traditional legends and stories. The Talmud consists of 63 sections (*tractates*), which are divided into 6 orders. Each order deals with a different subject, such as civil and criminal law and cleanliness. The study of the Talmud has been the core of Jewish education for over 1,000 years. After the Bible, the Talmud stands as the second most important and influential written work of the Jewish religion.

Tamarack *See:* Larch.

Tamarin, one of 14 monkey species belonging to the tamarin and marmoset family, native to the rain forests of Central and South America. Somewhat larger than the marmoset, it lives in groups of about 40 and uses various high-pitched calls to communicate. Tamarins are generally multicolored and grow up to 12 in (31 cm) long, excluding the tail, which may extend to 17 in (44 cm). As a result of the deforestation of the Amazon rain forest, the lion tamarin—so-called because of its long gold mane—is in danger of extinction.

Tamarind (*Tamarindus indica*), tropical tree belonging to the pea family. The fruits are made into preserves and laxative drinks. The wild tamarind of Florida is the only native representative of related trees from the U.S. tropics.

Tambourine, percussion instrument comprising a skin stretched across a hoop fitted with bells, or "jingles," that rattle as it is tapped or shaken. Originating in the Middle East, it is used in folk and popular music and in some orchestral scores.

Tamerlane, or Timur the Lame (c.1336-1405), Mongol conqueror, descendant of Genghis Khan. Tamerlane succeeded to the throne of Turkestan in 1369 and from his capital at Samarkand set out on a series of conquests, including Afghanistan, Persia, and southern portions of what is now the USSR. In 1398 he invaded India and sacked Delhi, where it is believed he and his troops massacred 80,000 people. Three years later he moved against Syria and captured Baghdad. The following year (1402) his armies defeated the Ottoman Turks and captured their sultan, Beyazid I. After capturing Damascus and defeating the Egyptian army, he plotted to overrun China but died before he could implement his plans. His empire, centered in Turkestan, crumbled after his death.
See also: Mongol Empire.

Tamil, Dravidian language spoken by some 40 million people, principally in southeast India and northeast Sri Lanka. It is the main language of Tamil Nadu (formerly Madras) state. Tamil has its own script and a rich ancient literature.

Tammany, Society of, or the Columbian Order, New York City Democratic political organization. Founded in 1789 as a "fraternity of patriots" dedicated to preserving the nation's independence, it evolved into the most powerful political machine in New York City's Democratic party. Tammany Hall, as it came to be known, drew much of its strength from newly arrived immigrants willing to pledge their votes for services and political favors. Scandals clouded much of its existence, the most infamous being the corruption of William M. "Boss" Tweed, convicted of defrauding the city of millions of dollars in 1871. Tammany Hall regained much of the power it lost after Tweed's conviction, but in the early 1930s state investigations weakened it, and the organization suffered defeats in the 1932 elections. It had a brief resurgence following World War II but, by the 1970s, ceased to exist as a political force.
See also: Bucktails; Nast, Thomas; Tweed, William Marcy 'Boss'.

Tampa (pop. 285,300), city in Florida, at the head of Tampa Bay, an arm of the Gulf of Mexico. Inhabited by Native American tribes when Spanish explorer Hernando De Soto landed there in 1539, the area did not see European settlement until 1823. In the late 19th century Tampa grew as a manufacturing center and as home to a prosperous cigar industry; it became a tourist center following the arrival of the railroad. Today Tampa is a major seaport, industrial hub, and retirement center, and houses 2 universities and numerous cultural and tourist attractions, including Busch Gardens and the Florida State Fair.
See also: Florida.

Tanaka, Kakuei (1918-93), Japanese prime minister (1972-74). He built up a construction business, headed the Liberal Democratic Party from 1965, and held cabinet posts from 1968. He was forced to resign in 1974 because of

financial misconduct and was convicted in 1983 of having accepted bribes from Lockheed Corporation.
See also: Japan.

Taney, Roger Brooke (1777-1864), chief justice of the U.S. Supreme Court (1836-64) whose decision in the Dred Scott case (1857) helped bring on the Civil War. As President Andrew Jackson's secretary of the treasury (1833-35), he crushed the Second Bank of the United States. As chief justice, he steered a middle course on States' Rights and continued Chief Justice John Marshall's liberal interpretation of the Constitution.
See also: Dred Scott case; Supreme Court of the United States.

Tang dynasty, rulers of China from A.D. 618 to 907. The Tang period is regarded as the golden age of Chinese civilization by many historians. During this period, Tang rulers centralized the government and unified the country. The capital city, Chang'an (now Xian), served as a worldwide center for scholarship and the arts. During this time, the Chinese invented block printing and produced the first block-printed book (A.D. 868). Emperor Tang Taizong, who ruled for 22 years, led the rise of the Tang dynasty. He conquered foreign lands and opened trade routes that brought the country great wealth and prosperity. Empress Wu followed Emperor Taizong's rule with great skill and came to be known as the second greatest Chinese leader. An 80-year war with the Tibetans in northwestern China, coupled with years of internal fighting, weakened the Tang dynasty, and it came to an end in 907.
See also: China.

Tangelo, citrus fruit produced by crossing a tangerine with a grapefruit. The name *tangelo* is a combination of *tangerine* and *pomelo* (another word for grapefruit). Like the tangerine, the tangelo has a thin peel and sweet pulp. The Minneola and the Orlando are North American varieties, and the Ugli is a Jamaican strain common to the West Indies.

Tangerine, fruit in the rue family, related to the orange. In shape, color, and taste the tangerine resembles the orange, but is smaller and easier to peel. Although originated in Southeast Asia, tangerines are grown in the southeast and western United States and Brazil, Italy and Spain. Clementine and Dancy are two popular varieties of tangerine.

Tangier (pop. 554,000), seaport and residential and commercial city of Morocco, facing the Strait of Gibraltar. Tangier is a major center of tourism and shipping and is considered Morocco's main passenger-vessel port. It is heavily populated by Arabs and Berbers. The city has its origins in the settlements built by the Phoenicians and Romans in ancient times. It was under Arab control in the 700s. From the 1400s to the late 1600s, when the sultan of Morocco acquired the power to guide Tangier, it was held, at different times, by France, Portugal, and England. In 1912 the city again fell under the control of Spain and France, and in 1923 it was put under international control. In 1956 Tangier became fully independent of France and Spain, gave up its international status, and came under the full control of Morocco.
See also: Morocco.

Tank, combat vehicle, armed with guns or missiles, and self-propelled on caterpillar treads; the chief modern conventional ground assault weapon. Tanks were first built in 1915 by Britain and used from 1916 against Germany in World War I. These early tanks were very slow, and development between the wars greatly improved speed and firepower. The Spanish Civil War and World War II showed the effectiveness of concentrated tank attacks. Amphibious and airborne tanks were developed. Heavy tanks proved cumbersome and were generally abandoned in favor of the more maneuverable (though more vulnerable) light and medium tanks. Improved models are now used where heavy guns are needed. Light tanks (less than 25 tons/23 metric tons) are used mainly for infantry support.
See also: Army.

Tanker, ship designed to carry liquid cargo in bulk, notably crude oil, gasoline, or natural gas. The first tanker (1886), a 300-ft (90-m) vessel, carried 3,000 tons (272 metric tons) of oil. Some tankers today hold 100 times as much: a 483,939-ton (439,029-metric ton) vessel (the *Globtik London*, 1975) has been built in Japan. Ships this size greatly reduce per-ton transport costs but cannot enter many ports; some large tankers transfer their cargo to smaller tankers offshore. In gross tonnage tankers account for over a third of all merchant shipping.

Tannhäuser (c.1200-70), German poet and legendary character who wrote poems that were sung. A number of dance songs, love songs, and lyric songs of his still exist. He supposedly participated in the Crusades (1228-29) and traveled widely throughout Europe. The composer Richard Wagner based his opera *Tannhäuser* on the poet's life. As legend has it, Tannhäuser lived in a mountain with the goddess Venus for 7 years. During a visit to Rome, Tannhäuser asked the pope to forgive his sins, but the pope responded that just as his staff could never blossom, never could Tannhäuser's sins be forgiven. Dejected, Tannhäuser returned to Venus. Three days later the pope's staff blossomed into flowers.

Tannic acid, or tannin ($C_{76}H_{52}O_{46}$), organic substance extracted from the bark of certain trees (e.g., oak, hemlock, and chestnut). In a process known as tanning, tannin is added to animal hides to resist decomposition. Tannin is also used to manufacture inks and is used as a fixative (mordant) for dyes. It can also be used as a medicine for treating burns and as an astringent. Most of the tannin used in the United States today is obtained from the quebracho trees of Argentina and Paraguay.

Tantalum, chemical element, symbol Ta; for physical constants see Periodic Table. Tantalum was discovered by A.G. Ekeberg in 1802. It occurs in the mineral microlite. It is obtained commercially from columbite-tantalite, a mixed oxide with niobium and iron and manganese. The element is prepared by the high-temperature reaction of tantalum (V) oxide with tantalum carbide in a vacuum. Tantalum is a gray, hard, malleable, ductile metal. It is high-melting and resistant to chemical attack. A tantalum carbide-graphite composite is one of the hardest materials ever made. Tantalum and its compounds are used in laboratory apparatus, surgical prostheses, special glasses, electrolytic capacitors, nuclear reactors, aircraft, missiles, and catalysts.

Tantalus, in Greek mythology, king of Lydia and son of Zeus and the nymph Pluto. Zeus banished him to Hades because of his cruel sacrifice of his son Pelops. Tantalus was punished by being forced to stand chin-deep in water under hanging fruit, each of which receded just beyond his reach whenever he wanted to eat or drink. The word *tantalize* is derived from his name.
See also: Mythology.

Tanzania, independent republic in East Africa consisting of the mainland, formerly Tanganyika, and the islands of Zanzibar and Pemba. The mainland of Tanzania has Mozambique, Malawi, and Zambia to its south; Zaïre, Burundi, and Rwanda to the west; Uganda and Kenya on the north; and the Indian Ocean to the east. Zanzibar and Pemba are separated from the mainland by the 22-mi- (35-km)-wide Zanzibar Channel. The capital is Dodoma.
Land and climate. Mainland Tanzania covers an area of 363,650 sq mi (942,626 sq km), including 20,650 sq mi (53,484 sq km) of inland water. The islands cover an area of 950 sq mi (2,461 sq km). A coastal belt, fringed by sand beaches, coral reefs, and mangrove swamps, leads inland to plains and plateaus 2,000 to 4,000 ft (1,219 km) above sea level with vast expanses of grasslands and open woodlands, as well as isolated hills and hill ranges. In this area is the Serengeti Plain, site of one of several national parks. To the north is Lake Victoria, and above the plateaus rise the Usambara, Pare, Kilimanjaro, and Meru mountains. Mt. Kilimanjaro (19,340 ft/5,895 m) is Africa's highest peak. The uplands extend to the south where they meet Lake Nyasa and the Ufipa Highlands. To the west lies Lake Tanganyika. Zanzibar and Pemba are coral islands and fertile. Their climate, like that of the coastal belt, is tropical. The inland climate is hot and dry for most of the year, and most humid in the highlands and along the western shore of Lake Victoria.
People. The vast majority of the people are black Africans, but there are also people of Asian, Arab, and European descent. Christianity and Islam, in roughly equal proportions, account for some three-quarters of the population. The rest of the people adhere to traditional beliefs. The official language is Swahili.
Economy. Tanzania's economy is chiefly agricultural. Coffee and cotton are primary exports, but other important exports include cloves from Zanzibar, pyrethrum, sisal, tobacco, and tea. Manufacturing is limited principally to processing agricultural products and industry is dominated by mining. Tanzania is a producer of diamonds.
History. Olduvai Gorge in North Tanzania is the site of the fossil remains of the earliest hominid. The remains have been dated to some 1.7 million years ago. In historical times, the coast and Zanzibar came under Arab control some time in the 8th century A.D. The Portuguese established a presence in the 16th and 17th centuries and introduced the slave trade, but were driven out by natives in 1698. Arabs from Oman established control of Zanzibar and set up on the mainland as well, conducting a flourishing trade in slaves and ivory throughout the 18th and 19th centuries. The Germans established a mainland protectorate in 1891, but, after World War I, the regions passed to Britain through a League of Nations mandate. Tanganyika gained its independence in 1961 and was joined with Zanzibar in 1964. The capital was transferred from Dar-es-Salaam to Dodoma in 1975. Tanzania was directly involved in the overthrow of the regime of Idi Amin Dada in neighboring Uganda in 1978-79. During the 1980s, Tanzania's economic difficulties, brought about

Tanzania

Capital:	Dodoma
Area:	364,804 sq mi (945,087 sq km)
Population:	30,609,000
Language:	English, Swahili
Government:	Federal presidential republic
Independent:	1961: Tanganyika; 1963: Zanzibar; 1964:
Head of gov.:	Prime minister (1 of 2 Vice-Presidents)
Per capita:	U.S. $120
Mon. unit:	1 Tanzanian shilling = 100 cents

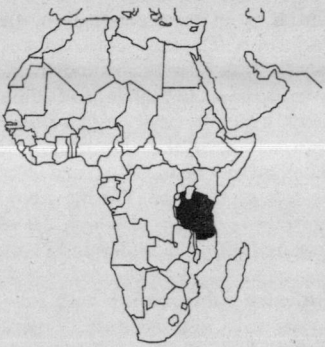

by trade deficits and debt , resulted in a decreased emphasis on a government-controlled economy. In 1985 Nyerere left office and was replaced by his recommended successor, Ali Hassan Mwinyi. In 1998 Muslim fundamentalists carried out a bomb attack on the American embassy in Tanzania.

Tanzanite, zoisite mineral and semiprecious gem unearthed in Tanzania (1967). This stone is popular for use in jewelry because its polished surfaces, created through a cutting process, reflect beautiful color. When a heat process is applied to tanzanite, it reflects a blue color. Before the heat treatment, tanzanite shines purple, blue, or yellow, depending upon the way light hits it.

Taoism, or Daoism (from Chinese *tao* or *dao*, "the way"), philosophy that originated in China (c.300 B.C.); also, a religion that had its beginnings c.100 B.C. Taoism as a philosophy is chiefly derived from 2 books: the *Lao-tzu* (renamed *Tao Te Ching, The Classic of the Way and the Virtue*), traditionally ascribed to Lao-tzu, and the *Chuang-tzu*. The *Lao-tzu* is a collection of writings by several unknown authors containing ideas that are in direct opposition to the Confucian philosophy. Confucianism stresses a life guided by definite rules of conduct, whereas Taoism emphasizes simplicity and spontaneity. Tao was considered impossible to describe save in cryptic imagery. Chinese literature and art were greatly influenced by Taoism.

Taos (pop. 3,369), historically significant city in New Mexico, located at the base of the southern Rocky Mountains, 75 mi (121 km) north of Santa Fe. It was the site of an ancient Pueblo Indian village as well as a farming center for early Spanish settlers. Taos was also a Spanish and Indian trading post and the center of the Pueblo Revolt of 1680. During the 1900s, the city achieved popularity as an artists' colony. Taos is frequently visited by artists and tourists.
See also: New Mexico.

Tao Te Ching *See:* Taoism.

Tape recorder, instrument for sound recording on magnetic tape and subsequent playback. A microphone changes sound to an electric current, which is in turn changed in the recording head into magnetic flux variations. The tape, consisting of small particles of iron oxides on a thin plastic film base, is wound from the supply reel to the takeup reel by a rotating capstan that controls the speed. The tape passes in turn: the erase head, which by applying an alternating field reduces the overall magnetization to zero; the recording head, which magnetizes the particles; and the playback head. Most recorders use two, four, or even more tracks side by side on the tape. The most common form of audio tape recorder is the cassette recorder, in which the cassette (a small plastic case) is simply snapped into a recorder and is ready to be played.

Tapestry, fabric woven with colored threads to form a design and used to cover walls and furniture. Vertical threads, which make up the warp are stretched on a loom, and horizontal threads, which make up the weft, are woven over and under them and then compacted. Tapestries were known in ancient Egypt, Syria, Persia, and China. North Europe's great era of tapestry-making began in the 1300s, notably at Arras in Flanders. It reached a peak in the Gobelin tapestries of the 1600s. Great painters who have made tapestry designs include Raphael and Rubens. The Peter Paul Bayeux tapestry is in fact embroidery.

Tapeworm, any of numerous flatworms (class *Cestoda*) that live as parasites in the intestines of humans and other animals. Some tapeworms measure less than 1 in (2.5 cm) long, while others reach 30 ft (9 m) or more. A person can be infected by a tapeworm by eating undercooked meat or fish containing tapeworm larvae. An adult tapeworm can sometimes cause diarrhea, nausea, and other ill effects in a person. Tapeworm larvae pose a more serious threat because they can develop into young worms and spread to other organs of the host body.

Tar, thick, dark, viscous liquid obtained through distillation of organic matter, primarily coal, petroleum products, and wood. Coal tar, obtained at high temperatures and condensed from vapors given off during the manufacture of coke from bituminous (soft) coal, is used for roofing and waterproofing materials, synthetic drugs, disinfectants, dyes, perfumes, and plastics. Coal gassifier tar, a source of organic chemicals, is a byproduct of the process that converts coal into a natural gas substitute. Wood tar is made from the condensed vapors created during the wood-burning process; pine tar, the major derivative, is used to manufacture soap, disinfectants, and turpentine. Other types of coal- or petroleum-derived tar are used to seal road surfaces and produce asphalt paving material.
See also: Pitch.

Tarabulus *See:* Tripoli.

Tarantula, popular name, originally of the large wolf spider (*Lycosa tarantula*), but now used for various unrelated giant spiders throughout the world. All are long and hairy and eat large insects or small vertebrates. Their venom seldom has serious effects on humans.
See also: Spider.

Tarascan, Native American tribe of Mexico. The Tarascan controlled a powerful empire from the late 14th to the early 16th century. With early settlements dating to c.500 B.C., their tribal holdings bordered the Aztec Empire at the time of the Spanish arrival in the 1520s. Along with the Aztecs, they were conquered by the Spanish, but only after great resistance. Hunters, farmers, and fishermen, many of the 60,000 Tarascans surviving today, inhabitants of the state of Michoacán, follow traditional ways of life. They are skilled craftspeople, weavers, and woodcarvers. Many still speak the Tarascan language, which bears no relationship to any other known language.

Tarbell, Ida Minerva (1857-1944), U.S. author and reformer. She was one of the leading muckrakers of the late 19th and early 20th centuries, exposing corruption and unsafe or unsanitary working conditions. Her *History of the Standard Oil Company* (1904) blasted monopoly practices in major industries and helped lead to reforms in corporate practices. Other writings include biographies and an autobiography, *All in a Day's Work* (1929).
See also: Muckraker.

Tariff, customs duty on an export or, more commonly, an import. The aim is generally to protect home industries from foreign competition, though it may be merely to provide revenue. During the 17th and 18th centuries the European powers created tariff systems that gave their colonies preferential treatment, but Britain's tariffs, by limiting North America's trade, helped provoke the Revolutionary War. In the early 1800s the free trade movement, bolstered by the economic philosophy of laissez-faire, helped limit the spread of tariffs. However, U.S. federal tariffs imposed to aid Northern industry damaged the South and contributed to the Civil War. U.S. and European tariffs were moderate in the early 1900s but, after the Great Depression, both the United States and the United Kingdom adopted high tariffs, with a consequent decline in international trade. In 1947 the United States and 22 other nations signed the General Agreement on Tariffs and Trade (GATT), aimed at reducing trade discrimination. GATT and the Common Market have been responsible for generally lower tariffs throughout the world.
See also: Taxation.

Tarkenton, Fran (Francis Asbury Tarkenton; 1940-), U.S. football player. A quarterback known for his passing and scrambling ability, Tarkenton holds the career records for pass attempts (6,467), pass completions (3,686), touchdown passes (342), and passing yards (47,003). He played in the National Football League (NFL) for the Minnesota Vikings (1961-66, 1972-79) and New York Giants (1967-71). Tarkenton was inducted into the Pro Football Hall of Fame in 1986.

Tarkington, (Newton) Booth (1869-1946), U.S. writer noted for novels reflecting midwestern life and character, for example, *Penrod* (1914). He won Pulitzer prizes for *The Magnificent Ambersons* (1918) and *Alice Adams* (1921). Tarkington also served as an Indiana state representative (1902-03).

Taro, plant (*Colocasia esculenta*) of the arum family whose rhizomes provide a starch food for millions of people in eastern Asia and the Pacific.

Taros have to be peeled to remove a poisonous acid compound, and they do not provide an adequate diet by themselves. In Hawaii taro is fermented to make poi.

Tarot, pack of 78 playing cards used mainly for fortune-telling. There are four suits (cups, pentacles, swords, and wands), each of 14 cards and a major arcana (heavily symbolic "picture cards") of 22 cards. There are various systems of interpretation.

Tarpon (*Tarpon atlanticus*), game fish that can survive in salt or fresh water. Tarpon of over 100 lb (45 kg) are often caught, and they can grow up to 840 lb (381 kg). The body bears large, silvery scales up to 2 in (5 cm) across, and the dorsal fin has a long ray protruding from the rear end. Tarpon live in warm seas from Florida to Brazil and also off West Africa. The eggs are laid in shallow water and the larvae grow up in stagnant lagoons and marshes.

Tarragon (*Artemisia dracunculus*), plant whose aromatic leaves provide a pleasant characteristic flavor to various meats, vegetables, sauces, and stuffings.

Tarsus (pop. 146,500), city in central Turkey on the Mediterranean coast. Archeological studies date the city to Neolithic times. The Assyrians built here in the early 8th century B.C. The Romans once took control of Tarsus (67 B.C.). The city claims to be the place of the first meeting of Antony and Cleopatra (41 B.C.) and the birthplace of St. Paul. Cotton and agriculture are products of the modern city and were the foundation of the ancient economy of Tarsus.

Tartan, checkered fabric of Scotland's native dress. Each clan is ascribed a particular tartan, though often in more than one variety: the hunting tartans are usually somber blues and greens, while reds generally predominate the dress tartans. The authenticity of ascriptions to clans is questioned, and some tartans are of comparatively recent origin.

Tartaric acid ($C_4H_6O_6$), naturally derived plant acid, used extensively for making jellies, jams, and carbonated drinks. There are tartaric salts—cream of tartar, Rochelle salt, and tartar emetic. The first is used in baking powder, hard candies, and for cleaning brass. Rochelle salt is used to silver mirrors and electronically cover metals with gold or silver; tartar emetic (antimony potassium tartrate) is used in medicines. Tartaric acids and their salts are solids, colorless, and water soluble.

Tartars, or **Tatars**, people of Turkish descent who live in the Russian Federation, Bulgaria, Romania, China, and Turkey. Originally a nomadic people, they turned to agriculture in the 16th century and have since figured prominently in the history of the Russian people. Many Tarters now live in the Tatar Autonomous Soviet Socialist Republic; most are Sunni Muslims.

Tartu (German: *Dorpat*), city in eastern Estonia, lying on the Emajogi River. It was a fortified settlement in the 5th century A.D. From the 11th century it was at different times held by the Russians, Swedes, and Poles; Russian

control was established in 1704. Its university, founded 1632, is now an important center for the study of botany and agriculture.
See also: Estonia.

Tashkent (pop. 2,000,000), capital of Uzbekistan, located in Chirchik Valley west of the Chatkal Mountains. One of the oldest cities in Asia, it was an important trading center for Arab, Muslim, and Mongol empires. Major products are textiles and agricultural machinery. Rebuilt after a devastating earthquake in 1966, it is an important cultural center.
See also: Uzbekistan.

Tasmania, smallest Australian state (26,383 sq mi/68,332 sq km). The 150-mi (253.5-km) Bass Strait separates Tasmania from the southeastern mainland. It includes King, Flinders, and Macquarie islands, as well as the main island. Tasmania's forests contain two unique marsupials, the Tasmanian devil and the thylacine. Chief cities are Hobart (the capital), Launceston, Burnie, and Devonport. Important industries are livestock (dairying, wool), horticulture, lumber and newsprint, mining, and mineral processing (zinc, copper, and lead).
See also: Australia.

Tasmanian devil (*Sarcophilus harrisi*), mammal of the marsupial family, native to the Australian island of Tasmania. This nocturnal, 4-legged animal measures 3-4 ft (0.9-1.2 m) long. Like other marsupials, the female gives birth to underdeveloped babies who grow to maturity in pouches on the mother's belly. Noted for their fierceness, they have been known to attack livestock and poultry, and have been hunted for that reason.

Tasman Sea, arm of the South Pacific Ocean, between Australia and Tasmania (east) and New Zealand (west). Named for the Dutch explorer Abel Tasman, the Tasman Sea is about 900,000 sq mi (2.3 million sq km). An underwater cable on its floor provides a key communication link between Australia and New Zealand.

TASS (Telegraph Agency of the Soviet Union), state news agency of the former USSR. Founded in 1925, it was managed by the Propaganda Department of the Communist Party's Central Committee.

Taste, special sense concerned with the differentiation of basic modalities of food or other substances in the mouth; receptors are distributed over the surface of the tongue and are able to distinguish sweet (generally at tip), sour, salt (along the sides), bitter (mainly at the back), and possibly water as primary tastes. Much of what is colloquially termed taste is actually smell perception of odors.

Tate, (John Orley) Allen (1899-1979), U.S. writer, critic, and teacher. He edited the literary magazine *Fugitive* (1922-25) and later *Sewanee Review* (1944-46) and advocated the "New Criticism," with its stress on a work's intrinsic qualities. His own work includes several collections of poetry and essays, biographies, and a novel.

Tatum, Art (1910-56), U.S. jazz pianist. With the physical handicap of only slight vision, he became a master of piano technique and various forms of jazz. As an accompanist to jazz singers and as a member of his own jazz trio, he performed mainly in New York City nightclubs, beginning in 1932.
See also: Jazz.

Tatum, Edward Lawrie (1909-75), U.S. biochemist awarded the 1958 Nobel Prize for physiology or medicine, with G.W. Beadle and J. Lederberg, for work with Beadle showing that individual genes control production of particular enzymes (1937-40) and for work with Lederberg showing genetic recombination in the bacterium *Escherichia coli* (1947).
See also: Biochemistry; Genetics.

Taube, Henry (1916-), Canadian-born U.S. chemist who won the 1983 Nobel Prize for chemistry for his work in the mechanisms of electron transfer reactions, especially in metal complexes.
See also: Chemistry.

Taussig, Helen Brooke (1898-1986), U.S. pediatrician and cardiologist. With Alfred Blalock she developed the "blue baby operation" (1945), which increases blood circulation to the lungs and stimulates research on the surgical correction of congenital heart defects.
See also: Blue baby.

Tautog *See:* Blackfish.

Tawney, Richard Henry (1880-1962), English historian and social theorist. His best-known book, *Religion and the Rise of Capitalism* (1926), connects the hard work and individualism of the Protestants of North Europe in the 16th and 17th centuries with the growth of capitalism there.

Taxation, raising of revenue to pay for government expenditure. Broadly speaking, a tax can be described as direct or indirect: income tax is paid directly to the government, but sales taxes are collected indirectly through government charges on goods or services. A tax is progressive or regressive; income tax is usually progressive (its rate rises as the taxable sum increases); sales taxes tend to be regressive (their burden decreases as the taxpayer's income increases).

Taxation without representation *See:* Revolutionary War in America.

Taxco (pop. 27,100), town in Mexico, 70, mi (113 km) southwest of Mexico City. A replica of an early Spanish town, it attracts many tourists and people in the arts. Founded (1529) by Hernando Cortés, it has been an important silvermining town since pre-Columbian times; it is still the center of Mexico's silver industry. Other minerals, such as copper, lead, and zinc are also mined there. Taxco also serves as a commercial center for the region, which is largely agricultural.

Taxidermy, stuffing and mounting animal skins to make lifelike replicas. Taxidermy is now practiced mainly in large museums, though it originated in the production of hunting trophies; in modern taxidermy, rather than stuffing, the animal's skin is streched over an artificial skeleton.

Taxonomy *See:* Classification.

Taylor, Elizabeth (1932-), English-born U.S. film actress. Beginning her career as a child actress (*Lassie Come Home*, 1943; *National Velvet*, 1944), she went on to become a major Hollywood star in such films as *Little Women* (1949), and *A Place in the Sun* (1951). She received Academy Awards for her roles in *Butterfield 8* (1960) and *Who's Afraid of Virginia Woolf?* (1966); in the latter she co-starred with her then-husband, British actor Richard Burton. In 1992 she received a Jean Hersholt Humanitarian Award for her dedication to the struggle against AIDS.

Taylor, George (1716-81), Irish-born member of the Continental Congress and signer of the Declaration of Independence. Taylor emigrated to Pennsylvania in 1736, serving there in the provincial assembly (1764-69, 1775) the militia (1775), and the First Supreme Executive Council (1777).

Taylor, John (1753-1824), U.S. political theorist and agricultural reformer, known as John Taylor of Caroline. An early exponent of States Rights, he was elected three times as U.S. senator from Virginia (1792, 1803, 1822).

Taylor, Lawrence (1959-), U.S. football player. A linebacker known for his quickness and powerful hits, he was the National Football League (NFL) Player of the Year (1986) and the National Football Conference (NFC) defensive player of the year 3 times (1981, 82, and 86). Taylor plays for the New York Giants (1981-) and has led the team to 2 Super Bowl victories (1987, 1991).

Taylor, Maxwell Davenport (1901-87), U.S. Army general who largely organized the U.S. Army's first airborne units in World War II. He commanded the 8th Army in Korea (1953-55), headed the U.S. and UN Far East commands (1954-55), was U.S. Army chief of staff (1955-59), and served as ambassador to Vietnam (1964-65).

Taylor, Paul (1930-), U.S. modern dance choreographer. He debuted with Merce Cunningham in 1953 and danced with Martha Graham's company (1955-61) before founding the Paul Taylor Dance Company in the mid-1950s. His work includes *3 Epitaphs* (1956), *Aureole* (1962), *Esplanade* (1975), and *Last Look* (1985).

Taylor, Zachary (1784-1850), war hero and 12th president of the United States. Taylor was a bold and resourceful general in the Mexican War and one of the most popular presidents of the period. His brief term in office—he died 16 months into his term—has been all but forgotten. However, he took a bold stand on the extension of slavery, the burning issue of his day, and—had he lived and prevailed—the Civil War might have broken out 11 years earlier than it did.

Early life. Taylor grew up on a wilderness farm. There were no schools, but his parents and tutors gave him some education. In 1810, he married Margaret Mackall Smith. They had six children, two of whom died in infancy.

Zachary Taylor

12th president of the United States

Born:	Orange Co., Va.; Nov. 24, 1784
Term:	Mar. 1849-July 1850
Vice president:	Millard Fillmore
Political party:	Whig
Spouse:	Margaret Mackall Smith Taylor
Children:	6
Died:	Washington, D.C.; July 9, 1850

Military career. In 1808, Taylor became a 1st lieutenant in the U.S. Army. During his 40-year army career, he moved from one end of the nation to the other, and did a great deal to open the West to settlement. He fought Native Americans and the British in the Northwest Territory during the War of 1812, served in the Black Hawk Indian War (1832), and spent three years fighting the Seminole in the Florida Everglades. He commanded Army posts, built roads and forts, and—along the way—purchased land and slaves for himself in Mississippi and Louisiana. "Old Rough and Ready," as his troops affectionately called him, won a reputation for skill, daring, and fairness as a commander and fighter.

The Whig Party, which saw the war hero as a sure winner, nominated Taylor as its presidential candidate in 1848. Taylor and the Democratic candidate each took a two-sided stand on slavery; the Free-Soil Party's candidate opposed slavery in new territories. Taylor and his running mate, Millard Fillmore, won the election.

President. In Dec. 1849, Congress was faced with California's request to enter the Union as a free state. Unexpectedly, Taylor urged Congress to accept California and New Mexico as free states. This, coming from a Southerner and slave owner, outraged militant Southerners. There was talk of secession, but Taylor declared that, if there was any rebellion, he would personally lead the army to put it down. Like many older-generation Southerners, Taylor believed that the Union must be preserved, even if it meant slavery would be kept from expanding beyond its existing borders. He probably was also swayed by the antislavery attitudes of his Whig advisers.

Senator Henry Clay offered a set of bills—later called the Compromise of 1850—that would admit California as a free state, with no provisions against slavery in Utah and New Mexico, and would prohibit the slave trade in the District of Columbia. To appease the South, they provided a rigorous law for the return of fugitive slaves. There was a great debate in the Senate; Taylor held firm and tensions grew. Then on July 9, 1850, Taylor died suddenly of acute gastroenteritis. Had Taylor lived, his uncompromising stand might have provoked a war by Aug. However, Millard Fillmore, his successor, allowed the compromise bills to go through, postponing the conflict.

Tay-Sachs disease, inherited disorder that occurs primarily in Jewish people from eastern Europe. Children born with the disease have little or no active hexosaminidase enzyme, the lack of which causes fat to accumulate in the brain's ganglions (bundles of nerves). The consequences are mental retardation, paralysis, blindness, and cherry-red spots on the retina of the eye. The disorder is usually fatal before the child reaches the age of four.

TB *See:* Tuberculosis.

Tbilisi, or Tiflis (pop. 1,268,000), capital city of the Republic of Georgia, situated on the Kura River south of the Caucasus Mountains. Tbilisi, founded in the 4th century B.C., was subsequently ruled by the Persians, Arabs, Khazars, and Turks into the Middle Ages and was the capital of an independent Georgia (1096-1225). It was then conquered by the Mongols, Iranians, and Turks again before it was finally ceded to Russia in 1801. Following the Bolshevik Revolution (1917), Tbilisi again served as capital of an independent Georgia, but the Communists soon overran it and its neighboring states (1920). Much of the older section of the city remains. Today it is a center for agricultural products and manufacturing. Warm springs, for which the city is named in the Georgian language, are nearby. *See also:* Georgia.

Tchaikovsky, Peter Ilich (1840-93), Russian composer. He studied with Anton Rubinstein, became professor at Moscow Conservatory, and gave concerts of his own music in Europe and the United States. His gift for melody and brilliant orchestration, plus the drama, excitement, and emotional intensity of his music, place him among the most popular composers. Orchestral works include *Violin Concerto in D Major* (1878) and *Symphony No. 6*, or the the "Pathétique" (1893). His ballets, *Swan Lake* (1876), *Sleeping Beauty* (1889), and *The Nutcracker* (1892), have become classics. His operas include *Eugene Onégin* (1879) and *The Queen of Spades* (1890).

Tea (*Camillia sinensis*), evergreen shrub, related to the camellia; also, the leaves of the plant and the beverage made from the leaves. The drink is prepared by pouring boiling water over dry processed tea leaves. Types of tea drunk include green, black (which is fermented), and oolong (which is partly fermented). Tea has been drunk in China since early times, but it was not until the early 1600s that the Dutch introduced it into Europe. Although expensive, it soon became fashionable. In the United Kingdom and the British colonies, the East India Company enjoyed a monopoly of the China tea trade until 1833; it was the attempt of the British government to levy a tax on tea imports into the American colonies that led to the Boston Tea Party of 1773. Today, the chief producers are India and Sri Lanka (Ceylon). Tea contains the stimulant caffeine. The term *tea* is also used to describe many other local drinks produced from the leaves of a vast array of plants.

Teach, Edward *See:* Blackbeard.

Teaching, range of activities used to demonstrate skills, impart information, and guide individuals in learning. Informal teaching, which takes place in any setting and without any requisite structure, may come from parents, employers, colleagues, or other persons. Formal teaching generally occurs in a structured setting and is administered by professional teachers. In the United States since the beginning of the 19th century, teaching procedures for elementary and secondary schools have been increasingly formalized by teacher-training programs and state certification (varying from state to state). Training in education includes general coursework in the subject areas the teacher will specialize in, special courses in educational theory and practice, and practice or student teaching in real classrooms. Both training programs and certification are particular to the grade level and the subject area. Uncertified support personnel are known as teacher aides or paraprofessionals. State certification requirements vary widely, and many states do not accept certificates issued in other states. Many school systems now require evaluations of professional teachers to maintain their level of competence. Teachers are generally hired by the local school board, often under regulation of the master agreement between the board and the teachers' union. In some states teachers are then protected by tenure agreements and cannot easily be fired. The National Education Association (NEA) and the American Federation of Teachers (AFT) are the main professional organizations that deal with working conditions and salaries.

Teak (*Tectona grandis*), deciduous tree whose wood is among the most valuable. Teaks grow in tropical climates from India to Malaysia. The hard, oily (thus water-resistant) wood is used for house construction, furniture, railroad ties, etc. Several other trees produce a similar hardwood also called teak.

Teal, name for various species of river ducks (genus *Anas*) related to the mallard. The blue-winged teal of North America is one of the fastest flying migratory ducks, able to travel over 3,500 mi (5,632 km) in a month. Other teal include the Cape teal of Africa and the Laysan teal, which lives only on the island of Laysan, west of Hawaii.

Teamsters Union (International Brotherhood of Teamsters, Chauffeurs, Warehousemen and Helpers of America), largest U.S. labor union, whose members are largely truckers. Formed by an amalgamation in 1903, the union grew during the presidency of Daniel Tobin (1907-52). Two of his successors, Dave Beck and J.R. Hoffa, were jailed for corruption, and in 1957 the Teamsters were expelled from the AFL-CIO.
See also: Labor movement.

Teapot Dome, scandal over government malpractice under President Warren G. Harding. The naval oil reserve at Teapot Dome, Wyo., was leased in 1922 by agreement of Secretary of the Interior Albert Fall to the Mammoth Oil Co. with no competitive bidding. A Senate investigation followed, and the lease was canceled. Fall was later convicted of receiving another bribe in a similar transaction.

Tears, watery secretions of the lacrimal glands situated over the eyes, which provide continuous lubrication and protection of cornea and sclera. A constant flow runs across the surface of the eye to the nasolacrimal duct at the inner corner, where tears drain into the nose. Excess tears produced in states of high emotion or because of conjunctival or corneal irritation overflow over the lower eyelid.

Teasel, or **teazel** (*Dipsacus fullonum*), European plant found in fields in North America. The small blue flowers grow on a conical head that remains as a prickly head after they have died. It was formerly cultivated, its dead heads used to raise the nap on cloth (fuller's teasel).

Tebaldi, Renata (1922-), Italian operatic soprano. A major rival of Greek-American soprano Maria Callas, she was known for the beauty and purity of her tone. She made her operatic debut in Italy in 1944 and her U.S. debut in 1950. Tebaldi, who performed many roles in the repertoire of Italian opera, sang frequently at the Metropolitan Opera in New York from 1955 to 1973. *See also:* Opera.

Technetium, chemical element, symbol Tc; for physical constants see Periodic Table. Technetium was discovered by C. Perrier and E.G. Segrè in 1937. It was the first element to be produced artificially. It was produced in the Berkeley cyclotron by bombarding molybdenum with deuterons. It is present in some stars. It has not been found in any ores on earth. Technetium is prepared by reducing the sulfide with hydrogen at 1,100°C. Technetium is a silvery-gray, reactive metal. Its chemistry is said to be similar to that of rhenium. Potassium pertechnetate is a corrosion inhibitor for steel. Technetium and its compounds have limited commercial use because of its high radioactivity.

Technology, application of science to practical human ends—particularly, to increase productivity and the availability of leisure and to improve the quality of life. Although technology includes developments since ancient times, such as occurred in the metallurgy involved in tool making, the term generally refers to industrial technology of the past 200 years. In agriculture, technology has improved crop yields and reduced the need for labor with the advent of farm machinery. Technology applied to manufacturing has made available goods in large numbers at the same time that industrial labor has become less strenuous and hazardous and work hours have been reduced. Major technological innovations of the past century have included the internal combustion engine used in automobiles and the harnessing of electricity for light, heat, and power. In the 20th century radio communication and powered flight, and more recently, the computer, laser, and atomic fusion and fission have created profound changes in many aspects of life. Technology applied to the field of medicine has greatly increased life expectancy. The extremely rapid changes caused by technology have also created serious problems. Population shifts to cities result in overcrowding. Natural resources have been depleted due to the industrial use of raw materials and the population explosions made possible by technology. Segments of the labor force are suddenly unemployed due to mechanization and automation, in a phenomenon known as technological unemployment. The assembly line that has made possible efficient production has also created boring and repetitive jobs, and the resulting loss of pride in work has created quality problems in U.S. industries. Most seriously, technology has resulted in many forms of environmental pollution, including toxic industrial waste, air pollution from motor vehicles, noise pollution, and the destruction of ecosystems by the use of insecticides.

Tectonics, branch in geology that studies the earth's structural deformations, the forces involved, and the resulting forms. The most popular theory used to

explain the origin of tectonic forces is the plate tectonic theory, developed in the 1960s. This theory holds that the movement of the rigid plates that line the surface of the earth's outer shell (either aigainst one other or away from one another) produces the crustal deformations in the earth. A second theory contends thet the earth originated from molten rock, which cooled as it shrunk; this shrinking in turn produced the tectonic forces. A third theory maintains that the earth began as a cold mass, and as it warmed it produced forces that fractured the crust.
See also: Volcano.

Tecumseh (1768?-1813), Shawnee chief. From their home in Ohio, Tecumseh and his brother Tenskwatawa (the Prophet) attempted to unite the Native American tribes of the upper Midwest in a confederacy, calling upon them to maintain their ancient culture and beliefs and to oppose, by force if necessary, all attempts by European-Americans to settle on tribal lands. At the Battle of Tippecanoe (Indiana) in 1811, the Prophet was defeated by a U.S. force led by Gen. William Henry Harrison, a victory that led to Harrison's election as president in 1840. Tecumseh, noted for his military prowess, joined the British army against the United States in the War of 1812 and was made a brigadier general. He was defeated and killed at the battle of the Thames River in Ontario.

Teeth, specialized hard structure used for biting and chewing food. The number of teeth varies from species to species and from age to age, but in most cases an immature set of teeth (milk teeth) is replaced during growth by a permanent set. In humans the latter consists of 32 teeth, comprising 8 incisors, 4 canines, 8 premolars or bicuspids, and 12 molars, of which the rearmost are the late-erupting wisdom teeth. Each tooth consists of a crown (the part above the gum line) and a root (the insertion into the bone of the jaw). The outer surface of the crown is covered by a thin layer of enamel, the hardest animal tissue. This overlies the dentine, a substance similar to bone, and in the center of each tooth is the pulp, which contains blood vessels and nerves. The incisors are developed for biting off food with a scissor action. The canines are for maintaining a hold on an object. The molars and premolars are adapted for chewing and macerating (separating) food. The most common disease of the teeth is dental decay, ot caries, in which acid produced by bacteria dissolves the tooth enamel, causing a cavity.

Tegu, or **Teju**, bold, quick and muscular South American lizard (genus *Tupinambis*). They weigh about 5 lb (2.3 kg) and grow up to 4 ft (1.2 m) in length. They have small square scales on their black-colored bodies with yellow horizontal bands over their backs.

Tegucigalpa (pop. 678,000), capital and largest city of Honduras, situated on the Choluteca River and on the slopes of Mt. Picacho in southern-central Honduras. Founded by the Spaniards in the late 1570s as a gold- and silver-mining center, in 1880 Tegucigalpa replaced Comayagua as the national capital. The 2 cities, on opposite banks of the Choluteca, merged in 1938. Today Tegucigalpa is a major manufacturing and agricultural hub, as well as the governmental center. The National University of Honduras is on the outskirts of the city.
See also: Honduras.

Teheran, or **Tehran** (pop. 5,734,000), capital and largest city of Iran. It is situated in northern Iran, south of the Elburz Mountains. It is believed that the area known today as Teheran was settled some 3,000 years ago; it began as a small town, but by the 1200s it had grown significantly. It received prominence after the Mogol destruction of nearby Ragy (1220) and became capital of Iran in 1788. Teheran is Iran's chief center of commerce and industry, employing a majority of the Iranian working population. Under Reza Shah Pahleve the city was modernized and is considered today to be one of the most modern cities in the Middle East. Teheran has two major universities.
See also: Iran.

Teheran Conference, inter-Allied conference of World War II, held in Teheran (Nov.-Dec. 1943) and attended by Soviet premier Joseph Stalin, U.S. president Franklin D. Roosevelt, and British prime minister Winston Churchill. Important items were the coordination of landings in France with a Soviet offensive against Germany from the east, future Soviet entry into the war against Japan, agreement on Iran's future independence, and international cooperation after the war.
See also: World War II.

Teilhard de Chardin, Pierre (1881-1955), French Jesuit, philosopher, and paleontologist. In China (1923-46) he studied Peking Man (*Homo erectus*). *The Phenomenon of Man* (1938-40, published 1955) attempted to reconcile Christianity and science with a theory of human evolution toward final spiritual unity. His superiors held his views to be unorthodox and warned against them; fame came to him and his ideas only posthumously.
See also: Paleontology.

Teju *See:* Tegu.

Te Kanawa, Dame Kiri (1944-), New Zealand operatic soprano. Her portrayal of the Countess in Mozart's *The Marriage of Figaro* won her international acclaim in 1971. She made her Metropolitan Opera debut in 1974 as Desdemona in Giuseppe Verdi's *Othello*. Widely recorded, she is known for her roles in works by Wolfgang Amadeus Mozart, Giuseppe Verdi, Giacomo Puccini, Georges Bizet, and Richard Strauss.
See also: Opera.

Tel Aviv-Jaffa (pop. 353,200), second-largest city in Israel, on the Mediterranean coast northwest of Jerusalem. It is a modern city-port and Israel's chief manufacturing center, as well as a tourist resort. Tel Aviv was Israel's first capital (1948-49). Jaffa (Hebrew: *Yafo*), an ancient port, was incorporated with Tel Aviv in 1950; the city officially became Tel Aviv-Yafo, but it is generally referred to as Tel Aviv. Tel Aviv has two museums and several educational institutions, including Tel Aviv University and Bar Ilan University.
See also: Israel.

Telegraph, electrical apparatus for sending coded messages. The term was first applied in the 18th century to Claude Chappe's semaphore. Experiments began on electric telegraphs after the discovery (1819) that a magnetic needle

was deflected by a current in a nearby wire. In 1837 W.F. Cooke and Charles Wheatstone patented a system using six wires and five pointers that moved in pairs to indicate letters in a diamond-shaped array. It was used on English railroads. In the same year Samuel Morse, in partnership with Alfred Vail and helped by Joseph Henry, patented a telegraph system using Morse code in the United States. The first intercity line was inaugurated in 1884. In 1858 Wheatstone invented a high-speed automatic Morse telegraph, using punched paper tape in transmission; the telex system, using teletypewriters, is now most popular. In 1872 Jean-Maurice-Emil Baudot invented a multiplexing system for sharing the time on each transmission line between several operators. Telegraph signals are now transmitted not only by wires and land lines, but also by submarine cables and radio.
See also: Morse, Samuel Finley Breese; Wheatstone, Sir Charles.

Telegraph plant (*Desmodium motorium*), plant of the pea family, native to tropical Asia. It is sometimes cultivated for its unusual behavior in response to touch—the leaves droop abruptly, like the arms of a railroad semaphore signal (hence its name). The plant grows about 4 ft (1.2 m) high and bears small purple flowers.

Telemann, Georg Philipp (1681-1767), German composer. He was a prolific composer who worked well with musical forms popular in his day. He wrote operas, including *Der geduldige Socrates* (1721) and *Pimpinone* (1725); orchestral music, including *Musique de Table* (1733); concertos; and cantatas. His work was influenced by Italian opera as well as by earlier baroque composers, principally Johann Sebastian Bach. He served as musical director for the 5 churches of Hamburg (1721) and the Hamburg Opera (1722-38).

Teleology (from Greek *telos*, "end"), study of an action, event, or thing with reference to it's purpose or end. Plato and Aristotle argued that the purpose, perfection, and good of a thing, which Aristotle called its "final cause," was the ultimate explanation of the thing. The teleological view of nature has declined since the rise of science. The teleological argument, or argument "from design," argues that the order and perfection of nature requires the existence of a divine Creator who effected that order.

Telephone, apparatus for transmission and reproduction of sound by means of frequency electric waves. The telephone was invented in 1876 by Alexander Graham Bell. Bell's transmitter worked by the voltage induced in a coil by a piece of iron attached to a vibrating diaphragm; the same apparatus, working in reverse, was used as a receiver. The carbon microphone (invented by Thomas Edison, 1878) provided a more sensitive transmitter. In 1878 the first commercial exchange was opened in New Haven, Conn.; local telephone networks spread rapidly in the United States and elsewhere. Repeaters, or amplifiers, made long-distance telephone calls possible. Today, microwave radio links, communications satellites, and optical fibers are used. Telephone subscribers are connected to a local exchange, these in turn being linked by trunk lines connecting a hierarchy of switching centers so that alternative routes may be used. When a call is dialed, each digit is coded as pulses or pairs of tones that work electromechanical or electronic switches.
See also: Bell, Alexander Graham.

Telescope, instrument used to detect or examine distant objects. It consists of a series of lenses and mirrors capable of producing a magnified image and of collecting more light than the unaided eye.
The refracting telescope (refractor) essentially consists of a tube with a lens system at each end. Light from a distant object first strikes the objective lens, which produces an inverted image at its focal point. In the terrestrial telescope the second lens system, the eyepiece, produces a magnified, erect image of the focal image, but in instruments for astronomical use, where the image is usually recorded photographically, the image is not reinverted, thus reducing light losses.
The reflecting telescope (reflector) uses a concave mirror to gather and focus the incoming light. The various types of instruments use different combinations of mirrors and lenses to view the focal image with fewer optical aberrations.
The size of a telescope is measured in terms of the diameter of its objective. Up to about 12 in (30 cm) diameter, the resolving power (the ability to distinguish finely separated points) increases with size, but for larger objectives the only gain is in light gathering. A 200-in (508-cm) telescope can thus detect much fainter sources but resolve no better than a 12-in (30-cm) instrument. Because mirrors can be supported more easily than large lenses, the largest astronomical telescopes are all reflectors.
See also: Galileo Galilei.

Television, communication of moving pictures between distant points over wire or by means of electromagnetic waves. In television broadcasting, centrally prepared programs are transmitted to millions of individual receivers. Closed-circuit transmissions, which rely upon signals carried over wire rather than electromagnetic waves broadcast at large, are most often used for industrial and educational applications.
The moving picture on a television screen originates with a television camera, which forms an optical image of the scene to be transmitted and then breaks the image down into electrical signals. The signals may be amplified and transmitted directly over a cable, or they can be converted into electromagnetic waves. As electromagnetic waves, they are transmitted by antennas, like radio waves, picked up by receiving antennas, and then conveyed to a television set equipped to reconstitute the electromagnetic waves into an optical image on the screen of a cathode-ray tube.
In the early days of television technology, most cameras used the iconoscope, but the iconoscope technology has since been replaced by orthicon or vidiscope. In order for an image to be transmitted and received electronically, it must be broken down into discrete but organized electrical signals and then reassembled or reconstructed by the receiver. The image formed by the optical lens system of a television camera is scanned as a sequence of 525 horizonal lines. As an image is scanned, variations in the light intensity along each line are converted into a fluctuating electrical signal, the brightness signal, which gives the image its gradations from light to darkness. Each scan is then repeated 30 times a second to create the illusion that the image is moving and without noticeable flicker. When reassembled on the television screen, the image appears whole and in fluid motion because of the persistence-of-vision effect of the human eye.
In color television, the image is not only resolved into brightness, but into hue and saturation as well. The light entering the camera is analyzed into red,

green, and blue components, the 3 primary colors. Both hue and saturation are converted to electronic information, which is added to the brightness signal and transmitted. In the color receiver, this information is recovered and used to control 3 electron beams fired within the television set. The beams are projected through a shadow mask, a screen containing some 200,000 minute, precisely positioned holes, and they excite the mosaic of red, green, and blue phosphor dots, which reproduce the color image on the television screen.

The possibility of television was conceived in the early days of the electric telegraph, but the realization had to await several key developments. First was the discovery of the photoconductive properties of selenium, followed by the development of the cathode-ray tube in 1897 and the electron tube in 1904. Crucial to both systems and at the heart of television technology was scanning. The first practical television system, demonstrated in London in 1926 by J. L. Baird, used a mechanical scanning method devised by Paul Nipkow in 1884. Electronic scanning dates from 1923 when Vladimir Zworykin filed a patent for his iconoscope camera tube. Television broadcasting began in London in 1936 using a 405-line standard. In the United States, public broadcasting began in 1941, and regular color broadcasting in 1954. U.S. television broadcasts are made in the VHF (Channels 2-13) and UHF (Channels 14-83) regions of the RF spectrum. Recent technology, both in Japan and the United States, has led to the development of High Definition TV with greatly increased scanning capacities making possible images that are much cleaner and much larger.

See also: Sarnoff, David; Videodisc; Videotape recorder.

Tell, William, legendary 14th-century Swiss hero. Ordered by the Austrian bailiff Gessler to bow to a hat on a pole as a symbol of Austrian supremacy, he refused and was forced to shoot an apple from his son's head, using a cross-bow; in this almost impossible task he succeeded. Later he killed Gessler, starting a revolt that overthrew the bailiffs. The story was the basis of a drama by Friedrich von Schiller and an opera by Giacomo Rossini in the early 19th century.

Teller, Edward (1908-), Hungarian-born U.S. nuclear physicist who worked with Enrico Fermi on nuclear fission at the start of the Manhattan Project, but is best known for his fundamental work on, and advocacy of, the hydrogen bomb. He also helped create the Strategic Defense Initiative (SDI) program in the 1980s.

See also: Manhattan Project; Nuclear weapon.

Tellurium, chemical element, symbol Te; for physical constants see Periodic Table. Tellurium was discovered by Franz von Reichenstein in 1782. It occurs in nature as metallic tellurides. It is obtained commercially from the anode mud obtained in the electrolytic refining of copper. Tellurium is a silvery-white, brittle, reactive metalloid. It can be amorphous or crystalline and is a *p*-type semiconductor. Tellurium and its compounds are used in alloys with copper, steel, and lead, blasting caps, ceramics, and thermoelectric devices. Tellurium and its compounds are probably toxic.

Telstar, U.S. artificial satellite, launched July 10, 1962. The first to relay television signals across the Atlantic Ocean. Telstar weighed 170 lb (77 kg).

Broadcasts ended (Feb. 1963) after Van Allen belt radiation damaged some of the 1,000 transistors.

Temperature, degree of hotness or coldness, as measured quantitatively by thermometers. The various scales used are arbitrary: the Fahrenheit scale was originally based on the values 0°F for an equal ice-salt mixture, 32°F for the freezing point of water, and 96°F for normal human body temperature. There are certain primary calibration points corresponding to the boiling, freezing, or melting points of particular substances, whose values are fixed by convention. The thermodynamic, or absolute, temperature scale, is not arbitrary; starting at absolute zero, at which there is no kinetic energy, and graduated in kelvins, it is defined with respect to an ideal reversible heat engine working on a Carnot cycle between two temperatures, T_1 and T_2. If Q_1 is the heat received at the higher temperature T_1, and Q_2, the heat lost at the lower temperature T_2, then T_1/T_2 is equal to Q_1/Q_2. Absolute temperature is independent of a body's mass or nature; it is thus only indirectly related to the heat content of the body. Heat always flows from a higher temperature to a lower. On the molecular scale, temperature may be defined in terms of the statistical distribution of the kinetic energy of the molecules.

Temperature, body, measurement of body heat in animals. Warm-blooded animals (including human beings, other mammals, and birds) are able to maintain a fairly constant body temperature, which does not significantly fluctuate with the temperature of the environment. Body temperature in warm-blooded animals may change slightly over the course of a day: an adult human being's normal temperature, 98.6°F (37.0°C), may be slightly lower in the morning and slightly higher by late afternoon. In warm-blooded animals, body temperature is controlled by the hypothalamus, a part of the brain that includes autonomic regulatory centers. The workings of the hypothalamus enable warm-blooded animals to balance the amount of heat lost to the environment with the heat produced by burning food. Cold-blooded animals, including reptiles, cannot regulate body temperature this way and must use other methods to maintain it. For example, snakes lie in the sun or shade, depending on whether they need to raise or lower their body temperature.

Templars, Knights *See:* Knights Templars.

Temple, building or place dedicated to the worship of a deity. Temples have been common to most religions; they date back to c.2000 B.C. in Egypt. In Eastern Asia, temples (pagodas) are towerlike structures built with many stories, each story a symbolic representation of a different level in the Buddhist religion. Worship in temples usually involves traditional ceremonies and at times may even contain sacrifices. The first of the three successive temples built by Solomon in ancient Jerusalem became the central shrine where sacrifice could be legally offered. This First Temple, destroyed in the Babylonian invasion 586 B.C., is considered the most important temple in Western history.

Temple, Shirley (1928-), U.S. child film star, later a politician. She made her movie debut at 3 and became phenomenally popular through such films as *Little Miss Marker* (1934) and *The Little Colonel* (1935). She retired from films in 1949. After working on television in the 1950s, Shirley Temple Black (her married name) took up Republican politics. She became a U.S. delegate to the United Nations (1969), ambassador to Ghana (1975), and U.S. chief of protocol (1976).

Tenant farming, system by which agricultural land holders, known as landlords, rent land to farmers, known as tenants, to produce crops. Landlords may either collect an agreed-upon payment for rental of the farm land and buildings or they may share other production costs and investments, as well as the harvested crop, with the farmer. This method of farming has been especially successful in the British Isles and the United States.

Ten Commandments, or the *Decalogue*, moral laws delivered by God to Moses on Mt. Sinai, as recorded in the Bible (Ex. 20:2-17; Deut. 5:6-21). They provide the foundation for Jewish, Christian, and Muslim teaching.
See also: Bible.

Tendon, fibrous structure at the ends of most muscles that transmits the force of contraction to the point of action (usually a bone). Tendons facilitate mechanical advantage and allow bulky power muscles to be situated away from small bones concerned with fine movements, as in forearm muscles acting on the hands.
See also: Muscle.

Teng Hsiao-p'ing *See:* Deng Xiaoping.

Tennessee, state in the south-central United States; bordered by Kentucky and Virginia to the north, North Carolina to the east, Georgia, Alabama, and Mississippi to the south, and the Mississippi River (with Arkansas and Missouri on the other side) to the west.
Land and climate. Tennessee has seven main land regions. The Blue Ridge region, a narrow strip along the state's eastern border, is a heavily forested, mountainous area. To its west is the Appalachian Ridge and Valley Region, a fertile farming area of minor ridges and wide valleys. The next westward region, the Appalachian (or Cumberland) Plateau, has flat-topped peaks, rocky cliffs, and narrow valleys. From there, the land drops into a high-plain region called the Highland Rim. In the center of the Highland Rim lies a region of fertile farmland and plain called the Nashville Basin. The westernmost region, the Gulf Coastal Plain, stretches from the Tennessee River to the Mississippi River. Its terrain ranges from rolling hills to a low, flat, narrow area called the Mississippi Alluvial Plain. Tennessee is drained by three major river systems: the Cumberland, Tennessee, and Mississippi. Most of the larger lakes were formed by dams built on the Tennessee and Cumberland rivers. Forests cover about half of the state. Tennessee has a humid, temperate climate. Principal cities are Memphis and Nashville.
Economy. Manufacturing leads Tennesee's economy, followed by wholesale and retail trade and other service industries. Chief manufactured goods are chemicals, processed foods, nonelectrical machinery, electric and electronic equipment, apparel, fabricated metal products, transportation equipment, and rubber and plastic products. Agriculture and mining are less important to Tennessee's economy. Chief crops are soybeans, tobacco, cotton, corn, and

Tennessee

Capital:	Nashville
Statehood:	June 1, 1796 (16th state)
Familiar name:	Volunteer State
Area:	42,114 sq mi (109,152 km); ranks 34th
Population:	5,368,000 (1997); ranks 17th
Elevation:	Highest—6,643 ft (2,025 m), Clingmans Dome; Lowest—182 ft (55 m), along the Mississippi River
Motto:	Agriculture and Commerce
Flower:	Iris
Bird:	Mockingbird
Tree:	Tulip poplar
Songs:	"The Tennessee Waltz" and "Rocky Top"

wheat. Chief livestock products are beef and dairy cattle and hogs. Chief mining products are coal, marble, limestone, and zinc.

Government. Tennessee's present constitution was adopted in 1870. The governor serves a 4-year term. The state's legislature, called the General Assembly, consists of 33 senators serving 4-year terms and 99 house members serving 2-year terms. In the U.S. Congress, Tennessee is represented by 32 senators and 9 representatives.

History. About 1,000 years ago, an ancient Native American tribe known as the Mound Builders lived in the area. When the first Europeans, Spanish explorers, arrived in 1540, it was populated by the Cherokee, Chickasaw, Shawnee, and other tribes. The area, claimed by France in 1682, was ceded to Britain in 1763. European settlers began building permanent settlements; in 1772 the Watauga Association was established to govern the area. Some of the area, considered part of North Carolina, broke away to form the independent state of Franklin (1784-8). In 1796, Tennessee became the 16th state. Bitterly divided over slavery, Tennessee was the last state to join the Confederacy (June 8, 1861) and the first readmitted to the Union (July 24, 1866). More Civil War battles were fought in Tennessee than in any other state except Virginia. In the first half of the 1900s, industry developed rapidly, aided by the 1933 establishment of the Tennessee Valley Authority (TVA). A plant built in the 1940s at Oak Ridge became an important center for atomic-energy research during World War II. Today, Tennessee seeks new industries to boost its flagging economy.

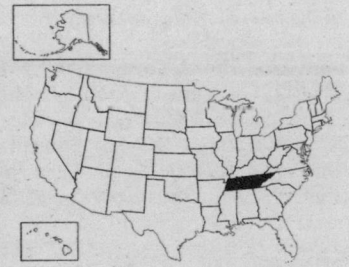

Tennessee River, principal tributary of the Ohio River. Formed by the junction of Holston and French Broad rivers near Knoxville, Tenn., it flows southwest into Alabama, then northwest and north across Tennessee and into Kentucky. The Tennessee is 652 mi (1,049 km) in length, and it drains some

40,000 sq mi (103,600 sq km). The river's many dams and power facilities are under the control of the Tennessee Valley Authority (TVA).

Tennessee Valley Authority (TVA), U.S. federal agency responsible for developing the water and other resources of the Tennessee River Valley, established (1933) as one of the early measures of President Franklin D. Roosevelt's New Deal. The TVA has 26 major dams on the Tennessee River and its tributaries. The dams and reservoirs have made it possible to eliminate major flooding. Locks make the Tennessee navigable throughout, and TVA hydroelectric and steam plans provide most of the region's electricity. TVA projects have also involved conservation, agriculture, and forestry.
See also: New Deal.

Tennis, racket game played on a rectangular court by two or four players. The court, divided by painted lines into sections (78 ft-23.8 m long and 27-31.5 ft-8.2-9.6 m wide) is bisected by a net 3 1/2 ft (107 cm) high. The object is to hit the hollow ball of cloth-covered rubber, about 2 1/2 in (6.4 cm) in diameter and 2 oz (57 g) in weight, over the net into the opposite court such that the opposing player is unable to return it. The racket has a metal or laminated wood frame, with gut or nylon strings forming an oval "head"; it is about 27 in (69 cm) long and weighs 12 oz (340-454 g). Tennis originated in 15th-century France as indoor court tennis and took its present form, lawn tennis, in 1870. It was first played in the United States in 1874. In 1877 England held the first Wimbledon Championship. Dwight Davis donated the Davis Cup in 1900. The International Lawn Tennis Federation regulates rules and play in over 80 countries.

Tennyson, Alfred, Lord (1809-92), English poet. His *Poems* (1842) established him as a major poet. His philosophic elegy *In Memoriam* (1850) became the favorite of Queen Victoria, who appointed him poet laureate. *Idylls of the King* (1842-85) is an epic based on the legends of King Arthur. Tennyson's mastery of sound and rhythm is perhaps best seen in haunting lyrics like "The Lotus-Eaters" and "The Lady of Shalott," which appear in *Poems* (1832).

Tenochtitlán, capital of the Aztecs, now in Mexico City. Founded c. 1325 on an island in Lake Texcoco, connected to the mainland by causeways, it was a rich city of brick houses, palaces, canals, aqueducts, and a great square of temple-topped pyramids. It was destroyed by Hernán Cortés in 1521.
See also: Aztecs; Cortés, Hernando.

Tenpins *See:* Bowling.

Tenskwatawa *See:* Shawnee Prophet.

Tent caterpillar, larval stage of moths (genus *Malacosoma*) in the Lasiocampidae family. Striped, colorful, and hairy, the tent caterpillar is so-called because most of its species spin communal, tentlike webs in the forks of trees. Notorious for damaging trees in which they live, these caterpillars are capable of killing a small tree by eating all of its leaves. The female moth lays 150-350 eggs during the summer that hatch the following spring. Common to the southeastern and central United States, these caterpillars feed on oaks and other shade trees, as well as on conifers and fruit trees.

Terbium, chemical element, symbol Tb; for physical constants see Periodic Table. Terbium was discovered by C.G. Mosander in 1843. It is found in cerite, and gadolinite and is obtained commercially from monazite. The metal is prepared by reducing the anhydrous fluoride with calcium. Terbium is silvery-white, soft, malleable, ductile metal. Ion-exchange and solvent extraction techniques have led to much easier isolation of the so-called rare-earth elements. Terbium and its compounds are finding use in laser materials, solid-state devices, color TV phosphors, and fuel cells.

Terence (195?-159? B.C.), playwright of Roman comedies, written in Latin. His 6 plays, based on earlier Greek comedies, still exist: *The Woman of Andros, The Self-Tormentor, The Eunuch, Phormio, The Mother-in-Law,* and *The Brothers.* These plays display his wit and his realistic understanding of human nature. He was brought from his native Carthage as a slave to Rome, and a Roman senator secured his education.

Teresa, or **Theresa, Saint** (1515-82), also known as Theresa of Ávila, Spanish nun and Doctor of the Church. She worked toward reforming the Carmelite order, which she believed was lacking in self-denial and austerity, and in 1562, with approval from the pope, established her own convent. She was a leading figure in the Catholic Reformation. Her writings rank among the greatest in mystical literature. St. Teresa was considered a miracle worker and was canonized in 1622. Her feast day is Oct. 15.

Teresa, Mother (1910-97), Roman Catholic nun, Albanian parents, who worked as a missionary in Calcutta, India. For her work with the poor of India, which began in 1950, she was awarded the Nobel Peace Prize (1979). The religious order she joined (1928) sent her to India, where she at first worked as a teacher. Her convent later permitted her to work among the poor people of Calcutta (1948), and she became an Indian citizen. She has received global recognition for her work, including the Pope John XXII peace prize (1971) and the Jawaharlal Nehru award for international understanding (1972).

Tereshkova, Valentina Vladimifouna (1937-), Soviet cosmonaut, the first woman to orbit the earth. Simultaneously with a fellow cosmonaut, Very F. Bykovsky, she circled the earth 45 times in her spacecraft *Vostok VI* (June 16-19, 1963). Her orbits, which she controlled manually, took less than 1 1/2 hours each.

Terman, Lewis Madison (1877-1956), U.S. psychologist. The popular term *IQ* (intelligence quotient) is a result of his development of an English-language version of the French Binet-Simon intelligence tests (1916, revised in 1937 and 1960). Terman's studies concluded that gifted children with high intelligence experienced healthy and stable development from childhood to adulthood. The findings were discussed in his book *Genetic Studies of Genius* (1925-59). He was a professor at Stanford University (1921-42).
See also: Intelligence quotient.

Termite, or white ant, primitive insect (order Isoptera) closely related to the cockroach, found in all warm regions. Termites have a complicated social system and live in well-regulated communities, with different castes taking distinct roles. They build large nests of soil mixed with saliva, in which the colony of king, queen, workers, soldiers, and juveniles live. Soldiers and workers are sterile individuals, their development arrested at an early stage. Termites feed on wood and vegetation, digesting the food with the aid of symbiotic protozoa or bacteria in the gut.

Tern, or sea swallow, slender, graceful seabird related to, but smaller than, the gull. Terns have a bounding, butterfly-like flight and feed on small fish that they catch by diving from the air. They are found in all seas from the Arctic to the Antarctic and also on some lakes and marshes. They nest on the ground in large, noisy colonies. The Arctic tern migrates from the Arctic to the fringes of the Antarctic.

Terra cotta (Italian, "baked earth"), any fired earthenware product, especially one made from coarse, porous clay, red-brown in color and unglazed. Being cheap, hard, and durable, it has been used from ancient times for building and roofing, and for molded architectural ornament and statuettes. Its use for sculpture and plaques was revived in the Renaissance and in the 18th century.

Terrapin, turtle (family Testudinidae) of fresh or brackish water, with diamond-shaped plates on its shell. It grows to 8 in (20 cm) and is found from Massachusetts to Mexico. At one time a cheap food for slaves, it became a luxury dish as *Terrapin à la Maryland*. The name is sometimes given to all brackish and freshwater turtles.

Terrell, Mary Church (1863-1954), U.S. activist in the movement for equal rights for African Americans. The daughter of a wealthy ex-slave, she graduated from Oberlin College (1884) before settling in Washington, D.C. She became one of the first 2 women and the first African American on the city's school board (1895), and helped found the National Association of Colored Women (1896). Throughout her life she continued to act as an adviser and advocate on racial issues and helped end the city's racial discrimination in public facilities in 1953. Much of her life is detailed in her autobiography, *A Colored Woman in a White World* (1940).

Terrier, class of dogs. Most of the 24 kinds of terrier were originally bred in England. They were developed specifically to hunt or flush out from the ground rats and burrowing animals. Terrier breeds include the fox terrier, the schnauzer, and the Scottish terrier.

Territoriality, behavioral drive causing animals to set up distinct territories defended against other members of the same species (conspecifics) for the purposes of establishing a breeding site, home range, or feeding area. It is an important factor in the spacing out of animal populations. Territoriality is shown by creatures of all kinds: birds, mammals, fish, and insects. A territory may be held by individuals, pairs, or even family groups.

Territorial waters, in international law, the belt of sea adjacent to a country and under its territorial jurisdiction. Important for control of shipping, seabeds, and fisheries, such limits used to extend 3 mi (4.8 km), and more

recently 12 mi (19.3 km), from low-water mark. A 200-mi (322-km) limit has been accepted by some countries.
See also: High seas.

Territory, in politics, area under a government's control, but with limited self-government. Territories have lower status than the states of the mother country. All but 19 U.S. states were first territories; Alaska and Hawaii were the last incorporated territories (with full Constitutional rights) to gain statehood. U.S. territories include the Virgin Islands, Guam, and American Samoa. Federated States of Micronesia, formerly a UN Trust Territory administered by the United States, became a self-governing territory in association with the United States in 1981.

Terrorism, actual or threatened violence for political ends. The level of terrorism increased markedly in the 1970s as antigovernment groups throughout the world turned to violent acts such as bombing, hijacking, kidnapping, and murder. Terrorism attracted increased international attention through the stepped up activities of Palestinians and their allies, who gave up hope of defeating Israel by conventional military tactics after the rout of the Arab nations in the 1967 war. The more active terrorist groups of the period included the Provisional wing of the Irish Republican Army, the Japanese Red Army (3 of whose members killed 28 people and wounded 76 at Tel Aviv's Lod airport in 1972), the Palestinian Black September group (responsible for the deaths of 11 Israeli athletes at the 1972 Munich Olympics), the Baader-Meinhof Gang in Germany, the Italian Red Brigades (who kidnapped and killed the former Italian premier, Aldo Moro, in 1978), the Tupamoros in Uruguay, and the Weathermen in the United States. While receiving much publicity—one of their aims—terrorists actually account for relatively few deaths (less than 2,000 in the 1980s) compared with other causes (nearly 10 times as many people are murdered every year by ordinary criminals in the U.S. alone). Terrorists are very hard to catch, however, because their groups are small, tightly organized, and highly mobile. As a major measure to curb the involvement of Libya in terrorism worldwide, President Ronald Reagan on January 8, 1984, issued an executive order severing virtually all U.S. economic ties to Libya.

Terry, Dame Ellen Alicia (1848-1928), English actress. Throughout more than 50 years on the stage, she performed often as Sir Henry Irving's leading lady, and is remembered for her roles as Beatrice in *Much Ado About Nothing*, Juliet in *Romeo and Juliet*, and Desdemona in *Othello*.

Tertiary Period, the lower division of the Cenozoic era, extending from the end of the Cretaceous to the beginning of the Quaternary, from 70,000,000 to 2,000,000 years ago. It is divided into 5 epochs: Paleocene, Eocene, Oligocene, Miocene, and Pliocene. The early Tertiary period was characterized by a large amount of mountain building (Andes, Alps, Hymalayas). In this period marsupials and placental mammals diversified and began to take a more modern appearance. Also during this time, worldwide climates began to gradually change into today's climatic zones.

Tesla, Nikola (1856-1943), U.S. electrical engineer, inventor of the induction motor. His innovative motor used alternating electric current. This concept, purchased by a George Westinghouse company, was used to

develop a successful commercial motor. Tesla worked on other successful inventions, including the Tesla coil, an arc-lighting system, and various generators and transformers. He was a forerunner in the field of communications with his work on wireless radio transmissions. He was born in Croatia, and moved to the United States in 1884.
See also: Electric motor.

Testes *See:* Testicle.

Testicle, or testis (plural: testes), one of paired male sex glands. The testes are contained in the scrotal sac just between the legs. They have two functions. As ductless glands, they secrete testosterone, the male sex hormone. This substance is responsible for maintenance of the accessory reproductive organs and also for the secondary sexual characteristics—deep voice, strong muscles, and facial hair. Their other function is to produce the sperm needed to fertilize the female egg. Sperm is produced in a series of long coiled tubes called seminiferous tubules. In higher mammals, this process requires a temperature lower than normal body temperature, a condition provided by having the scrotal sac outside the body cavity. Mature sperm are stored in a coiled tube, the epididymis, up to 20 ft (6 m) long, which leads from the rear of the testis to the ejaculatory duct.

Testing, in education and psychology, procedures to evaluate individuals with respect to intelligence, skills, perceptions, or other parameters. Testing in the classroom is generally nonstandardized, designed by the teacher to measure the achievements of the students in assimilating subject matter. Standardized testing in education is used to compare individuals to group norms, as in Graduate Record Examinations (GREs), or to measure them against predetermined standards, as in tests used to license professionals in law and medicine. Achievement tests measure learning in specific subject areas. Aptitude tests, which include intelligence tests that measure intelligence quotient (IQ), attempt to evaluate potential while eliminating factors of previous experience. Psychologists use a variety of personality tests, including both standardized tests that determine categories of personality profile and projective tests, like the Rorschach inkblot test, which can be evaluated only by a trained professional. Because test results are widely used to determine an individual's future in education and work, the validity of test procedures and contents must be scrutinized. Testing may inadvertently favor those of particular socioeconomic groups or otherwise express cultural biases.

Testosterone, androgen steroid produced by the testes under the control of luteinizing hormone. It is responsible for most male sexual characteristics—voice change, hair distribution, and sex organ development.
See also: Steroid.

Tetanus, or lockjaw, disease of the nervous system caused by toxins produced by the bacterium *Clostridium tetani*. The bacteria enter the body through breaks in the skin. The first symptom is often painful contraction of jaw and neck muscles; trunk muscles, including those of respiration, and muscles close to the site of injury are also frequently involved. Untreated, many cases are fatal, but artificial respiration, antiserum, and penicillin have improved the outlook. Regular vaccination and adequate wound cleansing are important in prevention.

Tet Offensive, in the Vietnam War, a coordinated cluster of attacks against cities and bases in South Vietnam by Vietcong and North Vietnamese forces, beginning on Jan. 30, 1968, the first day of the Tet (New Year) holiday. The offensive, which included a brief occupation of part of the U.S. embassy in Saigon, was costly to the enemy; nevertheless, it converted many Americans to the view that the war could not be won.
See also: Vietnam War.

Teton, Grand *See:* Grand Teton National Park.

Teton Range, mountain range located in Wyoming and Idaho in Grand Teton National Park. This rugged range, part of the Rocky Mountains, stretches for 40 mi (64 km) in length and up to 15 mi (24 km) in width. Grand Teton (13,770 ft, 4,197 m) is the highest peak. John Colter, part of the Lewis and Clark expedition, discovered (1808) the Teton Range.

Tetracycline, name for broad-spectrum antibiotics that can be given by mouth. They are useful in bronchitis and other minor infections and especially valuable in diseases due to rickettsia and related organisms; they can also be used in acne.
See also: Antibiotic.

Teutonic Knights, group of German crusaders. Founded in the Middle East at the end of the 12th century, this organization of knights worked to conquer and convert areas of central and eastern Europe to Christianity. Prussia was converted in the 1200s as were the neighboring countries of Estonia and Livonia, where the Livonian Knights were founded. Lithuania was eventually converted (1387), but with Poland later defeated the Teutonic Knights (1410). The order continued to weaken and, beginning in Prussia (1525), its various branches were eventually dissolved.
See also: Knighthood, Orders of.

Teutons, Northern European tribes that attacked the Roman empire early in the 1st century B.C. Though the Teutons, with the Cimbri, were badly beaten by the Romans under General Gaius Marius, both Caesar and the historian Tacitus wrote of the Teutons' warlike nature. As the Teutons moved south, southeast, and west, what is known as the Teutonic languages came to encompass the Scandinavian as well as Germanic languages, including Dutch, English, and Flemish.

Texas, the largest state in the southwestern region of the United States and the second-largest state in the nation; bordered by Oklahoma and the Red River to the north, Arkansas, Louisiana, and the Sabine River to the east, the Gulf of Mexico to the southeast, the Rio Grande (with Mexico opposite) to the south and southwest, and New Mexico to the west.
Land and climate. Texas has five main land regions. The Gulf Coastal Plains in the east and the southern horn cover a low-lying area with timberland in the northeast and fertile farmland in the south. West of that timberland is the Prairie Plains, a hilly, forested region. In the Rolling Plains region, another

Texas

Capital:	Austin
Statehood:	Dec. 29, 1845 (28th state)
Familiar name:	Lone Star State
Area:	266,807 sq mi (691,030 sq km); ranks 2nd
Population:	19,439,000 (1997); ranks 3rd
Elevation:	Highest—8,751 ft (2,667 m), Gaudalupe Peak; Lowest—sea level, along the Gulf of Mexico
Motto:	Friendship
Flower:	Bluebonnet
Bird:	Mockingbird
Tree:	Pecan
Song:	"Texas, Our Texas"

hilly area, elevations rise from east to west. The Great Plains, stretching southward from the northern Panhandle, is a high, level, grassland. In Texas's extreme southwest is the Basin and Range Region, a high, dry area that includes high spurs of the Rocky Mountain range. The Rio Grande, which forms the entire border between Texas and Mexico, is one of the largest in the nation. Other major rivers include the Pecos, Brazos, Red, Canadian, Colorado, Nueces, and Trinity. Forests cover about 14% of the state. Texas's climate ranges from temperate in the Panhandle region to subtropical in the Rio Grande delta. Principal cities are Houston, Dallas, and San Antonio.

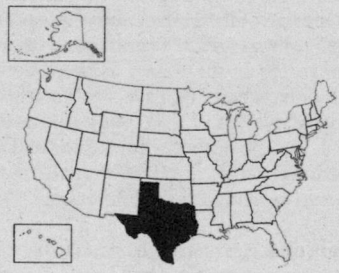

Economy. Texas's economy depends heavily on its oil and natural gas resources, among the richest in the world. Other mineral resources include sulfur, helium, coal, clay, salt, asphalt, limestone, gypsum, and sand and gravel. Service industries and manufacturing are also important to the economy. Chief manufactured goods are nonelectrical machinery, chemicals, processed foods, oil and coal products, electrical equipment, fabricated metal products, transportation equipment, and apparel. A leading agricultural state, Texas produces beef cattle, cotton, grain sorghum, rice, wheat, vegetables, and citrus and other fruits.

Government. Texas's present constitution was adopted in 1876. The governor serves a 4-year term. The state legislature consists of 31 senators serving 4-year terms and 150 representatives serving 2-year terms. In the U.S. Congress, Texas is represented by 2 senators and 30 representatives.

History. Several Native American peoples were living in Texas when Spanish gold-seekers, the first Europeans in the area, arrived in the early 1500s. In 1685, the French explorer La Salle arrived and claimed the area, which France sold to the United States as part of the 1803 Louisiana Purchase. In 1821, Texas became part of the newly independent Empire of

Mexico. But U.S. settlement in the area continued to grow; the Texas Revolution—a rebellion of U.S. settlers against Mexico—began in 1835. In 1836, after the famous battle at the Alamo, the independent Republic of Texas was formed. It became the 28th state in 1845. The Mexican War (1846-48) ended all Mexican claims to Texas. In 1861, Texas seceded from the Union and fought on the Confederate side during the Civil War; it was readmitted to the Union in 1870. Texas played a major role in the expansion of the western frontier during the late 1800s. The 1901 discovery of oil near Beaumont spurred rapid industrial growth, as did World War II. During the 1960s and 1970s, growth was centered in the U.S. space program and the oil and oil-related industries. Falling oil prices during the mid-1980s dealt Texas a heavy blow; it has been working to diversify and attract new industries.

Texas fever *See:* Cattle tick.

Texas Rangers, law enforcement body, part of the Texas department of public safety. The first Rangers were 10 men employed (1823) by S.F. Austin to protect settlers from Native American and Mexican raiders. In 1935 the Rangers were merged with the state highway patrol.

Textile, fabric made from natural or synthetic fibers, whether knitted, woven, bonded, or felted. The fibers (silk, wool, cotton, linen, or synthetics) are prepared and spun into yarn, which is formed into fabric by weaving or other methods. Finished processes include bleaching, calendering, mercerizing, dyeing, brushing, sizing, fulling, and tentering. Chemical processes are used to impart crease-resistance, fireproofing, stain resistance, waterproofing, or non-shrink properties.

Thackeray, William Makepeace (1811-63), English novelist, essayist, and illustrator. He did much to shape *Punch* and was first editor of *the Cornhill Magazine* (1860). His best-known novel is *Vanity Fair* (1848), a gentle satire of the early 19th-century middle classes. His other novels include *Barry Lyndon* (1844), *Pendennis* (1850), and *Henry Esmond* (1852).

Thailand, Kingdom of Thailand, formerly Siam, constitutional monarchy in Southeast Asia. Thailand is bordered by Myanmar (Burma) to the west and northwest, Laos in the north and east, Cambodia to the southeast, and Malaysia and the Gulf of Siam to the south. The capital is Bangkok.
Land and climate. Thailand takes up an area of 198,115 sq mi (513,115 sq km) and is divisible into 3 main areas. The principle region is a fertile plain approximately in the center of the country. It is here that most of the people live. To the north and northeast is a region sometimes called the Khorat Plateau. It is a high red sandstone plateau that drains eastward to the Mekong. It has poor clay, sand soils, and scrub vegetation and is dry and dusty about half of the year. The region is thinly populated. To the south, Thailand extends into the long narrow Malay Peninsula, which it occupies with Myanmar and Malaysia. In places where it borders Myanmar, Thailand's peninsular territory is not more than 10 mi (16 km) wide. The region is mostly mountainous and forested, but has rice-producing plains and mineral deposits. The many islands along its coast include Phuket, important for its tin. The climate of Thailand is monsoonal.

Thailand

Capital:	Bangkok
Area:	198,115 sq mi (513,115 sq km)
Population:	60,037,000
Language:	Thai (Siamese)
Government:	Parliamentary monarchy
Independent:	1939 (as Thailand)
Head of gov.:	Prime minister
Per capita:	U.S. $2,740
Mon. unit:	1 Thai baht = 100 satangs

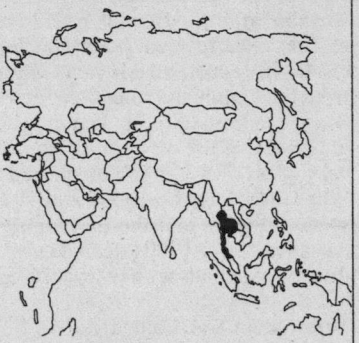

People. The Thai people are of Mongol origin. Ethnic Chinese are an important minority, and there are hill peoples in the north and Malays, most of them Muslim, in the south. Hinayana Buddhism is the official religion and Thai, a Sino-Tibetan language is the official language.
Economy. Rice is the chief crop in Thailand's predominantly agricultural economy, but sugarcane, cotton, corn, coconuts, rubber, and tobacco are also cultivated. Fishing is important and forestry yields teak, oils, resins, and bamboo. Among the few manufactures is quality silk production. Thailand is one of the world's largest exporters of rice. Other exports include corn, rubber, and teak. Tourism is also important to the economy.
History. The Thai people migrated from South China c.1000 B.C. The center of their culture and civilization moved south under the successive dynasties of the Sukho Thai (c.1220-1350), Ayuthai (1350-1778), and Chakri (1782-). The coming of the Portuguese in the 16th century eventually led to an enduring association between the kingdom of Siam and the Western powers. The only country of Southeast Asia that has never been a colony of a European power, Siam lost territorial influence in the 1800s to the British in Burma and Malaya and to the French in Laos and Cambodia, but kept its independence. Thailand was invaded and occupied by the Japanese in World War II. In the early 1950s it sent troops to Korea and joined the South East Asia Treaty Organization (SEATO) in 1954, which is headquartered in Bangkok. Thailand supported the United States in Vietnam, providing troops as well as air bases. King Prajadhikop was forced to grant the country a constitution in 1932 and Siam became Thailand in 1939. The post-World War II years saw political instability and military coups. A new constitution was promulgated in 1978 and general elections were held in 1979. The civilian government was brought down by a coup in 1991 and was restored in 1992. In 1997 a new constitution was adopted. In the same year the country experienced a serious economic crisis.

Thalassemia, inherited blood disorder in which hemoglobin is not adequately produced. Without hemoglobin—the red pigment in blood that carries oxygen through the body—children become sick and, with some varieties of the disease, die. This disorder most often affects people from the Mediterranean, along with Asian and Middle Eastern people as well as Black

Americans. A mild form of the disease called thalassemia minor may cause a person to transmit the disorder to the next generation. With thalassemia major, or Cooley's anemia, a child may suffer various symptoms that often become fatal by early adulthood. Thalassemia intermedia is a serious but not always fatal variation of the disorder. Although not a cure, blood transfusions may relieve symptoms if administered on a regular basis.

Thales (625?-546? B.C.), first known Greek philosopher. His ideas are known to us through the writings of others, such as the Greek philosopher Aristotle. Thales approached subjects through what he could scrutinize and logically reason about them—an approach quite different from the Greek tradition of explanations through supernaturally directed myths. Because of this approach, he is considered the first philosopher in the Western tradition. His observations led him to the conclusion that water was the cornerstone of all things on earth. He also introduced geometry to Greece. His school of thought is called either Milesian (based on Miletus, his birth place) or Ionian (based on Ionia, city-state of Greece in which Miletus was located).
See also: Pre-Socratic philosophy.

Thalidomide, mild sedative introduced in the late 1950s and withdrawn a few years later when it was found to be responsible for congenital deformities in children born to mothers who took the drug. This was due to an effect on the embryo in early pregnancy, in particular causing defective limb bud formation. Stricter regulations for testing new drugs in the United States resulted.

Thallium, chemical element, symbol Tl; for physical constants see Periodic Table. Thallium was discovered spectroscopically by William Crookes in 1861. It occurs in crookesite, loandrite, orbaite, and other minerals. It is obtained commercially from flue dusts remaining from pyrite calcination. Thallium is a tin-white, soft, reactive metal. It is soft enough to be scratched with the finger nail. The metal oxidizes in air and should be kept covered by an inert liquid. Thallium is a suspected carcinogen. The element and it compounds are poisonous, and contact with the skin should be avoided. The sulphate has been used as an insecticide and rodenticide, but its use in the United States is now prohibited. Thallium and its compounds are used in photo cells, infrared detectors, low-temperature mercury switches, and special glasses.

Thames River, England's chief waterway, winding east from the Cotswolds to its North Sea estuary. The Thames is 210 mi (338 km) long. On its banks lie Oxford, Reading, Eton, Windsor Castle, Runnymede, Hampton Court Palace, and Greenwich. Canals link it to the West and Midlands. Above London it displays fine, gentle scenery; below London it is of considerable importance for shipping. It is tidal up to Teddington (10 mi/16 km west of London).
See also: England.

Thanksgiving Day, since 1863, an annual U.S. national holiday to give thanks for blessings received during the year. It is celebrated on the fourth Thursday in November with feasting and prayers. The tradition was begun by the colonists of Plymouth, Mass., in 1621, and can be traced back to the

English harvest festivals. In Canada, it is celebrated on the second Monday in October.

Thant, U (1909-74), Burmese diplomat, United Nations secretary-general (1961-71). A cautious and unassertive negotiator, he was involved in the Cuban missile crisis (1962), and in peace negotiations in Indonesia (1962), the Congo (now Zaïre; 1963), Cyprus (1964), and the India-Pakistan war (1965).
See also: United Nations.

Thar Desert, also called the Indian Desert, located in northwest India and eastern Pakistan. This desert covers 74,000 sq mi (192,000 sq km). Even though rainfall is scarce (10 in/25 cm per year on average), the Indian government has developed the Indian Gandhi canal for irrigation (completed 1986), so that crops and people may thrive in this arid region. Nuclear power facilities of India are located within the desert in Kota.

Tharp, Twyla (1941-), U.S. choreographer and dancer. After 2 years as a dancer with the Paul Taylor Company (1963-65), she began to create original, expressive dances for her own company (founded 1965) and later the American Ballet Theater (joined in 1988). She uses various aspects of dance genres (ballet, tap-dance, social dance) and genres of music (classical, jazz, rock and roll). Some of her well-known dances are *Re-Moves* (1966), *Deuce Coupe* (1973), *Short Stories* (1980). She has also choreographed movies, such as *Hair* (1979) and *Amadeus* (1984).

Thatcher, Margaret Hilda (1925-), English prime minister (1979-90). She entered Parliament in 1959 and served (1970-74) as secretary of state for education and science. In 1975 she was elected Conservative Party leader, and in 1979, when the Conservatives won a parliamentary majority, Mrs. Thatcher became Britain's first female prime minister. To fight inflation she introduced austerity measures, but this kept unemployment high and contributed to domestic unrest. She took a firm line against the hunger strikes and terrorist tactics of the Irish Republican Army. Her vigorous defense of the Falkland Islands against Argentina in 1982 contributed to her party's solid electoral victory in 1983. She resigned in 1990 after failing to win the Conservative Party's leadership election.
See also: United Kingdom.

Thayer, Sylvanus (1785-1872), U.S. Army officer. He served as the superintendent of the U.S. Military Academy at West Point (1817-33), becoming known as the father of West Point.
See also: Army, U.S.

Theater, term used to refer to drama as an art form, as well as to the building in which it is performed. According to Aristotle, the drama of ancient Greece, the ancestor of modern European drama, grew out of the dithyramb (choral song). The form of tragedy credited to Thespis was refined successively by Aeschylus, Sophocles, and Euripides in Periclean Athens. Comedy developed separately. The plays of Aristophanes are the only remains of Greek Old Comedy (5th century B.C.), a form that was extremely licentious and close to its ritual origins. Middle and New comedy (4th and 3rd centuries

B.C., respectively) became increasingly sentimental. Greek drama was performed at religious festivals in amphitheaters built into hillsides; that at Epidaurus is still used each summer.
The Roman plays of Plautus, Terence, and Seneca were influenced by Greek theater. However, mime and pantomime were the popular theatrical forms in the Roman Empire. After the fall of the Empire, theater was banned by the Church until the 9th century. Medieval drama evolved from musical elaborations of the church service. Eventually these developed into mystery plays and were moved outdoors onto play wagons. Miracle plays, based on the lives of the saints and on scripture, also developed; cycles of plays were performed at religious festivals. Morality plays (such as *Everyman*) and interludes (comic plays) appeared in the 15th century.
During the Renaissance the rediscovery of Greek and Roman dramatic texts led directly to the growth of secular drama. Buildings for the performance of plays were erected in Elizabethan times. One of the most famous was the Globe Theatre (associated with Shakespeare), a multistory roofed building inside which the audience ranged around an open stage.
The modern form of the stage, with painted scenery and a proscenium arch across which a curtain falls between acts, was established by the 17th century. However, in the 20th century attempts have been made to eliminate the distancing of audience from the dramatic action, using such new theatrical designs as theater in the round.

Theater of the Absurd, term to describe plays in which traditional values are unable to fulfill emotional and spiritual needs. Human experience is seen as chaotic and without purpose, and people are often depicted as victims of technology and bourgeois values. Samuel Beckett, Eugéne Ionesco, Jean Genet, Edward Albee, and Harold Pinter have been identified with this genre.

Thebes, ancient Greek city located on same site as the modern-day Greek city of Thivai. It headed an alliance, or confederacy, of Greek city-states called Boeotia. As a rival of Athens—a southeastern neighbor about 30 miles away—Thebes supported an invasion of Athens by Persia (480 B.C.). Thebes also sided with Sparta against Athens in the Peloponnesian War (431-404 B.C.). After this war Thebes was dominated by Sparta until a Theban victory by Epaminondas (371 B.C.) made Boeotia powerful once again. Thebes was controlled by other city-states after the death of Epaminondas. Alexander the Great sacked Thebes (336 B.C.); the city was rebuilt 20 years later.
See also: Greece, Ancient.

Thebes, southern city in ancient Egypt, located on the Nile River; present-day city of Luxor. Temples to the god Amon-Re as well as elaborate pyramids constructed for the burial of kings from the Eighteenth Dynasty (1554-1304 B.C.) are found here. The temples of Karnak and Luxor still stand. Thebes served as the capital for many of these rulers, including Tutankhamen, whose remains were unearthed in the 20th century (1922). Remnants of tombs are still apparent in the nearby Valley of the Kings. Thebes was destroyed by the Assyrians (661 B.C.) and the Romans (29 B.C.).
See also: Egypt, Ancient.

Theism, philosophical system, as distinguished from deism and pantheism, that professes the existence of a personal, transcendent God who created,

preserves, and governs the world. Orthodox Christian philosophy is a developed form of theism.
See also: Religion.

Themistocles (514?-449? B.C.), ancient Greek politician and military strategist of Athens. He endorsed the development of the Athenian navy, which helped bring victory to Athens in their war against Persia. Themistocles is best known for his participation in the Athenian victory against the Persians in the battle at Salamis (480 B.C.). Suspicions due to political intrigues resulted in his exile to Persia, where he died on an estate presented to him by the Persian king.
See also: Salamis.

Theocracy, government in which power and authority are seen as derived directly from God and rulers are considered either incarnations or representative of divine power. In ancient times theocracy was widespread. During the Middle Ages in Europe the pope claimed ultimate authority in governing based on his religious authority, and later kings used the "divine right of kings" to justify their absolutist rule. Early Puritan colonies in New England like Massachusetts Bay and New Haven had leaders who claimed to derive their authority from God. While today secular and religious authority are for the most part separated in the Western democracies, their fusion in such political units as the Iranian Islamic Republic is still strong.

Theocritus (c.3rd century B.C.), poet of ancient Greece. He expressed himself through the idyll—a short, lyrical and emotional poem that describes the virtues and beauty of the countryside. This form of poetry is also called a pastoral. He worked in Alexandria, Egypt, a literary center of his time. Of his life's work, 30 written poems remain. Theocritus was influenced by the Alexandrian librarian and poet Callimachus, and in turn influenced the work of the Roman poet Vergil.

Theodoric (A.D. 455?-526), conqueror of Italy, king of Ostrogoths. He inherited the crown from his father Theodemir (A.D. 471). With the help of the Byzantine emperor, Zeno, Theordoric and his barbarians defeated Odoacer, the ruling barbarian of Italy (A.D. 493). Rather than tyrannize the Italians, Theodoric respected Roman citizens and used their political and legal institutions during his peaceful rule. He allowed Catholics to practice their religion even though his Arian beliefs conflicted with the beliefs and doctrines of the church. His elaborate tomb is located in Ravenna, Italy. Theodoric was known in Germanic legends as Dietrich of Bern.
See also: Ostrogoths.

Theodosius I (A.D. 346-395), emperor of Rome. Theodosius was of Armenian descent, born in Spain. He rose through the ranks of the Roman military. Later with Emperor Gratian he ruled Rome, becoming responsible for provinces in the east (A.D. 379). He would not allow religious practices that were not Christian, but he did allow the formation of an independent nation for the non-Christian Visigoths (A.D. 382) within the eastern provinces. He became emperor of all of Rome when he conquered the non-Christian peoples that populated the west (394 A.D.).
See also: Rome, Ancient.

Theology, science of religious knowledge; the formal analysis of what is believed by adherents of a religion, making its doctrine coherent, elucidating it logically, and relating it to secular disciplines. Most religions have no well-developed theology. The concept arose in Greek, but its elaboration took place only in Christianity. The early Church Fathers and Doctors formulated doctrine in contemporary philosophical terms, and major advances were made by resolving controversies. In the Middle Ages Scholasticism developed, partly in reaction to the influence of Neoplatonism, and divided theology into natural theology and revealed theology. From the Reformation each branch of Protestantism began to develop its own distinctive theology. From the Enlightenment rationalist theology became dominant, leading to modernism and the modern critical view of the Bible. Partly in reaction, neo-orthodoxy and the existentialist theology of Reinhold Niebuhr and Paul Tillich arose.
See also: God; Religion.

Theorell, Axel Hugo Teodor (1903-82), Swedish biochemist awarded the 1955 Nobel Prize for physiology or medicine for his studies of enzyme action, specifically the roles of enzymes in biological oxidation and reduction processes.
See also: Biochemistry; Enzyme.

Theorem *See:* Geometry; Pythagorean theorem.

Theosophy (Greek, "divine wisdom"), mystical system of religious philosophy claiming direct insight into the divine nature. The speculations of such philosophers as Plotinus, Jakob Boehme, and Emanuel Swedenborg are often called theosophical, as are many Eastern philosophies. The Theosophical Society was founded in 1875 by Madame Helena Petrovna Blavatsky.
See also: Besant, Annie (Wood).

Theotokopoulos, Domenikos *See:* Greco, El.

Therapy *See:* Occupational therapy; Physical therapy; Psychotherapy.

Theresa, Saint *See:* Teresa.

Thermal pollution, ecologically harmful warming of rivers, lakes, or oceans. In the past, this pollution was most often caused by heated wastewater discharged from nuclear power plants or factories into streams, rivers, or other bodies of water, resulting in elevated water temperature that endangered both plant and animal life in the water. The Environmental Protection Agency (EPA) established regulations requiring such parties either to cool the heated wastewater before discharging it or to release small amounts of it into many different places. Both precautions are aimed at maintaining normal temperatures in rivers and lakes to protect the life in them.
See also: Pollution.

Thermal springs *See:* Hot springs.

Thermocouple, electric circuit involving two junctions between different metals, or semiconductors. These junctions create a small electromotive

force (emf) in the circuit (known as the Seebeck effect). Measurement of this electromotive force provides a sensitive, if approximate, temperature reading ranging from 70°K to 1,000°K. Thermocouples can be run in reverse as small refrigerators. A number of thermocouples connected in series with one set of blackened junctions form a thermopile, which measures radiation. Thermoelectricity embraces the Seebeck and other effects relating heat transfer, thermal gradients, electric fields, and currents.
See also: Electric current.

Thermodynamics, division of physics concerned with the interconversion of heat, work, and other forms of energy, and with the states of physical systems. *Classical thermodynamics* is basic to engineering, parts of geology, metallurgy, and physical chemistry. Building on earlier studies of temperature and heat, Sadi Carnot pioneered the science with his investigations of the cyclic heat engine (1824), and in 1850 Rudolf Clausius stated the first two laws. Thermodynamics was further developed by J.W. Gibbs, H.L.F. von Helmholtz, Lord Kelvin, and J.C. Maxwell.
In thermodynamics, a system is any defined collection of matter: a closed system is one that cannot exchange matter with its surroundings; an *isolated system* can exchange neither matter nor energy. The state of a system is specified by determining all its properties, such as pressure, volume, etc. A *process* is a change from one state to another, the path being specified by all the intermediate states. A *state function* is a property or function of properties that depends only on the state and not on the path by which the state was reached.
See also: Physics.

Thermography, method to measure the slightest variations in temperature of soft tissue in the body using infrared heat sensors. The technique is often used in mammography (breast examination) to detect any growth in the breast (the mass will have a different temperature from other breast tissue). Thermography can also be used on an extremity, particularly the leg, to help diagnose a thrombus (clot) in a vein. The area of the body to be tested is usually placed on a heat-detection device that reacts to specific temperatures, either by color changes or by a direct display of temperatures.

Thermometer, instrument for measuring the temperature of a substance or object. Clinical thermometers are made of a glass tube with a bulb containing liquid (usually mercury) that expands and rises in the tube as the temperature increases. A scale on the tube indicates the object's temperature by measuring how high the liquid rises. The type of thermometer used in a given application depends on the temperature range.

Thermopylae (Greek, "hot gates"), narrow mountain pass that in ancient Greece led from the north to the south. This pass between Mt. Oeta and the Maliac Gulf was the scene of a famous battle from the Persian Wars (480 B.C.) that the Spartans lost against the invading Persian forces. Although this area is a marshy plain rather than a mountain pass, it contains hot springs as it did in ancient times.

Thermosphere, outermost layer of the earth's atmosphere, at altitudes between approximately 53 mi (85 km) and 300 mi (480 km). The heat, caused by radiation of the sun, varies from –135°F (–93°C) at the lowest altitude to

2,700°F (1,500°C) and more at the highest altitude. The thermosphere is different from the layers of the atmosphere closest to earth in that the pressure is much lower (1 million times lower than at sea level) and the chemical makeup includes mostly atoms of helium and hydrogen.
See also: Atmosphere

Thermostat, device for maintaining a material or enclosure at a constant temperature by automatically regulating its heat supply, which is cut off if the temperature exceeds and reconnected if it falls below that required. A thermostat comprises a sensor whose dimensions or physical properties change with temperature and a relay device that controls a switch or valve accordingly.

Theropod *See:* Dinosaur.

Theseus, in Greek mythology, son of King Aegeus and princess Aethra, renowned for his heroism. As a youth he went to Crete with other youths to be sacrificed to the Minotaur, but instead succeeded in killing the beast. On his voyage back to Athens, he failed to fly his ship's white sails, a symbol of his safe return. Aegeus thought his son was dead and killed himself in his grief. Theseus was then declared king.
See also: Mythology.

Thespis (c. 6th century B.C.), ancient Greek actor. Among his many innovations was that of allowing a character to speak dialogue separately from the words spoken by the chorus. The use of make-up and masks is also attributed to him. Most importantly, through an innovative performance in honor of the Greek god Dionysus at an Athenian festival (c.534 B.C.), Thespis became known as the originator of tragedy. A word for actors, thespians, honors his contributions to drama.

Thessalonians, Epistles to the, books 13 and 14 of the New Testament Bible. After the founding of the church at Thessaloniki in Greece, the apostle Paul wrote a letter (c.A.D. 50) to its members, explaining the purpose of the resurrection of Christ. A second letter, attributed to Paul but more likely written by one of his followers, indicated the lengthy time that would elapse before Christ's second coming. These letters represent the first Christian writings.
See also: Bible; New Testament.

Thessaloniki *See:* Salonika.

Thessaly, northeast region of Greece in which Mount Olympus of ancient Greek legend is located. This region was the home of the legendary Achilles, hero of the Trojan War, and Jason, head of the Argonauts. Lack of cooperation among its own people kept Thessaly weak militarily. It was conquered (344 B.C.) by Philip of Macedon, father of Alexander the Great. Later rulers included the Romans (146 B.C.), the Turks (1355), and the Greeks (1878). In ancient times, Pherae, Crannon, and Larisa were its major cities. Today, its major cities are Volos and Larisa.
See also: Greece.

Thiamine *See:* Vitamin.

Thibault, Jacques A.F *See:* France, Anatole.

Thiers, Louis Adolphe (1797-1877), French author and diplomat. Among his writings are *History of the French Revolution* (1823-27), a 10-volume study, and *History of the Consulate and the Empire* (1845-62). He helped organize the July Revolution (1830), which opposed the rule of Charles X. He served in the government of Louis Philippe, successor of Charles X. He opposed the rule of Napoleon II in the Second Empire. Later, after the Franco-Prussian War, he served 2 years as the first president of the Third Republic of France (1871-73).
See also: France.

Thieu, Nguyen Van (1923-), president of South Vietnam (1967-75). An army officer, he helped overthrow Ngo Dinh Diem (1963), becoming premier in 1965 and president in 1967. He was re-elected (1971), but after U.S. troops were withdrawn his dictatorial regime gradually collapsed, and he resigned in April 1975. He fled to Taiwan and later to Great Britain, after South Vietnam fell to the North.
See also: Vietnam.

Thiopental, drug used in general anesthesia. It is commonly known by its trade name, Pentothal or Sodium Pentothal. It was first demonstrated in 1934. Because it will not burn or explode, it is preferred over combustible anesthetics, such as ether. It is often used, usually by injection, to begin the anesthesia process. Small doses tend to release emotional inhibitions, and it is sometimes used in the treatment of psychiatric patients.
See also: Anesthesia.

Third International *See:* International, The.

Third Reich *See:* Germany; Reich.

Third World, term often applied to the nonaligned (and mostly developing) nations of Africa, Latin America, and Asia as opposed to Western and Eastern (Communist) countries.

Thirty-Nine Articles, doctrine issued by the Church of England to bridge the gap between Roman Catholic and Protestant Reformation groups in 16th-century England. The Articles, approved by Parliament in 1571, are still accepted today by the Anglican Church. Among the tenets are the condemnation of such Roman Catholic beliefs as purgatory, transubstantiation, and reverence for saints. Because the language of the Articles is intentionally vague, interpretations have been various.
See also: Anglicans.

Thirty Tyrants, or The Thirty, term used to identify the group of Athenians who ruled Athens after it fell to Sparta (404 B.C.). The oligarchy was set up by the Spartan general Lysander. Under the leadership of the Athenian politician Critias, the group terrorized the Athenian citizenry and seized their

property. In 403 B.C., Sparta reinstated Athens's democratic form of government.
See also: Athens; Greece, Ancient.

Thirty Years' War, series of European wars (1618-48). Partly a Catholic-Protestant religious conflict, they were also a political and territorial struggle by different European powers, particularly France, against its greatest rivals, the Habsburgs, rulers of the Holy Roman Empire. War began when Bohemian Protestants accused 2 government ministrers of wrongdoing and threw them out a window (a customary Bohemian punishment for offending officials). This event became known as the Defenestration of Prague (from Latin *fenestra*, "window") and triggered a civil war in Bohemia that rapidly spread to all of western Europe. The Bohemians were defeated by General Tilly (1620), who went on to subjugate the Palatinate (1623). In 1625 Denmark, fearing Habsburg power, invaded North Germany but was defeated in 1629. The emperor Ferdinand II issued the Edict of Restitution, restoring lands to the Roman Catholic Church. In 1630 the Swedish king Gustavus Adolphus led the Protestant German princes against Ferdinand. He was killed at Lützen (1632). By 1635 the Swedes had lost support in Germany, and the German states concluded the Peace of Prague. But now France, under Cardinal Richelieu, intervened. Further wars ensued, with France, Sweden, and the German Protestant states fighting in the Low Countries, Scandinavia, France, Germany, Spain, and Italy against the Holy Roman Empire, Spain (another Habsburg power), and Denmark. Peace negotiations, begun in 1640, were completed with the Peace of Westphalia (1648).

Thistle, common name for many prickly, herbaceous plants (family Compositae). They normally have purple or yellow flowers. When the seeds are ripe, they are dispersed as fluffy thistledown. Thistles normally produce a thick taproot that can be eaten or used as a coffee substitute.

Thomas à Becket *See:* Becket, Saint Thomas à.

Thomas, Dylan (1914-53), Welsh poet who first achieved recognition with *Eighteen Poems* (1934). His prose includes the quasi-autobiographical *Portrait of the Artist as a Young Dog* (1940) and *Adventures in the Skin Trade* (1955); his poetry includes *Deaths and Entrances* (1946) and *Collected Poems* (1952). His drama *Under Milk Wood* (posthumously published, 1954) was originally a radio play.

Thomas, George Henry (1816-70), U.S. Union general victorious at Mill Springs (1862) and dubbed the "Rock of Chickamauga" for his stand at that battle (1863). His Army of the Cumberland destroyed General John Hood's army at Nashville, Tenn. (1864).
See also: Civil War, U.S.

Thomas, Isaiah (1749-1831), U.S. printer and publisher. He printed books and magazines, and published the *Massachusetts Spy* (1770-1802), a colonial newspaper criticizing British policy before and throughout the Revolutionary War. He printed the first Bible and dictionary in the United States. His *The History of Printing in America* (1810) remains an informative work.

Thomas à Kempis (Thomas Hermerken von Kempen; 1380-1471), German religious writer and Augustinian friar at Zwolle in the Netherlands. He is the probable author of *The Imitation of Christ* (c.1427), one of the most widely read works of Christian literature.

Thomas, Martha Carey (1857-1935), U.S. leader in higher education and women's suffrage movement. She served as president of Bryn Mawr College (1894-1922), following 9 years as a dean and professor of English. The rigorous student requirements and course curriculum she endorsed upgraded academic possibilities for women in the United States. She also served as president of the National College Equal Suffrage League (1908-17), working to gain women the right to vote. Thomas earned a PhD at the University of Zurich in Switzerland, because few U.S. graduate schools accepted women at that time.
See also: Woman suffrage.

Thomas, Norman Mattoon (1884-1968), U.S. socialist leader who ran six times (1928, 1932, 1936, 1940, 1944, 1948) for the presidency of the United States as a Socialist Party candidate. He helped found the American Civil Liberties Union (1920) and the League for Industrial Democracy (1922). An ardent pacifist, he tried to keep the United States out of World War II. Many of his then radical proposals eventually became law.
See also: Socialism.

Thomas Aquinas, Saint *See:* Aquinas, Saint Thomas.

Thomas, Saint, one of the 12 apostles, known as "Doubting Thomas" because he would not believe Jesus' resurrection until he put his fingers in Jesus' wounds. His subsequent career and martyrdom at Madras are recounted in the apocryphal *Acts of Thomas*.
See also: Apostles.

Thompson, Sir John Sparrow David (1844-94), Canadian diplomat and prime minister (1892-94). He had previously served as justice of the Nova Scotia Supreme Court and minister of justice in the Cabinet of prime minister John MacDonald. He was renowned for his diplomatic skills and his successful negotiation of many treaties and controversies. He was named prime minister following the death of MacDonald and the resignation of MacDonald's successor.
See also: Canada.

Thomson, Charles (1729-1824), signer of the Declaration of Independence and secretary of the Continental Congress throughout its existence (1774-89).
See also: Declaration of Independence.

Thomson, Sir Joseph John (1856-1940), British physicist. The Nobel Prize in physics (1906) was awarded to him for his discovery of the electron. This discovery was made as he studied rays—known as cathode rays—that occurred in a vacuum in a glass tube when electric current was introduced. Eventually he proved that this phenomenon was due to moving particles rather than light rays; those particles were later named electrons. As professor

of physics at Cambridge in England, he helped develop their atomic research facilities. His son, Sir George Paget Thomson, also won the Nobel Prize for physics (1937), along with Clinton Davisson of the United States.
See also: Electron.

Thomson, Virgil (1896-1989), U.S. composer and music critic. Influenced by The Six in Paris, he became a leading "Americanist." His works include the operas *Four Saints in Three Acts* (1928) and *the Mother of Us All* (1947), in collaboration with Gertrude Stein, symphonies, and instrumental, chamber, and film music. He won a 1949 Pulitzer Prize for his *Louisiana Story* score.

Thor, in Norse mythology, god of thunder. Son of Odin, the king of the deities, Thor is depicted as a powerful warrior with a huge appetite. The fiercest adversary of the giants, Thor's strength is symbolized by his weapon, a magical hammer called Mjollnir, which unerringly hits its target and flies back to Thor. According to Norse myth, the world will be destroyed in a great war between the giants and the gods, which will also kill Thor. Thursday is named after Thor (Thor's day).
See also: Mythology.

Thoreau, Henry David (1817-62), U.S. writer, naturalist, and abolitionist. His book *Walden* (1854) was a philosophical essay that recounted Thoreau's experiences living close to nature in a cabin at Walden Pond, near Concord, Mass. His influential essay "Civil Disobedience" promoted the concept of passive resistance that inspired leaders such as Mohandas K. Gandhi and Martin Luther King, Jr. Thoreau's place in literature is as a major voice among the New Transcendentalists, led by his mentor Ralph Waldo Emerson. Self-direction and an intimate understanding of nature, as found within and outside of the individual, were Thoreau's consistent themes.

Thorium, chemical element, symbol Th; for physical constants see Periodic Table. Discovered by Jöns Jakob Berzelius in 1828. The element occurs in the minerals thorite, thorianite, orangite, yttrocrasite, and monazite and is obtained commercially from the latter. Thorium is obtained as a powder by reduction of its oxide with calcium. It is a gray-white, radioactive metal. It is pyrophoric in powder form and burns in air to form the oxide, which has the highest melting point of all oxides. It is a member of the actinide series. Thorium is used as a nuclear fuel source and for incandescent lamp mantles. It is estimated that the energy available from thorium in the earth's crust is probably greater than that from uranium and fossil fuels combined.

Thorn apple *See:* Jimsonweed.

Thorndike, Edward Lee (1874-1949), U.S. psychologist best known for devising tests to measure intelligence, learning, and aptitude. His system of psychology, *connectionism*, had a profound influence on U.S. school education techniques, especially his discovery that the learning of one skill only slightly assists in the learning of another, even if related.
See also: Psychology.

Thornton, Matthew (1714?-1803), signer of the Declaration of Independence. A New Hampshire delegate to the Continental Congress in 1776 and 1778, he previously had been the president of the first New Hampshire Provincial Congress.

Thorpe, Jim (James Francis Thorpe; 1888-1953), U.S. athlete. Known for his all-around athletic ability, he played major league baseball (1913-19), professional football (1915-30), and was the first athlete to win both the decathlon and pentathlon at the Olympic Games (1912). Thorpe was stripped of his gold medals after a controversy arouse involving his amateur status; the International Olympic Committee restored these medals in 1982. Thorpe was inducted into the Pro Football Hall of Fame in 1963.

Thoth, Greek name for Djhowtey, an ancient Egyptian moon god who became associated with civilization, learning, and healing. His sacred animals are the ibis and the baboon, and he is often depicted as a human with the head of an ibis or a baboon with the head of a dog. Said to be the inventor of writing, he was often considered the representative on earth and the scribe of the sun god, Re.
See also: Mythology.

Thothmes III *See:* Thutmose III.

Thousand and One Nights *See:* Arabian Nights.

Thousand Islands, group of over 1,500 islands—some Canadian, some U.S.—in the St. Lawrence River at the outlet of Lake Ontario. St. Lawrence Islands National Park includes 13 of them. Thousand Islands International Bridge (actually five bridges) is 8 1/2 mi (13.7 km) long and carries traffic across the river.

Thrace, ancient region in the eastern part of the Balkan Peninsula, southeastern Europe, bordering the Black and Aegean seas. It includes modern northeastern Greece, southern Bulgaria, and European Turkey.

Thrasher, any of 17 U.S. bird species belonging to the mockingbird family. A brownish, long-tailed bird, it is known for its raucous call. It forages on the ground for insects, worms, seeds, and fruit. The most familiar is the brown thrasher, found east of the Rocky Mountains.

Three Mile Island, site in the Susquehanna River, near Middletown, Penn., of a nuclear reactor that, on March 28, 1979, began to emit "puffs" of radiation as a result of malfunction of the cooling system, aggravated by problems with the computer monitors and some human error. Initial reports downplayed the crisis, but it developed that a core meltdown was a possibility and that a large, potentially explosive hydrogen bubble had formed in the reactor; also, it was learned that no workable plans existed for evacuating the area. Luckily, catastrophe was averted without fatalities or known injury.
See also: Nuclear reactor.

Three-mile limit *See:* Territorial waters.

Three Wise Men *See:* Magi.

Thrombosis, formation of a clot (thrombus) in the heart or blood vessels. It commonly occurs in the legs and is associated with varicose veins (thrombophelotist), but is more serious if it occurs in the heart or in the brain arteries. Detachments from a thrombus in the legs may be carried to the lungs as an embolus; this may have a fatal outcome if large vessels are occluded. Treatment includes anticoagulants.

Thrush, name for a family (Turdidae) of slender-billed songbirds found in most parts of the world. The plumage is often gray or red-brown, and many species have speckled or striated breasts. The tail is usually rounded or square and is held erect in some species. Birds of worldwide distribution, they feed largely on insects, worms, and snails, but many species also take fruit and berries. Species include the robin, the nightingale, the hermit thrush, and the bluebird.

Thrush, infection due to the fungus *Candida albicans*. It occurs usually in children and is characterized by small whitish spots on the tip and sides of the tongue and the lining membrane of the mouth.

Thucydides (460?-400 B.C.), historian of ancient Greece. His work *History of the Peloponnesian War* (441-404 B.C.) eloquently communicates an unbiased and accurate account of events in the first 30 years of that war. Both sides in the conflict are quoted, analyzed, and described in detail. Thucydides was an Athenian naval general who, upon failure to defeat the Spartan troops at Amphipolis in the Peloponnesian War, was exiled (424-404 B.C.).
See also: Greece, Ancient; Peloponnesian War.

Thugs, members of an Indian religious sect (13th-19th centuries) who murdered and robbed to honor the goddess Kali. All victims, usually wealthy travelers, were systematically strangled because the spilling of blood was forbidden. In 1831, British and Indian regimes collaborated to eliminate thug activities.

Thulium, chemical element, symbol Tm; for physical constants see Periodic Table. Thulium was discovered in 1879 by P.T. Cleve in crude erbium oxide. It occurs in the minerals gadolinite, euxenite, ytterspar, and monazite and is obtained commercially from the latter. It is prepared by reducing the anhydrous chloride with calcium. Thulium is a silvery, soft, reactive metal belonging to the series of elements known as the rare-earth metals. Thulium salts have a characteristic absorption spectrum. Ion-exchange and solvent extraction techniques have led to much easier isolation of the rare-earth elements. Thulium and its compounds are used in carbon-arc lighting, glass, and refractory materials.

Thunder Bay (pop. 112,300), city in Ontario, Canada, on the northwestern shore of Lake Superior. It has an excellent harbor, which makes it a major shipping center for grain and ore from western Canada. It is also the home of Lakehead University and of Confederation College of Applied Arts and Technology.
See also: Ontario.

Thurber, James (1894-1961), U.S. humorist and cartoonist. The sophisticated humor of his writing contrasts with the simplicity of his line drawings.

Several stories, such as "The Secret Life of Walter Mitty" (1942), were filmed. He contributed to *The New Yorker* from 1927. His collections include *My Life and Hard Times* (1933) and *The Thurber Carnival* (1945).

Thurmond, (James) Strom (1902-), U.S. political leader, senator from South Carolina since 1954. A hardline supporter of States Rights, he opposed federal civil rights legislation and federal welfare. He served as South Carolina's governor (1947-51) and was the 1948 States' Rights Democratic presidential candidate, carrying four states. During his Senate career he shifted to the Republican party. He served as chairman of the Senate's Judiciary Committee (1981-87).

Thutmose III, or **Thothmes III** (d.1450 B.C.), king (c.1490-36 B.C.) of ancient Egypt. Upon accession to the throne, his half sister and wife, Queen Hatshepsut, acted forcefully as his governing ruler. Upon her death he became sole ruler and a brilliant leader and conqueror, expanding Egypt's boundaries, increasing its wealth, improving its manpower, and building and enlarging numerous temples, including the temple at Karnak.
See also: Egypt, Ancient.

Thyme, pungent, aromatic herb (genus *Thymus*) of the mint family. It has pale purple flowers. *T. vulgaris* is commonly used in seasoning.

Thymus, lymphoid organ situated in humans in the chest cavity, behind the breastbone, and extending into the neck. It reaches its maximum weight at about puberty and then undergoes involution (shrinks). It is necessary in early life for the development of immunological functions.

Thyroid gland, ductless two-lobed endocrine gland lying in front of the trachea in the neck. The principal hormones secreted by the thyroid play a crucial role in regulating the rate at which cells oxidize fuels to release energy and thus strongly influence growth. Thyroid stimulating hormones (TSH) are released by the pituitary gland. Undersecretion (hypothyroidism) in adults leads to myxedema, with mental dullness and cool, dry, puffy skin. Oversecretion (thyrotoxicosis) produces nervousness, weight loss, and increased heart rate. Goiter, an enlargement of the gland, may result when the diet is deficient in iodine.
See also: Gland; Hormone.

Tianjin, or Tientsin (pop. 5,770,000), international port city on the Hai River in northeastern China. One of China's largest cities and Beijing's major port, it is a viable industrial center producing machinery, textiles, chemicals, and consumer products, in addition to offshore oil production. Tianjin was occupied by Western powers during the Boxer Uprising (1900) and was controlled by Japan from 1937 until the end of World War II. A major earthquake inflicted serious damage to Tianjin in 1976.
See also: China.

Tian Shan, or Tien Shan, major mountain system of central Asia. It runs some 1,500 mi (2,410 km) through Kirghizstan and China. Its highest peak, the Pobeda Peak, stands 24,406 ft (7,439 m) above sea level.

Tiberias, Lake *See:* Galilee, Sea of.

Tiberius (Tiberius Julius Caesar Augustus; 42 B.C.-A.D. 37), Roman emperor, successor of his stepfather, Augustus, upon his death in A.D. 14. Tiberius oversaw tax collections and selected capable administrators to supervise his provinces. However, due to unpopular financial reforms and his growing tyranny, he retired to the island of Capri, where he ruled until his death. *See also:* Rome, Ancient.

Tiber River, river in central Italy, flowing 252 mi (405.5 km) from the Appenines south through Umbria and Latium and southwest through Rome to the Tyrrhenian Sea near Ostia. Ancient Rome was built on its east bank.

Tibet, autonomous region of China in central Asia, bordering Myanmar (Burma), India, Nepal, Bhutan, and Sikkim. The capital is Lhasa.
Land and climate. Tibet's area is 471,662 sq mi (1,221,600 sq km), and the region averages 15,000 ft (4,570 m) in altitude. Tibet is often called the "Roof of the World." The tallest mountain in the world, Mt. Everest (29,028 ft/8,848 m above sea level), is in the Himalaya, the world's tallest mountain chain. The Himalaya rise along the southern end of the Plateau of Tibet. The Kunlun Mountains in the north are almost as high as the Himalayas. The Brahmaputra, Indus, and Yangtze rivers rise in Tibet. The winters are dry and intensely cold; summers, hot and humid.
People. Tibetans follow Buddhist Lamaism, headed by the Dalai Lama and the Panchen Lama. Until 1965 there were many monasteries, involving 20% of the male population as monks. After 1965, the Chinese Communists decreased emphasis on religion.
Economy. The pastoral, livestock-based economy has been affected by roadbuilding and new cement, chemical, paper, textile, and other industries. Tibet has deposits of coal and iron (exploited in the northeast) and other minerals.
History. Tibet was a powerful kingdom during the A.D. 600s, flourishing until the early eighteenth century, when it fell under Chinese control. In 1911 Tibet expelled the Chinese, but friction remained between the 2 countries until 1950, when China invaded again. An agreement signed in 1951 ended Tibetan sovereignty, but allowed self-government and freedom of religion and speech. However, Chinese rule became steadily more oppressive, and in the mid-1950s Chinese rule in eastern Tibet caused open dissent and a revolt (1959) that was ruthlessly suppressed. The Dalai Lama fled from the capital Lhasa to India, and in 1965 Tibet became an autonomous region. After 20 years of periodic rioting and unrest in Tibet, the Chinese began a policy of liberalization, decentralizing the economy and allowing a degree of freedom of religion. However, massive rioting again erupted during the late 1980s and the Chinese declared a state of martial law and sent in troups. Unrest continues in Tibet today. In 1993 there were talks between the Chinese government and the Dalai Lama, but this did not result in a change of Chinese policy. In 1995 the persecution of the followers of the Dalai Lama increased. *See also:* China.

Tick, name for a group of parasitic arthropods (order Acarina). Unlike most other arthropods, ticks have no head, and the thorax and abdomen are fused. All ticks are bloodsucking external parasites of vertebrates. They are divided into two main families: the soft ticks, Argasidae, and hard ticks, Ixodidae. Ticks transmit more diseases to humans and domestic animals than does any other arthropod group except the mosquitoes.

Tickseed *See:* Coreopsis.

Ticonderoga, village in northeast New York, near Lake George, site of Fort Ticonderoga, which commanded the route between Canada and the Hudson River valley. Taken (1759) by the British in the French and Indian Wars, it fell (1775) in the Revolutionary War to the Green Mountain Boys, led by Ethan Allen and Benedict Arnold. It was recaptured (1777) by General Burgoyne. The fort is now a museum.
See also: New York.

Tide, periodic rise and fall of land and water on the earth. Tidal motions are primarily exhibited by water: the motion of the land is barely detectable. As the earth-moon system rotates about its center of gravity, which is within the earth, the earth bulges in the direction of the moon, as well as in exactly the opposite direction owing to the moon's gravitational attraction and the centrifugal forces resulting from the system's revolution. Since the moon orbits the earth in the same direction that the earth rotates, the bulge "travels" round the earth each lunar day (24.83 hr); hence most points on the earth have a high tide every 12.42 hr. The sun produces a similar though smaller tidal effect. Exceptionally high high tides occur at full and new moon (spring tides), particularly if the moon is at perigee; exceptionally low high tides (neap tides), at first and third quarter. The friction of the tides causes the day to lengthen 0.001 sec per century.

Tien Shan *See:* Tian Shan.

Tientsiu *See:* Tianjin.

Tiepolo, Giovanni Battista (1696-1770), most renowned Venetian painter of his time, a capable craftsman, decorator, and artist of vivid, large murals. His frescoes in Labia Palace brought him widespread recognition. As a result he was commissioned by Emperor Frederick I of Bavaria and by the Spanish royalty of Madrid, where his work included the *Apotheosis of Spain*.

Tierra del Fuego (Spanish, "Land of Fire"), several small islands (28,476 sq mi/73,753 sq km) separated from the southern coast of South America by the Strait of Magellan. Named by Ferdinand Magellan in 1520, the islands belong to Chili and Argentina. The small population is supported by income from sheep and petroleum.
See also: Cape Horn.

Tiffany, Charles Lewis (1812-1902), U.S. jeweler and retailer. The stock in his first store, opened in 1839, was limited mainly to ordinary glassware and stationery, but it soon included bohemian glass, jewelry, silverware, and rare porcelain. Tiffany began manufacturing his own jewelry in 1848, and by 1870 had extended his operations to Paris and London.

Tiffany, Louis Comfort (1848-1933), U.S. artist and designer, a leader of Art Nouveau; son of jeweler Charles Tiffany. He created decorative objects of iridescent "favrile," or Tiffany glass.
See also: Art nouveau.

Tiflis *See:* Tbilisi.

Tiger (*Panthera tigris*), major cat of Asia with distinct races in different parts of that continent. Closely related to lions, they are the largest of all the cats. A tawny coat broken with dark, vertical stripes provides excellent camouflage against natural patterns of light and shade. Tigers do not chase after food, but prefer to stalk and spring. For the most part they are solitary animals, hunting in the cool of the day and otherwise lying in the shade to rest.

Tiger lily (*Lilium tigrinum*), plant of the lily family originating in eastern Asia and grown widely as a garden flower. The dark stem, 2-6 ft (0.6-1.8 m) tall, supports large red-orange flowers with black markings. The plant propagates by means of small, black, berrylike bulbs that form where the leaves join the stem and fall to the earth to produce new plants.

Tiglath-pileser, rulers of ancient Assyria. **Tiglath-pileser I** ruled from 1115-1077 B.C. A great military leader, he conquered territories from the Mediterranean coast to what are now Turkey and Iran. Historians know little about **Tiglath-pileser II**, who ruled from 967-935 B.C. during a seemingly stable reign. **Tiglath-pileser III**, who ruled from 744-727 B.C., founded the Assyrian Empire. He led a massive military and diplomatic campaign that extended into parts of what are now Iraq, Syria, and Turkey. In 728 B.C., he united the kingdoms of Assyria and Babylonia and declared himself king of Babylonia.
See also: Assyria.

Tigris River, easternmost of the two great rivers of ancient Mesopotamia. The Tigris-Euphrates valley was the cradle of Middle East civilizations. Baghdad, city of the Abbasids, now capital of Iraq, stands on its banks. It rises in the Taurus Mountains in Turkey and flows 1,180 mi (1,900 km) southeast through Iraq to join the Euphrates at Basra.

Tijuana (pop. 742,700), city in Mexico, near the U.S. border. Tijuana, its name derived from the Tia Juana (Spanish, "Aunt Jane") ranch in the area, was settled in the early 1900s. It is a popular tourist town, noted for its bullfights and racetracks.
See also: Mexico.

Tikhonov, Nikolai Aleksandrovich (1905-), soviet premier (1980-85). In 1940 Tikhonov joined the Communist Party. During the 1950s-70s he rose in the Soviet government, becoming a member of the Politburo in 1979. Failing health caused him to resign in 1985.
See also: Union of Soviet Socialist Republics.

Tilden, Bill (William Tatem Tilden, Jr.; 1893-1953), U.S. tennis player. Known for his powerful serve and strong forehand, from 1920 to 1930 he was the top-ranked U.S. player, and led the U.S. team to 7 Davis Cup titles (1920-26). Other victories include 3 Wimbledon titles (1920, 21, 30) and 7 U.S. Open titles (1920-25, 29).

Tilden, Samuel Jones (1814-86), U.S. lawyer and politician. An early leader of the Barnburners faction of the New York Democratic Party and of the Free Soil Party, he proved that there was corruption among New York City politicians led by William ("Boss") Tweed. He was governor of New York (1875-76). Even though he won more popular votes, Tilden lost the hotly contested 1876 presidential election to Republican Rutherford B. Hayes by one electoral vote.

Tilefish, colorful ocean fish belonging to the tilefish family, found along the New England coastline. It is about 3 ft (91 cm) in length and can weigh over 30 lb (14 km). It eats mostly crabs and other fish, and is considered to be a good food fish.

Tillich, Paul Johannes (1886-1965), German-born theologian and teacher. He attempted to synthesize Christianity and classical and modern existentialist philosophy in works like *Systematic Theology* (1951-63), *The Shaking of Foundations* (1948), and *The Courage to Be* (1948). Dismissed from Frankfurt University because of opposition to the Nazis, he taught at the Union Theological Seminary, New York (1933-59) and at Harvard and Chicago universities (1954-62 and 1962-65, respectively).
See also: Theology.

Timbuktu (pop. 20,500), city in central Mali, in the southern Sahara. It was settled in the 1100s by the Tuareg and used by merchants of the 14th century as a major trading center for gold, salt, ivory, and slaves. The 15th and 16th centuries saw the rise of the Songhai Empire and Timbuktu became a center of Muslim learning. It was sacked by the Moroccans (1593), and French rule was established in 1894. Today it continues to be an important marketplace (salt, handicrafts) for the nomads of the Sahara.
See also: Mali.

Time, measure of duration, whether past, present, or future; a particular portion or part of duration; period at which any definite event occurred or person lived; prevailing state or circumstances. Absolute time is time considered without relation to bodies or their motions. Relative time is the sensible measure of any portion of duration. Astronomical time is mean solar time reckoned through the 24-hour cycle. Civil time is mean time adapted to civil uses and distinguished into years, months, days, etc. A timetable is a table or register of times, as of the hours to be observed in a school, of the departure and arrival of railroad trains, buses, etc. Time-sharing is a method of operation in which a computer facility is shared by several users for different purposes at the same time. A time quantum, in a time-sharing system, is a unit of time allotted to each user. Time slicing is the allotment of a portion of processing time to each program in a multiprogramming system to prevent the monopolization of the central processing unit by any one program.

Timor, largest and easternmost of the Lesser Sunda Islands, 400 mi (644 km) northwest of Australia. Since Dec. 1975, when the former Portuguese (eastern) Timor was occupied by Indonesian troops, the whole island has been under Indonesian control. The terrain is largely mountainous. Crops include coffee, coconuts, and rice, and cattle are raised. Resistance against Indonesian occupation has been violently suppressed by the Indonesian army. In 1995 there were talks between Indonesia and Portugal on a diplomatic level. The latter represented eastern Timor. In 1996 bisshop Carlos Belo and José Ramos Horta received the Nobel Peace Prize for their support of the population's struggle for autonomy.

Timothy (*Phleum pratense*), perennial coarse grass grown for hay harvesting and animal grazing. Its nutritional value is increased when alfalfa or clover seed is added to its fields. Also known as herd's-grass, it grows 1.5-3.5 ft (46-107 cm) high and thrives in the northern United States (especially New York state) and Canada.

Timothy, disciple of the Apostle Paul; also, 2 epistles of the New Testament addressed to Timothy. They became part of the Pastoral Epistles, providing guidelines and advice on governing a church.
See also: New Testament.

Timpani, or kettledrums, drums having a calfskin head over a hollow brass or copper hemisphere. They were first used in orchestral music in the 1600s. A set of timpani usually consists of three drums. Pitch is governed by the tension of the head, which can be adjusted. Tone may be varied by the type of stick used for play and by the region of the head struck.

Timur the Lame *See:* Tamerlane.

Tin, chemical element, symbol Sn; for physical constants see Periodic Table. Tin was known to the ancients. It occurs in cassiterite, stannite, and tealite. The element is produced by reducing the oxide with coal in a reverberatory furnace. Tin is a silver-white, soft, malleable, ductile metal. It is resistant to corrosion and is used extensively for coating other metals. Tin exists in 2 forms: alpha (gray) and beta (white). Change to the unusable gray form, called tin pest, is prevented by the addition of small amounts of antimony or bismuth. Pewter, bronze, type metal, and soft solder are some important tin alloys. Stannous chloride is an important reducing agent. Tin and its compounds are used in electrically conductive coatings, dyeing, and super-conductive magnets.

Tinbergen, Jan (1903-94), Dutch economist who in 1969 shared the first Nobel Prize for economic science with Ragnar Frisch for work in developing dynamic models (econometrics).
See also: Economics.

Tinbergen, Nikolas (1907-88), Dutch ethologist awarded, with Konrad Lorenz and Karl von Frisch, the 1973 Nobel Prize for physiology or medicine for their individual, major contributions to the science of animal behavior.
See also: Ethology.

Tinnitus, sensation of sounds not derived from the outer environment, such as ringing, roars, or banging in the inner ear. It is a common symptom of most ear disorders. Tinnitus is not a severe or disabling problem, but a medical diagnosis is important in determining whether an underlying cause requires treatment.

Tintoretto (Jacopo Robusti; 1518-94), Venetian mannerist painter of the Renaissance. His popular name, Tintoretto ("Little Dyer"), refers to his father's occupation. Influenced by Titian and Michelangelo, Tintoretto's paintings and frescoes are characterized by free brushwork, dramatic viewpoint, movement, monumental figures, and rich colors. He sought to express drama through color and light, as in *Saint Mark Rescuing a Slave* (1548), the Scuola di San Rocco *Life of Christ* (1564-87), and his masterpiece, *The Last Supper* (1594).

Tippecanoe, Battle of *See:* Indian wars.

Tipperary (pop. 5,000), town in southern Ireland established in the late 12th century, located on the Ara River. Its chief industry is the processing of dairy products. Its name was made famous due to the popularity of the marching song "It's a Long, Long Way to Tipperary," sung by Allied soldiers during World War I (1914-18). Originally Tipperary was a small town encircling a castle built by the man who became King John of England.

Tiranë, or **Tirana** (pop. 244,200), capital of Albania, located about 20 mi (32 km) east of the Adriatic Sea. It was founded in the early 17th century and became the capital city in 1920. After the proclamation of Communist rule in 1946, the city grew as an industrial center. It is the home of many of Albania's cultural and educational institutions as well as the center of the country's publishing and broadcast industries. Most residents are Muslim.
See also: Albania.

Tirso de Molina (1584-1648), pen name of Spanish author and playwright, Gabriel Tellez. He is known as one of the greatest playwrights of the Golden Age of Spain. Among the hundreds of plays he wrote, 86 survive, most notably *The Deceiver of Seville* (1630), which introduced the legendary character of Don Juan. A friar and a respected theologian, he wrote plays, stories, and poetry that reflected his knowledge and understanding of history, religion, and human nature. These include *The Gardens of Toledo* (1624) and *Pleasure with Profit* (1635).

Tissue, in biology, similar cells grouped together in multicellular animals and plants. These cells are usually specialized for a single function; thus muscle cells contract but do not secrete, and nerve cells conduct impulses but have little or no powers of contraction. The cells are held together by intercellular material. Having become specialized for a single or at most a very narrow range of functions, they are dependent upon other parts of the organism for necessities like food and oxygen. Groups of tissues, each with its own functions, make up organs. Connective tissue refers to the material in which all the specialized body organs are embedded and supported.

Tissue transplant, permanent transfer of tissue or organs from one part of a body to another. It may involve transplanting tissue, such as skin or bone, within the same body (autografts); or it might involve more than one body, as when one person donates an organ to another person (allografts). Autografts are usually successful because the body normally does not reject its own tissues. Allografts, however, are often unsuccessful because the transplant recipient may reject the donor's tissue or organ. To avoid such rejections, physicians try to match donors and recipients with compatible tissues. People who have a number of similar proteins (HLA antigens) in the cells of the tissues to be exchanged are more likely to achieve a successful tissue transplant. Because HLA antigens are inherited, siblings have a higher rate of tissue transplant success.

Titanic, 46,328-ton British liner that sank in 1912 after hitting an iceberg on its maiden voyage. At least 1,500 of the 2,200 aboard drowned. After the disaster (caused mainly by excessive speed), lifeboat, radio watch, and ice patrol provisions were improved.

Titaniferous ore, blend of minerals rich in the metal titanium. The ore is black and granular and is usually composed of ilmenite and magnetite.

Titanium, chemical element, symbol Ti; for physical constants see Periodic Table. Titanium was discovered by William Gregor in 1791 (named after the Titans). It occurs in the minerals rutile, ilmenite, and sphene. Titanium is the ninth most abundant element in the earth's crust. It is prepared by reducing titanium tetrachloride with magnesium. Titanium is a white, lustrous, strong, corrosion-resistant metal. It is the only element that burns in nitrogen. It is as strong as steel, but 45% lighter. Titanium and its compounds are used in heat-resistant alloys, paint pigments, and chemical smoke screens.

Titans, in Greek mythology, offspring of Uranus and Gaea, including Cronus, Hyperion, Iapetus, Oceanus, Coeus, Creus, Theia, Rhea, Mnemosyne, Phoebe, Tethys, and Themis, as well as their descendants (e.g., Atlas, Prometheus). Cronus and his siblings overthrew Uranus. In turn one of Cronus's offspring, Zeus, led the Olympians to defeat Cronus and become rulers of the universe, banishing the Titans, except for Cronus (who ruled the Isle of the Blessed) and Atlas (who held up the sky), to Tartarus. Prometheus, who aided Zeus, was also allowed to remain.
See also: Mythology.

Titchener, Edward Bradford (1867-1927), English-born U.S. psychologist. A disciple of Wilhelm Wundt, he played a large part in establishing experimental psychology in the United States, especially through his *Experimental Psychology* (2 vol., 1901-05).
See also: Psychology.

Titi, small tree-dwelling monkey belonging to the New World monkey family Cebidae and found in Brazil's Orinoco River Basin. It lives in 2-parent family units and subsists on fruit, leaves, small birds, and insects. A characteristic of the titi is its habit, with others of its kind, of winding its tail around a tree branch when asleep or at rest.

Titian (Tiziano Vecellio; 1487-1576), Venetian painter, leading Renaissance artist. He worked for Giovanni Bellini and Giorgione, who influenced his early work, before becoming Venice's official painter (1516). His perceptive portraits, monumental altarpieces, and historical and mythological scenes are famous for their energetic composition, use of rich color, and original technique. Among his works are *La Gloria* (1554), *Rape of Europe* (1562), and *Adam and Eve* (1570).
See also: Renaissance.

Titmouse, forest bird of the family Pariclae, found mainly in the Northern Hemisphere. Related to the nuthatch and the chickadee, these small, brown-and-gray birds travel with other birds in flocks and are easily trained to do tricks.

Tito, Josip Broz (1892-1980), president of former Yugoslavia (1953-80), founder of the post-World War II republic. He became a Communist while a World War I prisoner of war in Russia, and later spent several years in Yugoslav jails. General secretary of the Communist Party from 1937, Tito organized partisan resistance to the Nazis in World War II, eclipsing the Chetniks, and after the war established a Socialist republic. He served as prime minister (1945-53) before becoming president. Tito broke with Joseph Stalin in 1948. He suppressed home opposition but worked for workers' self-management and the reconciliation of national minorities. Later years saw a substantial liberalization of his policies. On the international scene, Tito became an organizer and leading representative for Third World or neutralist countries.
See also: Yugoslavia.

Titus (Titus Flavius Sabinus Vespasianus; A.D.39-81), Roman emperor, successor (79) to his father Vespasian. A successful soldier, he captured (70) Jerusalem in the Jewish revolt (66-70). He was popular for lavish entertaining and for aiding victims of the eruption of the Vesuvius (79) and the fire at Rome (80).
See also: Rome, Ancient.

Titus, early Christian follower of St. Paul. He traveled with Paul to the Council of Jerusalem, and later went with him to Greece. Appointed by Paul as a special representative to the church in Corinth, he was later made the first archbishop of Crete. Paul's epistle to Titus, the 17th book of the New Testament, believed to have been written in A.D. 65 or 66, gave Titus instructions on how to organize the church in Crete.
See also: Paul, Saint.

TNT, or trinitrotoluene, [$CH_3C_6H_2(NO_2)_3$], pale yellow crystalline solid made by nitration of toluene. It is the most extensively used high explosive, being relatively insensitive to shock, especially when melted by steam heating and cast.
See also: Explosive.

Toad, name strictly referring only to members of the family Bufonidae, but generally distinguishing warty-skinned, tailless amphibians from smoother-skinned types, which are called frogs. Toads range in size from 1 to 7 in (2.5 to 18 cm). They are independent of water except for breeding, the larvae—tadpoles—being purely aquatic. Most toads feed nocturnally on insects.

Toadstool *See:* Mushroom.

Tobacco, plant of the nightshade family (especially genus *Nicotiana*); also, the dried and cured leaves of the plant, used for smoking and chewing and as snuff. Native to America, tobacco was introduced to Europe by the Spanish in the 16th century and from there spread to Asia and Africa. Today the United States remains the world's largest producer, followed by China, India, and the former USSR. Consumption is increasing despite the health hazards of smoking. Tobacco is grown in alluvial or sandy soils and may be harvested after about 4 months. Cultivation is dependent on hand labor.

Tobago *See:* Trinidad and Tobago.

Tobey, Mark (1890-1976), U.S. painter. Strongly influenced by Chinese calligraphy and Zen Buddhism, he developed his "white writing" style in the 1930s in small abstracts representing street scenes. His later, delicately colored abstracts have more intricate linear rhythms.

Tobin, Daniel Joseph (1875-1955), Irish-born U.S. labor leader. As president of the Teamsters Union (1907-52), he built it into one of the most powerful unions in the United States. He was also vice-president of the American Federation of Labor (1933-52).
See also: Labor movement.

Tobin, James (1918-), U.S. economist. He won the 1981 Nobel Memorial Prize in economic science for his research in relating the effects of financial markets to consumption, prices, production, and investment, as well as his studies of government monetary policies and budgets. He had served as one of President John F. Kennedy's economics advisors.
See also: Economics.

Tobit, or **Tobias, Book of**, in the Apocrypha, account of how Tobias, son of the devout but blinded Jew Tobit (or Tobias), successfully undertook a dangerous journey, helped by the angel Raphael, to exorcise a demon from, and marry, Sara. He then helped Tobit regain his sight.
See also: Old Testament.

Toboganning, sport of riding down snow or ice slopes on a sled or toboggan. Although sleds with runners are sometimes called toboggans, the term usually refers to runnerless sleds such as were originally developed by Native American hunters. The modern toboggan is generally 6-8 ft (1.8-2.4 m) long and 1 ft (46 cm) wide, and carries 4 people, one behind another. Artificial chutes for the initial acceleration have allowed high speeds. Bobsledding, a type of tobogganing, is a sport of the Winter Olympics.

Tocopherol *See:* Vitamin.

Tocqueville, Alexis de (1805-59), French historian and writer best known for the 2-volume *Democracy in America*, written after visiting the United States in the early 1830s. The book made him a leading European advocate of democracy, a system he believed would eventually replace the European monarchies and aristocracies. A philosopher, Tocqueville also saw the

Togo

Capital:	Lomé
Area:	21,925 sq mi (56,785 sq km)
Population:	4,906,000
Language:	French
Government:	Presidential republic
Independent:	1960
Head of gov.:	Prime minister
Per capita:	U.S. $310
Mon. unit:	1 CFA franc = 100 centimes

pitfalls of democracy, warning against a "tyranny of the majority" in which conformity would discourage individualism. He served in the French legislature (1839-51) and was foreign minister following the Revolution of 1848. *See also:* France.

Todd, Mary *See:* Lincoln, Mary Todd.

Tofu, or bean curd, soft, white, cheeselike food made by treating soybean milk with coagulants and pressing the curds into cakes. It originated in China more than 1,000 years ago and is widely used in Asia. Tofu is bland, high in protein, low in salt and calories, and cholesterol-free. It has thus become popular in the West as a substitute for cheese, cream, and other animal fat products.

Toga, robe worn in ancient Rome. Originally worn by both men and women, it gradually fell out of favor with women. Made of soft wool, it was loosely draped in abundant folds over an undergarment called a tunic. Its color delineated the status, rank, or age of the wearer. Because it limited movement, it eventually came to be worn by the upper classes and politicians.

Togo, republic in West Africa. Bordered by Ghana on the west, Benin on the east, Burkina Faso on the north, and the Gulf of Guinea on the south, Togo has an area of 21,925 sq mi (56,785 sq km) and is 340 mi (547 km) long and 70 mi (113 km) wide. The capital is the seaport of Lomè.
Land and people. From the central Togo Mountains a grassy plateau slopes east to the Mono River and south to the sandy coastal plain. North of the mountains is the savanna of the Oti Plateau. The climate is hot and humid. The people of Togo are almost entirely black Africans of the Ewe, Ouatchi, Mina, and Kabre ethnic groups. There are Christians and Muslims, but most people follow traditional beliefs. French is the official language.
Economy. Over 70% of the people live in rural areas, mostly in the south, and the economy is primarily agricultural. The chief exports are cocoa and coffee, but cassava, corn, and cotton are also important. Large phosphate deposits discovered northeast of Lomè have proven profitable and Togo ranks high in world production.

History. Togo was settled in the 1300s by a group of Ewe-speaking people, then further populated by invaders and refugees from various wars north of the area. As the slave trade grew, Togo became an important center for the buying and selling of slaves. Germany set up a protectorate (known as Togoland) in 1884; after World War I, it was administered by the French. Togo became an independent nation in 1960 with Sylvanus Olympio as president. After a long period of political turmoil, a military coup in 1967 installed Lt. Col. Gnassingbe Eyadema as the country's leader. He received popular support in a 1972 presidential vote and was reelected in 1979. With the first democratic elections in 1993, he was reconfirmed in office. In 1998, the presidential elections were won by Eyadéma. The opposition challenged the outcome.

Tojo, Hideki (1884-1948), Japanese military and political leader. He became minister of war in 1940, premier in Oct. 1941, and approved the bombing of Pearl Harbor on Dec. 7, 1941, leading Japan into World War II against the United States. Assuming totalitarian control over Japan during the early years of the war, Tojo was responsible for atrocities and the torture of Allied prisoners of war. He was forced to resign as premier in 1944 but continued to advocate a "no surrender" policy. After the war he was captured, tried as a war criminal, and hanged on Dec. 23, 1948.
See also: World War II.

Tokyo (pop. 7,927,100), capital of Japan. It lies at the head of Tokyo Bay on the southeastern coast of Honshu Island and contains over 10% of Japan's population. Founded in the 12th century as Edo, it became capital of the Tokugawa shoguns in 1603; it was renamed and made imperial capital in 1868. Reconstruction after earthquake and fire (1923) and the air raids of World War II transformed much of Tokyo. It is today a center of government, industry, finance, and education. The National Diet (parliament) meets here; most of Japan's great corporations have their head offices in the Maurunochi district; Tokyo University (founded 1877) is one of hundreds of educational institutions. Tokyo has many parks, museums, and temples, the Imperial Palace, and the Kabukiza theater. Industries (with large complexes to the west) include printing, shipbuilding, metal manufactures, automobile, chemicals, and textiles. The harbor and airport are Japan's busiest.
See also: Japan.

Toledo (pop. 329,300), city in northwestern Ohio, at the mouth of the Maumee River on Lake Erie. It was settled in the early 19th century after Gen. Anthony Wayne's victory over Native American forces at the nearby Battle of Fallen Timbers (1794) and the establishment of Fort Industry (1795). The settlements of Port Lawrence and Vistula, built near the site of Fort Industry, merged in 1833 to form Toledo. Today Toledo is an important Great Lakes port and manufacturing center (e.g., glass, oil products, machines), and a cultural center with 2 universities, a major art museum, symphony, opera, and one of the nation's best zoos.
See also: Ohio.

Toledo (pop. 62,800), city in central Spain 40 mi (64 km) southwest of Madrid, seat of Toledo province, former Roman and Visgoth capital. Pos-

sessing minimal industry, Toledo produces textiles, sabers, and firearms. The entire city has been declared a national monument and contains beautiful examples of medieval and Renaissance art and architecture. Toledo's many landmarks include the Alcázar (citadel), Gothic cathedral (the archbishop is Spain's primate), and El Greco's house, which serves as a museum for several of his paintings.
See also: Spain.

Tolkien, J(ohn) R(onald) R(euel) (1892-1973), English author and scholar, celebrated for *The Hobbit* (1937) and the trilogy *The Lord of the Rings* (1954-56), which present a mythical world of elves and dwarfs, partly based on Anglo-Saxon and Norse folklore. Tolkien was professor of Anglo-Saxon, then of English, language and literature at Oxford University.

Tolstoy, Aleksei Nikolaevich (1882-1945), Russian novelist and playwright, best known for his trilogy *The Road to Calvary* (1921-40), the novella *Nikita's Childhood* (1922), and the novel *Peter the First* (1929-45). A nobleman distantly related to Leo Tolstoy, he left Russia in 1917 but returned in 1922 and became a supporter of Joseph Stalin's regime.

Tolstoy, Leo (1828-1910), Russian novelist. Educated at Kazan University, he served in the army, married in 1862, and spent the next 15 years on his estate at Yasnaya Polyana near Moscow. In this period he produced his masterpieces, including *War and Peace* (1865-69), an epic of vast imaginative scope and variety of character, telling the story of five families against the background of the Napoleonic invasion of Russia. *Anna Karenina* (1875-77), the tragic story of an adulterous affair, is remarkable for its psychological portrayal. In later years Tolstoy experienced a spiritual crisis, recounted in his *Confession* (1882), and embraced an ascetic philosophy of Christian anarchism. His other works include *Childhood* (1852), *The Cossacks* (1863), and *Resurrection* (1899).

Toltec, Native American civilization dominant in the central Mexican highlands between the 900s and 1100s. The Toltec god was Quetzalcoatl, for whom they performed human sacrifice. The Toltecs, sophisticated builders and artisans, erected their capital at Tollán (ruins near modern Tula, 60 mi [96.5 km] north of Mexico City). The dominant group were Nahuati speakers. Aztecs and others overran the area and adopted various aspects of Toltec culture.

Toluene ($C_6H_5CH_3$), liquid hydrocarbon related to benzene. Made from treated petroleum or distilled coal tar, it is commonly used in the production of a wide range of industrial chemicals, such as the preservative benzoic acid and the explosive trinitrotoluene (TNT). Because it is toxic, federal guidelines exist to regulate its use in the workplace.
See also: Benzene.

Tomato (*Lycopersicon esculentum*), herbaceous plant of the nightshade family, native to South America but introduced to Europe in the 16th century and now cultivated worldwide; also, the fruit of the plant. Most of the crop is canned or processed to make prepared foods, a relatively small proportion being grown for salad use. In northern latitudes, tomatoes are grown under

Tonga

Capital:	Nukualofa
Area:	289 sq mi (748 sq km)
Population:	108,000
Language:	Tongan, English
Government:	Constitutional monarchy
Independent:	1970
Head of gov.:	Prime minister
Per capita:	U.S. $1.630
Mon. unit:	1 Pa'anga = 100 seniti

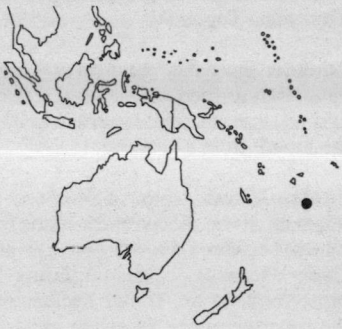

glass, but the bulk are grown as a field crop. Italy, Spain, Brazil, and Japan are among the leading producers.

Tombstone (pop. 1,632), city in southeastern Arizona, founded in 1879 after the discovery of silver veins in the nearby mountains. Once billed as "the town too tough to die," Tombstone was one of the most notoriously lawless settlements of the American West. In Oct. 1881 Tombstone's O.K. Corral was the site of a famous gunfight pitting Wyatt Earp, 2 of his brothers, and Doc Holliday against a rival faction. Today Tombstone is a major tourist attraction and in 1962 was designated a national historic landmark.
See also: Arizona.

Tom Thumb, General (1838-83), stage name for the U.S. entertainer Charles Sherwood Stratton. Stratton, a midget whose adult height was 40 in (101.5 cm), toured Europe and the U.S. with P.T. Barnum.

Tonegawa, Susumu (1939-), Japanese biologist. An expert in immunology, he won the 1987 Nobel Prize for physiology or medicine for his discovery of techniques to study the response of the body's immune system in order to protect against new disease agents. Formerly at the Basel Institute for Immunology in Switzerland, he has worked at the Massachusetts Institute of Technology since 1981.
See also: Biology; Immunity.

Tonga, or Friendly Islands, constitutional monarchy in the South Pacific. The kingdom comprises over 150 islands of which the chief groups are Tongatapu, Háapai, and Vaváu. The climate is tropical. The capital is Nukùalofa on Tongatapu. The population is mainly Polynesian, with a small number of Europeans. The economy is agricultural, with copra, banana, and vanilla the chief exports. Promising petroleum deposits were located near Tongatapu in 1977. The islands were discovered in 1616 by the Dutch explorer Jakob Lemaire and later visited by Abel Tasman (1643), and James Cook (1773), who named them the Friendly Islands. The present kingdom was founded in 1845 by George Tupou I and became a British protectorate in 1900. It achieved independence in 1970. The present king (since 1965) is Taufaahau Tupou IV.

Tongue, muscular organ in the floor of the mouth, concerned with the formation of food boluses and self-cleansing of the mouth, taste sensation and voice production. In certain animals, the tongue is used to draw food into the mouth from a distance.

Tonkin, historic region of Southeast Asia, now comprising most of northern Vietnam. It was the European name for the region around the Red River delta, which became a French protectorate in 1883, part of French Indochina. Under Japanese occupation during World War II and thereafter a French protectorate again, Tonkin became part of independent North Vietnam with the departure of the French in 1954.

Tonsil, name for either of two small oval-shaped, fleshy bodies, situated on each side of the back of the throat (palatine tonsils). They act as filters of disease organisms. Similar lymphoid masses are the phalangeal tonsils (adenoids) between the back of the nose and throat, and the lingual tonsils, on the back of the tongue.
See also: Adenoids.

Tonsillitis, inflammation of the tonsils due to virus or bacteria infection. It may follow sore throat or other pharyngeal disease, or it may be primary tonsil disease. Sore throat and red swollen tonsils, which may exude pus or cause swallowing difficulty, are common; lymph nodes at the angle of the jaw are usually tender and swollen. Quinsy is a rare complication. Antobiotic treatment for the bacterial cause usually leads to a resolution, but removal of the tonsils is needed in few cases.

Topaz, aluminum silicate mineral of composition $Al_2SiO_4(F,OH)_2$, forming prismatic crystals (orthorhombic) that are variable and unstable in color and valued as gemstones. The best topazes come from Brazil, Siberia, and the United States.

Topeka (pop. 119,000), state capital of Kansas, located on the Kansas River in the northeastern part of the state. Topeka was laid out by Free Staters in 1854, following passage of the Kansas-Nebraska Act that opened the territory to popular sovereignty, and in 1861 was chosen as the state capital. Headquarters of the Atchison, Topeka & Santa Fe Railroad, Topeka is also a major agricultural, livestock, and manufacturing center, and is home to the Menninger Foundation, one of the world's leading psychiatric facilities and research centers.
See also: Kansas.

Topology, branch of mathematics that studies properties of geometrical figures or abstract spaces that are independent of shape or distance. Point-set topology deals with ways of defining "nearness" of elements, or points, of a set without necessarily assigning numerical distances to pairs of points. Such a definition is called "a topology on the set," and the set is called a topological space. The topology makes it possible to define continuous functions on the space. Algebraic topology, or combinatorial topology, uses abstract algebra to treat the ways in which geometrical figures fit together to form figures of higher dimension, disregarding shape. For example a sphere is topologically the same as a cube, but it is distinct from a torus (doughnut) because if the surfaces of the figures are divided into triangles, the algebraic relationships between the triangles will be different in the two cases.

Torah (Hebrew: "law, teaching"), the Pentateuch (first five books of the Bible) kept in the ark of every synagogue. In a wider sense it is the whole body of the oral and written teaching central to Judaism and includes the rest of the Hebrew Bible, rabbinic codes, the Talmud, and the Midrash.
See also: Bible.

Tornado, violent whirlwind cloud of small diameter, extending downward from a convective cloud in a severe thunderstorm, generally funnelshaped. Air rises rapidly in the outer region of the funnel, but descends in its core, which is at very low pressure. The funnel is visible owing to the formation of cloud droplets by expansional cooling in this low-pressure region. Very high winds spiral in toward the core. There is almost total devastation and often loss of life in the path of a tornado, which may move at speeds up to 656 ft (200 m) per sec. Though generally rare, tornadoes occur worldwide, especially in the United States and Australia in spring and early summer.

Toronto (pop. 3.893,000), capital of Ontario province and York County, second-largest city in Canada (after Montreal), on the northwestern shore of Lake Ontario. It is a major port, as well as a commercial, manufacturing, and educational center. The cultural focus of English-speaking Canada, Toronto is home to the Royal Conservatory of Music, the Canadian Music Center, the Royal Ontario Museum, and a parks system that covers 6,000 acres (2,400 hectares). Its industrial products include chemicals, machinery, electrical goods, and clothing. The French settled the area and built Fort Rouillé (1750), which was replaced by the English city of York (1793). Sacked in the War of 1812, York was renamed Toronto in 1834.
See also: Ontario.

Torpedo, flat, broad fish of the Torpedinidae family, found in tropical and temperate regions of the Atlantic and Pacific oceans. Also known as the electric ray, it emits electricity to stun fish for food and to protect itself. The shock from the torpedo is not lethal to humans but has been known to stun them.

Torpedo, self-propelled streamlined missile that travels underwater, its explosive warhead detonating when it nears or strikes its target. The torpedo was invented (1866) by Robert Whitehead, a British engineer. Torpedoes are now chiefly antisubmarine weapons.

Torpedo boat *See:* PT boat.

Torquemada, Tomás de (1420-98), Spanish Inquisition leader. A Dominican monk, he became the confessor to Queen Isabella and was named inquisitor general (1483), responsible for the executions of more than 2,000 people considered heretics (primarily Muslims and

Jews). He was largely responsible for the expulsion of more than 200,000 Jews from Spain in 1492. Torquemada established rules and procedures for the Inquisition, some of which involved torture and other cruel methods of execution; his name has become synonymous with excessive cruelty.
See also: Inquisition.

Torricelli, Evangelista (1608-47), Italian physicist and mathematician who invented the barometer in 1643. He also improved the effectiveness of the telescope and the microscope. His work in the field of pure mathematics was influential in the development of integral calculus. He was inspired by the work of his friend and mentor, Galileo.
See also: Barometer.

Torsion balance, device for measuring the force of a twisting motion. These measurements are registered on a gauge that is calibrated—readings adjusted for correct measurement. In a torsion bar, stretched fibers (usually gold, quartz, or steel) are attached to heavy noncorrosive balls (usually gold, lead, or stainless steel) that twist and turn to compensate for the introduced push-and-pull actions. A balanced zero reading is the desired result. In automobiles, a torsion bar, through torsion balance, compensates for bumps and holes experienced on the road.

Torsion bar suspension, system designed to absorb front-end shock in automobiles. There is one torsion bar for each of an automobile's 2 front wheels. One end of the torsion bar is attached to the car's frame. The other end is attached to the axle near the wheel. When the car hits a bump, the torsion bar, which somewhat resembles a straightened spring, twists and then untwists. This movement absorbs the shock and makes the ride smoother.
See also: Shock absorber.

Tort (French, "wrong"), in law, a wrongful act against a person or their property for which that person can claim damages as compensation. It is distinguished from a crime, which the state will prosecute; it is up to the injured party to sue for redress of a tort. The same wrongful act, an assault for example, may be both actionable as a tort and prosecuted as a crime. Torts range from personal injury to slander or libel; they include trespass and damage or injury arising through negligence. Wrongful breach of an agreement, however, is covered by the law of contract.

Tortoise, name for slow-moving, herbivorous, heavily armored terrestrial reptiles of the family Testudinidae, found in the tropics, subtropics, and warmer temperate regions. The body is enclosed in a boxlike shell into which the head and limbs can be withdrawn. The shell is covered with horny plates, or scutes. Toothless, the tortoise's jaws are covered to form a sharp, horny beak. There are many species, ranging from the familiar garden tortoises to the 5-ft (1.5-m) giant tortoises of the Galapagos and Seychelles.

Tory Party, popular name of the Conservative and Unionist Party, one of Britain's two chief parties. The term (originally describing Irish highwaymen) was applied in 1679 to supporters of the future James II of England. In the main, Tories became staunch royalists and supporters of the Church of

England. "Tory" was applied to Loyalist colonists in the American Revolution. Taking a reactionary stance because of the threat to authority posed by the French Revolution, the party lost its support after the Reform Bill of 1832 and became the Conservative Party.

Toscanini, Arturo (1867-1957), Italian conductor, one of the greatest of his time. He became musical director of La Scala in Milan (1898) and went on to conduct the New York Metropolitan Opera (1908-14) and New York Philharmonic orchestras (1926-36). The NBC Symphony Orchestra was created for him in 1937.

Totalitarianism, system of government in which the state exercises wide-ranging control over individuals within its jurisdiction. Usually, a totalitarian state has only one political party, led by a dictator, and an official ideology; dissent is suppressed. Nazi Germany epitomized the repression of totalitarian states.

Totem, object, animal, or plant toward which a tribe, clan, or other group feels a special affinity, often considering it a mythical ancestor. Killing of the totemic animal or animals by members of the group is taboo, except, with some peoples, ritually during religious ceremonies. Totem poles, on which human and animal shapes representing a particular warrior's heritage, were common among the Native Americans.

Toucan, exotic bird of the family Ramphastidae, native to the tropical regions of Latin America. It is noted for its huge, brightly colored bill. About forty varieties exist, ranging in size from 13-25 in (33-64 cm). It subsists on fruits, often using its saw-edged bill to tear off small pieces. It lives in small flocks and is believed to be highly social.

Touch, sensory system concerned with surface sensation, found in all external body surfaces including the skin and some mucous membranes. Functional categories of touch sensation include light touch (including movement of hairs), heat, cold, pressure, and pain sensation. Receptors for all the senses are particularly concentrated and developed over the face and hands. When the skin receptors are stimulated, they activate nerve impulses in cutaneous nerves; these pass via the spinal cord and brain stem to the brain, where coding and perception occur.
See also: Senses.

Touch-me-not, wild flower of the balsam family, related to the impatiens. Its seed pods pop open when touched, hence its name. It grows in damp, shady regions of the eastern and central United States, reaches 3-5 ft (0.9-1.5m) tall, and bears pale yellow or spotted flowers. The pale yellow variety is thought to prevent poison ivy rashes when the juice from its stems and leaves are rubbed on the skin.

Toulon (pop. 170,200), port city in southeastern France. It is the administrative seat of the district of Var and an important French naval base. Historic landmarks include medieval churches and a 16th-century fish market. Toulon is the site of a Roman colony founded in the 100s B.C. Chief economic activities include shipbuilding, fishing, wine making, and chemical and machine manufacturing.
See also: France.

Toulouse (pop. 365,900), historically significant city in southwestern France, located on the Garonne River. It is the capital and administrative seat of the district of Haute-Garonne. During the Middle Ages, it served as an artistic and cultural center of Europe. Many medieval buildings, including the University of Toulouse, still stand. The city supports many economic activities, including the manufacture of electronics, aircraft, chemicals, and textiles.

Toulouse-Lautrec, Henri de (1864-1901), French painter and lithographer who portrayed Parisian nightlife. Born into an old aristocratic family, he was crippled at 15, studied art in Paris, and settled in Montmartre to paint the entertainers and circus performers who lived there, such as Jan Avril and Aristide Bruant. Influenced by Edgar Degas and by Japanese prints, his work did much to popularize the lithographic poster.

Touré, Sékou (1922-84), president of the Republic of Guinea (1958-84). A labor leader in French colonial times, a Marxist, and a political writer, Touré was the winner of the 1960 Lenin Peace Prize.
See also: Guinea.

Tourette syndrome, disorder of the central nervous system characterized by muscular tics, or twitches, and uncontrollable vocalizing. Symptoms first appear in childhood between 2 and 15 years and, if not treated, continue throughout the person's life, sometimes becoming more severe and other times less so. People with Tourette syndrome may also suffer from hyperactivity. Though no cure is yet known, symptoms can be alleviated by drug therapy.

Tourmaline, hard, complex silicate mineral containing such elements as boron, aluminum, and silicon. Colors include pink, green, blue, yellow, violet, red, and black. Transparent stones are considered semiprecious and are used as gems in jewelry. Tourmaline is found in granites, schists, and crystalline limestone of Brazil, Asia, the former USSR, and parts of the United States.

Tournament, or tourney, series of games; originally a combat between armored knights, usually on horseback. Popular in Europe in the Middle Ages, it provided both entertainment and training for war. In the 13th century the dangerous melée was replaced by the joust contest between only two knights, who tried to unhorse each other with lance, mace, and sword.

Tours (pop. 133,400), city in west-central France along the Loire River. Established by the Romans in 50 B.C., it served in medieval times as a center for Christian learning. The great Battle of Tours was fought nearby in 732 by the Christian Franks and Muslim armies, effectively stopping the Moorish advance in Europe. During World War II the city became the French government's headquarters. Today Tours is an important wine market and tourist and business center, with banking, insurance, medical- and electrical-equipment manufacturing industries.

Toussaint L'Ouverture (Pierre Dominique Toussaint-Bréda; c.1774-1803), emancipated Haitian slave who led the 1791 slave rebellion on the island of

Haiti. The slaves won their freedom in 1793, while the French in Haiti were fighting against British and Spanish troops there. Toussaint, who joined forces with the French and forced the British to evacuate, became ruler of the island in 1799. He suppressed a mulatto uprising (1799) and resisted Napoleon's attempt to reimpose slavery on Haiti. Ultimately, Toussaint was captured and imprisoned until his death. His popular name, L'Ouverture, is French for "The Opening." He has remained a symbol of the struggle for freedom.
See also: Haiti, Republic of.

Tower of Babel, mythical tower built in the ancient Mesopotamian city of Babylon. The myth popularly connected with it is related in the Bible (Genesis 11.1-9). According to this version the tower was built by the descendants of Noah and was intended by these peoples to reach heaven. God, however, disapproved of the tower and, as a consequence, confused the builders by causing them to speak in different languages. As a result of their confusion, the people stopped work on the tower and wandered off to various parts of the world. Many people believe today that the myth was an attempt by ancient peoples to explain the origin of different languages.

Tower of London, ancient fortress on the Thames River in the eastern part of London. Built 1078-1300, mainly by William the Conqueror and Henry III, its massive stone buildings are enclosed by high walls and a moat. It has been palace, prison, arsenal, and mint. Today it houses the crown jewels and an armor museum. Here Thomas More, Anne Boleyn, and Roger Casement were executed. Convicted Nazi war criminal Rudolf Hess was its last prisoner.

Townes, Charles Hard (1915-), U.S. physicist awarded the 1964 Nobel Prize for physics, with Nikolai Basov and Aleksander Prokhorov, for independently working out the theory of the maser and, later, the laser. He built the first maser in 1951.
See also: Laser; Maser.

Town meeting, direct democratic form of local government, mainly in New England (Massachusetts, New Hampshire, and Vermont). In colonial days, all enfranchised citizens met to choose officials, decide taxes, and discuss affairs. In the 1800s meetings became an annual event called by warrant. Today, many town meetings are attended only by officials and elected representatives, but others are fully attended by the public when significant local issues are discussed.

Townsend, Francis Everett (1867-1960), U.S. reformer, author of the Townsend Plan (1933), a share-the-wealth program by which citizens over 60 were to receive $200 a month, the money to be raised by a federal tax. Townsend claimed supporters of the plan numbered 5 million, but Congress rejected it.

Townsend, Willard Saxby (1895-1957), one of the first African-American labor leaders. He served as the first president of the Auxiliary of Redcaps (1936), a union that represented railroad baggage porters. In 1955, when the American Federation of Labor (AFL) merged with the Congress of Industrial

Organization (CIO) to form the AFL-CIO, Townsend became the new union organization's first vice president.
See also: Labor movement.

Toxemia of pregnancy, or preeclampsia, disease caused by bacterial toxins or other toxic substances in the blood, usually referring to a condition that attacks women in the last stages of pregnancy or just after childbirth. It occurs in about 5% of all pregnancies and, unless treated, may lead to eclampsia (convulsions and coma) and other complications, including death of the mother and fetus. Toxemia is characterized by an increase in blood pressure, excessive protein in the urine, and swelling of the body, and can be treated by drugs if diagnosed in time.

Toxic shock syndrome (TSS), rare and sometimes fatal bacterial disease associated with the use of tampons. TSS is characterized by high fever, vomiting, and diarrhea, followed by a sharp drop in blood pressure that may bring on fatal shock. At greatest risk are women under 30 during their menstrual periods. The incidence is low, with a frequency of about 3 cases per 100,000 women annually in the United States, and the mortality rate is about 10%.

Toxic wastes *See:* Hazardous wastes.